OXFORD STUDIES IN EUROPEAN LAW

*Series Editors*

PAUL CRAIG
*Professor of English Law at St John's College, Oxford*

GRÁINNE DE BÚRCA
*Professor of Law at New York University School of Law*

# The EU Deep Trade Agenda

OXFORD STUDIES IN EUROPEAN LAW

*Series Editors:*
Paul Craig, Professor of English Law at St John's College, Oxford and
Gráinne de Búrca, Professor of Law at New York
University School of Law

The aim of this series is to publish important and original research on EU law. The focus is on scholarly monographs, with a particular emphasis on those which are interdisciplinary in nature. Edited collections of essays will also be included where they are appropriate. The series is wide in scope and aims to cover studies of particular areas of substantive and of institutional law, historical works, theoretical studies, and analyses of current debates, as well as questions of perennial interest such as the relationship between national and EU law and the novel forms of governance emerging in and beyond Europe. The fact that many of the works are interdisciplinary will make the series of interest to all those concerned with the governance and operation of the EU.

OTHER TITLES IN THIS SERIES

**Economic Governance in Europe
Comparative Paradoxes and
Constitutional Challenges**
Federico Fabbrini

**Foreign Policy Objectives in European
Constitutional Law**
Joris Larik

**Private Regulation and
the Internal Market
Sports, Legal Services, and Standard
Setting in EU Economic Law**
Mislav Mataija

**The Human Rights of
Migrants and Refugees in
European Law**
Cathryn Costello

**An Ever More Powerful Court?
The Political Constraints of
Legal Integration in the
European Union**
Dorte Sindbjerg Martinsen

**The Concept of State Aid
under EU Law
From Internal Market to Competition
and Beyond**
Juan Jorge Piernas López

**Justice in the EU
The Emergence of Transnational
Solidarity**
Floris de Witte

**The Euro Area Crisis in Constitutional
Perspective**
Alicia Hinarejos

**The European Fundamental Freedoms
A Contextual Approach**
Pedro Caro de Sousa

**National Identity in EU Law**
Elke Cloots

**The Constitutional Foundations of
European Contract Law
A Comparative Analysis**
Kathleen Gutman

**The Criminalization of European Cartel
Enforcement
Theoretical, Legal, and Practical
Challenges**
Peter Whelan

**Fundamental Rights in Europe
Challenges and Transformations in
Comparative Perspective**
Federico Fabbrini

**The Principle of Loyalty in EU Law**
Marcus Klamert

**Constitutional Pluralism in the EU**
Klemen Jaklic

**EU Consumer Law and Human Rights**
Iris Benöhr

**The Principle of Mutual Recognition in
EU Law**
Christine Janssens

# The EU Deep Trade Agenda

*Law and Policy*

BILLY ALEXIS MELO ARAUJO

*Lecturer, Queen's University Belfast*

OXFORD
UNIVERSITY PRESS

OXFORD
UNIVERSITY PRESS

Great Clarendon Street, Oxford, OX2 6DP,
United Kingdom

Oxford University Press is a department of the University of Oxford. It furthers the University's objective of excellence in research, scholarship, and education by publishing worldwide. Oxford is a registered trade mark of Oxford University Press in the UK and in certain other countries



First Edition published in 2016



Published in the United States of America by Oxford University Press
198 Madison Avenue, New York, NY 10016, United States of America

British Library Cataloguing in Publication Data
Data available

Library of Congress Control Number: 2016930707

ISBN 978–0–19–875338–4

Para a minha filha Suzana Rose

# Series Editors' Preface

This book provides a thorough and informed account of the pursuit by the European Union since 2006 of a 'deep trade agenda'. The author describes how this agenda, whose introduction was marked by the publication of the Global Europe strategy that year, has meant a shift away from the multilateral trade regime to pursue a new generation of bilateral and regional trade agreements containing a whole range of regulatory provisions on matters such as competition, services, intellectual property, procurement, health and safety but also a whole host of other areas of domestic regulation.

The author identifies his objective as being to explore the rationale of this deep trade agenda of the EU from a political economy perspective and to critically examine its implementation, as well as to reflect on its implications for the way the EU is characterized and viewed as an international actor, and its implication for the multilateral trade regime more broadly.

Following an introduction to the post-war international trade system and the eventual creation of the WTO, the book depicts the shift in the international economic system 'from shallow to deep integration' and in particular the EU's move in this direction in its trade policy. It provides an account of the legal framework governing the EU's trade policy, and how that legal framework potentially affects and frames its pursuit of a deep trade agenda. This is followed by five chapters which examine the EU's promotion of particular issues or disciplines within its deep trade agreements: the first focusing on services, the second on investment, the third on intellectual property, the fourth on competition, and the fifth on procurement. The analysis contained in these five chapters focuses on a range of the new-generation EU trade agreements, in particular those concluded with Korea, Singapore, Peru–Colombia, Canada, the CARIFORUM states, and the Central America Association agreement.

The author concludes that the EU is indeed using these new generation trade agreements as a way of expanding its regulatory space and of aggressively pursuing its commercial interests. He finds that the EU does not generally use these agreements to promote its own norms but rather norms based on already existing international legal instruments, except that where the regulatory standards imposed within the EU are more burdensome than those imposed at the international level, it tends to promote its own norms abroad to try to level the playing field. Overall, he describes the EU's promotion of deep disciplines abroad as operating through a 'feedback loop system' whereby the EU 'participates in the development of international rules, which are then incorporated into the EU regulatory framework and re-exported into its deep trade agreements'. Thus the EU's self-confessed aim is to set rules at a plurilateral level so that they can later be multilateralised. He notes that in some cases when it regulates subject matters in trade agreements which were not previously covered by EU law, it may actually be harmonizing Member States laws and in so doing circumventing more cumbersome (but also possibly more participatory and democratic) domestic decision-making rules.

The findings of Melo Araujo's study suggest that, at least in this field, the EU is not distinctive in any way as an international actor, and that it acts in many respects as the kind of 'market power' that has been described in some of the international relations literature. Further, he suggests that while the EU has not given up on the promotion of multilateral standards, it has effectively given up on the multilateral *process*. Thus the EU in its deep trade agreements promotes *certain* aspects of the WTO agreements but makes no attempt to address the disagreements over contentious issues and instead seeks to impose its own preferred solution to these contentious issues. His conclusion is crisp and biting: that 'the EU advocates multilateral trade liberalization whilst actively contributing to the fragmentation of the international trading system and advocates market openness whilst considering protectionist policies'.

This is both a highly informative and also a timely book, coming as it does at a moment when the EU and the US are negotiating the Transatlantic Trade and Investment Agreement, and the US is advancing towards the conclusion of a Trans-Pacific Partnership.

The book should be of considerable interest to lawyers and political scientists alike, and in particular to students of EU and international trade law and policy, as well as all those interested in the EU as an international actor.

The book attempts to state the law and case law as of June 2015.

Paul Craig and Gráinne de Búrca

# *Acknowledgements*

This book is an updated version of my PhD thesis completed in 2014 at King's College London. First and foremost, I would like to thank my thesis supervisor Professor Piet Eeckhout for his encouragement and friendship. His expertise and guidance have been invaluable and I feel immensely privileged to have been given the opportunity to work under his tutelage. I am also grateful to King's College London's Centre of European Law for the grant of a three-year scholarship which enabled me to undertake my doctoral studies. I am greatly indebted to Professor Joanne Scott and Professor Markus Krajewski—my doctoral examiners—who made my examination such a rewarding experience and were so enthusiastic in encouraging me to publish my thesis.

Queen's University Belfast has been my employer for the past year, and I am very grateful for the support, time, and space that were given to me to complete this endeavour.

In writing this book I have benefited tremendously from insights from various colleagues and friends, and in particular: Dr Federico Ortino, Dr Charilaos Nikolaidis, Dr Maris Kask, Baskaran Balasingham, Dr Esin Kusk, and Dr Emily Lydgate. I would also like to thank Dr Werner Zdouc, Jesse Nicol, Judy Cowell, and everyone else at the WTO Appellate Body where I conduced an internship which shaped the direction of my research.

I would like to thank my mother, Sonia, my brother, Marc, and my grandmother Suzana, for their love and continuous support. Last but by no means least I would like to thank Sara, my wife, who somehow has managed to put up with me for the last five years. It is no hyperbole to say that this work would have not been completed without her.

# *Table of Contents*

# *Table of Cases*

## *EUROPEAN COURT OF JUSTICE*

### Cases



### Opinions



## *GATT/WTO*



## INTERNATIONAL INVESTMENT TREATY AWARDS

# *Table of Legislation*

*INTERNATIONAL TREATIES AND CONVENTIONS*

## *EU LAW*

### ***Basic Treaties***

**Proposed Legislation**



**European Parliament Resolutions**



*Guidelines*

# *List of Abbreviations*

| | |
|---|---|
| ACP | African Caribbean Pacific |
| ACTA | Anti-Counterfeiting Trade Agreement signed on 1 October 2011 in Tokyo, Japan |
| ASEAN | Association of South East Asian Nations |
| BIT | Bilateral Investment Agreement |
| CAP | Common Agricultural Policy |
| CARICOM | Caribbean Community and Common Market |
| CARIFORUM | The Forum of the Caribbean Group of African, Caribbean and Pacific States |
| CCP | Common Commercial Policy |
| CEPA | Economic Partnership Agreement between the CARIFORUM States, of the one part, and the European Community and its Member States, of the other part signed on 15 October 2008 in Bridgetown, Barbados. |
| CETA | Comprehensive Economic Trade Agreement between the EU and Canada |
| Colombia–Peru FTA | Trade Agreement between the European Union and its Member States, of the one part, and Colombia and Peru, of the other part signed on 26 June 2012 in Brussels, Belgium |
| Cotonou Agreement | Partnership Agreement between the members of the African, Caribbean and Pacific Group of States on the one part and the European Community and its Member States on the other part signed on 23 June 2000 in Cotonou, Bénin |
| Doha Round | Doha Development Round |
| ECJ | European Court of Justice |
| EEC | European Economic Community |
| ENP | European Neighbourhood Policy |
| EPA | Economic Partnership Agreement |
| EU | European Union |
| EU–CA FTA | Agreement establishing an Association between the European Union and its Member States, on the one hand, and Central America signed on 29 June 2012 in Tegucigalpa, Honduras |
| FDI | Foreign direct investment |
| FTA | Free Trade Agreement |
| G8 | Group of Eight (comprising Canada, France, Germany, Italy, Japan, Russia, the United Kingdom, and the United States) |
| GATS | General Agreement on Trade in Services |
| GATT 1947 | General Agreement on Tariffs and Trade in force between 1948 and 1994 |
| GATT 1994 | General Agreement on Tariffs and Trade in force since 1995 |
| GDP | Gross domestic product |
| GPA | Government Procurement Agreement |
| ICN | International Competition Network |

| | |
|---|---|
| ICSID | International Centre for Settlement of Investment Disputes |
| ILO | International Labour Organization |
| IMF | International Monetary Fund |
| IP | Intellectual property |
| KOREU FTA | Free Trade Agreement between the European Union and its Member States, of the one part, and the Republic of Korea, of the other part signed on 10 May 2010 in Brussels, Belgium |
| MERCOSUR | Mercado Comun del Sur (Southern Common Market) |
| MFN | Most-favoured nation |
| NAFTA | North American Free Trade Agreement |
| NGOs | non-governmental organizations |
| OECD | Organisation for Economic Co-operation and Development |
| PTA | Preferential Trade Agreement |
| SMP | Single Market Programme |
| TDCA | Trade, Development and Cooperation Agreement |
| TEU | Treaty on the European Union |
| TFEU | Treaty on the Functioning of the European Union |
| TRIMs | Agreement on Trade Related Investment Measures |
| TRIPS | Agreement on Trade Related Aspects of Intellectual Property Rights |
| UNCITRAL | United Nations Commission on International Trade Law |
| UNCTAD | United Nations Conference on Trade and Development |
| UNESCO | United Nations Educational, Scientific and Cultural Organization |
| UNESCO Convention | UNESCO Convention on the Protection and Promotion of Diversity on Cultural Expressions signed on 20 October 2005 in Paris, France |
| WIPO | World Intellectual Property Organization |
| WPDR | Working Party on Domestic Regulation |

# 1
# Introduction

## 1.1 Research Question

On 24 June 2013, the EU Council gave the Commission a mandate to negotiate what would be a historic Transatlantic Trade and Investment Partnership (TTIP) with the US (European Commission (2013b)). The idea of a transatlantic free trade agreement (FTA) itself is nothing new—it has been in the making for the better part of the last two decades (Hindley (1999), pp. 45–60). However, although EU and US leaders have previously been reticent about the prospect of signing a full-blown FTA, they have proved more receptive to the idea in the aftermath of the global economic downturn—an agreement between these two of the world's largest trading blocs may provide a much-needed boost for these flagging economies. And beyond the potential benefits that could be accrued from further trade liberalization, a transatlantic deal would be significant because of what it represents for international trade relations. It signals a recognition of the need to respond to the challenges posed by a multipolar international order where the trade power that was once exerted by the US and (to a lesser extent) the EU in international trade politics is being eroded by the rising importance of Asia and the BRIC (German Marshall Fund, 2012). It is also indicative of how far down in terms of choice of venues for trade liberalization the WTO has fallen since the turn of the century. In the absence of common ground between 'established and emerging powers' (US National Intelligence Council (2012), p. 7), multilateralism has clearly given way to bilateralism and regionalism as the main instruments for trade governance.

One area where 'common ground' is lacking concerns the direction of future trade liberalization. Developed countries, led by the EU and the US, have over the course of the past three decades consistently called for 'deeper integration'—that is, the convergence of behind-the-border or domestic policies and rules such as competition, public procurement, intellectual property (IP), investment, health and safety standards, and financial regulation (Lawrence (1996a), p. XVIII). Underlying the need for deep integration are fundamental changes that have occurred in the international trading system; from the diversification of international economic exchanges and the successive multilateral rounds of tariff cutting (complemented by unilateral tariff reductions) which have highlighted the importance of barriers resulting from divergences in domestic regulation, to the significant advances in transportation and information technology which have enabled the fragmentation of production processes. These factors have all contributed to an increased focus on the harmonization and dissemination of pro-competitive regulatory frameworks in order to facilitate market access and the operation of firms doing business abroad. Developing countries have by and large not heeded such calls, however, arguing—inter alia—that the type of regulatory reforms entailed by deep integration would deprive them of the autonomy and flexibility to implement policies that address their developmental needs (Gallagher (2012), p. 17). This fundamental rift is certainly one of the principal reasons behind the collapse of the WTO Doha Development Round (Doha Round).

The EU has been one of the strongest proponents for the inclusion of deep disciplines within the realm of the WTO both during the Uruguay Round (e.g. services, intellectual property, and investment) and the Doha Round negotiations (e.g. 'Singapore issues'—investment, public procurement, competition, and trade facilitation) (WTO (1996)). Notwithstanding the successful conclusion of the WTO 'Bali package', comprehensive reform of the type envisaged in the Doha Round remains an unlikely prospect (Donnan (2014a)), and the focus of the EU's deep trade agenda—that is, the EU's attempts to introduce regulatory disciplines within the sphere of international trade law (Peterson and Young (2007), pp. 795–814)—has shifted towards bilateralism and regionalism. In 2006, the EU launched the Global Europe strategy (European Commission (2006a)), which signalled a significant change in its external trade policy by putting the emphasis on the conclusion of deep and comprehensive FTAs (DCFTAs). The departure from the EU's previous policy approach is twofold: first, the EU has abandoned its policy of focusing exclusively on multilateral trade liberalization by following the lead of the US and Asia in concluding bilateral and regional trade agreements; and secondly, whereas the EU had historically tended to conclude FTAs as a means to achieve political and security goals (e.g. trade agreements concluded with neighbouring countries), the FTAs envisaged by the Global Europe strategy are 'commercially driven' (Woolcock (2007b)) insofar as they seek to increase market access in the lucrative markets in Asia and the emerging economies more generally.

With this new generation of DCFTAs, the EU is keen to pursue its deep trade agenda by going beyond what is currently provided at WTO level and regulating behind-the-border issues, including the Singapore issues. Because tariff barriers between the EU and the US are already relatively low, it follows that any agreement would put tackling barriers resulting from divergences in domestic regulation at the very top of its agenda. In this sense, the TTIP may possibly come to represent the culmination of the EU's deep trade agenda. If these two economic powerhouses are able to agree on the adoption of key common deep disciplines, it is likely that these rules will set the standard that will be followed by the rest of the world. At one fell swoop, the EU and the US could singlehandedly determine the rules of international trade and the core features of domestic market regulation in liberal economies.

Of course, all of this remains very speculative. Given their considerable differences of opinion on key trade issues, as well as the increasingly hostile domestic opposition to the TTIP, there is no guarantee that the EU and the US will sign the agreement, and even less that such an agreement would contain the sort of deep disciplines put forward by the EU. In the meantime, the EU is happy to continue signing EU DCFTAs with the smaller fish in the pond. The fact that these EU DCFTAs are being concluded in the context of considerable power asymmetries in favour of the EU means that, theoretically, they offer an opportunity for the EU to implement the type of deep disciplines it has always wanted to push through at the multilateral level. They therefore present an opportunity to analyse whether and how the EU's deep trade agenda can materialize in practice. Such is the overarching objective of the present book.

The main question that the book seeks to answer is the nature and content of the disciplines being grafted onto the new generation of EU DCFTAs. Do they simply require the adoption of basic common regulatory disciplines or—like the Europe Agreements, which were designed to ease the process of integration of candidate Member States into the EU—are they being used as tools for the expansion of the EU's regulatory space? Are the rules being sourced from the EU acquis, regulatory models found in other existing international instruments, or a mixture of both, or can the EU DCFTAs be seen as a laboratory for the development of innovative rule-making? A second, related, question concerns how the EU's deep trade agenda, as formulated and implemented in the aftermath of the Global Europe strategy, impacts on perceived notions of what the EU is and how it acts in the international sphere. As a foreign policy power, the EU has typically been portrayed in opposition to the US's hegemonic power based on military power and self-interest. The EU has been variously described as a civilian power, a normative power, or even an ethical power, whose foreign policy goals are achieved through the dissemination of rules and the promotion of governance structures that replicate its own normative values, rather than through military power or other forms of coercion (Bickerton (2011), pp. 75–80). This question has become all the more relevant since the Treaty of Lisbon confirmed the idea of the EU as an external actor motivated not only by mere self-interest but also concerned by the promotion of supposedly European values. Article 3 TEU provides that the EU's external action must contribute 'to the sustainable development of the Earth, solidarity and mutual respect among peoples, free and fair trade, eradication of poverty and the protection of human rights, in particular the rights of the child, as well as to the strict observance and the development of international law, including respect for the principles of the United Nations Charter'. Article 21 TEU then acknowledges the distinctiveness of the EU as an international actor that promotes its values and norms abroad by providing that the EU's external action must 'be guided by the principles which have inspired its own creation, development and enlargement', namely 'democracy, the rule of law, the universality and indivisibility of human rights and fundamental freedoms, respect for human dignity, the principles of equality and solidarity, and respect for the principles of the United Nations Charter and international law'. Finally, in order to remove any doubts that the EU's trade policy should be used to pursue the overall objectives of the EU, it is specified in Article 207 TFEU that the common commercial policy must be conducted 'in the context of the principles and objectives of the Union's external action'. In the context of the deep trade agenda, this approach to foreign policy has in the past manifested itself through a policy of 'managed globalisation' (Meunier and Abdelal (2010), pp. 350–67), which—drawing inspiration from the balance struck between liberalization and social policies in the internal market—seeks to accommodate free trade imperatives with the need to promote non-trade values such as the promotion of democracy, rule of law, human rights, multilateralism, sustainable development, and environmental protection. Yet, as will be seen throughout this study, as the EU's trade policy becomes ever more commercially driven and, arguably, less imbued with narratives concerning non-trade values, it may be questioned whether such representations of the EU's approach to external relations are entirely reflective of reality. By looking at the type of deep disciplines included in its deep FTAs and how the regulatory reforms implicit in these deep disciplines take (or do not take) into account non-trade values, the book aims to shed some light on the nature of the EU's 'actorhood' (Telò (2007), p. 302) in international trade relations.

This book attempts to provide the first comprehensive examination of the deep disciplines included in the new generation of EU FTAs. It provides a legal analysis of the implementation of the EU's supposed deep trade agenda through these FTAs and, in doing so, determines whether there is any substance behind the EU's foreign policy rhetoric regarding the need to introduce regulatory issues within the remit of international trade law. A further distinctive feature of the book relates to the interdisciplinary nature of the research, as the doctrinal legal analysis is conducted in the context of political economy and international relations literature. The objective thus pursued is, on the one hand, to explore the rationale of the EU's deep trade agenda from a political economy perspective and to enquire whether the implementation of the agenda in the FTAs is justifiable and, on the other hand, to question whether the various conceptualizations of the EU as an international actor correspond to the EU's current practice in the context of its FTAs.

## 1.2 Research Methodology

The book undertakes a doctrinal legal analysis of the EU's current attempts to disseminate regulatory disciplines in the context of its trade relations. The main objective is to establish how the EU's deep trade agenda is being implemented in practice. There is, furthermore, a constitutional dimension to the research as it aims to determine the extent to which the EU's deep trade agenda complies with the new requirement under the Treaty of Lisbon for EU trade policy to complement the values and general objectives of EU external action. The legal analysis relies on a number of primary sources such as WTO agreements, EU Treaties, existing bilateral trade agreements entered into by the EU, and the relevant case law of the European Court of Justice (the Court) and of the WTO Dispute

Settlement Body. Moreover, the research also focuses on soft law sources such as communications, speeches and working documents issued, individually or jointly, by the EU and its trading partners. The book also refers to existing legal literature relating to EU external relations law, international trade law, IP law, competition law and public procurement law.

However, the very nature of the deep trade agenda means that the research must adopt an interdisciplinary approach. First, since the rationale for the deep trade agenda is rooted in political economy, the legal analysis must also take into account wider political economy considerations by way of context. Although there is broad recognition among political economists concerning the welfare gains associated with trade liberalization through non-discriminatory treatment ('shallow integration'), the same cannot be said with regard to deep trade integration. This is reflected by the difficulties encountered by the EU in pushing through deep disciplines in the context of the WTO, particularly during the Doha Round. An analysis of the political economy underlying deep trade issues is required in order to understand the objectives pursued by the EU's current policy and to determine the extent to which such policy takes into account objections expressed by various actors (states, non-governmental organizations, academics, etc.). The book thus explores the rationale for the promotion of the various regulatory areas (services, public procurement, IP rights, and competition) in trade policy, examines the arguments for and against the introduction of regulatory disciplines in international trade rules as well as the difficulties encountered by the EU in pushing through this policy in the past. In order to achieve this, recourse is made to existing political economy literature concerning international trade and the external trade relations of the EU. Finally, the book analyses the EU deep trade agenda in the wider context of international relations literature which has over time developed numerous narratives regarding the manner in which the EU seeks to act and influence other international actors through its foreign policy. As external trade policy is one of the core components of the EU's foreign policy, the research aims to contribute to such literature by examining whether the implementation of the EU's deep trade agenda fits with any of the prevailing conceptualizations of the EU as an international actor.

## 1.3 Boundaries of the Research

A few preliminary comments regarding the limits of the present study are required. Although the book aims to examine the EU's deep trade agenda as a whole, it will focus mostly on the EU DCFTAs. This is, first, because time and space constraints render an in-depth analysis of the multitude of tools and fora utilized by the EU in the context of its deep trade agenda impossible. Secondly, this is because, following the Global Europe strategy, it has become clear that EU DCFTAs now take pride of place in the EU's trade policy. Multilateral trade liberalization might still be identified as the number one priority of the EU's trade policy but the reality is that the prospects of accomplishing the comprehensive reforms initially envisaged in the Doha Round in the short to medium term are—to put it kindly—very slim. In the meantime, the EU's enthusiasm for EU DCFTAs shows no signs of abating. Thirdly, the EU DCFTAs envisaged by the EU are comprehensive, covering both border and behind-the-border measures and essentially revisiting all of the regulatory issues that it sought to include in the Doha Round. As a result, contrary to unilateral instruments such as the General System of Preferences (GSP), which tend to focus on the promotion of good governance reforms, protection of labour rights, and environmental protection, as well as multilateral agreements such as the World Intellectual Property Organization (WIPO) conventions, soft law arrangements such as the UNCITRAL Model Law on Public Procurement, which are all single-issue legal instruments, the EU DCFTAs provide a window into the deep trade agenda as a whole. This is not to say that the study turns a blind eye to other legal instruments where these represent an important avenue for the EU to pursue its deep trade agenda or where these complement in a significant manner what is being done in EU DCFTAs. For example, in the context of IP enforcement regulation, the book examines certain aspects of the Anti-Counterfeiting Trade Agreement (ACTA) (European Commission (2011d))—a plurilateral agreement requiring higher enforcement standards than those set under TRIPS—which was rejected by the European Parliament but has had a considerable impact on the content of EU DCFTAs.

Since 2006, the EU has launched FTA negotiations with a number of countries or country groupings which broadly fit the economic profile set out by the Global Europe strategy in that all such agreements are justified by commercial considerations. These include ASEAN, Canada, Gulf Cooperation Council (GCC), India, Korea, MERCOSUR, and, more recently, the US (European Commission (2013c)). So far, the EU has struggled to turn these negotiations into fully fledged FTAs. Most of the negotiations remain ongoing processes whilst some have been abandoned (the FTA negotiations with GCC were suspended in 2008, whilst the negotiations with the idea of an ASEAN–EU FTA has been temporarily abandoned in favour of bilateral negotiations with individual ASEAN member states).[1] To date, the EU has only signed one FTA with one of the priority partners originally identified under the Global Europe strategy: the EU–Korea FTA (KOREU FTA) which was signed on 10 May 2010 and entered into force on 1 July 2011. Both parties had significant vested interests in the swift conclusion of an agreement. From the EU's side, there was the fact that Korea and the US were negotiating an FTA which, once concluded, could lead to the discrimination of European firms in favour of their US competitors. For Korea, the main driver for the negotiations was the promise of enhanced access to the EU market, particularly in the automotive sector (Elsig and Dupont (2010), pp. 500–1). The final

[1] Negotiations are currently ongoing with India, Japan, Malaysia, MERCOSUR, Thailand, the United States, and Vietnam.

outcome is a comprehensive and WTO-plus FTA covering trade in manufactured goods (including standardization of safety and environmental automotive standards eliminating tariffs for most manufactured goods), trade in agricultural goods, services, IP and public procurement, competition, and sustainable development (Cooper (2011); Harrison (2013), pp. 57–65). That the EU has thus far failed to conclude FTAs with the majority of the countries identified by the Global Europe strategy suggests that its comprehensive deep liberalization agenda may have been too ambitious from the outset. This is particularly relevant in the context of negotiations with emerging economies in Asia and South America that have opposed the EU's attempts to introduce deep disciplines at the multilateral level.

However, the EU has concluded, and continues to negotiate, a number of FTAs which, whilst being driven primarily by political and development considerations and not targeting countries identified by the Global Europe strategy, apply the Global Europe ethos insofar as they are comprehensive in scope and have a strong regulatory dimension focused on WTO-plus issues (European Commission (2006b)). This is the case of the economic partnership agreement signed by the EU and the CARIFORUM group of states[2] (CEPA), the FTA signed with Peru and Colombia (Colombia–Peru FTA) and the FTA component of the EU–Central America Association Agreement (EU–CA FTA). The CEPA is underpinned by the Cotonou Agreement signed on 23 June 2000[3]—an association agreement governing the trade, development cooperation, and political relationship between the EU and the countries currently making up the African, Caribbean and Pacific Group of States (ACP) (Bartels (2007), pp. 715–56). The signing of the Cotonou agreement signalled a shift away from the focus on trade and development that had characterized the previous EU–ACP regime under the successive Lomé Conventions (Ibid) as they (i) provided for the expiry of the non-reciprocal trade preferences (which were deemed to violate the General Agreement on Tariffs and Trade[4]) which are to be replaced with FTAs which will be signed with separate regional groupings (so-called economic partnership agreements) and (ii) added a political pillar to EU–ACP relations which places greater emphasis on strengthening dialogue concerning security issues, including conflict prevention and peacekeeping, respect for human rights, and good governance. The CEPA, signed on 15 October 2008, was the first and remains to date the only economic partnership agreement concluded with an ACP regional grouping. It departs from the Lomé trade regime in two fundamental aspects. First, insofar as it puts an end to the non-reciprocal preferential access of Caribbean States to the EU market. Secondly, the negotiations of the CEPA were informed by the Global

[2] The CARIFORUM Group refers to the Caribbean States currently including the Member States of the Caribbean Community and the Dominican Republic. See http://www.caricom.org/jsp/community_organs/cariforum/cariforum_main_page.jsp?menu=cob.

[3] Partnership agreement 2000/483/EC between the members of the African, Caribbean and Pacific Group of States of the one part, and the European Community and its Member States, of the other part, signed in Cotonou on 23 June 2000, OJ, L 317.

[4] GATT Panel Report, *EEC—Import Regime for Bananas*, DS38/R, 11 February 1994.

Europe strategy as the agreement is a comprehensive, WTO-plus FTA covering a number of deep disciplines in the area of services, IP, public procurement, and competition (Sauvé and Ward (2009)). In fact, as the first deep FTA concluded by the EU following the Global Europe strategy, the CEPA has set the template for all subsequent EU DCFTAs (Hoffmesiter (2013), p. 13).

Likewise, in 2007 the EU launched negotiations for the conclusion of Association Agreements with the Andean Community (Bolivia, Colombia, Ecuador, and Peru) and six Central American countries (Costa Rica, El Salvador, Guatemala, Honduras, Nicaragua, and Panama) in order to provide a framework for political dialogue, cooperation, and trade. The negotiations with the Andean Community were suspended in 2008 because of disagreements between Andean countries and were thereafter re-launched only with Colombia and Peru, which, led to the signing of the Colombia–Peru FTA on 26 June 2012.[5] The EU–Central America Association Agreement was signed on 29 June 2012, although it is yet to be ratified by all Central American countries involved (European Commission (2013c), p. 4). Again, it must be noted that the content of the Colombia–Peru FTA as well as the EU–CA FTA follow the template set out in the KOREU FTA and the CEPA by including rules that far exceed what is currently provided under WTO law. Finally, the book also examines the EU–Singapore FTA concluded in December 2012.[6] The EU–ASEAN FTA negotiations, launched in 2007, collapsed two years later partly because the ASEAN countries were unable to agree on a common negotiating position and partly because they were reluctant to acquiesce to the EU's demands that countries whose economic development was deemed insufficient (Cambodia and Laos) or whose human rights record was considered poor (Burma) should be excluded from the negotiating process. This forced the EU to pursue negotiations on an individual basis with Singapore, Malaysia, and Vietnam. The EU–Singapore FTA remains to date the only trade agreement concluded by the EU with an ASEAN country. Significantly, it is one of the first EU DCFTAs to make use of the extension of the EU's external competence in the area of foreign direct investment by including investment protection provisions and investment arbitration clauses. Negotiations were concluded on 17 October 2014 but the approval and the ratification of the EU–Singapore FTA have been delayed as a consequence of the Commission's decision to request an opinion of the Court of Justice on whether the EU has the competence to conclude the agreement alone.[7] The outcome of this procedure will have a huge bearing on the future development of the EU's external trade policy

[5] The Colombia–Peru FTA will enter into force once ratified by all Member States. It has been provisionally applied with Peru since 1 March 2013 (IP/13/173) and with Colombia since 1 August 2013 (IP/13/749).

[6] The EU–Singapore FTA is yet to be formally approved by the Commission, the Council of Ministers and the European Parliament. Ratification is expected at the end of 2014 at the earliest (European Commission (2014)).

[7] Commission Decision, requesting an opinion of the Court of Justice pursuant to article 218(11) TFEU on the competence of the Union to sign and conclude a Free Trade Agreement with Singapore, C(2014) 8218 final.

as the main focus of the opinion will be on the delineation of the EU's exclusive competence in the area of foreign direct investment. Finally, the EU concluded negotiations on the EU–Canada Comprehensive Economic Trade Agreement (CETA) on 26 September 2014 (European Commission (2014)). The negotiation of this agreement was motivated by a desire to provide a boost to the economies of both parties in the post-financial crisis era as a reaction to stasis that characterizes negotiations at the multilateral level. However, like the EU–Singapore FTA, the CETA contains clauses relating to investment protection and the parties have opted to wait for the outcome of the Court's opinion on the EU's competence before proceeding with the ratification of the agreement. These agreements constitute the main, albeit not exclusive, focus of the present study.

The EU has also concluded a number of deep FTAs with third countries within its periphery. However, such FTAs are being negotiated in the context of the European Neighbourhood Policy (ENP) which predicates an integration process covering both political issues and economic issues and where, in some cases, future accession to the EU is openly being contemplated. The market concessions and regulatory reforms the EU is able to secure from countries covered by the ENP are, naturally, greater than anything the EU could possibly expect to obtain either at the WTO level or in purely economically and development-driven FTAs (for example, trade agreements concluded in the context of the ENP require the adoption of a wide array of EU norms by third countries so as to allow increased participation in the internal market). Although part of the EU's deep trade agenda, FTAs concluded in the context of the ENP are therefore not particularly instructive as to the type of deep disciplines the EU wishes to or is able to realistically promote in the context of international trade relations and are therefore excluded from the present study.

The second limitation relates to the type of disciplines that are examined in the research. Although the deep trade agenda covers a wide range of areas of domestic regulation, the book will focus on services, investment, IP, public procurement, and competition. The focus on this select group of disciplines is justified by the special strategic importance accorded to them by the EU in its trade policy. The EU was one of the main proponents of the TRIPS and GATS in the Uruguay Round and public procurement and competition were part of the Singapore issues which the EU fought so assiduously to include in the Doha Round. All of them have been identified by the Global Europe strategy as new trade areas where stronger rules are required (European Commission (2006a), p. 8). Labour rights and environmental protection standards (part of the EU's agenda during the Doha Round) will be addressed summarily because of their reduced importance in the context of the EU's current focus on commercially driven FTAs.

Finally, each of these regulatory areas presents different challenges in the context of the deep trade agenda. The liberalization of public procurement markets has typically been rejected by developing countries because of concerns that opening such markets to foreign competition would curtail their ability to promote domestic industries. IP—an area typically associated with development concerns—also raises issues of human rights violations. As for services, the regulatory diversity and complexity that characterizes this area make any attempts at horizontal harmonization difficult, eliciting problems that go beyond the North/South divide in international trade negotiations. The inclusion of investment protection and investor arbitration clauses in trade agreements is a highly controversial practice that has been opposed by developing countries in the context of WTO negotiations and is increasingly being contested by developed countries, who have come to realize that such provisions can undermine their right to regulate in the public interest. Finally, competition law, an issue close to the EU's heart, is an area that has equally divided developed and developing nations for reasons varying from its impact on development to disagreements resulting from differing regulatory approaches.

Although all of the FTAs covered by the study now include binding dispute settlement provisions, this particular issue will not be addressed in the book. The EU has typically relied on diplomacy and conciliation mechanisms to solve conflicts that may arise as a result of the implementation of trade agreements. This diplomatic approach can be explained by a variety of factors (Garcia Bercero (2006), pp. 404–5)—not least the fact that the EU has hitherto mostly signed trade agreements with small economies and that most subject areas (e.g. anti-dumping, countervailing duties, sanitary and phytosanitary) that typically cause disputes at WTO level are exempted from the scope of dispute settlement provisions included in EU FTAs. As the EU increasingly signs WTO-plus FTAs with larger economies it may be that the dispute settlement provisions become more relevant. However, to the best of the author's knowledge, neither the EU nor its trading partners have invoked the dispute settlement mechanisms provided under the FTAs covered by the present study.

The third limitation concerns the non-trade values that are examined in the research. As explained above, the EU's trade policy has traditionally been peppered with references to political and social objectives that seek to counterbalance the adverse effects of trade liberalization and that incorporate the gamut of varying foreign policy goals that it pursues. Article 21 of the Treaty on the European Union lists some of these goals. The EU is enjoined to conduct its external action to

> safeguard its values, fundamental interests, security, independence and integrity, [...] consolidate and support democracy, the rule of law, human rights [...] foster the sustainable economic, social and environmental development of developing countries [...], encourage the integration of all countries into the world economy, including through the progressive abolition of restrictions on international trade, [...] help develop international measures to preserve and improve the quality of the environment and the sustainable management of global natural resources, in order to ensure sustainable development [...] assist populations, countries and regions confronting natural or man-made disasters; and [...] promote an international system based on stronger multilateral cooperation and good global governance'.[8]

[8] Article 21 TEU.

Rather than addressing the various EU foreign policy objectives systematically, for each of the disciplines covered, the book identifies those non-trade issues that have caused tensions in the context of multilateral trade negotiations and examines how these are tackled in the context of the EU's deep trade agenda. As explained, such issues may vary from the need to promote development (this is relevant because the main objections against further trade liberalization during the Doha Round related to concerns from developing countries that this would reduce policy space) to the protection of human rights. The book also examines to what extent the deep trade agenda undermines the EU's commitment to multilateralism. Political economists have historically identified FTAs as a threat to multilateral trade liberalization, partly because they cause trade diversion, but also because they divert attention away from multilateral negotiations. Yet despite its current emphasis on signing EU DCFTAs, the EU has consistently maintained that multilateral trade liberalization remains its first priority and that the EU DCFTAs will not constitute a stumbling block but rather a stepping stone towards further multilateral trade liberalization (European Commission (2006a), p. 10). The book therefore also considers the extent to which the deep disciplines proposed by the EU in its EU DCFTAs either undermine or assist multilateral trade liberalization.

## 1.4 Structure of the Book

The book is subdivided into seven chapters, including the introductory chapter which seeks to situate the issue of trade liberalization and domestic regulation from an historical and legal perspective. Chapter Two examines the evolution of the international trading system that emerged in the post-Second World War period and attempts to explain how the evolution of international economic exchanges has caused a significant shift in the priorities of the international economic system that led to the creation of the WTO. The chapter then examines the EU's deep trade agenda at multilateral, regional, and bilateral level. Chapter Three analyses the legal and institutional framework of the EU's external trade policy and, in particular, how rules regarding competence, decision-making process and objectives shape the EU's deep trade agenda. Chapters Four, Five, Six and Seven will deal with the EU's attempt to promote the deep disciplines in the areas of services, investment, IP, competition, and public procurement respectively. Each of these chapters will include a description of the EU and WTO regulatory framework for the field concerned, the ongoing debates concerning WTO reform, the content of the EU's policy, and provisions included in existing EU DCFTAs. Chapter Eight outlines the main findings of the research.

# 2

# The EU's Deep Trade Agenda Contextualized

## 2.1 Introduction

This introductory chapter provides an overview of the major issues surrounding the EU's deep trade agenda. It looks at the reasons behind this policy, how it has evolved over time, the issues it raises in terms of the future direction of the international trading system, and how it reflects on the EU's self-perception of its role in international relations.

Section 2.2 describes the evolution of the international trading system after the Second World War and highlights the various inter-connected changes that have occurred since that time, from the increasing demands for deeper forms of economic integration and the resulting loss of domestic regulatory autonomy to the rise and fall of multilateral trade liberalization. Section 2.3 contextualizes the evolution of the EU's own trade policy in the light of the external factors outlined in the preceding section. It explains, in particular, how the EU's trade policy has changed from a protectionist, inward-looking, and reactive policy to one that is aggressively pursuing deep integration, and how the EU has moved on from a deep trade agenda focused on multilateral trade liberalization to one that is focused on commercially-driven bilateral free trade agreements (FTAs). Finally, Section 2.4 examines the prevailing international relations theories concerning the nature of the EU's power as an international actor and questions whether these theories adequately account for the recent changes in the EU's trade policy.

## 2.2 Evolution of the International Trading System Post–Second World War

### 2.2.1 From shallow to deep integration

The international trading system designed in the aftermath of the Second World War was intended to avoid the national trade restrictive measures of the interwar period, which were widely believed to have been one of the main contributing factors behind the conflict (Simmons (2013), pp. 442–3). The type of free trade predicated by the General Agreement on Tariffs and Trade (GATT) 1947 was based on the principle of non-discrimination, as embodied by both the most-favoured nation (MFN) rule and its complement, the national treatment rule. Although

GATT 1947 urged its members to keep trade-restrictive measures to reasonably low levels, there was no obligation to reduce them, rather an obligation to remove any measure that would discriminate between products of the members of the organization and between domestic products and foreign products. The primary aim of GATT 1947 was to promote free trade in goods by focusing on the removal of border measures constituting barriers to trade, such as tariffs and import quotas. However, it did not concern itself with the content of domestic measures, so long as they did not discriminate against imported products (Heiskanen (2004), p. 3). This model for economic integration—where countries enter into international cooperation arrangements to remove exclusively discriminatory barriers to trade—has been referred to alternatively as 'negative integration' (Tinbergen (1954), p. 4) or 'shallow integration' (Lawrence, Bressand, and Ito (1996b), p. 5).

Negative integration remained the predominant model for the regulation of international trade relations for the two decades that followed the conclusion of GATT 1947, with successive rounds of GATT negotiations (Dillon Round and Kennedy Round) focusing essentially on the reduction of tariffs worldwide (Evans (1971)). However, by the 1970s it had become apparent that trade liberalization could no longer be seen purely in terms of removing trade barriers at borders, but should also encompass those domestic non-tariff regulatory (behind-the-border) measures that affect trade. This was partly due to the overwhelming success of the GATT in removing tariff barriers, which put the spotlight on barriers resulting from domestic regulatory measures that had hitherto received little attention. Often, these behind-the-border measures simply sought to achieve legitimate national policy goals, but it was not uncommon for countries to resort to domestic regulations such as technical barriers to trade (TBTs)—rules regulating the production of products to achieve health, safety, and environmental goals—for protectionist purposes (WTO (2012b), pp. 41–2). Therefore, starting with the Tokyo Round negotiations in the 1970s, which introduced minimal and voluntary disciplines in areas such as TBTs, subsidies, and public procurement (Heiskanen (2004), pp. 5–6), and culminating with regional and multilateral economic integration arrangements such as the EU's internal market and the WTO agreements, more recent attempts to liberalize international trade have increasingly moved away from the negative integration approach associated with GATT 1947 and focused on 'positive integration' (Tinbergen (1954), p. 4) or 'deep integration' (Lawrence (1996a)) models, where greater emphasis is placed on disciplining domestic regulation, particularly through the development of common or harmonized market rules and policies (Jovanovic (1998), pp. 5–10).

The change in approach towards trade liberalization also reflects a more fundamental upheaval in the international trading system from the 1980s onwards, resulting from the advances in transport and information technology which have enabled firms to be more footloose—that is, able to up sticks and move production and processing facilities to where consumers are located or, increasingly, where cheaper labour is available (Welfens (2000), pp. 13–33). This 'internationalisation of supply chains' (Baldwin (2012), p. 5) has become an increasingly prevalent concern in international trade politics. The ease with which firms are able to relocate means that countries that wish to attract foreign investment must be wary of the potential impact of domestic regulation on the ability of foreign firms to access their domestic markets. Market access may, for example, be impeded by the existence of onerous establishment or incorporation requirements, by the absence of a fully functioning antitrust or competition law system, or even by the lax enforcement of intellectual property (IP) laws. Moreover, mere differences in regulations may increase the costs of market access for foreign firms and thus place them at a competitive disadvantage compared to domestic market operators (Lawrence, Bressand, and Ito (1996b), pp. 49–52). The emphasis is on enhancing market contestability and minimizing 'the regulatory constraints to enter, operate in and exit from markets' (Hoekman and Kostecki (2011) pp. 414–15). As a result, the push for deeper integration aims to go beyond non-discrimination requirements by improving both market contestability and rules of operation for multinational firms by requiring the adoption of 'internationally compatible' business-friendly domestic regulatory frameworks (Maur (2008), p. 16; Baldwin (2012), p. 7).

Deep integration represents an important paradigm shift in the international trading system. It was already present in the context of the EU's internal market, which was based on the free movement of goods, services, capital, and persons, realized through the juxtaposition of negative integration and a brand of positive integration relying on regulatory harmonization and mutual recognition. But this paradigm shift was most potently materialized in the form of the World Trade Organization (WTO) which, as Dymond and Hart explained, 'shifted the centre of gravity of international trade rules from negative prescription to positive rule-making [...]. The WTO not only requires governments to live up to their GATT commitments, but also to implement specific policies, practices, and procedures' (Dymond and Hart (2000), p. 22). The best illustration of the WTO's push for regulatory harmonization can be found in the Agreement on the Trade Related Aspects of Intellectual Property (TRIPS), which includes minimum standards of protection and enforcement for an extensive list of IP rights (e.g. copyrights, trademarks, patents, and geographical indications) that must be incorporated into the domestic legislation of WTO Members (Reichman (1998), p. 21). In other words, TRIPS effectively obliges WTO Members to enact a comprehensive IP regulatory system. The Agreement on Technical Barriers to Trade (TBT) and the Agreement on Sanitary and Phytosanitary Measures (SPS) are also geared towards regulatory harmonization, as they both incentivize WTO Members to adopt regulations that are in line with existing international standards (Marceau and Trachtman (2002), pp. 811–82). Under the TBT, WTO Members are implored to use the relevant international standards 'as basis for their technical regulations except when such international standards [...] would be an ineffective or inappropriate means of fulfilling the legitimate objectives pursued'[1] and, under the SPS, WTO Members are told to 'base their sanitary and phytosanitary measures on international standards, guidelines and recommendations where they exist',[2] and may only apply

[1] Article 2.4 TBT. [2] Article 3 SPS.

higher standards of protection 'if there is a scientific justification or if an appropriate risk assessment has been concluded'.[3] Finally, regulatory harmonization is also evident to a lesser extent in other agreements, such as the General Agreement on Trade in Services (GATS) which contains certain rules on competition policy[4] and requires WTO Members to establish tribunals and procedures that can provide remedies for administrative decisions affecting service suppliers.[5]

Following the completion of the Uruguay Round, there have been attempts to extend the WTO's foray into domestic regulation. Although these were met with some limited success, such as the plurilateral agreements on financial services and telecommunications, in general, proposals for negotiations of new issues such as competition, foreign investment, procurement, labour standards, and environmental protection ended up on the scrapheap. Many of these new issues (so-called 'trade and' issues) (Charnovitz (2002), p. 11) appear to only be vaguely related to what has historically been understood as the primary objective of international trade law—that is, the liberalization of the cross-border movement of goods and services and the removal of discriminatory domestic measures (Heiskanen (2004), p. 13). The rejection of these deep disciplines and the push for the establishment of globally harmonized regulatory systems reveal a deep-seated unease concerning the intrusion of international trade politics into areas that have hitherto been the preserve of national sovereignty, as well as the difficulties encountered by the current multilateral trade governance system in dealing with these issues.

## 2.2.2 The impact of deep integration on national autonomy

### *2.2.2.1 WTO and policy space*

Governments regulate markets for a number of reasons. Regulation can rectify market failures—that is, to redress the undesirable effects that would result from unfettered competition within the markets. It may be required to ensure that markets remain competitive, to compensate for information asymmetries between economic operators and consumers or to address externalities such as the potentially adverse impact of certain economic activities on the environment (WTO (2004b), pp. 150–74; Snidal (2011), p. 345). States may also adopt legislation designed to implement macro-economic policies aimed at spurring economic development or even to achieve non-economic goals such as wealth redistribution or to pursue policy preferences and societal choices (e.g. cultural heritage or the preservation of wildlife) (Krajewski (2003), pp. 118–20).

In a globalized economy, the ability of governments to autonomously and efficiently regulate and pursue national policy objectives—that is, their regulatory autonomy (or policy space) (Santos (2012), p. 553)—can be reduced in two ways. First, the effectiveness of national policy tools may be decreased as a result of

[3] Articles 2.2, 5.1, and 5.2 TBT.
[4] Articles XVIII and IX GATS.
[5] Article VI GATS.

the integration of the national economy into the global economy (Akyuz (2010), p. 35). Once domestic markets are liberalized and opened to the outside world, they inevitably become vulnerable to external factors and economic performance may depend as much on external economic conditions as on national economic policy. In the same vein, the increased reliance on foreign investment necessarily narrows the policy tools available to national governments: raise taxes too much or under-invest in infrastructure, and companies may just decide to take their custom elsewhere (Luyten (1991), p. 278). Secondly, by entering into bilateral, regional, plurilateral, and multilateral trade liberalization agreements, sovereign states decrease the number of policy instruments available to national authorities to achieve macro-economic or developmental goals. In fact, because international trade governance instruments typically have a liberalizing agenda, their rules have the effect of diminishing national sovereignty, both by enhancing global economic liberalization and by establishing disciplines that restrict the utilization of policy tools by national authorities (Mayer (2009), p. 376).

Loss of policy space or regulatory autonomy has long been a consideration in devising international trade rules. Even the GATT 1947 system, which was based mostly on tariff cutting and negative integration requirements, took into account the potential for this agreement to undermine national sovereignty. GATT thus adopted an approach which sought to recognize the tension between economic integration and regulatory autonomy. The substance of GATT was informed by the specific historical context in which the agreement was concluded. The economic protectionism of the earlier part of the twentieth century had, to a large degree, been a counter-reaction to the failure of attempts to liberalize trade in the second half of the nineteenth century (Abbot (2007), p. 574).

By the time the international community began negotiating GATT 1947, it had become abundantly clear that a completely unrestricted trade system would not—contrary to the claims of the proponents of economic liberalism such as Adam Smith and David Ricardo—benefit everyone, and that domestic intervention was necessary in order to redress the problems caused by trade liberalization (Stopler and Samuelson (1941), pp. 58–73; Bernstein (2008), pp. 289–315). The numerous exceptions to non-discrimination, such as the possibility of establishing preferential trade agreements; the safety valves available to WTO Members, including the imposition of quantitative restrictions when required to safeguard a country's foreign exchange reserves and its balance of payments; the exclusion from the scope of GATT of certain sectors of trade, such as textiles and agriculture, which were politically sensitive sectors for the US and the European nations; and the absence of a dispute settlement mechanism issuing enforceable decisions all represent an implicit acknowledgement that states were unwilling to undermine the stability of their national economies in the name of free trade.

The term 'embedded liberalism' was coined by Ruggie to describe GATT's cautious take on trade liberalization (Ruggie (1982), pp. 379–415; Ruggie (1994), p. 1). It was premised on the assertion that, contrary to popular belief, free trade was not the 'be-all and end all' of the GATT regime. Rather, it was devised to curb national protectionist impulses whilst preserving the powers of states to intervene in order to cushion the impact of liberalization. It is a compromise between economic liberalism and domestic interventionism that aims to ensure, on the one hand, that states retain their capacity to undertake stabilization measures and pursue legitimate policy objectives and, on the other hand, that protectionist impulses are constrained within a specific set of multilateral rules.

However, the diversification of international economic exchange, the emergence of global supply chains, and the significant lowering of taxes from the 1980s onwards have reduced the efficiency of the national policy measures permitted under the embedded liberalism compromise. Ruggie acknowledged the impact of these changes on the ability of states to implement national policy objectives in the concept of 'disembedded liberalism' (Ruggie (1994), pp. 8–11). These changes led to the introduction of deeper and wider international trade disciplines, which have further undermined the ability of states to maintain effective economic policy tools. In particular, the tension between deep integration and the need to maintain regulatory autonomy has been laid bare in the context of the WTO.

The loss of policy space resulting from the WTO is a natural consequence of deep integration. Regulatory harmonization of the type required under agreements such as TRIPS and GATS entail, at the very least, adherence to a fixed set of common minimum rules from which WTO Members must not deviate. It is also linked in large part to more restrictive rules concerning the use of national measures that favour domestic industry. The Agreement on Subsidies and Countervailing Measures (SCM) prohibits export subsidies and generally subjects subsidies to stricter controls than had previously been in place in the pre-WTO regime, whilst the Agreement on Trade Related Aspects of Investment Measures (TRIMs) prohibits the imposition of national quantitative restrictions such as local content requirements (Dymond and Hart (2000), p. 30); Santos (2012), p. 564). Moreover, GATT 1994 substantially reduces the ability of WTO Members to use the release valves (e.g. safeguard measures, the balance of payments flexibilities, and special and differential treatment for developed countries exception) (Santos (2012), pp. 566–70) that were so instrumental to Ruggie's embedded liberalism system.

Although such rules apply to all WTO Members, the resulting loss of policy space was more acutely felt by developing country members, who were left unable to implement policies favouring national industries in the same manner as developed countries had once done—notably the East Asian Tigers, which had utilized protectionist policies to ensure the development of domestic industries prior to their integration into the global economy (Gallagher (2008), p. 63). These included industrial policies excluding market entry of foreign firms in certain key industries, which shielded domestic industries from international competition until they were able to compete on an equal footing, and the enactment of IP protection legislation that was less stringent than that enacted in developed countries, so as to facilitate the ability of domestic firms to catch up with technological advances in the developed world. The most striking example of how WTO rules proved problematic for developing countries is TRIPS, which imposes developed country standards of IP protection and enforcement on developing countries

(Lamy (2004b), p. 947). By requiring the adoption of high levels of IP protection, TRIPS is said to have had the perverse effect of impeding developing countries from developing technology-intensive domestic industries, whilst simultaneously allowing developed country industries to extract significant rents from developing countries (Baldwin (2004), p. 50; Abbott (2005), pp. 80–3).

Unsurprisingly, one of the main criticisms levelled at the WTO is that developed countries have used it to enshrine rules that impede developing countries from resorting to the same protectionist measures that contributed to their own development (Khor (2004), p. 50), reinforcing the perception that the WTO agreements were drafted by developed countries with developed country interests in mind (Finger and Nogues (2002), pp. 321–40; Finger (2007), p. 443). The counterarguments in this debate are that the Uruguay Round was the result of a grand bargain where developed countries also made concessions which hugely benefited developing countries, that doubts remain concerning the welfare effects of protectionism on economic development (Dornbusch (1992), pp. 69–85), and that there is evidence that the trade liberalization elicited by the WTO had, overall, a positive effect on the economic performance of developing countries (Rolland (2012), pp. 266–7). Nevertheless, fears concerning further loss of policy space have remained very much at the forefront of developing country concerns in the context of the Doha Round, not least with regard to the introduction of new deep trade disciplines, as evidenced by the *en masse* rejection of the proposals for the introduction of investment, competition, and public procurement rules in the 2003 Cancun Ministerial Conference (Cho (2004), pp. 230–1).

#### 2.2.2.2 *New trade issues and policy autonomy*

Deep integration adds another dimension to the conflict between international trade policy and the domestic policies of national governments. Whereas the welfare gains that come from market opening through non-discrimination are backed up by a significant body of evidence (Heydon (2012), pp. 33–5), the case for a global harmonization of domestic rules is far from established and depends very much on the regulatory area at issue (Hoekman and Kostecki (2001), p. 415). International disciplines on regulatory areas which are only indirectly linked to trade policy, such as competition, procurement, environment, or labour, may be required in order to promote the contestability of markets, but in many cases it is debatable whether the negotiation of such international disciplines is feasible or even desirable. Roessler pinpoints the issue as follows (Roessler (1996), p. 42):

> Any proposal to harmonize domestic policies through GATT or the WTO raises the question of whether the optimal area for the harmonization of the policies at issue coincides with the area covered by the multilateral trading system. To propose that international policy harmonization to be achieved through the WTO is to propose policy harmonization on a worldwide scale. It cannot be assumed that an international harmonization of internal regulations increases efficiency, and—to the extent that it does—that multilateral harmonization of internal regulations is superior to harmonization within

regional groupings because differences in regulations between nations or regions may reflect differences in values, tastes and circumstances.

For example, linking international trade rules and labour rights is usually justified by the concerns of human rights advocates keen to raise global labour standards or of exporters (mostly from developed countries) desirous of removing the competitive advantages enjoyed by firms operating in countries where the cost of labour is low (Hudec (1996), p. 2). Historically, the solution proposed to address this problem is to impose minimum labour rights and to permit trade sanctions against countries that fail to comply with such standards (so-called 'social clause') (Leary (1996), p. 177). However, the rationale for the imposition of global labour standards in international trade rules is very much disputed. There is little empirical evidence showing that diverging low labour standards significantly affect trade flows (Burtless, Lawrence, Litan, and Shapiro (1998), p. 122). Moreover, from a political economy perspective, requiring an increase of labour standards abroad seems at odds with the idea that trade liberalization is intended to allow countries to exploit their respective comparative advantages. Rather than levelling the playing field, the incorporation of labour standards in international trade rules can be construed as a protectionist move designed to remove one of the very few competitive advantages developing countries have over developed countries (Hansson (2012), p. 285). Valid economic justifications for the use of trade sanctions as a means of enforcing labour standards are also hard to come by as these 'raise the prices of imports, thus imposing a welfare cost at home, while at the same time worsening the labour situation at home' (Hoekman and Kostecki (2003), p. 450). Finally, there is also the issue that different labour standards reflect the choices of different societies at different levels of economic development (Hoekman and Kostecki (2003), p. 450):

> It is not necessarily the case that high standards [...] will reduce the ability of firms to compete on world markets. If firms can ensure that the incidence of the implicit tax is borne by workers [...] labour costs may be unaffected. Moreover, insofar as the cost-raising effects of workers rights cannot be fully shifted to workers, the resulting increase in product prices (due to higher costs) will put pressure on the exchange rate (because foreign demand for exports falls as prices increase by raising the cost of imports—all other things equal). The resulting depreciation will lower the standard of living by raising the costs of imports. While the economy thus bears the burden of the high standards, the exchange rate adjustment allows the firms to compete on world markets. [...] [A]s labour standards in force reflect desires of voters, the cost of implementation simply reflect the trade off between monetary and non-monetary wealth that society has made. However if standards are unilaterally imposed on a country, it is very unlikely that they will reflect the preferences of the population.

It is therefore not a given that the minimum labour standards applied in one country will produce optimal results elsewhere. Developed countries adopt high standards because there is a demand from their constituents to do so and because they are able to absorb the ensuing costs. However, developing countries are generally in no position to demand or achieve the 'trade-off between monetary and non-monetary wealth' (Burtless, Lawrence, Litan, and Shapiro (1998), p. 122). Another example of the adverse consequences that the incorporation of regulatory areas in international trade rules can have on the regulatory autonomy of states can be found in the area of competition law. National competition laws vary widely from one country to another; regulatory diversity can be attributed to a variety of historical, economic, and cultural factors. In the US, competition law is focused on maximizing consumer welfare, in the EU on removing market access barriers created by firms and in developing countries, such as South Africa, competition law is also used to pursue non-economic objectives. Leaving aside the issue of the feasibility of finding common ground between these disparate regimes, there is also the question of whether it is desirable to impose a global regime in the context of the WTO, where market access would be the primary concern, to the detriment of other valid objectives. Certain competition law regimes, for example, permit practices adopted by private enterprises that restrict market access if these are demonstrated to create economic efficiencies. In a world where trade rules and competition are linked, states may see themselves forced into a situation where such practices are prohibited irrespective of welfare considerations.

### 2.2.3 Deep integration and trade governance

#### *2.2.3.1 From multilateralism to fragmentation*

The successful conclusion of the Uruguay Round negotiations may represent the apotheosis of multilateralism in international trade relations. In fact, the WTO agreements could be seen as the culmination of a shift in the conduct of international relations, from a focus on unilateralism and bilateralism to an increased emphasis on multi-state cooperation, a process which started with the establishment of the United Nations in 1945. When GATT was established two years later, it was, despite its multilateralist agenda, still very much a developed-country club (Simmons (2006), p. 443), justified as much by the US's desire to reinforce political links between a group of countries in opposition to the Communist bloc as by any economic rationales underlying trade liberalization. The end of the cold war removed this element of opposition, which opened the door for the establishment of the multilateral WTO. However, it also undermined its future progress. Without a common foe, there was no longer an incentive to push for multilateral trade liberalization, and countries began exploring bilateralism and regionalism as means to promote their economic and political interests. The rise of large emerging economies, and in particular the East Asian 'Tigers' and the powerful BRICS countries, has caused a fundamental shift in international trade relations, insofar as these can no longer be directed by a duopoly of the EU and US, but rather must accommodate a diverse group of interests. In the WTO, the impact of this diffusion of power on multilateralism can be seen in the failure of the Doha Round negotiations, where the BRICS countries—whose commitment to a multilateral trading order has been questioned—demonstrated their capability to both withstand pressures exerted by the US and the EU and to mobilize developing country opposition. The end of US hegemony and the resulting diffusion of power and interests are the major causes of the progressive decline of multilateralism in the international trading system (Young and Peterson (2006), p. 797).

The fall of multilateralism's stock in the international trading order is also a reflection of the difficulties resulting from the incorporation of deep trade disciplines. As the classic understanding of what constitutes trade is extended beyond the mere cross-border movement of goods to include new areas that impinge on domestic regulatory sovereignty, multilateral negotiations become ever more complex affairs. First, the WTO's mercantilist system of negotiations based on the reciprocal trading of concessions is ill-suited to the negotiation of complex regulatory systems (Heiskanen (2004), pp. 18–19). Secondly, during the Uruguay Round, GATT members agreed to adopt the 'single undertaking' provision, which required all parties to adopt all agreements as a package (Hindley (2002), pp. 158–9). In other words, WTO negotiations are underpinned by an 'all or nothing' rationale, which precludes the possibility of cherry-picking. This approach proved problematic in the Doha Round, where disagreements concerning the expansion of global trade rules led to the outright exclusion of many proposals from the negotiating table. Developing countries, already disappointed by the outcome of the Uruguay Round, were never likely to embrace the deep trade disciplines proposed by developed countries (e.g. Singapore Issues, proposed by the EU), and used the single undertaking to exclude them from negotiations. Thirdly, the introduction of deep trade disciplines within the sphere of the WTO also undermined the ability of WTO Members to negotiate and complicated the process of domestic approval and implementation. Depending on the legal and constitutional framework of the concerned WTO Member, these new issues, which had historically not been considered as relating specifically to trade, may fall under the competence of decentralized or federated entities, meaning that any negotiations at WTO level would typically involve the participation of a broader range of state actors (Garcia Molyneux (2001), p. 64).

The failure of the Doha Round, and ultimately of multilateralism in international trade relations, has led developed countries to explore alternative means to achieve their goals. One option that is rapidly gaining traction is the idea of 'variable geometry' (Cornford (2004); Heiskanen (2004), p. 20; Leal-Arcas (2011), p. 145) where WTO Members could pursue the signing of plurilateral agreements—that is, agreements providing for additional WTO rules, but which are only binding on those WTO Members who consent to them. Variable geometry does present the advantage of acknowledging the unlikelihood of further multilateral deep integration when huge levels of disparities in terms of economic development persist within the WTO Membership, and of allowing a way out for those Members that do not wish to head down the path of further integration. However, it also presents certain drawbacks, namely the danger that plurilateral agreements would cause trade diversion and eventually force developing countries to adhere to agreements in whose negotiation they did not participate (Cornford (2004), p. 11).

In the meantime, trade agreements concluded outside the scope of the WTO, in particular bilateral and regional trade agreements, known as preferential trade agreements (PTAs), have become an increasingly dominant trend in the international trading system. PTAs had already become ubiquitous in the world trading system by the time that the Uruguay Round negotiations were initiated—in fact, the US had paved the way towards their successful completion by concluding a number of bilateral trade agreements in advance, which secured liberalization reforms and created a groundswell of support for the imminent multilateral trade liberalization (Mercurio (2006), p. 218). Faced with developing country resistance towards further trade liberalization, trading powers such as the EU and the US have, since the turn of the century, turned to PTAs to secure the market openings and reforms that they could not achieve at multilateral level. Indeed, a recent study of the PTAs concluded 3by both the EU and US confirm that they typically include the new deep trade disciplines which were rejected in the Doha Round (Horn, Mavroidis, and Sapir (2009); WTO (2011), p. 53). Most of these PTAs are concluded with developing countries, on whom the EU and US are able to use significant bargaining leverage to impose their agenda (Simmons (2006), p. 445). These bilateral PTAs are used to expand the regulatory standards favoured by the EU and the US and, in doing so, incrementally ratchet up the regulatory standards of the international trading system (Ibid). The irony is that, whilst developing countries successfully rejected the adoption of deep trade disciplines within the multilateral context of the WTO, all that this achieved was to force them to accept equally or more intrusive disciplines in the context of PTAs.

#### 2.2.3.2 *Bilateralism as a threat to multilateral trade liberalization*

The idea that bilateralism holds the potential to undermine multilateral trade liberalization is based on Jacob Viner's work on the effects of tariff preferences (Viner (1950)). Viner observed that if Country A cuts its tariffs for exports originating from Country B, then the exports of the latter to the former will increase. A by-product of this is that the exports of third countries to which no similar cuts are extended will decrease, as Country B could export products to Country A at lower prices. The granting of preferential treatment to a limited set of countries thus results in an overall decrease in trade flows (or trade diversion) (Viner (1999), pp. 106–7). Although the original drafters of GATT 1947 were aware of the trade-diverting effects of PTAs, they had no choice but to incorporate an exception within the agreement allowing members to conclude preferential (or regional) trade agreements (PTAs)—which include FTAs and customs unions—since a number of countries participating in the negotiations were parties to existing customs unions (Haight (1972), p. 392; Devuyst and Sedarevic (2007), p. 18; Mavroidis (2011), p. 385). However, in order to ensure that the conclusion of

PTAs remained an exception to the rule of non-discrimination embedded into the MFN clause, the conclusion of PTAs was subjected to a number of restrictive legal requirements set out under Article XXIV GATT. One of these requirements specifically addresses trade diversion by providing that PTAs must liberalize 'substantially all trade'[6] among parties. The requirement was intended to address the assumption that if countries were allowed to pick and choose the areas where tariffs should be cut, there would be an incentive to focus on tariff lines that would engender trade diversion (Mavroidis (2011), p. 378).

Despite these restrictions, PTAs have become ubiquitous in the world trading system. The control mechanisms put in place by the WTO to assess the legality of PTAs have simply not worked (Devuyst and Sedarevic (2007), p. 44; Mavroidis (2011), pp. 377–8) and, even if they had, such controls would be fraught with difficulties in light of the ongoing lack of clarity surrounding the requirement that FTAs should liberalize 'substantially all trade' (Mitchell and Lockhart (2005), pp. 232–5). Noting the emergence of this 'spaghetti bowl' of PTAs, economists such as Jagdish Bhagwati argued that the discriminatory liberalization inherent in PTAs would not only lead to trade diversion but would also create stumbling blocks to further multilateral liberalization, as it would discourage countries from engaging in multilateral trade liberalization efforts that would ultimately yield greater global welfare gains, for fear of seeing the benefits of the preferential PTA treatments eroded (McCulloch (2012), p. 42).

The view that PTAs constitute stumbling blocks, rather than building blocks, to multilateral liberalization is not universally shared amongst economists. It has been contested most cogently by Richard E. Baldwin, who argues that Vinerian economics no longer provide an appropriate model to examine the potential impact of FTAs (Baldwin (2011), p. 1). Empirical studies indicate that multilateralism and regionalism are endogenous processes, insofar as involvement in multilateral trade liberalization tends to encourage countries to enter into PTAs, and vice versa (Freund (2000), p. 359). Furthermore, trade diversion through tariff cutting is not so much of a concern given that, in general, most countries have unilaterally engaged in significant tariff cutting since the 1980s (Baldwin (2011), pp. 16–18).

It is also argued that the 'stumbling block' approach is based on the outdated assumption that tariff measures remain the greatest barrier to international trade when, in fact, PTAs are increasingly focused on deep trade issues. Significantly, research has demonstrated that modern PTAs have, by and large, not led to trade diversion, and that most PTAs generally have a positive impact on trade exchanges with third countries (Mavroidis (2011), pp. 378–9). Trade diversion is minimized due to the fact that the preferential treatment accorded in PTAs is increasingly applied on a non-discriminatory basis (Baldwin, Evenett, and Low (2009), p. 79). This is due in part to the widespread use of so-called non-party MFN clauses in PTAs enjoining parties to provide no less favourable treatment to the other parties

[6] Article XXIV GATT.

than they accord to third countries (Fink and Jansen (2009), p. 246; Mirodout, Sauvage and Sudreau (2010)), as well as the fact that the rules of origin (ROOs) for services are defined in a much more liberal way than in the area of goods. Another key factor underlying the absence of trade diversion in deep PTAs is that the regulatory behind-the-border disciplines such as services, competition, and IP protection tend to engender less—if any—discriminatory treatment. The regulatory reforms typically triggered by deep PTAs are generally adopted in order to promote good governance and establish a more attractive regulatory environment for business. Any regulatory convergence mandated by means of a PTA will presumably be of benefit both to nationals of the contracting parties and to nationals of third countries (Baldwin (2011), p. 26). For example, the prohibition of anti-competitive practices is meant to improve the efficiency of the domestic markets which should in turn yield welfare gains (Baldwin (2011), p. 26). There is no need to limit the application of these reforms to PTA parties, and consequently firms originating from non-party countries will benefit from the increased contestability of the concerned market.

In the light of the non-discriminatory features of preferential liberalization in deep trade disciplines, deep PTAs do not seem to present a particularly significant threat to multilateral liberalization (Fink and Jansen (2009), p. 258). Instead, regulatory cooperation, whether achieved through harmonization or mutual recognition, seems to hold the biggest potential for discrimination. As major economies increasingly require the adoption by trading partners of their own norms and standards in their FTAs, there is a danger that the competing regulatory blocs created will further entrench diverging regulatory positions and, consequently, undermine multilateral efforts to negotiate solutions to regulatory incompatibilities (Prada and Rossi (2002), p. 183). By 'locking-in' countries to particular regulatory frameworks, deep PTAs may disincentivize efforts to engage in multilateral liberalization (WTO (2011), p. 180). In light of this, Woolcock has provided a basic blueprint to be followed in order to ensure that deep disciplines included in PTAs do not undermine multilateral trade liberalization (Woolcock (2009), pp. 14–16). He recommends that PTAs should require compliance with existing WTO rules, something that is already observed in practice in most deep PTAs concluded by the major trading powers. He also recommends that the PTAs add to the current WTO regime by promoting further regulatory transparency. This would have the double effect of facilitating market access for foreign firms (who would be better placed to understand the regulatory burdens imposed by the host country), but would also discourage national governments from implementing discriminatory and protectionist measures. The PTAs should also require compliance with existing international standards wherever possible, rather than promoting *sui generis* rules that reflect the regulatory culture or interest of one or a select group of countries. Finally, any PTA that includes a dispute settlement mechanism should ensure that the rulings of the latter conform to the WTO case law. The main objective is therefore to encourage compliance with multilateral rules and standards and, in doing so, to contribute to the fostering of common ground on economic regulation between states, which can then be exported to the WTO. However, undercutting the WTO's role in the development of regulatory disciplines runs the risk that the regulatory agenda in the sphere of international trade law will be irremediably set by the powerful few at the expense of developing countries (Baldwin (2011), pp. 31–2). The sidestepping of developing country involvement in international rule-making is, regrettably, an inexorable consequence of the increased emphasis on bilateralism and regionalism.

## 2.3 The EU's External Trade Policy—a Historical Perspective

### 2.3.1 The EU as a powerful protectionist

From its inception, the EU has been recognized as a major player in international trade negotiations. In 2012, the EU accounted for 15 per cent of international trade in goods and 11.5 per cent of international trade in services (European Commission (2014d), p. 3). Today it is the world's largest trading bloc and bears a great deal of responsibility for the current legal landscape of international trade relations (Young and Peterson (2006), p. 796; Pomorska and Vanhoonacker (2015), p. 5). Meunier and Nicolaidis explain that the EU's trade power has two components: structural power and bargaining power (Meunier and Nicolaidis (2006), p. 906). The structural power flows from the size of the EU's internal market and the importance of this market to the global economy (Meunier and Nicolaidis (2006), p. 908). The attractiveness of the internal market to third country economic operators means that the EU can use the promise of access to its lucrative market as a carrot, or the threat of the removal of such access as a stick in order to obtain trade concessions. The bargaining power relates to the EU's ability to act as a single entity when negotiating international trade agreements (Meunier and Nicolaidis (2007), pp. 908–9). The common commercial policy (CCP), the EU's foremost external trade policy instrument, creates an exclusive competence for the EU to act for and on behalf of the Member States in all affairs pertaining to trade policy. By consolidating trade power in the hands of a single entity, the CCP allows a more efficient use of the significant bargaining leverage at the EU's disposal.

Historically, the EU's exclusive competence in trade was required in order to comply with GATT rules. Article XXIV GATT provides an exception to the MFN rule by allowing WTO Members to enter into two types of PTAs: customs unions and FTAs. Article XXIV:8(a) defines customs unions as 'the substitution of a single customs territory for two or more customs territories [. . .] so that (i) duties and other restrictive regulations of commerce [. . .] are eliminated with respect to substantially all the trade between the constituent territories of the union or at least with respect to substantially all the trade in products originating in such territories', and (ii) 'substantially the same duties and other regulations of commerce are applied by each of the members of the union to the trade of territories not included in the union'. FTAs on the other hand are defined under XXIV:8(b) as 'a group of two or more customs territories in which the duties and other restrictive regulations of commerce [...] are eliminated on substantially all the trade between the constituent territories in products originating in such territories'. In both cases, the formation of a PTA requires the elimination of trade restrictions between its members. This is the so-called 'internal trade requirement'. However, unlike FTAs, customs unions must apply substantially the same duties and other regulations of commerce to the trade of territories not included in their respective territories. In other words, only customs unions are required to adopt a common external trade policy. A further fundamental difference between the two types of PTAs relates to the regulation of trade relations between PTA members and third countries ('external trade requirement'). Trade restrictive measures imposed by members of FTAs with regard to third countries must 'not be higher or more restrictive than the corresponding measures existing in the same constituent territories prior to the formation of the free-trade area', while in the context of customs unions, the same measures must not 'on the whole be higher or more restrictive than the general incidence of the duties and regulations of commerce applicable in the constituent territories prior to the formation of such union'.[7] In other words, while the formation of an FTA entails an absolute obligation on the part of its members not to raise trade barriers, the corresponding obligation for the formation of a customs union is less stringent in that it only requires that trade barriers not be raised as a whole.

When examining the various modes of economic integration available to them, the founding Member States were of course acutely aware of the distinction created by Article XXIV GATT and opted for the creation of a customs union (Frank (1961), pp. 92–7). The Spaak Report of 1956—the intergovernmental report setting the blueprint for the establishment of the EEC's common market—is particularly instructive in this regard (Spaak Report (1956)). The report considered that the establishment of a free-trade area would give rise to problems of a technical and economic nature. First, since each Member State would preserve its power to regulate imports from third countries, the free movement of products would only be achieved with regard to products originating from other Member States, as opposed to those originating from third countries and which entered the free-trade area via another Member State. This would mean that border controls would have to be maintained within the free trade area. Secondly, it was noted that the distortions of trade that would result from the flow of imports into higher-tariff members via the member countries with lower tariffs would run counter to the objectives pursued by the common market—that is, the fostering of conditions conducive to stability and prosperity—by allowing Member States to retain their own tariffs from third countries (Arbuthnott and Edwards (1989), p. 172). A common and unified external trade policy was therefore the result of the need for the EU to both comply with GATT 1947 obligations and to establish a truly integrated market within the EU (Spaak Report (1956), p. 3).

[7] Article XXIV:5(b) GATT.

However, even at such an early stage, the significance of the concentration of the handling of trade policy in the hands of the EU was fully appreciated. The ability of the EU—then the EEC—to speak with one voice and negotiate all matters relating to trade would enable it to more efficiently wield its significant market power to its advantage (Meunier (2005), pp. 21–40). This concern would be reflected in Article 113 EEC, which provided that the CCP should be based on 'uniform principles', translating the need for a common external trade policy in order to avoid distortions of trade within the common market that would result from the application of differing tariff and non-tariff measures by the various Member States (Bourgeois (1987), p. 2) and the fact that the EEC would only have *one* external trade policy to the exclusion of the various external policies hitherto conducted by the Member States (Cartou (1959), pp. 106–8). Foreseeing that it may not be feasible to guarantee the uniformity of the CCP at all times, especially during the EEC's formative years when the common market remained uncompleted, the drafters of the Treaty of Rome included Article 115 EEC, which allowed Member States to adopt national protective measures under certain restrictive conditions.

The exclusivity of the EU's competence in trade matters was acknowledged early on by the Court's case law. The Court found that the exclusion of Member State competence in the area of the CCP is not only required to ensure the establishment of the common market, but also to ensure that the Community is able to adequately defend its common interests against the world and that the balance of its institutional structure is not undermined. Many of the rulings affirming the Community's exclusive competence were confined to the specific area of tariff measures. This was to be expected, since the EU already had a fully operational common customs tariff by 1968 (Pelkmans (1984), p. 160). In this area at least, uniformity had seemingly been achieved early on, with the Community having the sole competence to set the levels of external tariffs. However, whilst exclusivity was identified as a constitutional cornerstone of the CCP, it was not applied in all areas of the EU's external trade policy. The slow progress in establishing a common market and the absence of common policies in a number of key areas meant that Member States continued to apply non-tariff barriers such as quotas on third country products, technical barriers to trade, rules on procurement and subsidies to protect national industries from foreign competitors. The upshot was that the use of Article 115 EEC as an exception to exclusivity was prevalent throughout the first three decades of the EU's existence, mainly to fill the normative void resulting from the inability of Member States to reach a political agreement on matters pertaining to external trade regulation (Lenaerts (1986), p. 45). Moreover, although the EEC Treaty provided that the CCP should be adopted by qualified majority voting, unanimity was the de facto rule for much of the EU's formative years, meaning that Member States were able to block the decision-making process and effectively impose their national protectionist interests (Hanson (1998), pp. 69–70). The lack of a truly common external trade policy meant that the EU's action in international trade negotiations was both reactive and defensive. It was reactive insofar as the lack of common policies meant that the EU was ill-equipped to formulate and push forward comprehensive trade agendas. It was also defensive because the EU's main task in the context of trade negotiations was to maintain the ability of Member States to pursue their defensive national policies. As a result, all attempts to promote trade liberalization and the adoption of new multilateral trade disciplines under GATT were initiated by the US, and whilst the EU actively contributed to trade liberalization in a number of areas, it was most concerned with the need to maintain the ability of Member States to protect and promote national 'champions' (Woolcock (2012a), p. 50).

### 2.3.2 The EU as a promoter of multilateral deep trade liberalization

The transformation of the EU from a defensive trade actor to an active proponent of multilateral trade liberalization during the Uruguay Round was caused by a conjunction of external and internal factors. The external factor was the change in US international trade policy. After seeing its proposals for the introduction of deep trade disciplines within the sphere of GATT rejected in the early 1980s, the US increasingly resorted to unilateral acts and bilateral FTAs to pursue its trade interests (Woolcock (2009), p. 2). The EU's strong engagement in multilateral trade liberalization can be seen, in part, as an attempt to force the US to re-commit to multilateralism and thus avoid the trade diversion that would result from bilateralism and regionalism in certain areas.

The internal factor was the completion of the single market. In June 1985, the Commission issued a White Paper entitled 'Completing the internal market' (European Commission (1985)), which outlined a comprehensive legislative programme (the Single Market Programme, or SMP) to be implemented with a view to removing all barriers (physical, fiscal, and technical) to the free movement of goods, services, persons, and capital. The completion of the SMP in 1992 was a launchpad for the emergence of a new EU external trade policy (Meunier (2000), pp. 126–9). With a more integrated internal market, the EU's market power was significantly increased, enabling it to wield more influence (Ibid). The EU's increased trade power was further enhanced by the fact that the SMP specifically sought to rectify the fragmented and, as has been seen, often defensive trade policy of the EU (Hanson (1998), pp. 67–71). By imposing the qualified majority rule and progressively removing national protective trade measures authorized under Article 115 EEC, the SMP paved the way for a more uniform EU trade policy (Hanson (1998), pp. 67–71). And finally, any trade disciplines that may have been imposed either by GATT or by its new incarnation held no fears for EU Member States, who, during the completion of the SMP, had gone through an economic integration process that was far more intrusive than anything that could be imposed at the multilateral level (Woolcock (2000), pp. 30–46). In fact, contrary to initial fears that Member States would demand a more protectionist stance with regard to imports from third countries in order to offset the increased intra-Community competition resulting from the completion of the SMP, quite the opposite would occur. The EU's external policy of the 1990s and thereafter is one that is incontrovertibly geared towards trade liberalization (Holmes (2008), pp. 191–206). National quantitative restrictions, voluntary export restraint agreements, and surveillance measures were progressively abandoned (Eeckhout (1994), pp. 145–85).

Buoyed by the success of the internal market as well as benefits reaped from external trade liberalization, the EU became one of the staunchest proponents of the Uruguay Round negotiations and the inclusion of new deep trade disciplines at the multilateral level (Cohn (2001), pp. 205–7). Following the conclusion of the WTO agreements, the EU continued its efforts to introduce deep trade disciplines at the multilateral level. Although the WTO agreements provided an in-built negotiation agenda for issues such as services and agriculture, the EU sought to expand this by including new issues. In the WTO ministerial meeting held in Singapore in 1996, WTO working groups were established in response to EU proposals, in order to discuss the possibility of negotiating multilateral disciplines on investment, competition, government procurement, and trade facilitation (the 'Singapore issues') (WTO (1996)). Although these issues were included in the negotiating agenda of the Doha Round in 2001, a number of factors, such as ongoing disagreements concerning the crucial issue of agricultural subsidies and developing country hostility towards the introduction of new liberalizing disciplines, contributed to their eventual demise (Evenett (2007), p. 392; Young (2007), p. 804). By the 2003 Cancun WTO Ministerial meeting, all but one of the Singapore issues—trade facilitation—had been removed from the negotiating agenda (WTO (2003b)).

Cancun may have sounded the death knell for the EU's ambitions to reshape the multilateral trading system but, as pointed out by Peterson and Young, it also demonstrated the EU's unique response to the emergence of deep trade politics:

> Since the Uruguay Round the EU has been the most aggressive and persistent advocate of a broader international trade agenda and the strongest proponent of developing *common* disciplines on the making of domestic rules—what might be termed a 'deep' trade agenda—in areas including competition policy, environmental standards, labour rules and investment rules. Arguably, the EU has responded more quickly and energetically than any other major trading power to the new domestic politics of international trade, if not to the new balance of international power. (Peterson and Young (2006), p. 796)

Although it ultimately failed at the multilateral level, the EU's deep trade agenda was said to be very much informed by the EU's own experience of the internal market (Orbie, Gistielinck, and Kerremans (2008), p. 148). Having identified the need for deep integration within the multilateral trade regime, the EU was keen to ensure that such regime would be in line with the EU's own internal market rules. The adoption of such deep disciplines by the WTO would have caused the spread of EU-type regulatory principles worldwide and provided EU firms with an important competitive advantage in the global marketplace. Furthermore, the EU's broad agenda in the Doha Round was intended to secure WTO reforms in areas that would be beneficial for the EU and that would be seen as adequate trade-offs for the reform of its protectionist common agricultural policy (CAP) (Allen and Smith (2001), p. 97). Besides these political and economic considerations, the EU's deep trade agenda was linked to the more general trade policy objective of 'managing globalization'. The term was coined by Pascal Lamy during his tenureship at the helm of Directorate-General for Trade (DG Trade) to encapsulate two central but conflicting objectives of EU trade policy: to maximize the benefits of globalization by promoting trade liberalization on the one hand, and to develop mechanisms that minimize the negative effects of globalization on the other. In fact, managed globalization was the EU's proposed solution to the tensions between trade liberalization and the resulting loss of policy space. This solution entailed the incorporation within the global trading system of a comprehensive regulatory framework inspired by the EU's 'blend of market integration, common rules and social safety net mechanism' (Lamy (2002b), p. 2), insofar as it would establish a balance between liberalization and the need to promote non-trade objectives, such as multilateralism and sustainable development. Such concerns were clearly evident in the proposals made by Lamy in 2004 to introduce the concept of 'collective preferences' in WTO law (Lamy (2004a)). Collective preferences were defined as societal values that are the end result of practical decisions made by communities (e.g. international organizations, states, and sub-national entities). According to Lamy, the process of economic globalization and the multilevel trade regulation that resulted thereof represented a threat to such collective preferences. If public support for the WTO was to be garnered, the WTO should take due account of collective preferences, notably by avoiding liberalization in these areas and by considering the addition of a safeguard rule addressing social choices. However, the collective preferences proposal was criticized by legal scholars and never received substantial support from the wider WTO membership (Charnovitz (2005), pp. 449–72).

Managed globalization presented several defining characteristics, namely the widening of trade policy to cover new areas of rule-making, particularly the Singapore issues; the projection of the EU's regulatory model abroad (e.g. EU enlargement process and promotion of regional economic integration); and the redistribution of the benefits and costs of globalization through the granting of non-reciprocal trade preferences to developing countries or the implementation of domestic initiatives to mitigate the negative effects of globalization (Meunier and Abdelaal (2007), p. 8–9). Also crucial to managed globalization was the availability of a rules-based multilateral trading system. For the EU, managed globalization could only realistically be achieved through international institutions with a coherent set of rules and a strong institutional framework to ensure compliance with such rules. Managed globalization also provided the EU with a very handy rhetorical tool to promote its own economic interests. The emphasis on deep disciplines and the removal of regulatory barriers, in particular, fitted well with the fact that the EU has a strong services sector that would benefit immensely from the opening of international markets (Van den Hooven (2002), p. 17). Also, the calls for negotiations on the issues of labour rights and environmental protection opened the possibility of addressing the competitive advantage enjoyed by third countries—especially developing countries—in imposing comparatively low environmental and labour standards and removing the threat of social dumping (i.e. the lowering of social or environmental costs to attract foreign investment) or a race to the bottom (Brulahrt and Matthews (2007), p. 476). However, the EU sought to make its recipe for managed globalization more palatable to a multilateral audience by presenting it as a tool to promote sustainable development. The EU presented the adoption of deep disciplines as being in the interests of developing countries—trade liberalization should be underpinned by an overarching regulatory framework, including disciplines on issues such as competition and investment that would allow countries to better realize gains from trade liberalization whilst simultaneously taking into account other non-trade objectives such as the promotion of environmental and social standards (European Commission (2002)). This view was not shared by WTO developing countries who saw in proposals for disciplines on competition, procurement, and investment complex regulatory issues ill-suited to the WTO, as well as an attempt to further enhance access to developing country markets and therefore an unwelcome constraint on their already dwindling policy space (Mehta (2003), pp. 22–9). Calls for negotiations on the relationship between trade and environmental protection and labour rights were also rejected because of the perception that the real objective pursued was to protect developed countries against the competitive advantage of the availability of low-skilled labour in developing countries (Di Matteo, Dosanijh, Frantz, and Bowal (2003), p. 124), and to allow developed countries to block imports from developing countries that failed to comply with onerous environmental standards set at the international level (Schaeffer (2005), p. 6). The dismissal of the Singapore issues and the subsequent collapse of the Doha Round put paid to the grand objectives of managed globalization—at least at the WTO level.

### 2.3.3 Global Europe strategy—shift towards competitive liberalization

#### *2.3.3.1 The EU's renewed emphasis on bilateralism*

From 1999 until 2006, the EU's external trade policy shunned bilateralism in favour of multilateralism (Woolcock (2009), p. 4). Under the stewardship of Pascal Lamy, the EU put into effect a moratorium on the negotiation of FTAs:

> Since I joined the Commission in 1999, my policy [...] has been to pursue all existing mandates for regional negotiations with vigour and fairness, but not—in general terms—to begin any new negotiations. We have not ruled out doing so, but remain very much sceptical of the benefits of doing so.
>
> The principal reason is that the priority has to remain the multilateral agenda. Now that we have successfully launched the Doha Development Agenda, and particularly given that we are pushing for its conclusion by the end of 2004, it is very important that we do not take any initiative which might detract from the completion of the DDA. A secondary reason, given our strong preference for deep integration is that these agreements

are themselves complex and time-consuming to negotiate. If FTAs are not to be rolled off the press cheaply, and are to be done properly, it follows that there are grounds for hesitating before plunging into new negotiations. (Lamy (2002a), pp. 1412–13)

The WTO was viewed as a more attractive regulatory venue than FTAs, given the size of its membership and the existence of its dispute settlement mechanism that can issue legally binding rulings (De Bievre (2006), pp. 851–66). Negotiating FTAs on a bilateral or regional basis was viewed as a distraction from the far bigger prize of multilateral liberalization. In fact, throughout the 1990s and the early 2000s the EU tended to only sign FTAs where this was required to promote its political rather than economic interests. Thus the EU signed agreements with countries to ensure their political and democratic stability (e.g. Europe Agreements with central and eastern European countries or the Trade and Development Cooperation Agreement with South Africa) or to counterbalance the economic influence of the US and NAFTA abroad (e.g. FTAs signed with Chile and Mexico) (Woolcock (2005), p. 377).

However, two events put paid to Lamy and the EU's FTA moratorium. First, the implausibility of achieving any considerable progress at WTO level in the short- to medium-term has become all too evident, with the Singapore issues being moved off the negotiating table in response to objections from developing countries. In 2006, with little progress being made, Lamy—by then WTO Director General—announced the suspension of negotiations.[8] Secondly, while the EU put all of its eggs in the multilateral basket, its main competitor, the US, pursued a policy of 'competitive liberalization' which favoured the negotiation of FTAs (Hilaire and Yang (2005), p. 603; Evenett and Meier (2007)). One of the underlying rationales behind competitive liberalization was that the US could use its higher bargaining power in the context of bilateral FTA negotiations to push through a US-style approach to economic liberalization (Sbragia (2010), pp. 376–7). The term 'competitive' reflected two fundamental aspects of the policy. First, that the US was competing against other major trading powers also engaged in bilateral trade negotiations and was seeking to re-establish its leadership in the international trading system—the more FTAs the US signed, the more support would be gathered for its positions at WTO level (Evenett and Meier (2007), p. 5). Secondly, that trading partners would have to compete against each other to gain access to the US market. Indeed, the US's approach to competitive liberalization was that it would only negotiate with countries that were willing to make substantial market opening concessions. By making it clear that those countries that were not willing to play by the rules would be left behind, the US sought to further increase its leverage in negotiations (Evenett and Meier (2007), p. 20).

Once it became clear that the Doha Round was faltering, and in a bid to make up for lost ground against the US, the EU was forced to reconsider its approach towards the negotiation of FTAs. The shift in policy was crystallized in the 2006

[8] See http://www.wto.org/english/news_e/news06_e/gc_27july06_e.htm.

Global Europe strategy, which outlined a new EU strategy with regard to its trade agreements (European Commission (2006a)). The policy notes that whilst the EU has focused on the Doha Round, its 'main trading partners and priority targets have been negotiating FTAs with [the EU's] competitors' (European Commission (2006b), p. 14) and bemoans the fact that '[t]he current geography of FTAs mainly covers our geography and development objectives well but our trade interests less well' (European Commission (2006b), p. 14). Therefore, much like the US's competitive liberalization policy, the EU seeks to enhance its position in comparison to its competitors. The Global Europe strategy is also similar to the US's competitive liberalization in terms of the ambitious levels of harmonization being pursued, as it clearly maintains the EU's focus on deeper integration. The EU's position is that, in the absence of any real progress in the Doha Round negotiations, the EU should look to enter into FTAs promoting 'deep integration' (European Commission (2006b), p. 19), which it defines as 'WTO-plus in terms of width and depth' (European Commission (2006b), p. 19). With this in mind, the EU's strategy to further facilitate its own access to foreign markets consists essentially of entering into deep FTAs that are comprehensive insofar as they are not limited to tariffs but extend to 'non-tariff barriers [...], including services, intellectual property, SPS, TBT, public procurement, competition and investment' (European Commission (2006a), p. 16). In this respect, however, the EU's policy may go further than that of the US, because whilst the latter has concluded a multitude of FTAs that go beyond what is currently provided by the WTO (including in areas such as IP, investment, and public procurement) (Heydon and Woolcock (2009), pp. 155–6), it has also been noted that with regard to regulatory issues, these FTAs also shy away from promoting regulatory harmonization and requiring the adoption of international norms (Heydon and Woolcock (2009), p. 156).

A further difference between the EU's current trade policy and US competitive liberalization relates to the fact that, whereas the US adopted an open door policy where all countries are welcome to enter into negotiations, the EU initially focused on large emerging economies with big market potential and which maintain a certain level of protection against EU exports:

> Based on these criteria, ASEAN, Korea and Mercosur (with whom negotiations are on-going) emerge as priorities. They combine high levels of protection with large market potential and they are active in concluding FTAs with EU competitors. India, Russia and the Gulf Co-operation Council (negotiations also currently active) also have combinations of market potential and levels of protection which make them of interest to the EU. China also meets many of these criteria, but requires special attention because of the opportunities and risks it presents. (European Commission (2006b), p. 16)

The Global Europe strategy had initially targeted emerging economies not only because of a desire to secure a substantial share of fast growing markets, but also because many of these countries (in particular Brazil and India) acted as ringleaders for the opposition to the reforms proposed by developed countries in the Doha Round (Messerlin (2012), pp. 1–2). If the EU could use bilateral trade negotiations to get these countries onside and develop a common agenda, then these FTAs could be used as basis for a multilateral consensus. However, it has since become clear that the very same issues that led to the collapse of the Doha Round are also proving major stumbling blocks in the context of the bilateral trade negotiations with rising economic powers such as India and MERCOSUR, with progress slow and some simply grinding to a halt. The EU–MERCOSUR negotiations have proved an arduous process. Initially launched back in 1995, the talks were suspended in 2005 because of an inability on both sides to significantly compromise on key defensive areas of interests (agriculture for the EU and services for MERCOSUR) (Robles (2008), p. 336). The negotiations were re-launched, yet despite nine negotiation rounds, have also struggled to make much headway, with the EU maintaining a protectionist stance in the area of agriculture whilst MERCOSUR remains reluctant to make significant concessions on services, investment, procurement, and IP. The EU–India FTA negotiations, which were launched in June 2007, have seemingly stuttered along with no end in sight. India's extensive lists of concerns include fears that the EU's TRIPS-plus agenda may constrict its ability to manufacture and sell generic drugs, concerns that the enactment of EU-inspired competition laws would undermine developmental objectives, and objections to the liberalization of a government procurement market that accounts for a huge chunk of the national GDP (Modwel and Singh (2012), pp. 13–16). On the other side, the EU is unwilling make significant market access concessions in areas where India has strong offensive interests, namely the agricultural sector and the temporary movement of persons (Wouters, Godderis, Natens, and Ciortuz (2013), pp. 7–10). In the meantime, the US's decision to pivot its foreign policy to the Asia-Pacific region in order to counteract the growing influence of China led to the launch of trade negotiations on the so-called Trans-Pacific Partnership (TPP) (a trade agreement that would include countries such as Australia, Canada, Malaysia, Mexico, Singapore, and Japan) which left the EU in the unenviable position of being outside looking in on what could be not only the most lucrative trade arrangements in the world but also—as the TPP seeks to achieve deep liberalization—one that would set the template for future deep trade disciplines. The EU has recently launched FTA negotiations with Japan and the US (TTIP), and has mooted the possibility of signing an investment agreement with China (De Gucht (2013b), p. 2), partly in response to the economic downturn which has affected the EU, but also in order to mitigate the potential for the TPP to divert trade away from the EU and to ensure that it also has a hand in setting the new deep disciplines of the free-trade system. In the context of negotiations with Japan and the US, the EU has made it clear that dismantling non-tariff barriers is its primary objective. With regard to the negotiations with Japan, the EU has already stated its intention to address disciplines in areas such as 'services, investment, procurement, intellectual property rights and regulatory issues' (De Gucht (2013b), p. 2) and has demanded the harmonization of Japan's notoriously *sui generis* technical, safety and environmental regulations with existing international standards (Stoble (2013)).

### *2.3.3.2 Deep trade agenda and 'commercially driven' FTAs*

#### 2.3.3.2.1 FTAs and EU global competitiveness

Whilst the conclusion of deep FTAs was central to the Global Europe strategy, it did not encompass the policy in its entirety. The Global Europe strategy was designed to provide an external dimension to the EU's Lisbon Growth and Jobs Strategy (Lisbon strategy) (European Commission (2005c)), which focused on enhancing the EU's global competitiveness by promoting further market integration and fostering internal policies on competition, research and development, and education. The notion of 'competitiveness' is at the very heart of this overall economic strategy. The EU's belief is that increased exposure to international competition benefits domestic consumers by driving down prices and EU firms will become more efficient by incentivizing these (Hay (2007), p. 29). Trade liberalization is not just viewed as a tool to gain access to foreign markets but also as a means to expose EU firms to international competition and emphasize the need for the type of structural reforms envisaged by the EU in the Lisbon strategy (Hay (2007), p. 32). Another feature of the strategy is that it recognizes the blurring of the distinctions between domestic and international policies and rulemaking by making an explicit link between internal economic policy and external trade policy. To further enhance the EU's competitiveness, the Global Europe strategy acknowledges the need to ensure consistency between internal and international rules. The objective (to minimize difficulties encountered by EU firms doing business abroad) is to be achieved by playing a 'leading role in sharing best practice and developing global rules and standards' (European Commission (2006a), p. 12) and also by taking 'account of the external dimension in making our regulatory and other standards' (European Commission (2006a), p. 12). In other words, while the EU's external trade policy must promote EU rules and standards abroad, EU legislators must also make efforts to incorporate international rules into the EU legal framework.

There is, in particular, recognition of the need to address two phenomena that are intrinsically related to globalization. First, the increased importance of global supply chains in international trade has resulted in a need to go beyond what is currently provided by the WTO by addressing non-tariff barriers. Thus, the Global Europe strategy proposes a trade policy which will look at

> the whole operating environment in third countries and reduce the barriers and transactional costs derived from fragmentation for the productive processes. Regulatory barriers to trade and investment are a major challenge for several key sectors, including services, food, cosmetics, pharmaceuticals, building materials, electronic communications, medical devices and motor vehicles and they are still of direct relevance for chemicals, textiles, tyres, electric and mechanical engineering (European Commission (2006b), p. 6).

Beyond trade in goods there is also a call to strengthen the presence of EU companies through permanent establishment, to open up procurement markets and to ensure the enforcement of IP rights abroad.

Secondly, there is the need to improve the EU's competitive position with regard to the BRIC countries. Here, the policy notes that whilst the EU has progressively opened its market to third countries, these countries have maintained significant barriers to trade. This puts the EU at a disadvantage in trade negotiations since, in many areas, it has little to offer in terms of market access to tempt third countries to open their own markets. To redress this imbalance, the Global Europe strategy suggests a two-pronged approach which includes the conclusion of FTAs with emerging economies and the development of internal mechanisms that stop third countries from free-riding on the openness of the EU's market, where such third countries are unwilling to provide reciprocal market access (European Commission (2006b), p. 14). From this perspective, there is an inherent contradiction in the EU's rhetoric insofar as, on the one hand, it erects competitiveness through trade liberalization as a good per se whilst at the same time contending that too much openness (and therefore competition) is a problem that may have to be addressed internally.

The Global Europe strategy identifies a number of fora and tools that may be used to achieve these objectives. For example, it encourages regulatory dialogue and cooperation with trading partners such as China and the US on issues such as IP rights enforcement and financial regulation, and proposes the reform of existing EU trade defence instruments to take into account the treatment of EU economic operators abroad, as well as reform of the EU procurement rules to allow restrictions on market access for firms originating from third countries that do not provide reciprocal market access. It is, however, in the context of FTAs that the EU's deep trade agenda comes into its own. The FTAs must be comprehensive, aim for the highest possible degree of trade liberalization and, where partners have signed FTAs with competitors, achieve at the very least full parity. Whilst border measures must be addressed, the main focus is on non-tariff barriers, particularly disciplines that are beyond the current remit of the WTO. FTAs must contain extensive provisions on investment, intellectual property, public procurement, and competition. Furthermore, the regulation of these issues within the FTAs should be geared towards the development of common regulatory frameworks. This is very clear in the case of IP enforcement provisions, which should be in line with the EU rules (European Commission (2006b), p. 11), and competition provisions, which should 'promote greater conversion of competition laws and enforcement' (European Commission (2006b), p. 18). Regulatory convergence, mutual recognition arrangements and regulatory transparency are also suggested as methods that should be explored with trading partners to address non-tariff barriers (European Commission (2006c), p. 7). Finally, the trade liberalization commitments and regulatory frameworks established by the FTAs are to be supported by an institutional framework—including a dispute settlement mechanism—that will monitor the implementation of the FTAs. In other words, the FTAs imagined by the Global Europe strategy closely resemble the type of multilateral trading system that the EU would have wished to see in place.

In short, the Global Europe strategy cannot be reduced to a mere change in the EU's choice of venue in which to pursue its deep trade agenda. It also reformulates and adapts the substance of the deep trade agenda to reflect a new reality where multilateral trade liberalization no longer presents itself as a viable outlet for the

EU's trade policy goals and where competition from other trading powers means that it must undertake an increasingly aggressive stance in terms of promoting its economic interests abroad. As a result, although the Global Europe strategy still aims at the adoption of 'common disciplines on domestic regulation', these disciplines seemingly cover a more extensive range of areas than those proposed in the context of the Doha Round, whilst the tools proposed for the development of these disciplines are more varied and sophisticated (e.g. harmonization, mutual recognition, regulatory dialogue, transparency, etc.). Moreover, the Global Europe strategy demands that both internal EU policy and external trade be geared towards increasing the EU's leverage, so as to enable it to extract more market access concessions and domestic reforms from its trading partners.

###### 2.3.3.2.2 Non-trade goals of the Global Europe strategy and the concept of differentiation

The Global Europe strategy has been described as a 'clear neo-liberal strategy in that it assumes that large-scale liberalisation will increase competitiveness and, thus, make production more efficient and profitable leading ultimately to a general increase in wealth and the creation of new jobs in Europe' (Bieler (2012), p. 206). The purported neo-liberal underpinnings of the strategy raise questions as to whether the compromise of 'managed globalization' is still relevant to the EU's deep trade agenda, or whether these commercially driven FTAs signal an abandonment of attempts to square liberalization with non-trade goals (Bieler (2012), pp. 203–6). However, although the references to collective preferences are gone, many of the old social and pro-development values of managed globalization can be found in the policy documents relating to the EU's current trade policy. The EU reassures us that 'completing the Doha Round remains [the EU's] top priority' (European Commission (2010c), p. 9), that it is 'committed to promoting sustainable development, international labour standards and decent work also outside the EU' (European Commission (2010c), p. 8) and that, internally, in addition to 'the right flanking social, educational and labour market policies' (European Commission (2010c), p. 8) which must be adopted by Member States to meet the challenges of globalization and market opening, the EU will also 'contribute additional support through a number of instruments (including structural funds)' (European Commission (2010c), p. 8). More specifically, in the context of the new FTAs, the EU recognizes that '[c]ountries have the right to establish their own levels of public policy protection and regulate accordingly, such as maintaining a high level of human health and safety and environmental protection' (European Commission (2010c), p. 7) and that it will 'continue to give particular attention to the sustainable development chapters in [its] trade agreements' (European Commission (2010c), p. 8). Clearly then, the EU's deep trade discourse remains very much imbued with the social and pro-development narrative of managed globalization. Multilateralism, the promotion of sustainable development, the importance of policy space and so forth—crucial features of managed globalization—are all seen as considerations that must be factored into the EU's deep trade agenda.

The EU's current trade policy also recognizes that its ambitious FTAs might be problematic for developing country trading partners and proposes that such agreements take into account the level of development (European Commission (2006a), p. 12) of its partners as well as offer 'flexible approaches tailored to their needs and the capacities of each country' (European Commission (2010c), p. 12). The idea that FTAs should be tailored to the particular development need of the trading partner borrows from the concept of differentiation initially developed in the context of the EU's development cooperation policy by requiring that assistance given to developing countries should be ' "tailor-made" to each partner country or region, based on the country's own needs, strategies priorities and assets' (European Commission, Council, European Parliament (2006), p. 9). In the Doha Round, the term 'differentiation' has been used primarily to address what, in the EU's eyes, constitutes a flaw of the current WTO legal framework: the absence of distinction between developing countries, which allows emerging economies to benefit from the same type of differential treatment as other 'poorer' developing countries (Mandelson (2005)). The EU would wish to introduce a classification of developing countries reflecting their heterogeneity in terms of economic development so that emerging economies in particular no longer benefit from developing country provisions in WTO agreements, and are obliged both to open their markets to other WTO Members on a non-discriminatory basis and to offer preferential schemes to least developing countries (Van den Hooven (2009), pp. 69–70). More recently, in the 2012 Communication on Trade, Growth and Development, the Commission restated the importance of the principle of differentiation in trade policy (European Commission (2010c), p. 5):

> The growing diversity of developing countries calls for more differentiation in the design and implementation of EU policies. Emerging economies and poorer ones have different potentials, needs and objectives thus requiring a different policy approach.

Therefore, the EU's trade policy based on the principle of differentiation still advocates a new role for emerging economies in the WTO. A recent application of the principle can be seen from the newly reformed General System of Preference regime, which no longer offers preferential market access to all developing countries as it excludes, inter alia, countries classified as upper-middle-income countries by the World Bank.[9] However, no guidance is provided as to how differentiation can be achieved in the context of FTAs, apart from the vague requirement to ensure that these take into account the level of development of the concerned trading partner. EU FTAs concluded with developing countries have traditionally included flexibilities such as transitional periods and asymmetrical liberalization commitments in terms of product coverage and timetables for tariff dismantlement. Presumably, one consequence of differentiation is that such flexibilities are unlikely to feature in FTAs concluded with emerging economies. It remains to be seen, however, whether the principle of differentiation holds wider

[9] Regulation No 978/2012 O.J. L 303/1.

implications for the content of EU FTAs. Given the general ambivalence of developing country WTO Members towards deep integration, it may be asked whether the EU should systematically operate a distinction in terms of the deep disciplines included in FTAs with developed and developing countries, or whether it should offer a one-size-fits-all model whose content will vary on a case-by-case basis as a result of the bargaining process. In the latter case, it is questionable whether differentiation adds anything of substance to the EU's current trade policy besides contributing to the EU's goal of ensuring that developing countries are no longer treated as a homogenous group irrespective of levels of economic development.

## 2.4 Trade Policy as a Vector for the EU's Identity in International Affairs

### 2.4.1 Civilian and Normative Power Europe

International relations scholars have long sought to conceptualize how the EU acts and exerts power on the global stage. In the midst of the Cold War, the EU's external action was initially categorized in opposition to that of the US—the capitalist hegemonic power largely premised on military might. The failure to establish a European Defence Community in 1954 left the Member States of the EEC without a discernible common defence policy and forced it to pursue its foreign policy goals through means other than military. What has since been referred to as 'Civilian Power Europe' (or 'CPE') denoted the perception of the EU as an international actor which sought to influence international affairs through non-coercive means (Duchene (1973), p. 19). This civilian form of power would be based on three pillars: economic power, diplomatic cooperation, and the promotion of rule-based international institutions (Maull (1990), pp. 91–106; Manners (2002), pp. 235–6). The idea of the EU as a civilian power was attractive because it provided a conceptual framework for the EU's identity in international relations which made sense of the EU's international action in light of the comparatively limited tools available to it, and provided a legitimizing narrative for the EU as an international political actor, offering a more palatable alternative to the military-focused power politics of the Cold War era. The exercise of the EU's civilian power abroad reflected the EU's self-perception as a construct designed to ensure democracy and peace by promoting economic integration. In the light of CPE, it should come as no surprise that the EU has placed so much stock in the WTO as a venue for conducting international trade relations, since the WTO's rules-based system, anchored to a binding dispute settlement system, fits perfectly with the EU's own identity as an international actor based on the rejection of power-based diplomacy (Meunier and Nicolaidis (2006), p. 912).

The idea of a CPE has had its critics. It was posited that the EU's power was based in large part on the military power of its Member States and that the

EU's ability to play an important role in international relations would continue to be undermined by the absence of military capabilities at an EU level (Bull (1982), pp. 149–70); Orbie (2006), p. 123). The continued validity of Civilian Power Europe has also been brought into question by the introduction in the 1992 Treaty of Maastricht of a defence and security component (Smith (2000), p. 11). Finally, the 'civilizing' mission implicitly associated with the EU's external action is one that has been criticized for holding unhelpful neo-colonialist connotations (Nicolaidis and Howse (2002), p. 770). The idea of the EU as a civilian power is one that has since been recalibrated to take into account changes in the self-perception of the EU and its self-projection in international relations. Manners argued that studying the EU's international action exclusively through the prisms of military and civilian power was based on underlying assumptions about the 'fixed nature of the nation-state, the importance of direct physical power, and the notion of national interest' (Manners (2002), p. 238). Whether power was exercised through military or economic means, there was still a reliance on forms of coercion through the wielding of 'physical power' to promote national interests abroad. In doing so, CPE appeared as an attempt to shoehorn the EU's international identity and action into outdated Westphalian-based notions of how national states can exert influence in international affairs. This approach, whilst not incorrect, was considered incomplete because it ignored fundamental differences between the EU and the traditional nation-state. According to Manners, the EU is a hybrid of supranational and international forms of governance whose existence was legitimized by its commitment to constitutional norms such as the respect of democracy, the rule of law, human rights, and social solidarity (Manners (2002), pp. 240–2). Such normative values recognize the common normative heritage from the disparate set of Member States and further serve the purpose of legitimizing the ever-increasing transfer of national sovereignty to the hybrid construct that is the EU (Nicolaidis and Howse (2002), pp. 778–80).

The normative basis of the EU—that is, the fact that its conception is based on the development of normative values—shapes its identity as an international actor. Besides the traditional use of civilian or military power, the EU also acts as a normative power ('Normative Power Europe' or 'NPE'), disseminating its norms, and therefore its very identity, across the globe. The dissemination of EU norms occurs in a variety of ways. For instance, EU norms can have an impact abroad just by existing, a process known as 'contagion', whereby norms are adopted by non-EU actors who view the EU as a regulatory model to aspire to. EU norms can also be promoted through policy documents or in the context of institutionalized international cooperation formats ('procedural diffusion'). More clear-cut forms of norm diffusion are the promotion of norms in the context of trade, development and cooperation relations ('transference'), the institutional presence of the EU abroad ('overt diffusion'), and the development of international norms (cultural filter) (Manners (2002), p. 245).

### 2.4.2 EU trade policy and narratives of self-projection

NPE recognizes trade policy as one of the many tools through which the EU exerts power by exporting its norms. In the context of the WTO, the projection of norms is exemplified by the EU's continuous attempts to ensure the compatibility of the multilateral trade regime with EU law and, strikingly, it appears that in many instances the EU is more concerned with the projection of its normative identity abroad than its immediate economic interests. For example, there was little internal demand from EU lobbyists and little support from other developed countries, notably the US, for the inclusion of competition disciplines—one of the cornerstones of the EU's internal market and one of the Singapore issues—in the Doha Round (Polleti (2012), pp. 195–6). The EU's insistence on introducing common competition policies was in fact motivated by institutional factors (the exportation of EU competition law enhances the Commission's status internationally and vis-à-vis Member States) (Aydin (2012), pp. 668–9) and by a belief that its approach to economic integration is necessarily the right approach globally (Poletti (2012), p.184). Outside the sphere of the WTO, the EU's trade policy has also consistently encouraged its trading partners to engage in regional economic integration processes. The promotion of regional integration as a good in itself is typically justified by the EU's own positive experience in economic integration and liberalization. In fact, there are misgivings about the rationale for the global harmonization of competition law as well as considerable debate as to whether the welfare benefits associated with the EU's regional economic integration can be replicated in other circumstances. These examples support the idea of the EU as an international actor whose trade policy is driven as much by an almost ideological desire to project its own regulatory model abroad as by purely economic interests.

However, narratives of self-projection, such as NPE, provide only an imperfect tool to understand the EU's role and identity in international trade relations. For Manners, just as important as the nature of the normative principles and rules that the EU promotes, is the *process* through which these are promoted (Manners (2008)). In order to assess whether the EU acts as a normative power, Manners posits that one must also examine the normative projection mechanisms through the prism of procedural normative ethics which can be subdivided into three separate approaches: (i) 'virtue ethics' which require normative actors to live by virtuous example by ensuring the coherence and consistency in policy making; (ii) 'deontological ethics' where the promotion of normative principles should not be achieved through force or coercion but rather through persuasion and processes of engagement and dialogue; and (iii) 'consequentialist ethics' according to which normative powers must give due consideration to the potential external impact of their policies on the welfare of others (Ibid, pp. 75–9). Therefore, the EU's NPE credentials depend in part on its ability to present itself as a credible model of the values, norms and processes that underlie its functioning (Nicolaidis and Howse (2002), p. 771). But it has been argued that, in practice, there is an apparent disconnect between what the EU is and how it is projecting itself. Meunier and Nicolaidis have stated in this regard that the sheer volume of goals being pursued by the EU's trade policy means that in many instances these goals may contradict each other, whilst in other cases such goals may conflict with the EU's own self-interest (Meunier and Nicolaidis (2006), pp. 922–3). This can be seen in the EU's simultaneous endorsement of multilateralism, regionalism, and more recently bilateralism, and in its push for deeper integration whilst maintaining a protectionist stance in the area of agricultural subsidies. They also contend that unless these internal contradictions that characterize the EU's trade power are resolved, the EU may continue to struggle to successfully wield its trade power effectively (Ibid). Clearly, a conflicted EU trade policy will undermine the EU's position in trade negotiations. During the Doha Round, for example, it was all too easy for developing countries to point out the EU's hypocrisy in demanding countries to embark on pro-market regulatory reforms whilst at the same time maintaining a protectionist stance in politically sensitive areas. In addition, the very idea that the EU seeks to export norms by convincing others of the legitimacy of such norms is heavily disputed (Nunes Ferreira (2011), p. 7). On this point, Zielonka has argued that the EU's normative agenda displays a number of features typically associated with empires insofar as it 'tries to assert political and economic control over various peripheral actors through formal annexations or various forms of economic and political domination' (Zielonka (2008), p. 475). This, Zielonka argues, is particularly evident in the area of external economic policy, where the EU 'tries to use its economic leverage to shape other countries' policies and 'imposes constraints on domestic conditions and operations of sovereign states' (Ibid, p. 479). The use of economic coercion to export norms for which there is little demand is incongruous with the notion of a NPE which expands the reach of its norms by the use of persuasion and deliberation and 'in the absence of obvious material gain' (Manners (2002), p. 253). It should be noted in this regard that although the conceptualization of the EU's foreign policy as CPE or NPE is typically understood in opposition to that of the US—based on power diplomacy—as far as trade policy is concerned, the narratives put forward by the US and the EU are not in fact too dissimilar. Consider the following statement from former US Trade Representative, Robert Zoellick, explaining some of the goals of competitive liberalization (Zoellick (2011)):

> [...] we need to align the global trading system with our values. We can encourage open and efficient markets while respecting national sovereignty. We can encourage respect for core labour standards, environmental protection, and good health without slipping into fear-based campaigns and protectionism. And we must always seek to strengthen freedom, democracy, and the rule of law.

Such phrasing would certainly not look out of place in EU trade policy statements—an indication that perhaps there is nothing intrinsically distinctive about the EU's foreign policy discourse based on norms and values.

### 2.4.3 Moving away from normative power

#### *2.4.3.1 Market Power Europe*

Recent scholarly work has focused on the emergence of a Market Power Europe (MPE), where the conceptualization of the EU's power as an international actor is based on the importance of the single market as a constituent element of the EU's identity. Damro explains that the idea of an integrated market was from the outset not only the central feature of the EU project, but also had an external dimension, since the establishment of the EEC as a customs union required a common external tariff (Damro (2012), p. 685). The success of the completion of the SMP only served to reinforce the perception of the EU as a construct intrinsically linked to the notion of a regulated market, and it is this 'market basis' for the EU's identity which informs the EU's role as a market power (Ibid). The first characteristic of MPE is that the sheer size of the EU's internal market enables it to act as a gravitational force pulling the norms of third countries towards it. The externalization of the EU's regulatory framework and policies can result from a deliberate policy by third countries to converge their regulations and standards with those of the EU in order to facilitate the task of economic operators wishing to take a bite of the EU market. As Bradford explains, this process (referred to as the 'Brussels Effect') 'captures a phenomenon where the EU does not have to do anything except regulate its own market to exercise global regulatory power' (Bradford (2012), p. 65). The EU may also force such convergence by blocking market access to economic operators from third countries that have not enacted similar regulatory standards to those that apply in the context of the Single Market (Ibid, p. 686). The second characteristic of MPE relates to the EU's significant regulatory institutional capacity. Because of the complexity of EU decision-making processes underpinning the adoption of market regulation, the EU has over time developed an array of tools that allow it to better take into account the external dimension of its internal regulation. Finally, the important role played by interest groups in the formulation of EU regulatory policies means that they can have a significant impact on the externalization of such policies. This is particularly relevant when 'pro-externalization coalitions' (Ibid, p. 689) take a prominent role in the conception of regulatory and policy initiatives.

The externalization of the regulatory dimension of the single market is a necessary consequence of the need to ensure that EU internal market rules do not place the EU at a competitive disadvantage in a globalized economy. In designing market regulation, EU legislators are required to balance market integration and diverging national interests and cultures and to incorporate often-opposing policy goals (liberalization, social, environmental, etc.). The pursuance of these regulatory goals can have the effect of placing regulatory burdens on EU economic operators—in comparison to less onerous requirements imposed outside the EU. Smith argues that there are three methods commonly used by the EU to reconcile the tension between market regulation and global competitiveness (Smith (2010), p. 937). The first of these methods is regulatory accommodation, which occurs whenever the EU rules are adapted to ensure that the regulatory burdens imposed on EU economic operators are not such as to undermine their ability to compete in the global market. The other two methods come into play when EU legislators have decided against regulatory accommodation and higher regulatory burdens are imposed on EU economic operators. Compliance deficits are observed where the EU chooses not to allocate its limited enforcement resources in areas where high regulatory burdens have an adverse impact. In other words, the EU will opt not to enforce burdensome regulatory standards that may affect the global competitiveness of its firms. Otherwise, where the EU enforces its legislation it may choose to level the playing field by 'uploading' its standards into the national or international regulatory frameworks (Ibid, p. 938). As Damro explains, this practice is particularly apparent in the context of trade agreements (Damro (2012), p. 695):

> The externalization of internal regulatory measures can take place if, for example, the EU attempts to include standards in bilateral and multilateral trade agreements (i.e., positive conditionality). Even if the EU employs the tools of positive conditionality with the intent of persuading changes in behaviour, the third parties in question may feel they have been coerced into changing their behaviour because they have no alternative: they must agree to undesirable terms in trade agreements because they need access to the large European single market; and they must abide by the EU's relevant internal regulatory measures or they will be subject to sanctioning under the associated implementing legislation.

MPE still contains the crucial element of NPE: power through projection of norms, whether as a result of a deliberate policy or as a result of the mere existence of the internal market. However, it makes sense of the EU's increasingly comprehensive and commercially driven trade (and economic) policy as embodied by the Global Europe strategy. The EU's power is derived from the strength and size of its internal market, the rules of which are designed to further the EU's interests abroad whilst the enhancement of the EU's competitiveness becomes an increasingly prominent justification and goal of its external action.

#### *2.4.3.2 Governance mode of EU foreign policy*

Another attempt to frame EU foreign policy which seeks to do away with the focus on the projection of norms and values has been developed by De Búrca (De Búrca (2012), pp. 39–58). She notes that whether in the pursuance of its material interests or the projection of its values, the EU's foreign policy typically displays a preference towards collective means of action based on cooperation between international actors, namely through the establishment of 'transnational and broadly participatory regulatory frameworks to coordinate and govern various issues [and] networks of stable, institutionalised and iterative relationships with other states entities and regions' (Ibid, p. 40). Moreover, such modes of governance 'replicate or externalize some of the modes of governance it has developed for similar policies in its internal realm' (Ibid). The emphasis is less on achieving 'specific forms of reciprocity' and more on 'the intensification of interdependence and institution-building' in order to achieve multiple inter-linked goals in different policy areas.

De Búrca provides numerous examples of arrangements which, whether at the bilateral level (e.g. partnerships on climate change), the regional level (e.g. European Neighbourhood Policy, ENP) or the multilateral level (e.g. promotion of the International Criminal Court) confirm the EU's desire to establish institutional and regulatory frameworks where common goals can be pursued in the long-term. The EU's governance mode of foreign policy borrows from NPE as it puts forward the idea of the EU as a power keen to project its identity (in this case its governance processes) abroad whilst avoiding unrealistic categorizations of the EU as an actor more virtuous than others. However, as De Búrca points out, the governance mode is not an all-encompassing conceptualization of the EU's conduct in foreign policy. The EU will seek to act unilaterally in some areas, and will demand immediate results from its interlocutors in others. There is also the question of the effectiveness of this particular approach to foreign policy, as well as of whether the externalization of EU processes is a means employed by the EU to impose its substantive norms by stealth (Ibid, pp. 57–8).

## 2.5 Conclusion

The international trading system has changed dramatically since the days of GATT 1947, from what is understood to constitute trade liberalization to the manner in which trade politics are conducted. Trade is no longer just about goods, and liberalization is no longer just about tariffs. A wider and more intrusive set of rules are therefore needed to regulate the complexities of international economic exchanges. These changes are evidenced both by the evolution of the EU's internal market and that of its external trade policy. Mindful of the inevitability of deeper integration, but wary of the adverse impact that may occur from the resulting loss of policy and regulatory autonomy, the EU has sought to develop policies that seek to shape the international trading system in its own image.

Beyond its altruistic overtones, the objective of managed globalization incorporated in the EU's deep trade agenda is at its core an attempt to promote an international trading system that works best for the EU. Managing or harnessing globalization is first and foremost about disciplining globalization so that it allows EU firms to reap the maximum benefits from trade liberalization whilst simultaneously delimiting clear pockets of sovereignty where the EU and its Member States can still pursue domestic policy objectives and preferences. In other words, it is globalization on the EU's terms. Viewed from this perspective, the EU's current trade strategy does not represent a significant departure from the EU's attempts to bring reform at the level of the WTO. The setting might be different, but the objectives are similar. The EU's deep trade agenda, deeper integration premised on the adoption of common regulatory disciplines, is still very much the order of the day.

However, the abandonment of multilateralism as the exclusive venue for trade negotiations and the emphasis on commercially or interest-driven EU Deep and Comprehensive Free Trade Agreements (DCFTAs) provide a different slant to the EU's deep trade agenda. References in EU trade policy statements to the 'WTO plus' nature and the various methods of 'regulatory convergence' that will be explored in the EU DCFTAs support the suspicion that the EU uses its economic leverage to include in these agreements disciplines that go further than those proposed in the context of the Doha Round. This raises the question of the nature of these disciplines and of the relevance of conceptualizations of how the EU acts in international politics—particularly the NPE literature, where the EU's attempts to spread its norms are, in contrast to other international actors, said to be based on its ability to present itself as a model to be emulated rather than through any means of coercion and requires the EU to 'think reflexively about the impact of its policies on partner regions and countries' (Manners (2008), p. 79). In that sense, it may be worth recalling the considerable similarities in the narratives put forward by the US in its approach to competitive liberalization and by the EU's Global Europe strategy. Both stress the importance of combining liberalization with the pursuance of other values and goals, and both argue that bilateralism and multilateralism are mutually reinforcing processes. However, competitive liberalization—a policy that has been in place for longer than the Global Europe strategy—has arguably failed to deliver on its promises, leading some to ask whether it 'amounts to little more than bilateral opportunism masquerading as high principle with an apparently compelling narrative' (Evenett and Meier (2007), p. 27).

# 3

# Legal Framework of the EU's Deep Trade Agenda

## Competence, Decision Making, and Objectives

### 3.1 Introduction

Although the trade agreements envisaged by the EU's deep trade agenda may be ambitious and comprehensive, they remain subject to a number of restrictions imposed by EU law. This chapter aims to provide an overview of the legal framework for the conduct of EU external trade relations, and to elucidate how this may impact on its ability to adequately pursue its deep trade agenda. Section 3.2 addresses the issue of the EU's external trade competence. As a rule, the EU may only act in the areas where a competence has been conferred on it in the EU Treaties by the Member States (principle of conferral).[1] In the context of external trade, the EU has traditionally been granted an exclusive competence under the common commercial policy (CCP), and as trade policy increasingly encroaches on domestic rules, the EU has been forced to expand the scope of the CCP. Even so, there are areas that are now understood as being an integral part of trade policy but which remain outside the CCP. Section 3.3 provides an overview of the rules relating to the decision-making process surrounding the negotiation and conclusion of trade agreements. Particular attention will be paid to the enhancement of the European Parliament's role in the conclusion of trade agreements following the signing of the Treaty of Lisbon and how its involvement may affect the content of such agreements. A further trade policy innovation brought by the Treaty of Lisbon is that the EU is now obliged to carry out the CCP in the context of various, and sometimes conflicting, trade and non-trade objectives (e.g. trade liberalization, protection of human rights, promotion of democracy, rule of law, and sustainable development).[2] Section 3.4 analyses the main Treaty-recognized objectives underlying the EU's external trade policy, attempts to determine the extent to which these may or may not affect the content of trade agreements, and examines a specific example of how such objectives are implemented in practice in the EU's DCFTAs by focusing on the sustainable development chapters included in such agreements.

[1] Article 5 TEU. [2] Article 207(1) TFEU.

## 3.2 EU External Trade Competence

### 3.2.1 General considerations

Traditionally, a distinction is operated between two types of competence in the context of EU foreign policy (Craig and De Búrca (2011), pp. 309–11). The EU can act on the basis of express competence, where its power to act internationally is explicitly enshrined in the text of the treaties (e.g. CCP,[3] trade and development policy,[4] and association agreements[5]). It may also act on the basis of implied competence (Eeckhout (2011), pp. 70–190)—that is, where the EU's power derives from the mere existence of internal EU competence. According to established case law (which the EU sought to codify in Article 216(1) TFEU), the EU has the power to conclude international agreements in any area where it has a corresponding internal competence and where the conclusion of the agreement is required in order to attain the objective set out by the internal competence.[6]

As far as the exercise of the EU's competence is concerned, there is a further distinction to be made: that between exclusive and shared (or mixed) external competences. The EU's competence is exclusive where it is the only body that can act internationally on a particular topic to the exclusion of Member States. Article 3(1) TFEU lists areas that are considered to be competences that are exclusive to the EU: customs union, the establishment of competition rules necessary for the functioning of the internal market, monetary policy for the Member States whose currency is the euro, the conservation of marine biological resources under the common fisheries policies, and the CCP. For these matters only the EU 'may legislate and adopt legally binding acts, the latter concept clearly extending to treaties, conventions and agreements under international law' (Eeckhout (2011), p. 121). The EU's exclusive competence can also be implied from the existence of an EU internal competence if such competence has been exercised or is being exercised simultaneously with the ongoing negotiation of an international agreement. Shared competences can be subdivided into concurrent competences, where the EU must act alone once it exercises its power, and parallel competences, where the EU and the Member States can act simultaneously. The Treaties count among the EU's concurrent competences areas pertaining to the internal market, social policy, agricultural policy, and the area of freedom and security.[7] Parallel competences include research, technological development and development cooperation, and humanitarian aid.[8]

According to EU case law, implied competence is considered exclusive if a specific EU act provides for the negotiation of an international agreement,[9] if the

[3] Article 207 TFEU. [4] Articles 208–211 TFEU. [5] Article 217 TFEU.

[6] Opinion 1/76, *European Laying-up fund for inland Waterway Vessels* [1977] ECR 741, paras 3–4.

[7] Article 4(2) TFEU. [8] Article 4(3) and (4) TFEU.

[9] Opinion 1/94 *Competence of the Community to conclude international agreements concerning services and the protection of intellectual property* [1994] ECR-I5267 para 95.

ability of Member States to act alone would undermine an internal EU act,[10] or if exclusive competence is necessary to either conduct a common policy or put into practice an internal competence (Opinion 1/76 doctrine). The Treaty of Lisbon sought to codify this case law by providing that exclusive competence for the conclusion of international agreements shall exist where 'the conclusion of an international agreement is provided for in a legislative act of the Union or is necessary to enable the Union to exercise its internal competence, or insofar as its conclusion may affect common rules or alter the scope'.[11] Moreover, it is also provided that the Union may conclude international agreements 'where the Treaties so provide or where the conclusion of an agreement is necessary in order to achieve, within the framework of the Union's policies, one of the objectives referred to in the Treaties, or is provided for in a legally binding act of the Union or is likely to affect common rules or alter their scope' (Eeckhout (2011), pp. 112–13).

## 3.2.2 Common Commercial Policy

### *3.2.2.1 Scope of the CCP: Beyond trade in goods*

The exclusivity of the EU's competence in the area of the CCP was confirmed by the Court at an early stage.[12] When asked to examine the existence and nature of the power, the Court noted that the CCP was conceived as a tool to ensure the proper operation of the common market by eradicating distortions of competition between Member States in relation to external markets. This, the Court added, would not be feasible if Member States were allowed to act unilaterally in this area. The concurrent exercise of powers by the Member States in this specific area could therefore not be entertained.

The scope of the CCP has, however, been the cause of much debate over the years. Under the Treaty of Rome, the CCP was described in rather loose terms. With regard to its objectives, Article 110 EEC (now Article 206 TFEU) stated that it should 'aim to contribute, in the common interest, to the harmonious development of world trade, the progressive abolition of restrictions on international trade and the lowering of customs barriers'. As for the policy tools available to the EU, Article 113 EEC provided an illustrative list[13] of instruments that were covered by it. These included, on the one hand, unilateral measures such as changes in tariff rates, export and import policies, and commercial defence measures and, on the other hand, the establishment of contractual relations with third countries. The provision did not specify the types of economic exchanges that would be covered by the CCP, and in particular whether this competence extended beyond the traditional focus on trade in goods. This apparent lacuna reflected the prevailing

[10] Case 22/70 *Commission v Council* (ERTA) [1971] ECR 263.

[11] Article 3(2) TFEU.

[12] Opinion 1/75 *Draft Understanding on a Local Cost Standard drawn up under the auspices of the OECD* [1975] ECR 1355.

[13] Opinion 1/78 *Natural Rubber Agreement* [1979] ECR 2871.

conception that trade was all about goods and border measures, and proved irrelevant in practice given that during the first three decades of its existence, the EU was unable to so much as simulate a semblance of an integrated market in any area other than that of goods. By the mid-1980s, the EU was yet to significantly address trade in services with third countries, even though services accounted for around 30 per cent of international trade (Bourgeois (1987), p. 12).

The SMP and the Uruguay Round negotiations, which both covered fields beyond trade in goods, brought the issue of the scope of the CCP to the fore. After the completion of these negotiations, the Commission submitted to the Court a request for an opinion on, inter alia, the EU's power to conclude GATS and TRIPS. With regard to services, the Court stated that Opinion 1/78 had established that the CCP should not be viewed as a static policy area but rather viewed as open-ended and progressive, by taking into account general developments in international trade. Therefore, 'as a matter of principle'[14] there was no impediment to the inclusion of trade in services within the scope of Article 113 EEC. However, to ascertain whether the areas covered by GATS came within the scope of Article 113 EEC, the Court analysed the extent to which the definition of trade in services under GATS was aligned with that of the EU. The Court found that of the four modes of supply for the delivery of services in cross-border trade covered by the GATS, only the first mode, cross-border supply (where the service is supplied by a supplier established in one country to a consumer located in another country), was within the scope of the CCP. The remaining modes of supply (consumption abroad, commercial presence, and presence of natural persons) could not be covered by the CCP since the treatment of third country nationals within the EU was an issue concerning the entry and movement of persons as demonstrated by the existence of specific Treaty chapters and provisions on the movement of natural and legal persons.

A similar analysis was followed with respect to TRIPS, as the Court rejected the notion that the EU had the exclusive competence to negotiate and conclude TRIPS on the basis of the CCP. The Court considered in the first instance that although IP laws did have an effect on trade, insofar as such rules allowed IP rights holders to prevent the use of such rights, this effect was not limited to international trade but also covered purely internal situations. The Court's view was that TRIPS was more focused on strengthening and harmonizing 'the protection of intellectual property on a worldwide scale' than regulating international trade per se.[15] The harmonizing brief of TRIPS was also problematic in light of the exclusive nature of the EU's competence under the CCP. At the time, the internal harmonization of rules on IP was subject to specific procedural rules involving unanimity and consultations with the European Parliament.[16] Extending the scope of the CCP to the sphere of IP protection would effectively allow the EU to determine the content of internal legislation in that area through the back door,

[14] Opinion 1/94, para. 41. [15] Opinion 1/94, para. 57.
[16] Opinion 1/94, paras 59 and 60.

since it would be able to circumvent the much more cumbersome procedural rules applicable for the harmonization of EU legislation. This reflects in part the difficulties encountered by the EU in the establishment of a European IP rights regime which, in turn, is a by-product of the reluctance of Member States to cede their competences in this area.

The Court also rejected the Commission's argument that exclusive external competence in the area of services and intellectual property could flow implicitly from the EU's existing internal powers. The Commission had argued that an implicit exclusive external competence was justified in this area since the EU did have the power to adopt internal harmonization measures and because the conclusion of an international agreement was necessary to achieve the EU's internal objectives. The existence of Treaty provisions granting powers for the adoption of harmonization measures relating to IP in the EU was deemed irrelevant to the extent that the internal power to harmonize had not been exercised. Further, the Court found that the Commission's argument that the joint competence of the EU and the Member States to conclude TRIPS would affect existing legislative acts could not be upheld, since harmonization of EU law in the areas covered by the GATS and TRIPS was only partial, if not non-existent. There were two reasons for the Commission's argument that exclusive external competence was necessary. First, the coherence of the internal market would be impaired without such competence and, secondly, the EU could not afford to remain inactive in the context of international trade negotiations. For the Court, however, Opinion 1/76 related to a very specific set of circumstances where the EU had no choice but to enter into an international agreement in order to achieve one of its objectives. This, the Court added, was not the case with services where 'the attainment of freedom of establishment and the freedom to provide services for nationals of Member States is not inextricably linked to the treatment to be afforded in the Community to nationals of non-member countries or in non-member countries to nationals of Member States of the Community'.[17] The same could be said in the area of IP regulation, where it was argued that the 'unification or harmonization of intellectual property rights in the Community context does not necessarily have to be accompanied by agreements with non-member countries to be effective'.[18]

The exclusion of GATS and TRIPS from the scope of the CCP posed serious practical difficulties for the EU. If, for example, no consensus could be reached with regard to an area where competence was to be shared between the EU and the Member States,[19] Member States could decide to act individually, thereby undermining the EU's unity of action and weakening its position in external trade relations. Therefore, subsequent Treaty reforms have all sought to expand the EU's competence under the CCP, culminating in the Treaty of Lisbon which provides under Article 207 TFEU that the CCP covers 'the conclusion of tariff and trade

[17] Opinion 1/94, para. 86. [18] Opinion 1/94, para. 100.
[19] Opinion 1/94, paras 98 and 105.

agreements relating to trade in goods and services, and the commercial aspects of intellectual property, foreign direct investment'.

### *3.2.2.2 Intellectual property*

In Opinion 1/94, the Court concluded that the EU's competence to conclude agreements in the area of IP was one that should be shared with the Member States. The Treaty of Nice would respond to Opinion 1/94 by explicitly extending the scope of the CCP to cover the 'commercial aspects of intellectual property rights'.[20] The extension was subject to a number of limitations. First, no guidance was provided as to what would be covered by these 'commercial aspects'. Secondly, although certain aspects of intellectual property regulation were brought within the scope of the CCP, it remained a shared competence. Thirdly, in terms of how the CCP would function in general, the Treaty of Nice introduced language which asserted the requirement of parallelism between internal and external powers in the area of IP as developed by the Court in Opinion 1/94. According to Article 133(5) EC, unanimity was required for the negotiation and conclusion of agreements in the field of the commercial aspects of intellectual property, where these agreements contained provisions for which unanimity was required for the adoption of internal rules, or which related to areas where the EU had not yet exercised the powers conferred upon it by adopting internal rules. Article 133(6) EC first subparagraph also provided that the Council could not conclude an international agreement in the areas of services and the commercial aspects of intellectual property if such agreement included provisions which exceeded the EU's internal powers.

The end result was an extremely cumbersome system which the Member States sought to rationalize in the Treaty of Lisbon. First of all, it should be noted that, in accordance with Article 4(2)(a) TFEU, IP remains an area of shared competence. This, allied with the continued lack of harmonization at the internal level, means that there is still no implied exclusive external competence for the EU in this area. Many international agreements on IP continue to be negotiated as mixed agreements (van Eechoud, Bernt, Hugenholtz, VanGompel, Guibault, and Helberger (2009), p. 17; Peers (2011), p. 231). However, with respect to the CCP, the new Article 207 TFEU retains the term 'commercial aspects of intellectual property' but removes any references to the possible existence of shared competences in the CCP and reduces procedural exceptions to the EU's power to act externally. Despite this, what is covered by or excluded from the concept of 'commercial aspects' is a question that remains unanswered. There appears to be a general consensus in the academic world that the term should encompass the areas covered by TRIPS (Herrmann (2002), p. 15; Cremona (2003), p. 1363; Muller-Graff (2008), p. 192; Piris (2010), p. 281; Bundenberg (2010), p. 131; Villata Puig and Al-Haddab (2011), p. 292; Gosalbo Bono (2011), p. 17).

[20] Article 133(5) EC.

This position was recently endorsed in the *Daiichi* ruling[21] in which the Court confirmed that the entirety of TRIPS rules now fall under the exclusive competence of the CCP. The Court had been asked whether, in accordance with case law preceding the entry into force of the Treaty of Lisbon,[22] Article 27 TRIPS regulating patentable subject matter remained a shared competence. The Court took the opportunity to determine the scope of the exclusive competence of the EU in matters relating to 'commercial aspects of intellectual property'. It reasoned, rather summarily, that only those matters that have a specific link to international trade can constitute 'commercial aspects of intellectual property' and that such link existed in the case of TRIPS since the agreement is an integral part of the WTO system.[23] The *Daiichi* ruling is at odds with the opinion delivered by Advocate General Cruz Villalón, which had concluded that not all rules included in TRIPS fell within the scope of Article 207 TFEU, including Article 21 TRIPS which dealt 'with an aspect of intellectual property which is directly concerned with establishing legal rules governing the rights in that special property which a legal system recognises and guarantees'[24] and had warned against a construction of Article 207 TFEU which would equate 'commercial aspects intellectual property' to all areas of IP regulation.[25] An over-expansive construction, the Advocate General warned, could allow the EU to indirectly harmonize IP laws through its exclusive external competence, a remark which echoes concerns present in Opinion 1/94 where the Court had considered that only a few TRIPS provisions—namely those regulating IP enforcement measures applied by customs authorities—could be said to be 'closely linked to trade'.[26]

The approach adopted in *Daiichi* can perhaps be explained by the Court's desire to give some meaning to the textual amendments resulting from the Treaty of Lisbon regarding the scope of the CCP—something to which the Court refers by reasoning that the similarity between the term 'commercial aspects of intellectual property' and 'trade-related aspects of intellectual property' was no mere coincidence and revealed the intention of the authors of the TFEU to ensure that the entirety of TRIPS was covered by the CCP.[27] The approach means that the scope of Article 207 TFEU is determined purely by reference to the content of TRIPS and presumably supports a dynamic interpretation of the 'concept of commercial aspects of intellectual property', where the term covers both the matters currently regulated under TRIPS, as well as any future amendment of TRIPS (Krajewski (2005), p. 91; Dimopoulos (2007), pp. 108–9). If this is indeed the case, then the concerns raised by Advocate General Cruz Villalón may turn out to be prescient.

Whilst the EU's exclusive competence under the CCP with respect to TRIPS appears to be firmly established, one question that remains unanswered is whether

[21] C-414/11 *Daiichi Sankyo and Sanofi-Aventis Deutschland v DEMO Anonymos Viomichaniki kai Emporiki Etairia Farmakon*, 18 July 2013.

[22] Case C-431/05 *Merck Genéricos—Produtos Farmacêuticos* [2007] ECR I-7001, para 33.

[23] Case 441/11, paras 53–54.

[24] C-441/11, Opinion of Mr Advocate General Cruz Villalón, 31 January 2013, para 80.

[25] Ibid. [26] Opinion 1/94 para 54. [27] Case 44/11, para 55.

such exclusive competence could also be extended to the negotiation of international agreements outside the sphere of the WTO. This question is of particular relevance with regard to the politically sensitive area of the criminal enforcement of IP rights, and has been the subject of some debate in the context of the signing by the EU of the Anti-Counterfeiting Trade Agreement (ACTA)—whose ratification has since been rejected by the European Parliament[28]—which contains extensive provisions relating to criminal enforcement (Ramalho (2011), p. 99). A further complication in the context of criminal enforcement arises from the uncertainty regarding the EU's internal competence in this area, the question being whether the lack of competence to legislate internally could preclude the exercise of the EU's competence in the CCP. Advocate General Kokott has provided some insights on this issue, albeit only in relation to the CCP as established in the Treaty of Nice.[29] The Advocate General's opinion was given in the context of a case concerning the EU's power to approve alone the accession of Vietnam to the WTO on the basis of Article 133(5) EC. Having established that the EU's power under Article 133(5) EC was a concurrent power—that is, one where the EU must act alone once it exercises its power—the Advocate General questioned whether the EU had the internal competence to legislate issues pertaining to, inter alia, the criminal enforcement of IP rights. The question was relevant to the extent that Article 133(6) EC specifically precluded the EU from negotiating provisions which exceeded the EU's internal powers from the scope of the CCP.[30] Up until the entry into force of the Treaty of Lisbon, the EU was not deemed to have competence in matters pertaining to criminal law and procedure. The Court had accepted that the EU could adopt criminal enforcement measures where this was necessary in order to ensure the effectiveness of rules it had laid down, but such competence did not extend to the possibility of determining the types and level of criminal penalties.[31] This means that even if the CCP was considered to cover the area of the criminal enforcement of IP, the EU would not be competent to exercise such competence for the lack of a corresponding internal power. This explains why the criminal enforcement component of ACTA had been negotiated by the Presidency on behalf of the Member States while the remainder of the agreement was negotiated by the Commission.

The Treaty of Lisbon has changed this situation. Not only are the 'commercial aspects of intellectual property' an exclusive external competence of the EU, but the requirement that the EU's external powers should not go beyond existing internal powers was removed and replaced by Article 207(6) TFEU which provides, inter alia, that the exercise of the EU's policy 'shall not affect the

[28] European Parliament legislative resolution of 4 July 2012 (12195/2011–C7-0027/2012–2011/0167(NLE)).

[29] Case C-13/07 *Commission v Council*, Opinion of Advocate General Kokott, 26 March 2009 (withdrawn following the entry into force of the Treaty of Lisbon).

[30] Case C-13/07, paras 152–157.

[31] Case C-176/03 *Commission v Council* [2005] ECR I-7879, para 48; Case C-440/05 *Commission v Council* [2007] ECR I-9097, para 66.

delimitation of competences'. This provision is being read as the application of the principle of limited conferred powers (Cremona (2003), p. 1363). Applied in the specific context of the CCP, the principle removes the possibility that the exercise of exclusive CCP competence in an area would lead to the establishment of an exclusive internal competence (Ibid). There is, however, some debate as to whether the new provision truly removes the requirement of parallelism between internal and external powers—that is, whether exclusive competence in the area of the CCP can now extend to areas where it has no corresponding internal powers (Eeckhout (2011), p. 61). With regard to the issue of the criminal enforcement of IP rights, this debate has become immaterial given that the Treaty of Lisbon also establishes a legal basis for the EU's internal competence in the area of criminal enforcement. Article 83(2) TFEU provides that the EU may adopt directives establishing minimum rules with regard to the definition of criminal offences and sanctions where the approximation of criminal laws and regulations of the Member States proves essential to ensure the effective implementation of a Union policy in an area which has been subject to harmonization measures. In other words, even if the Court was to find that the principle of parallelism as developed in the context of Article 133(6) EC was also applicable with regard to Article 207(6) TFEU, such requirement would be fulfilled because there is now a corresponding internal power.

During the negotiation process of ACTA, the EU's power to negotiate the provisions on criminal enforcement on the basis of Article 207 TFEU was criticized. Leaked drafts of the agreement had shown that the parties intended to prosecute certain IP infringements that had no direct or indirect motivation of financial gain.[32] It was argued as a result that ACTA's provisions on criminal enforcement did not necessarily concern trade or commercial activities (Ramalho (2011), p. 99). However, anyone fearing that the EU may have been looking to act ultra vires need not have worried. Even though the misgivings concerning the commercial character of ACTA's criminal enforcement provisions were addressed in the final draft of the agreement, which replicates Article 61 TRIPS by providing that criminal enforcement would apply to IP infringements on a 'commercial scale', the Commission has not sought to use Article 207 TFEU as the legal basis. On the contrary, the Commission's Proposal for a Council Decision on the Conclusion of the ACTA (ACTA Proposal) (European Commission (2011d)) assumes from the outset that criminal enforcement of IP rights is an area that remains outside the EU's exclusive competence under Article 207 TFEU, a view that is also endorsed by the European Parliament and the Council (Kamperman Sanders, Shabalala, Moerland and Pugatch (2011)). Clearly then, the current consensus is that criminal enforcement is one area which is not covered under the 'commercial aspects of intellectual property', despite its inclusion in TRIPS.

At first sight, the Commission's reluctance to explore the possibility of using Article 207 TFEU as a legal basis for the negotiation and conclusion of criminal

[32] Article 2.14, para 1(a) ACTA.

enforcement provisions in trade agreements seems surprising, given that the Court has not provided any inkling of what its position would be on the matter. In fact, in Advocate General Kokott's opinion above, there is an acknowledgement that the issue remains open for discussion. Ultimately, it may be that the politically sensitive nature of the issue, rather than purely legal considerations, was the determining factor. The possibility of using Article 83(2) TFEU as a legal basis for the EU's external competence was also discussed. Although the provision falls under an area of shared competence (Title V TFEU, area of freedom, security and justice[33]), it creates a firm legal basis for an implied external competence in the area of criminal enforcement, which would allow the EU to conclude agreements containing criminal enforcement provisions on its own. The exercise of such competence would be problematic in light of the EU's hitherto inability to harmonize national criminal law concerning IP rights infringements (Opinion of European Academics (2010), p. 4; Ramalho (2011), p. 98). It is also contended that the approximation of criminal laws in this area may fail the Article 83(2) TFEU test, insofar as it may not 'prove essential' to the effective implementation of the internal market (Ramalho (2011), p. 98). However, whilst the Commission stated in the ACTA Proposal that certain criminal enforcement provisions of ACTA do fall under the scope of Article 83(2) TFEU, it chose not to exercise such competence, as ACTA was never intended 'to modify the EU acquis or to harmonise EU legislation as regards criminal enforcement of intellectual property rights'.[34] The Commission's refusal to use Article 83(2) TFEU as a legal basis is undoubtedly a political decision and cannot be viewed as a template for future negotiations of criminal enforcement provisions in trade agreements. ACTA was signed and concluded as a mixed agreement but only to avoid accusations that the EU was seeking to harmonize criminal law of the Member States by stealth (Hoffmeister (2011), pp. 84–95). It may be that the Commission will wait until it is able to push through internal legislation on criminal enforcement of IP to seek to conclude an agreement on the basis of Article 83(2) TFEU. When (or if) that happens, Article 83(2) TFEU should provide a solid legal basis for the EU to act alone when negotiating criminal enforcement measures relating to IP rights infringements in its trade agreements.

### *3.2.2.3 Services*

Although both the Treaties of Amsterdam and Nice confirmed that the CCP covered 'trade in services', there were a number of areas pertaining to services that remained shared competences. As previously discussed, Article 133(6) EC first subparagraph provided that the EU could not conclude an international agreement in the areas of services and the commercial aspects of intellectual property if such agreement included provisions which exceeded the Community's internal powers (this would apply in particular to cases where the signing of an agreement

[33] Article 4(j) TFEU.

[34] ACTA Proposal, p. 6.

would lead to the harmonization of the laws and regulations of the Member States in an area where such harmonization was to be excluded). In such cases, we find ourselves in the domain of mixed agreements, where the signature of both the Community and the Member States are required. Article 133 6(2) EC was more forthright insofar as it provided that notwithstanding the extension of the CCP to trade in services, trade in cultural and audiovisual services, educational services, and social, and human health services would fall within the shared competence of the Community and its Member States. In case the explicit reference to 'shared competence' was not clear enough, the last two sentences of Article 133(6) EC, which provide that the negotiation of such agreements not only require the 'common accord of the Member States' but must also be 'conducted jointly by the Commission and the Member States',[35] drive the point home.

By the time of the Treaty of Lisbon, the references to shared competence in the areas of trade in cultural and audiovisual services, educational, social, and human health services that were introduced in the Treaty of Nice had disappeared. Therefore, it can be said that the entirety of trade in services now comes under the exclusive competence of the EU. However, there are two qualifications to this statement. First, Article 207(5) provides that the field of transport remains a shared competence. Secondly, although it is now clear that the fields of cultural, social, educational, and health services come wholly within the scope of the EU's exclusive competence under the CCP, they are, unlike the other areas of the CCP, subject to the rule of unanimity in certain circumstances, reflecting their ever politically sensitive nature: (1) 'in the field of trade in cultural and audiovisual services, where these agreements risk prejudicing the Union's cultural and linguistic diversity',[36] and (2) 'in the field of trade in social, education and health services, where these agreements risk seriously disturbing the national organisation of such services and prejudicing the responsibility of Member States to deliver them'.[37] This provision is problematic because of its vagueness. It is not clear, for example, what is encapsulated by the term 'cultural and linguistic diversity' nor, for that matter, how one would go about assessing a 'serious risk' to such diversity (Krajewski (2012), 306–7). There is also no guidance as to how, from a procedural point of view, Member States can exceptionally decide to act unanimously where a Member State has invoked the existence of a serious risk to one of the identified interests. Could the mere fact that a Member State has raised concerns as to the impact of an international agreement on cultural diversity or the organization of its social services suffice to trigger the requirement of unanimity, or must this view also be shared by other Member States? In the latter case, what level of Member State support is required in order to trigger unanimity? The suggestion that a Member State could unilaterally impose unanimous voting within the Council must be rejected as it would effectively mean that Member States have retained a right of veto with respect to the areas listed in Article 207 subparagraph 3 TFEU.

[35] Article 133(6) as amended by the Treaty of Nice.
[36] Article 207(4)(a).
[37] Article 207(4)(b).

This would bring us back to the situation that existed under the pre-Lisbon regimes and would render the amendments introduced by the Treaty of Lisbon ineffective. In any event, it appears that a de facto unanimity requirement will continue to apply in these areas, given the particular national concerns associated with them (Leal-Arcas (2012), pp. 266–7).

Irrespective of the uncertainties surrounding the decision-making process, it is no longer disputed that these fields are now firmly within the scope of the EU's exclusive competence. The schedules of the EU DCFTAs contain commitments in some of these fields, namely mode 3 service supply national treatment and market access commitments for health and social services (e.g. hospital and ambulance services). However, liberalization in the more sensitive sector of audiovisual services remains a no-go area. Not only are they explicitly excluded from the scope of the EU DCFTAs, but the EU has also developed a practice of concluding Protocols on Cultural Products with trade partners whose aim is to affirm the regulatory autonomy of each country to regulate this particular area.

#### *3.2.2.4 Foreign direct investment*

The most visible reform of the CCP under the Treaty of Lisbon relates to the expansion of its scope to cover 'foreign direct investment' (FDI). This development is illustrative of the progressive alignment of the scope of the CCP with that of the WTO rules and, in general, the diversification of the international economy (Cremona (2000), p. 13; Woolcock (2008a), p. 5). However, the exact contours of the concept of FDI under the CCP have caused some debate (Eilmansberger (2009), p. 446). International investment law is dominated by a multitude of bilateral investment treaties (BITs) and bilateral and regional FTAs (together international investment agreements, or IIAs). The regulation of investment under these IIAs typically covers two types of investment. On the one hand, there is FDI, which 'refers to an investment made to acquire lasting interest in enterprises operating outside of the economy of the investor' (IMF (2007)). On the other hand, there is portfolio investment—a less prominent feature of IIAs (Sornarajah (2004), p. 7)—defined as the 'movement of money for the purpose of buying shares in a company formed or functioning in another country' (Ibid). IIAs typically do not address issues pertaining to conditions of entry (Molinuevo (2012), p. 83), i.e. market access, but rather focus on promoting standards of protection that need to be applied with regard to foreign investment (Seid (2002), pp. 52–3; Schreuer (2007), pp. 2–6). These include, for example, non-discrimination obligations (national treatment, MFN), fair and equitable treatment standards (e.g. standards relating to due process and denial of justice), full protection and security, repatriation of profits, compensation for expropriation, and investor–state dispute settlement. The main discussion has centred on whether the concept of FDI under the CCP corresponds to the regulation of investment in these IIAs.

There appears to be a general consensus that the CCP does not cover portfolio investment (Eilmansberger (2009), p. 94). It seems unlikely that the drafters of the Treaty of Lisbon would have failed to appreciate the well-rehearsed distinction between these two types of investment, particularly when such distinction has important ramifications, since only FDI is subject to protection under customary international law (Sornarajah (2004), p. 8). Moreover, it has also been noted that the distinction is one that is recognized by the EU's own case law (Eeckhout and Ortino (2013), pp. 314–15). Within the specific remit of FDI, there is also a question as to whether the EU's competence covers only conditions of entry (Krajewski (2013), p. 303), or whether it also extends to the type of investment protection rules that are pervasive in IIAs. Here, again, the consensus seems to point towards the latter option (Eeckhout (2011), p. 64; Leal-Arcas (2012), p. 266), notably because GATS, in its current state, already contains significant rules relating to investment protection. Such rules include the obligation not to discriminate against foreign service suppliers who have a commercial presence within the territory of a WTO member (mode 3 service supply) (Eeckhout (2011), p. 65), as well as transparency, due process and fair administration obligations, which not only incorporate key features of the fair and equitable treatment standard found in IIAs, but also go further in certain aspects (Molinuevo (2012), p. 183). To the extent that the Treaty of Lisbon sought to expand the scope of the CCP by including FDI, limiting FDI to cover only market access issues when GATS already contains rules relating to investment protection would effectively render this supposed expansion of competence meaningless.

A final issue relates to whether FDI under the CCP would allow the EU to negotiate rules relating to expropriation. The issue has been raised because Article 345 TFEU provides that the EU treaties 'shall not prejudice the rules of member states governing the system of property ownership'. For some, this provision should be read as excluding any EU competence which pertains to property law (Ceyssens (2004), p. 281). Such a restrictive reading has not been considered convincing by most legal scholars (Shan and Zhang (2010), p. 1067; Bungenberg (2011), p. 36; Dimopoulos (2012), p. 408) namely because, as explained by Eeckhout, the EU's case law has repeatedly confirmed that this provision should not be read as a restriction on EU competence (Eeckhout (2011), p. 65).

Unsurprisingly, the Commission has sided with the more expansionist views of the scope of FDI under the CCP. In the 2010 Communication 'Towards a comprehensive European investment policy' (Investment Policy Communication), the Commission confirmed that FDI should not be read as encompassing portfolio investment (European Commission (2010b), p. 8) but added that, with regard to the latter, the EU may in any event imply its competence from the provisions on the free movement of capital (Dimopoulos (2012), p. 405). However, the existence of an EU external competence (exclusive or shared) with regard to portfolio investment which would be derived from such provisions is disputed (Eeckhout and Ortino (2013), pp. 315–18). The Commission also considers that the EU's external competence extends beyond issues of investment liberalization and that the EU may in future

IIAs negotiate provisions relating to standards of investment protection, such as fair and equitable treatment, full security and protection treatment, and expropriation issues, and include in such agreements investor-to-state dispute settlement mechanisms (European Commission (2010b), pp. 8–10). Based on the Investment Policy Communication there are, therefore, few areas currently covered by BITs that would remain outside the remit of the EU's exclusive competence (Dimopoulos (2012), p. 408).

## 3.3 Decision-making Process for EU Trade Agreements

Under EU law, the decision-making process relating to the negotiation, signing and ratification of trade agreements is one that requires the involvement of various institutions as well as the Member States (Eeckhout (2011), pp. 195–207). According to Article 207 TFEU, the conclusion of trade agreements is subject to the rules of the ordinary legislative procedure (OLP) set out under Article 294 TFEU. Formally, the right of initiative rests with the Commission, which submits recommendations to the Council, which in turn has the power to authorize the opening of trade negotiations.[38] If such authorization is received, the Commission conducts the negotiations on its own, although it must comply with the negotiating mandate (or 'directive') provided by the Council and has an obligation to keep both the Council (via the Trade Policy Committee or 'TPC') and the European Parliament (via the International Trade Committee or 'INTA') informed on the progress of negotiations.[39] Once the negotiations are finalized, the conclusion of the trade agreements requires the approval of the Council,[40] acting by qualified majority (barring those fields for which unanimity is required[41]) as well as the consent of the European Parliament by simple majority.[42]

Prior to the signing of the Treaty of Lisbon, the decision-making process for trade agreements had been essentially technocratic in its nature, with most decisions being taken by Commission and Trade Policy Committee (then known as the 133 Committee) whilst parliamentary scrutiny remained limited, given that the European Parliament was not given any power of substance in this area (Woolcock (2012a), p. 56). This meant that the EU's external trade policy was characterized by a serious democratic deficit, as in the areas of the CCP where competence was exclusive (Herrman (2011), p. 25), trade agreements were concluded in the absence of any parliamentary scrutiny of note. Moreover, although ratification by national parliaments was required in the areas of the CCP where the EU's competence was shared, the reality is that most national parliaments proved unable to effectively scrutinize the EU's external trade policy (Woolcock (2008a), p. 29), partly because of the technical nature of the issues involved in

[38] Article 207(3) TFEU. [39] Article 207(3) TFEU. [40] Article 218(8) TFEU.
[41] Article 207(4) TFEU. [42] Article 207(3) TFEU and Article 218(6) TFEU.

trade negotiations, and partly because the remoteness of EU trade negotiators created a belief among national parliamentarians that they could not impact on EU external trade policy (Leal-Arcas (2008), p. 25). By requiring regular reports to the European Parliament during the negotiating process and by requiring parliamentary consent, the Treaty of Lisbon sought to address this democratic deficit, which had become all the more relevant given the expansion of the EU's exclusive competence under the CCP (trade in services, commercial aspects of IP, and FDI).

Despite its increased powers, doubts have been cast over the European Parliament's ability to effectively influence the EU's external trade policy. Its powers remain modest compared to those of the Council. The fact that it still does not have the power to authorize negotiations (Leal-Arcas (2012, pp. 274–5), and therefore influence the Commission's negotiating mandate, is politically problematic since the European Parliament is unlikely to block the conclusion of a multilateral trade agreement in the context of the WTO, which is the result of years of arduous negotiations between a large number of countries (Woolcock (2012a), p. 61). Moreover, the initial impact of the INTA during the negotiation process is likely to be somewhat limited given its lack of expertise and technical capacity compared to the TPC (Leal-Arcas (2012), p. 275); Woolcock (2012) p. 275). Finally, history suggests that in practice the European Parliament tends to focus its scrutiny on a narrow set of issues: it is, by and large, in favour of trade liberalization and more interested in '[...] general issues such as human rights, labour standards, environmental standards, and development issues rather than the detail of tariff schedules or other parts of the agreement that can impact on specific sectors' (Woolcock (2012), p. 61). Nonetheless, the very existence of a veto power means that at the very least, the particular concerns of the European Parliament should be taken into consideration during the negotiation process of trade agreements (Leal-Arcas (2012), pp. 276–7). Early signs indicate that the Council and the Commission will ignore the European Parliament at their peril, since the latter will not shy away from using its veto power if its flagged concerns are not adequately addressed in the final drafts of the concerned agreements. This was the case, for example, when the European Parliament refused to give its consent to the signing of the ACTA[43] because it considered that concerns regarding the impact of the agreement on the protection of fundamental human rights had not been taken into account. More recently, the European Parliament has shown its readiness to flex its new-found muscles in the context of the TTIP negotiations. It was said to have pushed the Council to exclude audiovisual from the mandate for negotiations (De Ville, Orbie, and Van den Putte (2014), p. 2) and has issued recommendations requesting the reforms of some of the controversial aspects of the agreement, notably the inclusion of investor–state arbitration clauses (Vicenti (2015)).

[43] European Parliament legislative resolution of 4 July 2012 (12195/2011–C7-0027/2012–2011/0167(NLE)) [available at: http://www.europarl.europa.eu].

## 3.4 Objectives of EU External Trade Policy

### 3.4.1 Objectives of the CCP

Article 206 TFEU states that the 'Union shall contribute, in the common interest, to the harmonious development of world trade, the progressive abolition of restrictions on international trade and on foreign direct investment, and the lowering of customs and other barriers'. The references to 'the progressive abolition of restrictions' and 'the lowering of customs [...] barriers' date back to the text of the Treaty of Rome. At the time they constituted an acknowledgement of trade liberalization as one of the main principles underpinning the creation of the common market. They also served as a reminder that the common market is subject to the rules of GATT 1947 and, in particular, that the establishment of a customs union is an exception to the free trade imperatives set out under GATT and is therefore only allowed under the very restrictive conditions of Article XXIV GATT 1947.

Alongside the objective of trade liberalization, the CCP 'shall be conducted in the context of the principles and objectives of the Union's external action'.[44] In accordance with Article 21 TEU, these include a wide array of objectives ranging from the political and social to the environmental and economic. The fact that non-trade objectives are now to be incorporated in the CCP should not come as a surprise, since the EU's external trade policy has long been used as a tool to achieve goals that are not necessarily trade-specific. For example, the Court has long accepted that the incorporation of development objectives in CCP instruments (e.g. the successive Community Regulations applying schemes of general systems of preferences and the cooperation agreements concluded with developing nations (Flaesch-Mougin (1980), pp. 161–8) were primarily aimed at development cooperation and yet were based solely on Art. 133 EEC) were compatible with Article 110 EEC to the extent that in an ever-evolving international trade system, an overly restrictive interpretation of the purposes for which the CCP could be used would render it useless.[45] In this sense, the Treaty of Lisbon is merely formalizing a practice that is already well established (e.g. the references to the need to support democracy, the rule of law, human rights, and environmental development provide an unambiguous legal basis for trade conditionality) (Cremona (2007), p. 30).

### 3.4.2 Normative value of Treaty-recognized objectives

#### *3.4.2.1 Trade liberalization*

The proclamation of trade liberalization as a guiding principle of the CCP suggested that the EU was not created for protectionist purposes and that trade

[44] Article 207(1) TFEU.

[45] Opinion 1/78, paras 47–50); Case 45/86 *Commission v Council* [1987] ECR 1493, para 19).

restrictive measures adopted towards third countries in the context of a customs union should bear in mind the overall objective of GATT 1947 to promote the liberalization of trade. However, if it was true that the EU should aim to contribute to trade liberalization, it could not be said that the EU was in fact under a general obligation not to adopt trade restrictive and protectionist measures with regard to third countries and even less to extend the level of liberalization applied within the EU to third countries. In *EMI*,[46] the Court laid to rest the notion that the principle of liberalization under the CCP could be interpreted to mean that intra-EU liberalization must be extended to third countries:

> [...] the provisions of the Treaty on commercial policy do not, in Article 110 et seq., lay down any obligation on the part of the Member States to extend to trade with third countries the binding principles governing the free movement of goods between Member States and in particular the prohibition of measures having an effect equivalent to quantitative restrictions.[47]

*EMI* would thereafter be reinforced in the *Polydor* case,[48] where the Court found that even if a trade agreement contains trade liberalization language that is similar to that used in the provisions of the EEC Treaty, the same interpretation need not apply. Similarly, in *Durbeck*,[49] the Court would find that the objective of trade liberalization could be subjugated to inherently internal interests of the Community. However, the amendments brought by the Treaty of Lisbon questioned the continued validity of this case law. Whereas the pre-Lisbon regime provided that the EU '*aims* to contribute' to trade liberalization, Article 207 TFEU now states that it '*shall* contribute' to trade liberalization. *Prima facie*, the change in verb appears to suggest that the liberalization of trade with third countries should now be viewed as a binding objective of the CCP. One interpretation that has been mooted is that the reference to the gradual liberalization of trade in Article 206 creates an obligation to, at the very least, maintain the existing levels of liberalization (Dimopoulos (2011), p. 161). In other words, the EU would be bound by a standstill obligation which would preclude the introduction of new trade restrictive or protectionist measures. In fact, the exact nature of the obligation remains far from clear. It appears highly unlikely that Article 206 TFEU could be used to argue that intra-EU liberalization should be extended to third countries.[50] First of all, there is not an obligation to liberalize trade with third countries per se, but rather, an obligation to contribute to trade liberalization. The term 'contribute' implies that efforts to promote trade liberalization should be understood in the context of a collective effort on the international stage. It could be argued therefore that

[46] Case C-51/75 *EMI Records Limited v CBS United Kingdom Limited* [1976] ECR 811.

[47] Ibid. para 17.

[48] Case 270/80 *Polydor Limited and RSO Records Inc v Harlequin Record Shops Limited and Simons Records Limited* [1982] ECR 329.

[49] Case 112/80 *Firma Anton Dürbeck v Hauptzollamt Frankfurt am Main- Flughafen* [1981] ECR 1095.

[50] An argument that was rejected by the Court in the past. See Case C-51/75 *EMI v CBS* [1976] ECR 811.

the Union is merely under an obligation to endorse increased trade liberalization when negotiating trade agreements, whether at a bilateral, regional or multilateral level. Moreover, a reading of trade liberalization as an absolute obligation would not sit well with the rest of Article 206 TFEU which also states that world trade should be developed harmoniously.[51] Such language reflects the fact that trade liberalization is merely a means to an end, the latter being in general the improvement of economic, social, and environmental conditions. This would fit with the ethos of the general objectives of the EU's external action, which state for example that the EU must 'foster the sustainable economic, social and environmental development of developing countries, with the aim of eradicating poverty'[52] and 'encourage the integration of all countries into the world economy, including through the progressive abolition of restrictions on international trade'.[53] A very persuasive argument against the binding nature of the principle of trade liberalization is that changes to the EU's existing level of liberalization is an issue that is also regulated by WTO rules, which allow for the removal of concessions in certain circumstances.[54] Reading Article 206 TFEU as prohibiting an increase in existing levels of trade liberalization would deprive the EU of the ability to make full use of existing WTO rules (Krajewski (2013), p. 296).

In the light of the above, it is difficult to see exactly how the principle of trade liberalization, as formulated in Article 206 TFEU, signals a shift away from an aspirational objective towards a mandatory one. Whilst it must be assumed that in modifying the terminology of Article 206 TFEU the drafters of the Treaty intended to add a new dimension to trade liberalization, there is a distinct possibility that the amendment was simply a nod to the EU's avowed practice of promoting deeper and wider trade liberalization in its relations with third countries, and that the drafters of the treaty were acknowledging the political importance of economic integration (whether at multilateral, regional or bilateral level) for the EU. In short, the amendment to Article 206 TFEU may have a declaratory rather than binding nature.

#### *3.4.2.2 Non-trade objectives*

The proliferation of treaty-recognized objectives for the CCP is not without its problems. The Treaty of Lisbon does not institute a hierarchy between the general objectives of the Union's external action, meaning that one cannot discount the very real possibility that conflicts would arise between different objectives. Whilst the general assumption seems to be that the objectives and principles of Article 21 TEU are broad enough to fall within the margin of appreciation of the Union's institutions (Dimopoulos (2011), p. 166); Krajewski (2013), p. 298), one could easily envisage a conflict where, for example, a trade policy measure adopted by the EU pursuing one of the general objectives listed in Article 21 TEU would

[51] Article 206 TFEU. [52] Article 21(d) TFEU. [53] Article 21(e) TFEU.
[54] Article XXVIII GATT; Article XXI GATS.

adversely affect existing levels of trade liberalization with third countries. This would be problematic if the Court were to accept that the principle of trade liberalization as currently formulated is mandatory, since the Treaty language does not provide any meaningful guidance as to how to resolve the conflict between contradictory policy objectives. It has even been posited in this regard that where the pursuance of a non-trade objective leads to a trade-restrictive measure, such measure should only be permitted to the extent that it passes a proportionality test whereby it is demonstrated that the measure is required in order to achieve the non-trade objective, and that it does not exceed what is necessary to achieve said objective (Dimopoulos (2011), p. 166).

As we have already seen, Article 206 TFEU states that the CCP 'shall contribute' to trade liberalization whereas Article 207 TFEU that the CCP 'shall be conducted in the context of the general objectives of the Union's external action'. The language used in relation to trade liberalization ('shall contribute') is stronger than that used for the general objectives ('shall be conducted in the context of') making it possible to argue the primacy of trade liberalization over other non-trade objectives. Moreover, although it seems unlikely that the EU's institutions would ever countenance the notion that trade liberalization can override such fundamental interests as those of security, democracy and the rule of law in practice, some contend that Article 21 TEU does not actually list legally binding objectives, but rather well-meaning—although ultimately toothless—declarations reflecting the various objectives of the EU, that it should strive to pursue in the context of its foreign policy (Dashwood and Hyett (2011), p. 903). On the other hand, it is worth considering that it is not uncommon for national constitutions to include foreign policy objectives, which, whilst leaving executive branches a significant margin of discretion as to how to achieve such objectives, at least require a best endeavour obligation to pursue them (Larik (2011), p. 23).

The assumption that the Treaty of Lisbon has or has not conferred normative value to the various external action objectives listed in the Treaty is one that is contested (Cremona (2011), pp. 90–1) and that shall remain unverified unless a challenge is brought before the Court. Nevertheless, the fact remains that Article 21 TEU was included in the Treaty and that the language of this provision suggests ('[t]he Union *shall* define and pursue common policies and actions [...]'[55]) that it imposes some form of obligation on the EU. By stating that the CCP must be conducted in 'the context' of these objectives, Article 206 TFEU indicates that at the very least the CCP must conform to an overarching external policy framework. This makes sense when viewed in light of the abolition of the pillar structure which separated the supranational Economic Community from intergovernmental policy areas of the Common Foreign and Security Policy (CFSP) and Justice and Home Affairs. With the emergence of a de-pillarized EU, the Treaty of Lisbon sought to acknowledge the need for a unified external policy by listing all of the EU's objectives in a single provision and by requiring that the EU ensures

[55] Article 21(2) TEU. Emphasis added by the author.

'*consistency* between the different areas of its external action and between these and its other policies'.[56] The concept of consistency—which is referred to on a number of occasions in the EU Treaties—is key to understanding how the EU must conduct its various external policies. Consistency is understood as entailing not only an obligation to ensure the removal of contradiction between different external policy areas of the EU but also meaning that efforts should be made to develop policies that are mutually reinforcing and that create synergies (Hillion (2008), pp. 12–17; Marangoni (2012), p. 4). To promote such consistency, the Treaty of Lisbon creates the post of High Representative of the European Union for Foreign Security Policy, which occupies simultaneously the role of High Representative of the CFSP, Vice-President of the Commission, and Commissioner for External Relations, and in this way seeks to bridge the gap between the different external policies of the EU.[57] In this sense, Article 207 TFEU's call to conduct the CCP in the context of the general objectives of the EU's external action is a reminder that the EU's trade policy may not be carried out in a vacuum and that, at an operational level, the EU must take steps to ensure that trade policy takes into account other external policy areas by not undermining and, if possible, furthering the objectives pursued in these policy areas.

### 3.4.3 Current practice in EU DCFTAs—sustainable development chapters

The introductory chapters of the EU DCFTAs list the various objectives that are being sought by the conclusion of these agreements. The overwhelming majority relate, in some form or another, to trade liberalization concerns. They aim for the gradual and progressive liberalization of trade in goods and services, the facilitation of trade and investment, the opening up of public procurement markets, the promotion of free competition, and the enforcement of IP rights.[58] However, as with past FTAs entered into by the EU (Cremona (2011), p. 295), the EU DCFTAs also incorporate non-trade issues. Notable amongst these issues is the practice of including so-called 'essential element' clauses (Smith (1998), pp. 253–74; Bartels (2008), pp. 361–3), which require parties to respect existing international human rights obligations, the rule of law and democratic principles and permit the EU to withdraw concessions or even terminate the concerned agreement in the absence of such compliance.[59] Such clauses can be found in all EU DCFTAs, and although they have historically hardly been used in practice, they clearly fulfil the purpose of promoting the protection of human rights abroad by both requiring compliance with existing international obligations and providing

[56] Article 21(3) TEU. [57] Article 18(4) TEU.

[58] Article 1 CEPA; Article 1.1 KOREU FTA; Article 4 Colombia–Peru FTA; Article 78 EU–CA FTA; Article 1.2 EU–Singapore FTA.

[59] Case C-168/94 *Portugal v Council* [1996] ECR I-6177.

the EU with a strong tool to compel third countries towards compliance (Bartels (2013), p. 311).

Besides human rights issues, in recent years the promotion of sustainable development has occupied an ever-increasing place in the EU's trade relations. Sustainable development is not only a central objective of the internal market of the EU,[60] but also of the EU's external relations.[61] The concept itself was first developed in the Brundtland report of the World Commission on Environment and Development, which defined it as 'development that meets the needs of the present without compromising the ability of future generations to meet their own needs' (World Commission on Environment (1992), p. 43). Sustainable development as currently understood entails the incorporation of different inter-related concerns, from issues regarding economic development, social development, and environmental protection (United Nations (2002), para 2; Voigt (2009), pp. 28–31; Grosse Ruse-Khan (2010a), pp. 144–50). In the context of the EU's external trade relations, sustainable development has been identified as a crucial feature of the EU's managed globalization policy. As stated in the EU's communication 'Towards a Global Partnership for Sustainable Development', 'the objective of the European Union's sustainable development strategy must be to maximise the benefits of globalisation while minimising the costs' (European Commission (2002), p. 7). This is to be achieved through the integrated approach posited by the EU in the Doha Round, which recognizes the need to complement liberalization with a broad regulatory framework, including topics such as competition and investment as well as social and environmental issues (European Commission (2002), p. 8). The European Parliament also issued a resolution on 25 November 2010, which advocated the inclusion of human rights, social, and environmental standards in the EU's bilateral trade agreements.[62] The resolution recalled the EU's obligation to conduct the CCP in the context of the principles and objectives of the EU's external action and stated that trade policy be envisaged as a tool to promote 'fair trade that can bring into general practice the inclusion and implementation of social and environmental standards with all EU trade partners'.[63] These standards correspond to minimum labour standards established by the International Labour Organization (ILO) (e.g. ILO's eight Core Labour Standards as listed in the ILO Declaration on Fundamental Rights and Principles) and those international environmental agreements included in the EU's GSP scheme. The obligation to comply with such standards should be made legally binding and be subject to a dispute settlement mechanism which would allow for the imposition of fines or the removal of trade benefits in cases of non-compliance. Therefore, the European Parliament proposes that the EU adopts a prescriptive approach in its FTAs with regard to sustainable development issues, insofar as these agreements are to be used to impose compliance with existing international social and environment

[60] Article 3.3 TEU. [61] Article 21.2(d) TEU.

[62] European Parliament resolution of 25 November 2010 on human rights and social and environmental standards in international trade agreements (2009/2219(INI)) P7_TA(2010)0434.

[63] Ibid.

standards. Such an approach is largely followed in the existing EU DCFTAs (European Commission (2006a), p. 12). The importance of the principle of sustainable development to the EU's external trade policy is evidenced by the fact that this is the only listed objective of the EU DCFTAs that is not related to market opening and trade facilitation concerns.[64] All EU DCFTAs contain numerous provisions on the issue of sustainable development, including a specific chapter dedicated to this topic.[65] Such provisions require parties to commit to and uphold obligations under existing international treaties relating to social issues and environmental protection. All agreements contain provisions asserting the parties' commitment to core labour standards contained in the fundamental Conventions of the International Labour Organization, as well as the 2006 Ministerial declaration by the UN Economic and Social Council on Full Employment and Decent Work.[66] With regard to environmental standards, most EU DCFTAs contain provisions reaffirming the parties' commitment to complying with the multilateral environment agreements to which they are party.[67] However, the more recent EU DCFTAs concluded with developing countries (Colombia–Peru FTA and EU–CA FTA) contain more specific and far-reaching commitments. They both require the signatories to commit to implementing various multilateral environmental agreements, namely the Montreal Protocol on Substances that Deplete the Ozone Layer, the Basel Convention on the Control of Transboundary Movements of Hazardous Wastes and their Disposal, the Stockholm Convention on Persistent Organic Pollutants, and the Convention on International Trade in Endangered Species of Wild Fauna and Flora.[68] The EU–CA FTA goes further by requiring the ratification before the entry into force of the agreement of the amendment to Article XXI of the Convention on International Trade in Endangered Species of Wild Fauna and Flora (adopted on 30 April 1983) and the Rotterdam Convention on the Prior Informed Consent for Certain Hazardous Chemicals and Pesticides in International Trade.[69] The EU–CA FTA also contains commitments in the areas of sustainable management of forest resources[70] and sustainable development of fisheries,[71] including the obligation to, inter alia, adhere to the principles of the Agreement for the Implementation of the Provisions of the United Nations Convention on the Law of the Sea of 10 December 1982 relating to the Conservation and Management of

[64] Article 3 CEPA; Article 1.1(g) and (h) KOREU FTA; Article 4(j) and (k) Colombia–Peru FTA; Article 78(j) EU–CA FTA.

[65] Chapter Thirteen KOREU FTA; Title VIII Colombia–Peru FTA. Title VIII EU–CA FTA; Chapter Thirteen EU–Singapore FTA. The CEPA and the CETA contain two separate chapters, one dealing with social aspects (Chapter V CEPA; Chapter 24 CETA), the other with environmental protection (Chapter VI CEPA; Chapter 25 CETA).

[66] Article 191(1) and (2) CEPA; Article 13.4(2) and (3) KOREU FTA; Article 269 Colombia–Peru FTA; Article 286 EU–CA FTA; Article 13.3(2) and (3) EU–Singapore FTA; Article 3 Chapter 24 CETA.

[67] Article 13.5 KOREU; Article 13.6(2) EU–Singapore FTA; Article X.3 Chapter 25 CETA.

[68] Article 270.1 Colombia–Peru FTA; Article 287.2 EU–CA FTA.

[69] Articles 287(3) and (4) EU–CA FTA.

[70] Article 289 EU–CA FTA.

[71] Article 290 EU–CA FTA.

Straddling Fish Stocks and Highly Migratory Fish Stocks.[72] The requirement of compliance with specific international social and environmental rules is a significant departure from the EU's past practice with regard to FTAs, where references to existing standards were few and far between.[73] Therefore, under the guise of sustainable development objectives, the EU is pursuing a policy of dissemination of core labour and environmental protection standards. Although the agreements recognize the right of the parties to impose high labour and environmental standards, and even to further improve existing standards, they are also keen to stress that these standards should not be used for protectionist purposes. The agreements contain provisions that prohibit parties from reducing the existing levels of protection under labour or environmental law or from failing to enforce such laws in order to encourage trade and investment.[74] With the exception of the CEPA, commitments to uphold levels of protection are phrased in strong terms rather than the type of best endeavour language which is the hallmark of most other provisions found in the sustainable chapters. By combining the requirement to adopt international labour and environmental protection standards with a prohibition to increase or lower such standards for protectionist purposes or in order to gain a comparative advantage, the EU ensures that the EU DCFTAs promote sustainable development in a manner that does not conflict with the obligation to pursue trade liberalization in the context of the CCP. However, this approach is in contrast to that adopted in the Doha Round, where the focus was not so much on the promotion of labour and environmental standards but rather on an assessment of linkages between trade and labour and environmental standards (Orbie (2008), pp. 58–9). This is reflected in the Doha Agenda which included a mandate to promote 'the mutual supportiveness of trade and environment' (WTO (2001c), para 31) and negotiate the 'relationship between existing WTO rules and specific trade obligations set out in multilateral environmental agreements'[75] (negotiations on labour rights were excluded from the Doha agenda) (WTO (2005e), para 30). In the EU DCFTAs, however, there is no attempt to address the relationship between environmental rules and trade, only an obligation not to reduce such standards in order to gain a competitive advantage (Marin-Duran (2013), pp. 225–40). That being so, it may be questioned whether beneath the apparently selfless rhetoric concerning the promotion of sustainable development through trade, the imposition of social and environmental standards in EU DCFTAs is, in fact, much motivated by economic interests. The European Parliament let the cat out of the bag in this respect when it recognized that the link between trade and these non-trade concerns is integral to negotiations on FTAs notably because 'distortions of competition and the risks of environmental and social dumping are becoming

[72] Article 290(2) and (4) EU–CA FTA.

[73] Articles 50(1) and (3) Cotonou Agreement. See in this regard Bartels (2008), pp. 362–3.

[74] Articles 188 and 193 CEPA; Article 13.7 KOREU FTA; Article 277 Colombia–Peru FTA; Article 291 EU–CA FTA; Article 13.12 EU–Singapore FTA; Article 4 Chapter 24 CETA; Article X.5 Chapter 25 CETA.

[75] Ibid.

more and more frequent, to the detriment in particular of undertakings and workers in Europe who are required to comply with more stringent social, environmental and fiscal standards'.[76] These 'non-lowering clauses' may not be too problematic with regard to the social clauses included in the EU DCFTAs, since these relate to core labour rights, most of which are also considered to be fundamental human rights. However, the environmental standards of the type included in the EU DCFTAs, especially in the Colombia–Peru FTA and the EU–CA FTA, can impose onerous requirements which developing countries may struggle to uphold (Marin-Duran (2013), p. 237).

The one area where the EU DCFTAs depart from the recommendations of the European Parliament relates to the issue of dispute settlement. Only the CEPA currently subjects disputes concerning sustainable development provisions to its dispute settlement mechanism, although even in that case, the ability to suspend market access concessions as a result of the violation of any sustainable development objective is ruled out.[77] Instead, the EU DCFTAs provide an institutional framework within which issues and eventual disagreements concerning the implementation of obligations relating to sustainable development may be dealt with. Each agreement establishes joint committees or boards specifically dedicated to the issue of sustainable development, which are entrusted with the tasks of both monitoring compliance with the obligations of the agreement and of resolving any issues regarding the implementation of such obligations.[78] The agreements also provide that where the parties are unable to resolve an issue regarding the sustainable development provisions that arises through government consultations, the parties may request that the matter be examined by a panel or group of experts[79] whose task it is to issue a report containing recommendations. Although these recommendations are not binding, the KOREU FTA,[80] the Colombia–Peru FTA,[81] the EU–CA FTA,[82] the EU–Singapore FTA,[83] and the CETA[84] all provide that the sustainable development committee must monitor the implementation of the recommendations by the parties. Therefore, in the area of social and environmental protection standards, the EU DCFTAs do not envisage a dispute settlement mechanism or the retaliatory measures provided for under 'essential element' clauses—an approach largely dictated by the wishes of the EU's trade partners (Hoffmeister (2013), p. 20). By demanding that these provisions remain unenforceable, the EU's trade partners—especially those that are developing

[76] European Parliament, Resolution on Human Rights and Social and Environmental Standards in International Trade Agreements, 25 November 2010 (P7_TA(2010)0434, recital B).

[77] Article 213(2) CEPA.

[78] Articles 189 and 195 CEPA; Articles 283–285 Colombia–Peru FTA; Articles 294–297 EU–CA FTA; Article 13.15 EU–Singapore FTA.

[79] Articles 189.6 and 195.6 CEPA; Article 13.15 KOREU FTA; Article 284 Colombia–Peru FTA; Articles 297–301 EU–CA FTA; Article 13.16 EU–Singapore FTA.

[80] Article 13.15(2) KOREU FTA.

[81] Article 185(4) Colombia–Peru FTA.

[82] Article 301(3) EU–CA FTA.

[83] Article 13.17(9) EU–Singapore FTA.

[84] Articles 10(10) and (11) and 11 Chapter 24 CETA; Articles X.15(10) and (11) and X.16 Chapter 25 CETA.

countries—remove the possibility of being sanctioned by the EU in the event that they should fail to comply with the international standards listed in the EU DCFTAs.

## 3.5 Conclusion

This chapter has sought to provide an overarching view of the legal dimension of the EU's deep trade agenda. It has shown that in the pursuance of its deep trade agenda, the EU has to contend with a number of internal legal constraints. The first constraint relates to the limits of the EU's external competence to negotiate provisions in its trade agreements. Despite the continuous expansion of the CCP to cover trade in services, the commercial aspects of IP, FDI and the removal of the requirement of parallelism between internal and external competence, the CCP does not yet appear to encompass the entirety of matters dealt with in international trade politics. Therefore, a number of fields regulated by trade agreements remain areas of implied exclusive competence (e.g. competition policy) or shared competence between the EU and its Member States (e.g. intellectual property), whilst others are excluded from the scope of such agreements (e.g. audiovisuals and air transport). The sheer breadth of regulatory topics currently covered in the EU DCFTAs has created uncertainty concerning the exact scope of the EU's external trade competence. As a consequence of this lack of clarity, the EU used the conclusion of the EU–Singapore FTA to request an opinion from the court on the extent and nature of the EU's competence. This has led the Commission to request an opinion of the Court on the nature of the EU's competence with respect to certain elements of the agreement, including IP and investment protection.[85] The second constraint relates to governance. The enhanced role of the European Parliament in the CCP has reduced the democratic deficit that previously hampered the EU's external trade policy, but it also adds an extra layer of complexity in the decision-making process. The Commission's ability to implement a comprehensive and cohesive negotiating position is undoubtedly complicated by the requirement to accommodate the views of the European Parliament, in addition to those of the Member States. And already, despite misgivings regarding the limits of the powers conferred to the European Parliament and its ability to impact on the substance of the EU's external trade policy, it is clear that the latter is not for turning—as evidenced by its recent rejection of ACTA. A third set of legal constraints concerns the EU's obligation under Article 206 TFEU, together with Article 21 TEU, to pursue a series of trade and non-trade objectives in the context of its external trade relations. Historically, the EU has used trade policy to promote other foreign policy objectives. This continues to be the case in the context of the EU DCFTAs, which incorporate provisions relating to the protection of human rights and the promotion of labour rights and environmental

[85] Supra footnote 7.

protection. That this legal obligation to incorporate non-trade objectives into the EU's trade policy will not remain *lettre morte* can be seen from the number of resolutions issued by the European Parliament enjoining the EU to use trade as a tool to promote social and environmental standards, corporate social responsibility, and climate change imperatives. In this respect, the EU DCFTAs have not only continued the EU's well-established practice of incorporating an essential elements clause in its trade agreements, but also include chapters dedicated to the issue of sustainable development. However, most provisions concerning sustainable development are drafted in rather broad terms and are non-binding with two noteworthy exceptions: first, the commitment to implement and/or ratify a number of multilateral labour and environmental agreements rules, and secondly, the obligations to not lower the existing levels of protection provided under national law and not fail to enforce them in a manner affecting trade and investment between the parties. In other words, the EU uses EU DCFTAs to promote minimum social and environmental protection standards whilst also ensuring that such standards are not used in a manner that would adversely impact trade liberalization. The approach ensures that the sustainable development provisions of these agreements do not conflict with the CCP's overarching objective of liberalizing trade, and also shows that, from the EU's perspective, the global dissemination of social and environmental standards is not just an attempt to project constitutive values and norms of the EU but is also an important tool to protect the global competitiveness of EU firms.

# 4

# Services

## 4.1 Introduction

The liberalization of trade in services is a priority area of the EU's current external trade policy. The rationale is straightforward: the EU is the leading exporter and importer of services in the world (WTO (2012c)), and services are a vital component of the EU's economy. In 2013, EU services exports to third countries amounted to EUR 688.4 billion (Eurostat (2014)). The importance of the sector is clearly evident from the ongoing efforts to establish an internal market for services within the EU (European Commission (2012c)), as well as the renewed focus on the need to dismantle barriers to trade in services with third countries (European Commission (2010c), p. 10). However, both objectives are plagued by difficulties specific to the regulation of services industries, where behind-the-border measures represent the main barriers to trade, rather than tariffs and other border measures. Any attempt to liberalize trade in services requires countries to impose disciplines on domestic regulation that are often non-discriminatory, and thus constitute a substantial impingement on the regulatory autonomy of such countries. The task of disciplining domestic regulation is made even more difficult by the fact that, whilst it can be protectionist in nature, regulatory intervention can be necessary in order to meet legitimate social and economic objectives. Another difficulty arises from the regulatory diversity that pervades services. The nature and intensity of regulation will vary from sector to sector as well as from one regulatory system to another (Kox and Lejour (2007), p. 7).

The General Agreement on Trade in Services (GATS) was the first attempt to provide a multilateral framework for the liberalization of trade in services. However, the regulatory disciplines contained therein remain quite modest, with a significant focus on the discrimination-based approach to liberalization adopted in GATT. Even the EU's internal market, which has gone further than any other economic integration arrangement in the area of services, has struggled to tame regulatory barriers to trade in services. That significant barriers to intra-EU trade in services remain in place to this day illustrates just how difficult it is to overcome the attachment of countries to their own regulatory standards (Davies (2012), pp. 99–120).

The EU DCFTAs concluded to date include chapters dedicated to trade in services which include GATS-plus commitments and include horizontal and sector-specific regulatory disciplines. Moreover, on 15 February 2013, the Commission issued a press release proposing the opening of negotiations on a plurilateral Trade in Services Agreement (TISA) (European Commission (2013a)) with a number of WTO Members—referred to as 'Really Good Friends'[1]—with the hope that the outcome may eventually be multilateralized. The EU has already stated that, in addition to being comprehensive in scope and providing improved market access commitments, the TISA should (like the EU DCFTAs) also include GATS-plus regulatory disciplines. The aim of this chapter is to determine how the EU's stated desire to remove regulatory barriers in the area of services has manifested itself in its EU DCFTAs, and the extent to which the EU acts as an exporter of services rules in the context of such agreements. The chapter argues in particular that, in relation to its EU DCFTAs, the EU acts not as a promoter of detailed regulatory frameworks but rather of broad regulatory principles and institutional and cooperative mechanisms—rules developed with the intention of facilitating regulatory cooperation, which may in turn lead to regulatory convergence. Section 4.2 provides an overview of the major challenges faced in the pursuance of liberalization of trade in services, particularly with regard to regulatory barriers, and the various tools that can be used to discipline domestic rules in services. Section 4.3 describes the current legal framework on the regulation of international trade in services by focusing on the law of GATS. Section 4.4 describes the EU's current external policy in the area of trade in services. Section 4.5 examines the services chapters of the EU DCFTAs and assesses whether and how regulatory disciplines have been introduced.

## 4.2 Liberalization of International Trade in Services

### 4.2.1 The purpose of domestic regulation of services

Unlike goods, the main barriers to trade in services are not those resulting from border measures. The intangibility of services products, as well as the fact that services can be delivered by means other than cross-border trade (such as local presence of foreign service suppliers, FDI, movement of labour, e-trade, etc.), means that tariffs and quotas are not only difficult but impossible to impose in certain instances (Jackson (1988), p. 4; Marchetti and Mavroidis (2004), p. 547). Furthermore, with the exception of those services provided electronically, delivery will generally entail the cross-border movement of either capital or people (service suppliers or consumers), meaning that behind-the-border measures represent significant barriers to trade in services (Dee and Sidorenko (2006), p. 206; Delimatsis (2010), p. 6). Services are typically characterized by their regulatory diversity and intensity. Different economic sectors (for example financial, telecommunications,

[1] The coalition of Really Good Friends currently includes the following members: Australia, Canada, Chile, Chinese Taipei, Colombia, European Union, Hong Kong, Iceland, Israel, Japan, South Korea, Liechtenstein, Mauritius, Mexico, New Zealand, Norway, Pakistan, Panama, Peru, Switzerland, Turkey, the US, Uruguay, Costa Rica, Israel, Panama, Peru and Turkey.

transport, postal, or tourism sectors) require differing regulatory frameworks that will vary in terms of both their substance and intensity from country to country (Diebold (2010), pp. 30–1). In addition, national regulators will often seek to intervene in order to pursue efficiency and equity concerns (Krajewski (2003), pp. 11–19). Certain services sectors, including healthcare, legal, and financial services, are characterized by considerable information asymmetries between the services supplier and the consumer, with the result that regulatory intervention may be required in order to ensure that consumers receive a service that meets minimum standards of quality (Copeland and Mattoo (2008), p. 104). In the area of financial services, so-called prudential regulation is key to maintaining the financial stability of the economy and the protection of depositors. Equity concerns also come into play with regard to services whose social and economic impact is so crucial that they cannot be run purely for profit. Universal services obligations (USOs) are therefore typically imposed in the area of telecommunication and postal services to ensure that services are provided throughout a country's territory, with a minimum of quality and at a reasonable price (Fink (2009), p. 221). Competition law plays an important role in promoting market efficiency by ensuring the contestability of services markets. The efficient operation of networks in key infrastructure services, such as telecommunication and transport services, may be best achieved by one single service provider. In cases where such monopolies exist, legislation preventing anti-competitive practices by the network operators may be justified (Dee and Sidorenko (2006), p. 205). Regulatory intervention through competition law is required in the above-mentioned infrastructure services as they entail significant economies of scale and are consequently characterized by a large degree of market concentration (Choynowski (2004), pp. 28–9). Regulators can also intervene in order to address network externalities—that is, the 'benefit that a consumer derives from the use of a good depends on the number of other consumers purchasing compatible items' (Catz and Shapiro (1986), p. 822). In the case of telecommunication services, for example, the benefit derived by users as a whole from a network will be reduced if they are not able to communicate with consumers using other networks. In this context, regulation is needed to ensure the compatibility of the various networks provided by different service providers through standardization.

### 4.2.2 Domestic regulation as a barrier to trade in services

Domestic regulation measures impacting on trade in services are varied and range from entry controls such as licensing, qualification and other certification requirements to rules pertaining to the operation of services suppliers in the market, such as quality standards, information requirements and regulations on competition, pricing, and advertising (Krajewski (2003), pp. 13–16). These various types of domestic regulation need not necessarily be discriminatory to create barriers to entry for foreign services suppliers—mere differences in regulatory requirements can lead to additional costs for foreign services suppliers. For example, additional costs can result from the added burden placed on firms to familiarize themselves with foreign regulatory frameworks and to comply with higher regulatory demands (Sykes (1999), pp. 53–7). Often the issue may be as much about the nature of the regulation itself as it is about the way in which it is applied by the domestic authorities: regulatory opacity, administrative delays, and discriminatory procedures are all factors that can potentially affect trade. Also, the absence of a regulation may in itself, in certain instances, constitute a barrier to trade. This can occur, for example, in the context of infrastructure services such as telecommunications, transport, and energy, where a lack of legislation prohibiting anti-competitive practices may enable the operators of distribution networks to preclude services suppliers from accessing the market by applying excessive charges to access their distribution networks (Hoekman and Mattoo (2008), p. 26).

Kox and Nordas have shed light on the importance of addressing domestic rules that create up-front costs to market—that is, entry costs such as licensing, accreditation requirements, and restrictions on equity participation (Kox and Nordas (2007)). They explain that, whilst tariff measures (and measures equivalent to such tariffs) are variable trade costs insofar as 'tariffs increase the market price of imports and/or lower the unit price that the exporter receives', fixed trade costs have an 'impact on the export value necessary for the exporting firm to break even'. This means that services firms have to increase the volume of exports to reduce the fixed costs that come with domestic regulations forming barriers to market entry, and that as costs to market increase, so does the need of foreign service suppliers to increase their market share. Therefore, domestic regulations can have a negative outcome on both international trade, since they impede market access for foreign service suppliers, and domestic service suppliers, as they can lead to market concentration.

Three major types of tools are used to discipline services regulation in international trade law: general prohibitions, mutual recognition, and harmonization. General prohibitions prohibit measures that create barriers to trade by either discriminating against or causing additional costs for foreign services suppliers (Pelkmans (2012), p. 5). The EU, the WTO and the North American Free Trade Agreement (NAFTA) are all examples of international trade agreements that have implemented a prohibition system to varying degrees. Derogations from the general prohibition will typically be allowed in order to pursue legitimate policy goals, but these can be reviewed by the relevant judiciary bodies if it is thought that underlying the purported legitimate objective is a protectionist measure in disguise. The weakness of such prohibitions is that the multiplication of derogations can mean that many trade restrictive barriers remain in place. Furthermore, assessing the real motivation behind a national measure can be a difficult and politically sensitive task (Sykes (1999), p. 62).

Mutual recognition and the harmonization of standards and regulations are the most straightforward solutions to the costs of regulatory diversity (Kox and Lejour (2005), p. 7). Studies conducted in areas where the recognition of equivalence or harmonization in services legislation has been achieved within the EU indicate that these have had welfare-increasing effects (WTO (2012b), p. 151).

However, neither goal is easily achievable or even, in some instances, desirable. First, there is the obvious challenge of bridging the gap created by the regulatory diversity prevailing in most services sectors, which makes countries unwilling to adapt their legislation to facilitate market access. As Nicolaidis and Schaeffer note, cross-national regulatory compatibility is a 'function of the degree of convergence across regulatory cultures, policies, and standards which affect perceptions of regulatory effectiveness' (Nicolaidis and Schaeffer (2005), p. 286). Countries look upon each other's regulatory systems with a certain degree of mistrust, which is partly borne out of a concern that the regulatory standards of others may fail to adequately address crucial and legitimate objectives. There is also no optimal regulatory policy that could be imposed worldwide (Sykes (1999), p. 59). Domestic regulatory demands depend on a number of factors ranging from the country's level of development to its specific cultural preferences. Mutual recognition presents the advantage of removing barriers to trade whilst simultaneously allowing countries to maintain a degree of regulatory autonomy (Nicolaidis and Schaeffer (2005), p. 316; Pelkmans (2012), p. 2). However, there is a concern that mutual recognition arrangements incite regulatory competition and can cause a 'race to the bottom', where countries are forced to progressively lower their regulatory standards in order to attract businesses (Gkoutzinis (2005), p. 888). As a consequence, mutual recognition typically requires a harmonization of minimum or correct levels of standards as to the goals to be achieved by services regulation, and trust that these rules will be enforced, at the very least (Klerovic (1996), pp. 2249–61; Radaelli (2004), p. 3).

The obstacles to international harmonization and mutual recognition mean that international efforts to discipline domestic rules in technically complex regulatory areas such as services have increasingly focused on alternative methods to achieve economic integration. Rather than focusing on the desired outcomes—harmonization or mutual recognition—countries seek to establish legal and institutional frameworks that are conducive to the creation of mutual trust between national regulatory systems. In this context, integration is seen as a 'process of building increased levels of institutional based trust (or system trust) between actors across national boundaries' (Lianos and Le Blanc (2012), pp. 46–52). The process of trust-building is underpinned by formal or informal institutional mechanisms and processes such as the establishment of channels of communication between regulatory authorities and other relevant public or private actors, transparency, and monitoring. The regular exchange of regulatory information and experiences enables regulatory actors to better understand the rationale for each others' differing regulatory demands, decreasing mistrust between regulators and allowing countries to maintain legitimate regulatory differences. However, the establishment of communication channels also provides a forum for discussion and exchange of best regulatory practices, which can help to resolve the significant problems caused by regulatory diversity (Nicolaidis and Schaeffer (2005), p. 317). The exchange of best practices can further be a force for harmonization, as it allows regulators to determine the effectiveness of different types of regulation (Ibid). Regulatory transparency contributes to trust building by facilitating access to regulatory information and by easing the costs of compliance for foreign firms, whilst mutual monitoring can act as a disincentive to engage in uncooperative regulatory activities (Lianos and Le Blanc (2004), p. 50).

## 4.3 Legal Framework for the Regulation of International Trade in Services

### 4.3.1 GATS regulatory framework

During the Uruguay Round negotiations, there was some uncertainty as to how best to address the issue of services trade liberalization at the multilateral level (Marchetti and Mavroidis (2011), pp. 689–721). The relative novelty of the activity in the context of global trade relative to trade in goods and the inherent complexity of services regulation spawned debates as to whether GATT tools, based on a non-discrimination approach to trade liberalization, could be transposed in the area of services. Negotiators also had the elemental fear that committing to liberalization of trade in services would undermine the regulatory autonomy of WTO members, and thereby undermine their ability to intervene in order to ensure public policy objectives. This fear was one that was particularly prevalent among developing countries, some of which sought to completely dissociate services from the GATT legal framework (Howse (2012), p. 446). The final draft of GATS is a compromise between the desire to design a liberalizing framework that would apprehend both the complexity of services markets and the desire of WTO Members to maintain their ability to regulate services (Ibid).

The complexity of trade in services is reflected in the architecture of GATS, which departs from GATT on a number of key aspects. First, in recognition of the various ways in which services can be delivered, Article I:2 GATS distinguishes four modes of services supply: (1) services that are supplied from the territory of one WTO Member to another WTO Member (cross-border trade); (2) services that are supplied from the territory of one WTO Member to the consumer of another WTO Member (consumption abroad); (3) services that are supplied by a supplier from one WTO Member in the territory of another WTO Member (commercial presence); and (4) services that are supplied by a supplier from one WTO member through the presence of natural persons placed in the territory of another WTO Member (movement of natural persons). The scope of GATS is therefore wider than that of GATT, as it not only covers measures affecting services but also the suppliers of such services. GATS applies to all services sectors, barring certain exceptions and limitations (such as the Annex on Air Transport Services).

Evidence of the attempt to balance the tension between liberalization and regulatory autonomy can also be seen in terms of the obligations contained in the agreement. First, although the legal instruments used to promote liberalization in GATS are largely inspired by GATT, the manner in which such instruments operate differs significantly. Under GATS, the provisions on Most-Favoured-Nation

(MFN), national treatment and prohibition of quantitative restrictions can be subject to significant restrictions. The MFN obligation applies generally to all WTO Members and to all service sectors, except for measures that are listed in the MFN exemption list.[2] The restrictions that may be imposed on the market access obligation (Article XVI GATS), which fulfils the same function as Article XI:1 GATT prohibiting quantitative restrictions, and the national treatment obligation (Article XVII GATS), are even more far-reaching, insofar as WTO Members are only bound by such obligations with respect to those services sectors and modes of supply for which they have scheduled specific commitments. Once a market opening commitment is made, a WTO Member may still limit said commitment by listing any qualification or condition. GATS is said to follow a 'positive list' approach to the scheduling of commitments, in contrast to that followed by other trade agreements such as NAFTA, where all services sectors are assumed to be covered by the liberalization commitments unless a country has scheduled a limitation to the contrary. This exposes the desire of WTO Members to restrict the liberalization process of trade in services.

Whilst GATS recitals stress that the liberalization of trade in services should not come at the expense of WTO Members' right to regulate, the agreement includes a number of provisions which acknowledge the significance of non-discriminatory regulatory barriers to trade. For instance, Article XVI:1 GATS on market access prohibits certain non-discriminatory quantitative restrictions, Article III GATS includes a number of procedural obligations, such as the obligation to promptly publish all measures of general application pertaining to services by WTO Members seeking to ensure the transparency of domestic regulations, and Article VII GATS recognizes the right of WTO Members to enter into mutual recognition agreements (MRAs) on a non-discriminatory basis.

A more intrusive provision is found in Article VI GATS which contains disciplines on WTO Members' domestic regulation. Such disciplines include procedural standards that must be maintained in the administration of measures of general application affecting trade in services and applying to sectors where specific commitments have been made. More significantly, Article VI:4 GATS seeks to close the gap left by the market access and national treatment provisions—which have no impact on non-quantitative and non-discriminatory measures (Delimatsis (2007), p. 18)—by granting a mandate to negotiate cross-sectoral substantive standards, with the intention of ensuring that measures relating to qualification requirements and procedures, technical standards and licensing requirements do not constitute unnecessary barriers to trade in services (Wouters and Coppens (2006), p. 13; Adlung and Mattoo (2008), p. 67). In other words, Article VI:4 GATS complements the non-discrimination obligations by establishing procedural and substantive requirements that are intended to discipline overly burdensome domestic regulation undermining market access (Krajewski (2003), p. 130–1). In order to achieve this, WTO Members are invited to negotiate

[2] Article II.2 GATS.

disciplines ensuring that qualification requirements and procedures, technical standards and licensing requirements are '(a) based on objective and transparent criteria, such as competence and the ability to supply the service; (b) not more burdensome than necessary to ensure the quality of the service; (c) in the case of licensing procedures, not in themselves a restriction on the supply of the service'.[3] Subparagraph (b) contains the germ of a 'necessity test' which would pave the way for judicial assessments regarding the appropriateness of a domestic measure in order to secure a given public policy objective. However, Article VI:4 GATS only provides a mandate for negotiation, and progress on these negotiations has been slow. Disciplines in domestic regulation for the accountancy sector were finalized in 1998, and include a necessity clause that requires WTO Members to ensure that the domestic rules covered by Article VI:4 GATS are not more trade restrictive than necessary to fulfil a legitimate objective (WTO (1998b)). The accountancy disciplines provide a non-exhaustive illustrative list of such legitimate objectives, which include the protection of consumers, the quality of the service, professional competence, and integrity. These disciplines are not yet binding, as they will only enter into force once the Doha Round is concluded (Ibid). Meanwhile, on 26 April 1999, the Council for Trade in Services established the Working Party on Domestic Regulation (WPDR) to negotiate horizontal disciplines on domestic regulation. However, as the multiple negotiating drafts released by the Chair of the WPDR show (WTO (2011b); WTO (2011c)), negotiations on such rules remain an ongoing process with the application of a 'necessity test' to non-discriminatory regulation being the most salient sticking point (WTO (2011b), p. 17). Debates abound as to whether the terms 'not more trade restrictive than necessary' and 'not more burdensome' contained in Article VI:4 GATS equate to the necessity and proportionality tests developed under WTO case law (Krajewski (2003), pp. 144–5) and whether disciplines should include an exhaustive or open-ended list of legitimate objectives (Marchetti and Mavroidis (2004), p. 552).

The lack of progress in the negotiations on domestic regulations disciplines demonstrates the reluctance of the WTO membership to bring regulatory issues within the ambit of the GATS framework. Having gone to the trouble of providing a large scope of application to the agreement, and having conceived disciplines that go beyond the non-discrimination requirement, the GATS negotiators have so far proved unable to agree on the exact nature of such disciplines, let alone put them into effect. Furthermore, Article VI:4 GATS does not address all issues presented by domestic regulation in services. It is restricted in scope to a limited set of domestic measures, essentially those that represent an upfront cost to market entry, and does not address other issues that can impede trade in services in specific regulatory areas relating to efficiency and equity concerns (Ibid). In this regard, it is significant that for a trade agreement

[3] Article VI:4 GATS.

covering the area of services—characterized as it is by regulatory diversity and intensity—no real attempt has been made towards harmonization of minimum standards. The use of international standards under the TBT and SPS agreements and the regulatory convergence found in TRIPS are completely absent from GATS.

Finally, the WTO has also developed disciplines that apply to two specific sectors: financial and telecommunications services. With regard to financial services, the Understanding on Commitments in Financial Services ('Financial Services Understanding') imposes optional enhanced national treatment and market access commitments to WTO Members, and the GATS Annex on Financial Services ('Financial Services Annex'), which includes a carve-out allowing WTO Members to derogate from GATS in order to adopt prudential measures such as those ensuring the protection of depositors and the maintenance of financial stability. These justifiable prudential regulations have been developed over time by international standard-setting bodies—notable examples include minimum capital standards, legal lending limits, capital adequacy ratio requirements, and fit and proper test for management.[4] However, the Financial Services Annex has not provided any guidance as to the type of measures that could be covered by the prudential carve-out, nor on the operation of the carve-out itself. The key GATS instrument with regard to telecommunication services is the Reference Paper on Telecommunications Services ('Reference Paper') which provides a number of regulatory principles that must be incorporated into the regulatory framework of WTO Members who have made commitments in the area. However, contrary to the Financial Services Annex which is solely focused on recognizing the need to address equity concerns through prudential regulation, the Reference Paper is also concerned with market efficiency. The Reference Paper recognizes equity concerns specific to the telecommunications services industry by allowing WTO Members to impose USOs—measures that ensure that services are provided throughout their territory, with a minimum quality at reasonable prices. To ensure efficiency, it imposes a number of pro-competitive regulatory disciplines which were developed in the context of telecommunications liberalization in developed countries (Krajewski (2004), p. 171). It prohibits anti-competitive behaviour, requires procedural transparency in the granting of licences, sets out extensive rules on interconnection that ensure that new entrants in the telecommunications services markets are able to access existing infrastructure networks, regulates the allocation and use of scarce telecommunications resources (spectrum allocation, numbering, and right of way), and requires the establishment of independent regulatory authorities. In sum, the Reference Paper promotes a regulatory framework for telecommunications services based on principles of openness and competition and reflects, in particular, the experiences of developed nations in

[4] Financial Services Annex, para 2.

liberalizing the telecommunications sector in the final two decades of the twentieth century (Lang (2011), p. 285). These regulatory principles, whilst broad, have the potential to undermine regulatory autonomy. For example, the requirement that interconnection rates be 'cost-oriented' may undermine the ability of governments to apply additional charges to fund universal services obligations (Krajewski (2013), p. 176). Likewise, the obligation to maintain independent regulators can be problematic in countries whose constitutions require parliamentary accountability of administrative bodies (Ibid). However, the impact of the Reference Paper is lessened by the fact that it is a plurilateral instrument which provides a significant degree of flexibility for WTO Members. The regulatory principles included in the Reference Paper only bind WTO Members to the extent that they are included as part of their scheduled commitments. Moreover, WTO Members have the option to select which specific regulatory principles they wish to be bound by or even modify the Reference Paper in their commitments so as to reflect their particular interests and needs (Crowley and Klimenko (2002), p. 275).

### 4.3.2 Obstacles to further GATS liberalization

In its current incarnation, GATS does not provide adequate tools to address non-discriminatory regulatory barriers impacting on services trade. The lack of regulatory disciplines with any real bite is problematic for two reasons. The obvious reason is that the most significant barriers to services trade remain largely unaffected by GATS. The second reason is that negotiations on trade in services have taken a back seat to issues such as agriculture and industrial products and that the market access offers made thus far have been unambitious (Gootiz and Mattoo 2009, pp. 7–11). This is in part due to the divergent views held by developing and developed countries as to what should be the focus of negotiations on trade in services. For developing countries, Mode 4 liberalization (temporary movement of natural persons supplying services) is seen as an issue of utmost importance, namely because low-skilled labour is one of the few areas where developing countries hold a comparative advantage and because they stand to gain substantially from the remittances from temporary workers stationed in developed countries (Charlton and Stiglitz (2004), p. 305). Developed countries have, on the other hand, been reluctant to make Mode 4 commitments because of concerns that liberalization may undermine the implementation of immigration policy (Langhammer (2005), p. 316; Roberts (2007), p. 56). Where commitments have been made, they relate predominantly to highly skilled labour, which neither addresses the needs of most developing countries nor compensates for developing country commitments made with regard to other modes of service supply (Panizzon (2010), p. 1207). Another (less obvious) reason is that a key factor undermining efforts towards further multilateral liberalization of trade in services is the fear harboured by governments that the opening of domestic markets could prove detrimental to the national economy, if not accompanied by the adoption of appropriate regulatory standards to ensure that countries are able to reap the rewards of liberalization whilst also ensuring that equity concerns are addressed (Hoekman and Mattoo (2011), p. 10). In this context, domestic regulatory reform improving the contestability of markets and addressing equity concerns is a pre-requisite for the opening of services markets. For this reason, it has been suggested that GATS reform should focus on the establishment of cooperation mechanisms between regulatory authorities which would be complemented by aid programmes to assist countries in conducting regulatory reform and improving institutional capabilities (Hoekman, Mattoo, and Sapir (2007), p. 367).

## 4.4 EU External Trade Law and Policy in the Area of Services

### 4.4.1 General trends in FTA services liberalization

The conclusion of GATS did not lead to significant gains in the area of liberalization. Most market opening commitments made at the time of the Uruguay Round reflected the level of liberalization that had already been unilaterally implemented by WTO Members. In this sense, it has been argued that the major achievement of GATS had been to 'lock in' existing policy reforms and to provide a framework for further multilateral liberalization (Hoekman (1996), p. 4). Subsequently, although WTO Members have continued to liberalize their services markets, these policy reforms have not manifested themselves into the GATS commitments—the upshot being that, quite often, the commitments scheduled under GATS do not correspond with the applied level of liberalization (Roy (2009), p. 5).

In the absence of tangible progress at the multilateral level, countries have resorted to FTAs, which have tended to go much further not only than GATS in terms of market commitments, but also further than existing offers made by WTO Members in the Doha Round (Marchetti and Roy (2009), p. 82). Significant liberalization commitments are made across all services sectors, even those where only modest commitments have been made at the WTO level (Ibid, p. 89). The success of FTAs in securing GATS-plus commitments can be explained in part by their services chapters' structure. Whereas GATS assumes a positive list approach to scheduling where sectors are only subject to the rules of the agreement if a specific commitment is made, a considerable number of FTAs have opted to follow the example set by the NAFTA and adopted a negative-list approach to scheduling, where all sectors are assumed to be covered by an agreement unless it is specifically excluded by a party (Low and Mattoo (2000), pp. 467–8). However, despite the breadth of commitments typically undertaken in FTAs, sensitive services sectors for developed countries, such as health services, audiovisuals (for the EU) and maritime transport and professional services (for the US), remain off limits (Lim, Marchetti, and Roy (2010), p. 353). FTAs also tend to shy away from the major unresolved issues in GATS, such as public procurement, subsidies, and emergency safeguard measures (Hoekman and Mattoo (2008), pp. 7–9). Beyond certain provisions on transparency and mutual recognition, non-discriminatory regulatory barriers are also not high on the agenda. Disciplines on domestic regulation are barely touched upon, and even where references are made to Article VI GATS, few FTAs venture beyond what is currently provided under GATS (Krajewski (2006), p. 191). In sum, it appears that in the area of trade in services, FTAs focus essentially on national treatment and market access rather than disciplines on non-discriminatory domestic regulation.

### 4.4.2 Global Europe strategy and trade in services

As the largest exporter and importer of services in the world, the EU has understandably been keen to open services markets abroad—it was one of the proponents of GATS during the Uruguay Round (Deutsche (2001), p. 41). There are, however, certain limits to such openness. First, certain services sectors are no-go areas because of political sensitivities involved, namely cultural services—in particular, the audiovisual sector.[5] Secondly, most of the commitments relate to Modes 2 and 3 of service delivery. With regard to Mode 1, the EU's reluctance to provide market access can be attributed to concerns regarding inadequate levels of consumer protection that may be provided abroad (Langhammer (2005), p. 316). Mode 4 remains the area where the EU has made by far the fewest commitments largely because of concerns based on the potential impact of liberalization of labour mobility on national immigration policies (Hoekman, Mattoo, and Sapir (2007), pp. 364–5). Even as developing countries stressed the importance of Mode 4 liberalization in the context of the Doha Round, the EU's offer remained somewhat limited (Hufbauer and Stephenson (2007), p. 621). Commitments were made but only in areas of high-skilled labour (intra-corporate transfers, business visitors, contractual service suppliers, independent professionals) and subject to restrictive conditions (Dawson (2012), p. 12). Individual Member States impose sector-specific restrictions (e.g. nationality and language requirements) as well as market access limitations such as economic needs tests and numerical ceilings imposed with regard to certain categories of services suppliers (Murkherjee and Goyal (2013), p. 4). In addition there are horizontal obligations for beneficiaries of labour mobility to comply with all rules applied under EU and Member State law regarding work and social security, including minimum wage requirements and collective wage agreements (Natens (2013), p. 22).

[5] European Parliament resolution on the General Agreement on Trade in Services (GATS) within the WTO, including cultural diversity—12 March 2003, P5_TA(2003)0087.

The EU's recent focus on bilateralism has not led to a significant shift in its approach to services liberalization. In the Global Europe Communication, the European Commission sets out the objectives to be pursued in trade in services in its future EU DCFTAs. It explains the EU's offensive interest in this area (European Commission (2006a), p. 7):

> EU service producers are strongly competitive on world markets and therefore stand to gain from international market opening. The EU, for example, boasts the three largest firms in construction services worldwide, six out of the top ten global companies in telecommunication services, and similarly in distribution, finance, insurance, transport and environmental services. But they are prevented from providing their services in many parts of the world. The EU should push negotiations in sectors where it has a comparative advantage and where market access is hindered or where few commitments have been made so far by third countries.

This passage indicates that the increase of the breadth and depth of liberalization commitments made by third countries under the GATS framework is an important objective of EU DCFTAs, and the emphasis is, naturally, on the areas where the EU has a comparative advantage—as illustrated by the fact that at no point does the Global Europe strategy acknowledge Mode 4 liberalization. The issue is referred to later in the EU's 2020 Trade and Growth Strategy but once more, the focus is on promoting the temporary movement of 'highly qualified people' (European Commission (2010c), p. 7) rather than low- and medium-skilled workers. The EU DCFTAs also follow a similar path to liberalization as that formulated under GATS, which is essentially focused on securing national treatment and market access obligations in various services sectors. However, the Global Europe strategy goes further, as it is very much concerned with non-tariff regulatory barriers. It provides that 'tariff reductions are of little use if the market remains closed [...]' (European Commission (2010c), p. 8) and recognizes the need to 'look at the whole operating environment of third countries' (Ibid). It further adds that (Ibid):

> Although it is legitimate to regulate trade in products and services, for instance to protect human health or the environment, this has to be done in a way which is transparent, non-discriminatory and proportionate to the ultimate objective. And even then the companies might face undue supervisory or regulatory burdens which call for (long term) work on equivalence recognition or convergence of regulatory solutions.

Having recognized the need to remove barriers that are engendered by regulatory opacity and the existence of discriminatory domestic regulation, the EU clarifies that even where transparency and non-discrimination are achieved, barriers to trade may persist because of inefficient regulatory practices. The lack of common standards and mutual recognition represent business costs that inhibit the ability of EU service providers to exploit opportunities in third country markets. However, the EU's regulatory agenda is not purely defined in terms of the promotion of the EU's own economic interest. The EU packages its agenda for regulatory reform of services markets in third countries as a developmental tool. While discussing the need to obtain better market access in services, the EU also states (European Commission (2010c), p. 9):

> Progressive liberalization of trade in services, based on sound regulatory frameworks, will not only benefit the European economy, but it is essential to developing countries [...] No country can prosper today without efficient services markets, which help countries build up and modernise their infrastructure and foster an environment that is conducive to foreign investment.

The EU's approach to trade liberalization in the area of services is all-encompassing and, as a result, the means proposed to pursue this approach in the context of its EU DCFTAs are varied. Naturally, preferential treatment is to be sought in all modes of supply. Regulatory convergence and mutual recognition are mentioned on a number of occasions but such statements are usually accompanied by caveats that allude to the limits of such endeavours. Regulatory convergence, for example, 'is more likely to be achieved with neighbourhood partners' (European Commission (2010c), p. 15) while mutual recognition should be pursued 'where necessary and useful' (Ibid, p. 17). In fact, as far as regulatory convergence and recognition is concerned, the EU is ready to play the long game by promoting, through its EU DCFTAs, various types of regulatory cooperation mechanisms. The 2020 Trade and Growth Strategy contains references to the possibility of incorporating cooperation instruments between regulatory bodies (private or public) aimed at regulatory convergence and requesting and supporting the participation of trade partners in international standard-setting bodies within EU DCFTAs. Given the 'development' dimension attached to the EU's push for regulatory reforms, where agreements are concluded with poorer countries (developing countries and emerging economies), regulatory cooperation also encompasses technical assistance to address capacity constraints (Ibid, p. 11). Complementing regulatory cooperation are disciplines on regulatory transparency at the level of the adoption of domestic rules, as well as at the level of the implementation of such rules. In particular, the EU DCFTAs should ensure that the adoption of domestic rules is preceded by a prior consultation process or—at the very least—that regulators must announce their intent to adopt new regulations. This type of regulatory cooperation puts an emphasis on trust building through transparency of regulatory frameworks and the establishment of institutional frameworks where regulators can exchange ideas and negotiate possible avenues for regulatory convergence.

### 4.4.3 Liberalization of trade through EU DCFTAs

#### *4.4.3.1 Structure of services chapters in EU DCFTAs*

All EU DCFTAs contain a chapter or title dedicated specifically to trade in services and investment (Services Chapter(s)). Each typically cover five major issues: (i) general provisions dealing with the scope, institutional issues, and objectives of the provisions on services; (ii) cross-border supply of services (mode 1 and 2);

(iii) establishment or commercial presence (mode 3); (iv) temporary presence of natural persons for business purposes (mode 4); and (v) general and sector-specific disciplines on domestic regulation. In addition, these Services Chapters include sections dealing with various services sectors such as telecommunications, financial services, international maritime transport, and tourism services. The one exception to this practice is the CETA, which follows the NAFTA model (Lang and Conyers (2014), p. 16) in containing separate chapters dealing with cross-border supply of services and presence of natural persons (commercial presence is covered under the 'investment chapter' of the agreement) as well as chapters dealing with telecommunications and financial services.

The EU DCFTAs typically adopt the GATS positive list approach to trade liberalization. Market access or national treatment obligations apply only to the extent that specific commitments have been scheduled (Mirodout (2011), p. 323). Again, an exception must be made with regard to the CETA which departs from previous EU FTA practice by following the NAFTA in adopting a negative list approach (Lang and Conyers (2014), p. 16). In keeping with the global trend observed regarding FTAs, the EU DCFTAs seek to go further than GATS, both in terms of the breadth and depth of trade liberalization commitments. Each sub-section on modes of supply contains MFN, national treatment, and market access commitments and substantively, these commitments do not stray from those under GATS with wording based on that found in the GATS text. In other areas, not only do these agreements go beyond what is currently provided under GATS but they also go further than the levels of liberalization offered by the EU in the context of the Doha Round negotiations (Sauvé and Ward (2009), pp. 30–1). The EU DCFTAs contain extensive Mode 2 and 3 commitments in areas where the EU has strong offensive interests, including telecommunications, environmental, transport, construction, financial, retail, insurance, and professional services such as accounting and legal services. With regard to Mode 4 commitments, the picture is mixed. While the commitments included in the KOREU FTA are modest (e.g. no commitments for independent professionals and contractual service suppliers), those included in the CEPA and the Colombia–Peru FTA are more extensive than those offered by the EU in the Doha Round (Bartels, Stevens, and Woolcock (2012), p. 49). More specifically, in the CEPA, the EU has made concessions in 'non-traditional' (Chaitoo (2008)) categories of services suppliers (e.g. fashion models, chefs, and midwives) and in areas where CARIFORUM States have strong offensive interests, namely in the entertainment sector (Murkherjee and Goyal (2013), p. 14). Although the Mode 4 commitments in these agreements have been criticized for favouring developed country interests by focusing mostly on highly skilled labour, the willingness of the EU to negotiate Mode 4 commitments in areas of interest for developing countries is to be welcomed, as it contrasts with the conservative approach adopted by many developed countries in the context of the Doha Round and by major trading nations such as the US, which tend to adopt GATS-minus commitments in their trade agreements (Stephenson and Robert (2011), p. 16).

Certain areas are excluded outright from the Services Chapters, such as government procurement (covered in a separate chapter), services supplied in the exercise of governmental authority, subsidies or grants and measures relating to movement of persons in general. There are also specific carve-outs for each mode of supply. Audio-visual services, national maritime cabotage, and domestic and international air transport services are excluded from the scope of application of provisions on cross-border supply. With regard to commercial presence/establishment, in addition to those economic activities excluded from cross-border supply, there is a carve-out that applies to mining, manufacturing, and processing of nuclear materials. The EU DCFTAs also contain general exception provisions which largely replicate the text of Article XIV GATS. Signatories are permitted to adopt domestic measures deemed necessary to pursue policy objectives such as the protection of public security and public morals, human, animal or plant life, or health.[6] There is, however, one notable deviation from Article XIV GATS in, the Colombia–Peru FTA which includes horizontal exemptions on sector-specific commitments on establishment (commercial presence) for both Colombia and Peru. Colombia, for example, reserves the right to adopt or maintain any measure according rights or preferences to socially or economically disadvantaged minorities and ethnic groups, including with respect to the communal lands held by ethnic groups as well as any measure according rights or preferences to local communities with respect to the support and development of expressions relating to intangible cultural patrimony,[7] whilst Peru reserves the right to 'adopt or maintain any measure according rights or preferences to socially or economically disadvantaged minorities and ethnic groups'.[8]

### *4.4.3.2 Disciplines on domestic regulation*

#### 4.4.3.2.1 Cross-sectoral disciplines

*Article VI:4 GATS*

With regard to Article VI:4 GATS, with the notable exception of the Singapore FTA, EU DCFTAs are GATS-minus in nature. Although the CEPA, the KOREU FTA, the Colombia–Peru FTA and the EU–CA FTA contain a provision similar to Article VI GATS, none attempt to go beyond this and in general, the agreements provide even less than GATS. In the CEPA, there is no mention of the basic obligation to administer measures of general application in a reasonable, objective, and impartial manner (Article VI:1 GATS). Furthermore, neither the CEPA, Colombia–Peru FTA nor the EU–CA FTA make mention of disciplines to be developed in accordance with Article VI:4 GATS.[9] The KOREU FTA

[6] Article 2.24 CEPA; Article 7.50 KOREU FTA; Article 167 Colombia–Peru FTA; Article 103 EU–CA FTA; Article 8.63 EU–Singapore FTA.

[7] Annex II Section A Colombia–Peru FTA. For an analysis of the scope of this exception see J. Kelsey (2010), 96.

[8] Annex II Section C Colombia–Peru FTA.

[9] Article 87 CEPA; Article 131 Colombia–Peru FTA; Article 179 EU–CA FTA.

replicates most of Article VI GATS, including some elements of Article VI:4 GATS, which provides as follows:

With a view to ensuring that measures relating to qualification requirements and procedures, technical standards and licensing requirements do not constitute unnecessary barriers to trade in services, while recognising the right to regulate and to introduce new regulations on the supply of services in order to meet public policy objectives, each Party shall *endeavour* to ensure as appropriate for individual sectors that such measures are: (a) based on objective and transparent criteria, such as competence and the ability to supply the service; and (b) in the case of licensing procedures, not in themselves a restriction on the supply of the service.[10]

The above provision has two major limitations. First, it shies away from the more contentious issue of the necessity test by omitting any reference to Article VI:4(b) GATS—that is, the obligation to ensure that requirements are not more burdensome than necessary to ensure the quality of the service. Secondly, the parties must only endeavour to comply with the other, less intrusive, obligations of Article VI:4 GATS. Clearly, the EU DCFTAs are not viewed as an adequate testing ground for potential solutions to the current debate taking place at WTO level with regard to Article VI:4 GATS. In this sense, the EU DCFTAs are following the general trend observed in FTAs, where discussions on development of domestic regulatory disciplines are foregone in the belief that they can be best addressed at the multilateral level (Krajewski (2006), pp. 186–91). This stance seems to be confirmed by commitments from parties in both the KOREU FTA and the Colombia–Peru FTA to incorporate the results of any negotiation on the issue either at GATS level or any other multilateral fora.[11]

The CETA and the EU–Singapore FTA take a different approach to other EU DCFTAs in that instead of requiring the parties to incorporate the results of WPDR negotiations on cross-sectoral disciplines, they include a number of provisions found in the latest WPDR negotiating drafts relating to conditions and procedures for licensing and qualification. Such provisions include, inter alia, requirements to ensure that: (i) procedure and qualification requirements are pre-established and accessible to the public and interested persons;[12] (ii) licensing fees incurred by services suppliers should be reasonable and not in themselves restrict the supply of the service;[13] (iii) applicants are allowed a reasonable period of time for the submission of an application;[14] (iv) competent authorities must, within a reasonable period of time after receipt of an application which it considers incomplete, inform the applicant, and to the extent feasible, identify the additional information required to complete the application, and provide the opportunity to correct deficiencies;[15] or (v) authenticated copies should be accepted in lieu of originals.[16]

10 Article 7.23 KOREU FTA. Emphasis added by author.
11 Article 7.23.4 KOREU FTA; Article 131.4 Colombia–Peru FTA.
12 Article 8.19.19(c) EU–Singapore FTA; Article X.2(2)(c) Chapter 14 CETA.
13 Article 8.20(2) EU–Singapore FTA.
14 Article 8.20(3) EU–Singapore FTA.
15 Article 8.20(5) EU–Singapore FTA; Article X.2(14) Chapter 14 CETA.
16 Article X.2(12) Chapter 14 CETA.

All of the aforementioned provisions are ones for which disagreements persist at WTO level (WTO (2011b), pp. 2–5). These agreements seemingly represent a shift away from the EU's approach to the negotiation of disciplines on domestic regulation in its FTAs, which is based on deference towards ongoing WPDR negotiations. However, the significance of these GATS-plus provisions must be put into context. Both the CETA and the EU–Singapore only include broad GATS-plus transparency and administrative obligations for licensing and qualification procedures (which are already incorporated into the sophisticated regulatory systems of the signatories to these agreements) and make no reference to Article VI:4(b)'s necessity test. In that sense, at least, the EU–Singapore FTA and the CETA can still be viewed as another example of the conservative approach adopted in EU FTAs towards disciplines on domestic regulation.

*Transparency requirements under EU DCFTAs*

The Global Europe Communication identified the promotion of regulatory and procedural transparency as key to addressing the barriers created by domestic regulation. The manner in which the EU DCFTAs approach the issue varies in accordance with the level of development of the EU's trading partners. The agreements signed with developing countries do not go beyond the restatement of existing GATS obligations. However, the developed country EU DCFTAs impose significant GATS-plus obligations. A peculiarity of each of these agreements is that they contain transparency obligations that apply to all areas covered by the agreement. These 'horizontal' provisions are then sometimes complemented by transparency obligations that apply exclusively to areas covered by the services chapters of these agreements. Together, these provisions regulate a number of issues such as publication and notification requirements, administrative procedural standards, and the facilitation of access to information on services regulation by private parties. The KOREU, the EU–Singapore FTA and the CETA replicate the requirement to promptly publish measures of general application of Article III:1 and 2 GATS, whilst adding a number of GATS-plus clarifications pertaining to the modalities, means, content, and timing of such publications.[17] They provide that measures of general application must be made readily available to interested parties in a non-discriminatory manner.[18] The publication requirement is thus made subject to an obligation of non-discrimination, in contrast to the current GATS framework which allows differential treatment between domestic and foreign services suppliers.[19] In addition, there is some guidance on the manner in which the publication must be made. The measure must be published in 'an officially designated medium, preferably via electronic means'[20] and the publication must explain both the objective and rationale for the measure.[21] Although no specific deadlines are

[17] Article 12.3(a) KOREU FTA; Article 14.3(a) EU–Singapore FTA; Article X.01 Chapter 31 CETA.

[18] Article 12.3(a) KOREU FTA; Article 14.3(a) EU–Singapore FTA.

[19] Panel Report Canada—Provincial Liqueur Boards (US) BISD/39S/27.

[20] Article 12.3(1)(a) KOREU FTA; Article 14.3(1)(a) EU–Singapore FTA.

[21] Article 12.3(1)(b) KOREU FTA; Article 14.3(1)(b) EU–Singapore FTA.

provided, all three agreements are keen to stress that the publication must be timed to occur prior to the actual entry into force of the concerned measure.[22] This differs from GATS, which provides that publication can occur 'at the latest by the time of entry into force'.[23] Under the KOREU FTA, it is specified that the time lapse between publication and entry into force should be sufficient so as to allow the other party and interested persons to become acquainted with the measure and 'by taking into account the requirements of legal certainty, legitimate expectations and proportionality'.[24] Furthermore, both agreements open the door for the possibility of prior comment procedures. The parties must '(a) endeavour to publish in advance any measure of general application that it proposes to adopt or to amend, including an explanation of the objective of, and rationale for the proposal; (b) provide reasonable opportunities for interested persons to comment on such proposed measure, allowing, in particular, for sufficient time for such opportunities; and (c) endeavour to take into account the comments received from interested persons with respect to such proposed measure'.[25] Similarly, the CETA provides that, to the extent possible, parties must provide interested persons and parties a reasonable opportunity to comment on proposed measures.[26] Although parties are only *encouraged* to publish proposed measures in advance, where this occurs, there is an outright obligation to allow all interested parties to comment on the proposed measures. Such prior comment requirement would not only increase transparency but also allow foreign service suppliers the opportunity to actively participate in, and shape the development of, domestic regulation.

The KOREU FTA and the EU–Singapore FTA also mirror Article III GATS by requiring the establishment of enquiry points that can serve as contact points to provide information concerning measures falling under the scope of the agreement. However, whereas under GATS only WTO Members can request information from such enquiry points, in the KOREU FTA and the EU–Singapore FTA, they are required to respond promptly to all enquiries from interested parties regarding the application of an actual or proposed measure of general application.[27] There is also an obligation on both parties to establish contact or enquiry points dealing specifically with enquiries from interested persons of the other party concerning the problems encountered in the application of general measures of application.[28] Whilst the establishment of such 'specialized' contact points is only a best endeavour provision under the KOREU FTA, it is legally binding under the EU–Singapore FTA. In other words, these enquiry points are entrusted with the task of effectively resolving problems faced by foreign economic actors in the application of measures of general application.

22 Article 14.3(c) EU–Singapore FTA; Article X.01(2)(b) Chapter 31 CETA.

23 Article III(1) GATS.

24 Article 12.3(1)(c) KOREU FTA.

25 Article 12.3(2)(a), (b) and (c) KOREU FTA; Article 14.3(2)(a), (b) and (c) EU–Singapore FTA.

26 Article X.01(2)(b) Chapter 31 CETA.

27 Article 12.4(1) KOREU FTA; Article 14.4(3) EU–Singapore FTA.

28 Article 12.4(4) KOREU FTA; Article 14.4(7) EU–Singapore FTA.

With regard to the transparency provisions whose scope of application is limited to the measures covered by the Services Chapters, only the KOREU FTA contains provisions which go beyond what is currently provided in Article III GATS and the horizontal transparency provisions included in the agreement. It adds to the Article III.3 GATS and Article 12.3(a) KOREU FTA obligations to respond promptly to any requests from the other party for specific information on measures of general application or international agreements by clarifying that, in the area of services, this obligation covers '(a) international agreements or arrangements, including on mutual recognition, which pertain to or affect matters falling under this Chapter; and (b) standards and criteria for licensing and certification of service suppliers, including information concerning the appropriate regulatory or other body to consult regarding such standards and criteria. Such standards and criteria include requirements regarding education, examination, experience, conduct and ethics, professional development and re-certification, scope of practice, local knowledge and consumer protection'.[29] The KOREU FTA also contains provisions intended to ensure the respect of due process requirements and procedural transparency in the context of both administrative and judicial proceedings' due administration and prompt review. These provisions follow essentially what is currently provided under Articles VI:1, 2 and 3 GATS with the caveat that under the KOREU FTA, the obligations on procedural transparency are not solely limited to sectors where the parties have made specific commitments. The services-specific provisions on transparency also build on Article VI GATS by putting the emphasis on due administration and procedural transparency. Article 7.22 KOREU FTA provides additional safeguards that aim to ensure the transparency and fairness of application procedures relating to the supply of services. Regulatory authorities are thus enjoined to inform an applicant, upon request, of the status of its application and unsuccessful applicants shall, as far as possible, be informed of the reasons for the denial of their application. There is also an attempt to set a deadline for the completion of an application procedure—regulatory authorities are required to make an administrative decision relating to the supply of a service within 120 days.[30] Where it is not possible to comply with this deadline requirement, regulatory authorities must notify the applicant and endeavour to make a decision within a reasonable period of time.[31]

*Regulatory cooperation*

The EU DCFTAs establish institutional frameworks that can act as fora for the discussion of issues relating to the implementation of the services chapters, as well as the further development of the parties' relationships in this area. This is achieved through the establishment of 'trade committees' jointly composed of representatives from both parties, whose main task is to ensure the implementation

[29] Article 7.22(1) KOREU FTA. [30] Article 7.22(6) KOREU FTA. [31] Ibid.

of the agreements and to promote regulatory cooperation between the parties. The work of these committees is therefore conceived as proactive, insofar as they are encouraged to discuss all matters—including regulatory issues—that would advance the aim of progressive reciprocal liberalization.

The remit of these institutions varies from agreement to agreement. For example, whilst the KOREU FTA institutes a 'Committee on Trade in Services, Establishment and Electronic Commerce' (KOREU FTA Services Committee), the purpose of which is to supervise and assess the implementation of the provisions on services, discuss issues flagged by one of the parties, and provide opportunities for relevant authorities to exchange information on prudential measures,[32] the, Colombia–Peru FTA permits the establishment of working groups that could discuss a wider range of topics, such as regulatory issues concerning trade in services, the proposal of guidelines for Andean countries to become a safe harbour for the protection of personal data, establishing cooperation mechanisms for digital accreditation and certification for electronic transactions, and mutual recognition of digital certificates.[33] Besides their general supervisory tasks, these committees have a particular role to play in promoting regulatory cooperation in key areas of trade in services. For instance, they play a critical role in the promotion of mutual recognition agreements. The EU DCFTAs include provisions establishing a mechanism intended to facilitate the development of mutual recognition arrangements in services sectors between the parties.[34] The parties agree to encourage representative professional bodies to jointly provide recommendations on mutual recognition to be submitted to the Trade Committee, which will assess the compatibility of the recommendations with the Agreement and decide whether to negotiate a mutual recognition agreement. However, the provision has its limitations, as there is no requirement on the parties to kick-start discussions on any specific services sector, and no obligation to actually negotiate an agreement when a suitable recommendation is made.

Regulatory dialogue is also encouraged in specific services sectors. As noted above, in the area of financial services, the KOREU FTA Services Committee is identified as the forum where parties must work to facilitate the mutual recognition of prudential measures by providing 'opportunities for relevant authorities to exchange information on prudential measures'.[35] In the area of electronic commerce, all EU DCFTAs also agree to maintain a dialogue on a number of 'regulatory issues' (such as recognition of certificates of electronic signatures, liability of intermediary service providers, protection of consumers, development of paperless trading, etc.).[36] Likewise, under the CEPA, the Trade and Development

[32] Article 7.3 KOREU FTA. [33] Article 109 Colombia–Peru FTA.

[34] Article 7.21(2) KOREU FTA; Article 177 EU–CA FTA; Article 129 Colombia–Peru FTA; Article 8.16 EU–Singapore FTA.

[35] Article 7.3 KOREU FTA.

[36] Article 120 CEPA; Article 7.49 KOREU FTA; Article 163 Colombia–Peru FTA; Article 202 EU–CA FTA; Article 8.16 EU–Singapore FTA.

Committee must develop the modalities for regulatory dialogue between the parties concerning the tourism sector. Such dialogue includes the obligation to 'exchange experiences, information and best practices'[37] and to consult on issues relating to the tourism sector, and requires the participation of 'private and other relevant stakeholders'.[38]

Another facet of the administrative cooperation provided for under the EU DCFTAs concluded with developing countries can be found in the establishment of legal and institutional frameworks for capacity building and technical assistance. Both the CEPA and the Colombia–Peru FTA recognize the importance of cooperation between the parties as a means to further the objectives pursued by the agreements. The cooperation initiatives—which are to be conducted under the auspices of the relevant Trade Committee[39]—are thus intended to strengthen capacity in the supply of services, so as to facilitate the implementation of the commitments in the EU DCFTAs and to ensure that welfare gains are maximized. Regulatory reform is one of the areas targeted for such cooperation. The CEPA requires that technical assistance, training, and capacity building be provided, inter alia, to address 'quality and standards needs in those sectors where the signatory CARIFORUM States have undertaken commitments', to develop and implement 'regulatory regimes for specific services sectors at CARIFORUM regional level' and to promote the advancement of the tourism sector in CARIFORUM States, namely by facilitating participation of CARIFORUM States in international standard-setting bodies,[40] while the Colombia–Peru FTA mentions the need to 'strengthen institutional capacities'.[41]

*Horizontal regulatory disciplines in the TTIP*

The fact that the KOREU FTA and the EU–Singapore FTA go further than the other EU DCFTAs is logical, given that the EU has little to gain by including ambitious regulatory cooperation and transparency provisions in agreements with developing countries—some of which would likely not have the institutional capacity and expertise to fully comply with such obligations. For the EU, the benefits of regulatory cooperation are to be found in advanced economies with more sophisticated regulatory frameworks. Not only does the EU stand to gain more from the removal of regulatory barriers with such trading partners but it can also benefit from the influence of foreign regulation. The argument goes that, faced with a better quality of regulation, the EU is 'induced to improve its own regulations in order to face the challenges raised by the partner's better regulations' (Messerlin (2012c), pp. 5–6). The EU's desire to promote regulatory cooperation and transparency with larger economies is made clear in the context of the CETA and the ongoing negotiations for the TTIP, where the EU has proposed the adoption of horizontal disciplines and institutional provisions to 'eliminate, reduce

[37] Article 118.1 CEPA. [38] Article 118.2 CEPA.
[39] Article 326 Colombia–Peru FTA. [40] Article 119.3(d) CEPA.
[41] Article 324.2(d) Colombia–Peru FTA.

or prevent unnecessary "behind the border obstacles" to trade and investment' (European Commission (2013e)). The CETA includes a Chapter 26 on Regulatory Cooperation, which establishes an institutional framework for bilateral cooperation. The main objectives of such regulatory cooperation are to: (a) prevent and eliminate unnecessary barriers to trade; (b) enhance the climate for competitiveness and innovation; and (c) promote transparent, efficient and effective regulatory process.[42] The cooperative activities would include, inter alia, engaging in discussions on topics relating to regulatory governance that may impact on the relationship between the parties, exchanging information during the regulatory development process and contemplated regulatory actions,[43] examining the opportunities to minimize regulatory divergence,[44] conducting post-implementation reviews of regulations and policies[45] and exploring the possibility of reducing regulatory divergence through convergence, mutual recognition, minimizing the use of trade-distorting regulation, and the use of international standards.[46] In relation to the TTIP, the EU has published a 'Textual Proposal for a Legal Text on Regulatory Cooperation in TTIP' (Textual Proposal) (Commission (2015c)), which contains a number of broad constraints on the regulatory processes of the parties (e.g. advance publication planned regulatory acts,[47] involvement of stakeholder consultations,[48] the completion of impact assessments on planned regulatory acts[49]). Like the CETA, the EU's proposal for regulatory cooperation in the TTIP also envisages a framework for discussion and the exchange of information.[50] However, it is more specific with respect to the methods that may be used by the parties to promote regulatory compatibility as it states that parties may propose the development of mutual recognition mechanisms, harmonization (by applying international standards or by approximating rules on a bilateral basis), or the simplification of rules and procedures in a bilateral basis.[51] Particularly relevant, in the context of services, have been proposals for regulatory cooperation in the area of financial services where the EU would like to establish an institutional process within the TTIP through which the parties would work to ensure the 'timely and consistent' implementation of international standards, conduct mutual consultations in advance of new financial measures that may impact on the supply of financial services, examine where existing rules may constitute unnecessary barriers to trade, and assess the extent to which their respective rules on financial services are equivalent in outcomes (European Commission (2014b)). The ultimate goal of such regulatory cooperation would be to examine the possibility of securing recognition of equivalence in financial standards so as to ensure that EU service suppliers are not subject to the cumbersome US

[42] Article X.04(1) Chapter 26 CETA.
[43] Article X.03(2), (3), (4), (5) and (6) Chapter 26 CETA.
[44] Article X.03(7) Chapter 26 CETA. [45] Article X.03(15) Chapter 26 CETA.
[46] Articles X.03(9) and X.03(18) Chapter 26 CETA.
[47] Article 5 EU Textual Proposal. [48] Article 6 EU Textual Proposal.
[49] Article 7 EU Textual Proposal. [50] Article 9 EU Textual Proposal.
[51] Article 11 EU Textual Proposal.

prudential regulations that have followed the Dodd-Frank Act (Johnston and Schott (2013), p. 5). However, this proposal has been met with little interest on the part of US trade officials, who fear that a binding cooperative framework may hamper the ongoing reform of the US financial regulatory system or even be used to water down existing standards, and have stressed that any discussion on financial services regulation is off the negotiating table (Donnan (2014b)). In other words, there are limits to how far EU DCFTAs can go in disciplining domestic regulation with respect to certain services. As the case of financial services in the TTIP illustrates, even in the context of negotiations between parties presenting similar levels of economic development and regulatory approaches, such as the EU and the US, the regulatory mistrust that persists between states renders any proposal for regulatory convergence or significant cooperation a difficult sell.

#### 4.4.3.2.2 Sector-specific regulatory disciplines

In recognition of the difficulty of adopting a one-size-fits-all approach to the liberalization of services, the EU DCFTAs contain a number of provisions regulating specific service sectors of interest to the EU, namely financial services, telecommunication services, postal and courier services, computer services, international maritime services, and electronic commerce. In the CEPA, the EU also included a subsection dealing with tourism, which responded to the particular demands of the CARIFORUM countries. These sector-specific rules have been lauded as evidence of the EU's attempts to impose 'detailed regulatory frameworks' (Brown (2011), p. 306). Whilst it can be argued that these rules are indicative of the high level of trade liberalization sought by the EU in the EU DCFTAs as the EU is able to incorporate a number of items it has struggled to push through in the context of WTO negotiations, not all services sectors covered contain regulatory disciplines. The EU DCFTAs do not, for example, introduce any regulatory disciplines relating to computer services but instead focus on clarifying the scope of coverage of the term 'computer services'. The EU's principal priority in this area in the context of services negotiations at WTO level has been to ensure that the scope of 'computer services' as specified under the GATS Sectoral Classification List (GATT (1990b)) is understood broadly to incorporate new technological advances in information technology, such as web or domain hosting and data mining services and to ensure that any areas of potential overlap, such as in the telecommunication services sector, are clarified (WTO (2002a)). Such clarification of the scope of the term 'computer services' is incorporated into the vast majority of EU DCFTAs.[52] A similar reflection can be made with regard to the provisions on international maritime transport—a key industry sector in the context of international trade, where non-discriminatory regulatory barriers such as competition issues and the use of environmental and safety standards for protectionist uses are widespread (Fink, Mattoo, and Neagu (2002), p. 87; Nesterowicz

[52] Article 88 CEPA; Article 7.25 KOREU FTA; Article 132 Colombia–Peru FTA; Article 180 EU–CA FTA; Article 8.21 EU–Singapore FTA.

(2011), p. 629; OECD (2011)). In a policy document outlining the EU's strategy for maritime transport, the European Commission identified the increase of market access, the promotion of internationally-agreed standards relating to the safety and quality of shipping, and the alignment of substantive competition rules abroad as some of the primary objectives of the EU's current external policy (European Commission (2009c), p. 3). To pursue this approach, the EU looks beyond the WTO by engaging in bilateral dialogue and agreements (FTAs, Association Agreements, and special maritime transport agreements). However, if harmonization of competition and safety and environmental standards are part of the EU's external policy, this feature is certainly not present in the EU DCFTAs, which focus exclusively on market opening commitments.[53] Likewise, in the area of electronic commerce, the EU DCFTAs do not impose regulatory disciplines but establish a framework for future regulatory dialogue on a number of regulatory issues.[54]

Generally speaking, where regulatory disciplines *have* been imposed, these are concerned with the promotion of regulatory and procedural transparency, competition and, in certain instances, the recognition of prudential and equity concerns relevant to concerned services areas. Where possible, the EU DCFTAs use regulatory models already available at WTO level. As a result, all of the pro-competitive and regulatory attributes that apply, for example, to telecommunication and financial services under GATS are found in the EU DCFTAs.

Most of the Global FTA provisions disciplining domestic regulation on financial services are effectively taken from the WTO Financial Services Understanding and the Financial Services Annex. These include the prudential measures exception of the Financial Services Annex[55] as well as rules relating to new financial services[56] and access to self-regulatory organizations[57] from the Financial Services Understanding. The EU DCFTAs go further than the WTO texts in some instances. For example, with regard to the treatment of 'new financial services', the Financial Services Understanding provides that WTO Members must 'permit financial service suppliers of any other Member established in its territory to offer in its territory any new financial service'.[58] This means that a home state is required to allow the supply of a new financial service provided in the territory of another WTO Member even if such services are not provided in the territory of the former (Tietje, Finke, and Dietrich (2010), p. 30). However, all of the EU DCFTAs

[53] Article 7.47 KOREU FTA; Article 8.56 EU–Singapore FTA.

[54] Article 120 CEPA; Article 7.49 KOREU FTA; Article 163 Colombia–Peru FTA; Article 202 EU–CA FTA; Article 8.61 EU–Singapore FTA.

[55] Article 104 CEPA; Article 7.38 KOREU FTA; Article 154 Colombia–Peru FTA; Article 195 EU–CA FTA; Article 8.50(1) EU–Singapore FTA.

[56] Article 105 CEPA; Article 156 Colombia–Peru FTA; Article 197 EU–CA FTA; Article 8.53 EU–Singapore FTA.

[57] Article 7.40 KOREU FTA; Article 8.51 EU–Singapore FTA.

[58] Understanding on Commitments in Financial Services, Uruguay Round Final Act, GATT Trade Negotiations Committee Document MTN/FA II-AIB, General Agreement on Trade in Services, 15 April 1994 para 7.

significantly reduce the scope of this obligation by adding that the supply of the new financial service is only required if the host state allows the supply of such service under domestic law.[59] The upshot is that the FTA parties are not obliged to accept the supply of new financial products in their territories simply because their trading partners have decided to do so. Finally, the CETA regulates certain issues that cannot be found in any WTO instrument (e.g. rules on the composition of senior management and board of directors of financial institutions[60] and the establishment of prior comments procedures[61]) and which are seemingly inspired by the text of Chapter 14 on financial services in the NAFTA.

The section on telecommunication services is based on the GATS Reference Paper on basic telecommunication services. This sets out regulatory principles, such as prohibition of anti-competitive practices, rules on interconnection and allocation and use of scarce resources, licensing criteria, USOs, and independence of regulatory authorities, which are replicated verbatim in the EU DCFTAs. By transposing the text of the Reference Paper into its EU DCFTAs, the EU ensures that a voluntary set of rules established at WTO level becomes legally binding. However, the agreements go further in certain aspects by requiring higher standards of impartiality and transparency from regulators. Thus, the relevant regulatory authorities must be 'sufficiently empowered to regulate the telecommunications services sector'[62] and the tasks of such authority 'must be made public in an easily accessible and clear form'.[63] Additional rules are also provided with respect to licensing procedures. Where a licence is required to provide telecommunication services, the terms and conditions of such licence must be made publicly available[64] and the applicable licence fees must not exceed the administrative costs normally incurred for management, control, and enforcement of the applicable licences.[65] As regards interconnection, the EU DCFTAs also borrow from the Reference Paper whilst making certain additions which aim to avoid abuses from dominant market players in relation to negotiations on interconnection. It provides that 'any supplier authorised to provide telecommunication services shall have the right to negotiate interconnection with other providers of publicly available telecommunication services networks and services'[66] and that interconnection should be agreed on the basis of '*commercial negotiation* between the companies concerned'.[67] Such language is taken directly from EU legislation on interconnection, which states that organizations authorized to provide telecommunication networks or publicly available telecommunications

[59] Article 15.6 CEPA; Article 7.42 KOREU; Article 156 Colombia–Peru FTA; Article 197 EU–CA FTA; Article 8.53 EU–Singapore FTA; Article 13 Chapter 15 CETA.

[60] Article 8 Chapter 15 CETA. [61] Article 10 Chapter 15 CETA.

[62] Article 95 CEPA; Article 7.28(2) KOREU FTA; Article 143(3) Colombia–Peru FTA; Article 8.29(5) EU–Singapore FTA.

[63] Ibid. [64] Article 7.29(2) KOREU FTA; Article 8.41(2) EU–Singapore FTA.

[65] Article 7.29(3)(c) KOREU FTA.

[66] Article 7.29(3) CEPA; Article 96(2) KOREU FTA; Article 144(3) Colombia–Peru FTA; Article 187(3) EU–CA FTA.

[67] Ibid.

services should be free to negotiate interconnection agreements on a '*commercial basis*'.[68] The EU DCFTAs also replicate the obligation provided under EU law to ensure the confidentiality of information acquired by service suppliers during the process of negotiating interconnection.[69] By specifying the manner in which interconnection is to be negotiated, the EU DCFTAs build upon what is provided in the Reference Paper by borrowing from the principles found in EU law. The exportation of EU norms is even more salient in the context of the EU–Singapore FTA, which contains provisions taken from the EU directives on electronic communications networks and services. The agreement lists a number of obligations on major suppliers to provide access to, and use of, network elements and associated facilities[70] which replicates Article 12 of the Directive 2002/19/EC on access to electronic communications networks, and replicates requirements relating to facility sharing[71] included in Article 12 of Directive 2009/140/EC on a common regulatory framework for electronic communications networks and services. In its most recent EU DCFTAs—the EU–Singapore FTA and the CETA—the EU has included a range of provisions (transparency, independence of regulatory authorities, co-location, number portability, confidentiality of information obtained in the process of negotiating interconnection agreements)[72] that are not found on the Reference Paper. These provisions are based on standard language included in US FTA agreements; something that can be attributed to the fact that both Canada and Singapore have signed trade agreements with the US and tend to follow the US FTA model (Melo Araujo (2015)).

The EU DCFTAs also use the template provided by the Reference Paper in network services industries, where similar regulatory disciplines can be implemented. The EU has made clear its desire to push through the adoption of a reference paper akin to that relating to telecommunication services in the area of postal and courier services (WTO (2001a), p. 4). Such a reference paper would prohibit anti-competitive practices, set out minimum procedural guarantees in licensing procedures, require the establishment of independent regulatory authorities and grant the right to WTO Members to impose USOs (Ibid). These regulatory frameworks have been successfully transplanted into the CEPA, the Colombia–Peru FTA and the EU–CA FTA.[73] The EU–Singapore FTA contains broad requirements regarding the prohibition of anti-competitive practices[74] and the autonomy of regulatory bodies[75] whilst in the KOREU FTA, there is a commitment from the parties to set out similar disciplines in the three years after the entry into force of the agreement.[76] The provisions regulating tourism services in the CEPA were

[68] Directive 97/33/EC OJ [1992] L 76 Recital 5; Directive 2002/19/EC OJ [2002] L 108/7, Recital 5; Article 98 CEPA; Article 7.31(1) KOREU FTA; Article 145 Colombia–Peru FTA; Article 189 EU–CA FTA.

[69] Article 98 KOREU FTA; Article 4.2 Directive 2002/19.

[70] Article 8.32 EU–Singapore FTA.

[71] Article 8.35 EU–Singapore FTA.

[72] Articles 8.24–8.48 EU–Singapore FTA; Articles 17:2–17.13.

[73] Articles 89–93 CEPA; Articles 133–138 Colombia–Peru FTA; Articles 181–184 EU–CA FTA.

[74] Article 8.22 EU–Singapore FTA.

[75] Article 8.23 EU–Singapore FTA.

[76] Aricle 726 KOREU FTA.

intended to accommodate the specific offensive interest of CARIFORUM countries in this area. Developing countries have proved to be demandeurs for further multilateral trade liberalization in this area. Proposals for negotiations at WTO level have gone beyond requests for broader commitments in all modes of supply to emphasize the need to include disciplines to prevent anti-competitive practices and consumer protection and promote cooperation for sustainable development of tourism and the adoption of international standards developed by international bodies (WTO (2011b)). The CEPA incorporates a number of these disciplines. With regard to anti-competitive practices and consumer protection, there is a provision requiring the parties to adopt appropriate measures to prevent suppliers from materially affecting the terms of participation in the relevant market for tourism services by engaging in or continuing anti-competitive practices including, inter alia, 'abuse of dominant position through imposition of unfair prices, exclusivity clauses, refuse to deal, tied sales, quantitative restrictions or vertical integration'.[77] The special emphasis on distribution networks reflects the high degree of vertical integration in the global tourism market, which is dominated by few market players that are able to invest in extensive distribution networks incorporating holiday package providers, retailers, and tourism service providers (OECD (2008a), p. 30; UNCTAD (2010), p. 16). Since the EU has some of the major market players, there were significant concerns from the CARIFORUM tourism industry that in the absence of adequate competition legislation, large tour operators could drive down the margins of local tourist service suppliers and push them out of the market (ITC (2009), pp. 16–17).

#### 4.4.3.2.3 Plurilateralizing sector-specific disciplines on services

Although the negotiations on the TISA are still in their infancy, the EU has already set out its stall regarding its ambition to introduce regulatory disciplines in a number of services sectors. Such sectors include telecommunications, financial services, or postal and courier services (European Commission (2013a), p. 2), and the disciplines will cover 'issues such as the independence of regulators, fair authorisation processes or non-discriminatory access to telecommunication networks' (Ibid). The EU has also revealed that suggestions have been made to include new rules, covering domestic regulation (e.g. authorization and licensing procedures), international maritime transport, telecommunication services, e-commerce, computer-related services, cross-border data transfers, postal and courier services, financial services, temporary movement of natural persons, government procurement of services, export subsidies, and state-owned enterprises (Ibid).

One point to note is that this proposal seems no more ambitious than the current crop of GATS-plus FTAs. The objective is to increase national treatment and market access commitments across all modes of service supplies whilst eschewing the more problematic topics that have hampered multilateral

77 Article 127(1) CEPA.

negotiations, including the development of horizontal disciplines on domestic regulation. Instead, the references regarding the planned inclusion of 'regulatory disciplines' and 'rules' on a variety in specific services sectors acknowledges that the current Global FTA practice of using the types of disciplines included in sector-specific GATS instruments as a model for the regulation of other sectors (especially network industries) (Sauvé (2013), p. 14) might be a more realistic prospect. The agenda pursued by the TISA is therefore strikingly similar to that of the EU's own EU DCFTAs confirming the notion that major trading powers are resorting to bilateralism and plurilateralism to push through the reforms that have been rejected in the context of the multilateral process. Effectively, the EU wants to plurilateralize its EU DCFTAs which, in turn, could be multilateralized.

## 4.5 Conclusion

As far as services are concerned, the EU DCFTAs fit the general trend observed in recent FTAs, insofar as they contain GATS-plus commitments (except in particularly politically sensitive sectors such as audiovisual services) and—barring a few minor exceptions—reproduce the provisions of the GATS intended to safeguard policy space. Where the EU DCFTAs stand out is in their attempts to provide regulatory frameworks in a number of key services sectors. The EU has generally not used these agreements as tools to project its internal market rules in services. Although EU policy statements relating to EU DCFTAs refer to mutual recognition and regulatory convergence as goals to be pursued, provisions that create legally binding obligations that would approximate in any way the respective legislation of the EU and its trade partners are few and far between. Instead, the EU DCFTAs must rather be viewed as tools promoting compliance with the rules-based system of the GATS and making legally binding the voluntary commitments included in ancillary GATS-plus instruments promoting regulatory and pro-competitive disciplines, namely the Reference Paper on Telecommunications Services. If the EU is using EU DCFTAs to impose substantive norms, those norms are mostly being sourced from the shallow regulatory pool of plurilateral GATS rules. However, the EU DCFTAs go further in two ways: first, they add certain regulatory disciplines that are not found in either the Financial Services Annex or the Reference Paper on Telecommunications Services (e.g. procedural guarantees, transparency, data protection requirements, rules on electronic communications and services, etc.); and secondly they apply similar regulatory disciplines to other services sectors (e.g. postal and courier services and tourism services). The EU would like to follow a similar path in the context of the TISA and in this regard, it is not inconceivable that the EU DCFTAs currently being negotiated with other proponents of the TISA (e.g. US and Japan) will play a part in the future content of any future plurilateral agreement regulating trade in services.

A key question relating to the dissemination of regulatory disciplines on services through EU DCFTAs is whether such disciplines adversely impact the regulatory autonomy of the parties. This is especially the case with respect to agreements concluded with developing countries that have consistently opposed the development of further disciplines in the context of the GATS. Here, it must first be noted that most disciplines concluded in EU DCFTAs are intended to ensure that the liberalization commitments made by countries are not undone by overly burdensome and opaque non-discriminatory domestic regulation. In fact, although this chapter has highlighted some areas of concern for developing countries (notably with regard to financial and telecommunication services), most of these disciplines tend to be broadly termed regulatory disciplines that allow parties to maintain a significant amount of regulatory discretion. Secondly, the EU DCFTAs examined in this chapter show that the EU is willing to tailor disciplines on domestic regulations in accordance with the needs and peculiarities of developing country signatories. The EU adopts a flexible approach to the negotiation of regulatory disciplines where it is willing to deviate from its standard template to accommodate demands from FTA partners. The disciplines typically included in EU DCFTAs with developing countries are generally less onerous than those found in developed country EU DCFTAs and, in one instance, the EU has added regulatory disciplines at the specific request of developing nations (Sauvé and Ward, 2009, pp. 13–14). A note of concern should, however, be raised in light of the EU's plans to multilateralize its deep trade agenda in the area of services through the conclusion of the TISA. In doing so, the EU appears to be going down the one-size-fits-all approach to disciplining trade in services. There is an assumption amongst the proponents of the TISA that once the agreement is concluded others (including developing countries) will eventually follow suit. However, as the continuous inability of the EU to conclude trade deals with India and MERCOSUR indicates (Messerlin (2013)), convincing emerging economies to subscribe to rules that further undermine their regulatory autonomy and do little to address their most pressing concerns (e.g. Mode 4 liberalization) is far from a given. It may therefore be that the TISA will not be seen as a model for the new rules of the international trading system but rather as an agreement that further entrenches the divisions that exist between developed and developing countries.

Beyond the promotion of certain regulatory disciplines, the EU DCFTAs also implement regulatory cooperation mechanisms. Whilst harmonization is not sought outright, a particular attribute of the EU DCFTAs is that they incorporate institutional mechanisms that are intended to foster mutual trust between the regulatory systems involved. The transparency provisions in the KOREU and the EU–Singapore FTAs are GATS-plus in nature and each Global FTA establishes (or enables the establishment of) an institutional framework tasked with the supervision of the implementation of services chapters, and which serves as a forum for the regulatory dialogues mandated in specific services sectors. In addition the EU has sought to include ambitious horizontal regulatory cooperation chapters in the CETA and TTIP that promote 'good' regulatory practices, exchanges of information, and establish institutional bodies to facilitate cooperative activities.

The rationale is that the establishment of institutional frameworks for regulatory dialogues will foster mutual trust and discourage the adoption of trade-restrictive measures by reducing concerns relating to the dangers posed by national measures and by allowing regulatory authorities to solve any market access issues that may emerge. However, a note of caution should be sounded with regard to the regulatory cooperation provisions in the EU DCFTAs. First, soft forms of regulatory cooperation included in trade agreements have generally proved ineffective means to address regulatory divergence in the absence of strong enforcement mechanisms (Steger (2012), pp. 111–26). Secondly, pursuing any form of significant cooperation in the area of services regulation, which is characterized by domestic and cultural preferences, remains an extremely complex and politically sensitive endeavour. In this regard, when expounding the potential benefits of regulatory cooperation in the context of the CETA and TTIP, the EU has tended to focus mostly on the possibility of harmonizing or concluding mutual recognition arrangements with respect to technical standards and regulations, rather than services rules (European Commission (2015)). And, as seen in this chapter, on the one occasion where the EU welcomed regulatory cooperation in an important services sector (financial services in the TTIP) the suggestion was dismissed out of hand by the negotiating counterpart.

# 5
# Investment

## 5.1 Introduction

For a long time, investment protection was seen as the missing link in the EU's external trade policy. The EU could conclude trade agreements that facilitated market access for EU firms in third countries, but it could not negotiate terms that would ensure the protection of EU investments abroad. Conversely, whilst the EU was solely competent to determine the conditions under which third country firms accessed the EU market, the protection of foreign investments within the EU remained an issue that fell within the competence of Member States. The upshot is that investment protection in the EU was regulated by a multitude of separate bilateral investment treaties (BITs), each securing different levels of protection and undermining the uniformity of the EU's common commercial policy. However, with the extension of the EU's exclusive competence in this area in 2010 the EU can now 'fill the gap' in its trade policy by complementing its attempts to open foreign markets with agreements that ensure the same investment protection standards for all EU economic operators investing abroad (Commission (2010b), p. 5).

However, the EU's foray into the area of investment protection has not been plain sailing so far. As discussed in Chapter 2, the exact scope of the EU's exclusive competence in this area has been contested. In addition, the content, and in some cases the very existence of the investment chapters currently being included in the EU DCFTAs are also the subject of much criticism within the EU. Such criticisms—which vary in their scope from the very general (e.g. discontent towards globalization) to the more specific (e.g. contours of investment protection standards and lack of accountability of arbitrators)—are part of a much wider debate concerning the continued relevance and legitimacy of the international investment legal system.

The EU has so far negotiated two EU DCFTAs containing investment protection chapters: the CETA and the EU–Singapore FTA. It is a measure of the controversy that surrounds the investment protection issue that neither of these agreements is even remotely close to being ratified despite the fact that, in both cases, negotiations were concluded in 2014. Furthermore, the debate on investment protection has been at its most fierce in the context of the highly publicized TTIP negotiations, where a very effective campaign against the inclusion of an investment protection chapter including investor–state dispute settlement

(ISDS) clauses has led the EU to reconsider its negotiating stance. This chapter will therefore focus on the text of the investment chapters of the CETA and the EU–Singapore FTA as well as the various policy documents released by the Commission concerning the proposed language for the investment protection chapter in the TTIP. The objective of this chapter is to describe and assess the EU's attempts to negotiate investment protection and ISDS provisions in EU DCFTAs within the context of the wider debate concerning the future direction of international investment law. It finds that whilst the investment protection provisions included in the EU DCFTAs must be viewed as part of the new generation of 'recalibrated' international investment agreements (IIAs)—which attempt to ensure that protection of foreign investors does not come at the expense of the right of states to regulate, they still present a number of problematic features that could undermine the regulatory autonomy of parties. Section 5.2 considers the evolution of international investment law from the mid-twentieth century onwards. It explains the historical context within which modern international investment law emerged and the rise of international investment agreements (IIAs) characterized by strong investment protection standards and ISDS clauses. It then discusses how the system, which was primarily geared to protect the interests of capital exporting countries, is increasingly being questioned with a growing number of countries calling for the recalibration, and in some cases the eradication, of IIAs. Section 5.3 examines the EU's current policy with respect to the negotiation of investment protection chapters in its EU DCFTAs, highlighting the EU's stated intention to develop investment protection chapters that address the flaws typically associated with IIAs. Section 5.4 conducts a legal analysis of some of the main substantive and procedural features of the investment chapters included in the EU DCFTAs, and assesses the extent to which the agreements contribute to the further recalibration of international investment law.

## 5.2 Evolution of International Investment

### 5.2.1 The emergence of international investment law

Modern international investment law can best be described as a fragmented legal system composed of disparate IIAs promoting investment protection and liberalization and subjecting disputes to ISDS. This system is the result of a process of 'treatification' (Salacuse (2007), p. 156), which occurred in the post-colonial era when capital exporting countries sought to counter the prevalence of economic nationalism in decolonized developing countries by concluding comprehensive and enforceable BITs (Vandevelde (2005), pp. 166–7). Indeed, to this day, most BITs are concluded by and between developed and developing nations—the former to secure protection for investments and investors and the latter to attract foreign investment. The first generation of such BITs enshrined substantive provisions such as non-discrimination requirements, fair and equitable treatment (FET), and prohibitions against uncompensated expropriations, and provided for state–state dispute settlement (Newcombe (2013a), p. 16). A further crucial component of most modern BITs emerged in the 1960s with the replacement of state-to-state dispute settlement with ISDS mechanism. The signal event in this respect was the conclusion, under the auspices of the World Bank, of the 1965 Convention establishing the International Centre for the Settlement for Investment Disputes (ICSID), which provided facilities for the arbitration of disputes between investors and host states and formulated model investor-arbitration clauses that would subsequently be incorporated in most IIAs (Vandevelde (2005), p. 175). The introduction of ISDS within the realm of international investment law had a revolutionary effect. Whereas under the old system, challenges against violations of IIAs required the endorsement of the investor's claim by the home state (Ibid), ISDS allowed private investors to invoke IIA provisions and bring claims against host states directly before arbitration tribunals.

IIAs remained relatively few in number throughout the 1960s and the 1970s, however, because of the opposition of developing countries towards foreign investment and the perceived lack of balance of these agreements (Sornarajah (2010), p. 22). Indeed, as the terms of IIAs were set by capital exporting countries, the agreements tended to be somewhat one-sided, with the emphasis being placed on the protection of investor rights rather than investor responsibilities and the right of host states to regulate (Muchlinski (2013), pp. 216–19). However, from the early 1980s onwards, IIAs have increased exponentially, in part because of the emergence of a neo-liberal economic model promulgated by the Washington Consensus as the dominant economic paradigm, as well as the debt crisis of the 1980s that forced developing countries to consider foreign investment as a viable alternative to private lending (Vandevelde (2005), p. 177; Salacuse (2007), p. 160). These events also impacted on the substance and objectives of IIAs, which not only incorporated enhanced standards of investment protection but also increasingly pursued a strong liberalizing agenda (Alvarez (2011a), p. 231). The mixing of trade liberalization and investment protection issues was evidenced in the content of the BITs as well as the tendency to include investment protection agreements in bilateral and regional free trade agreements—a phenomenon that culminated with the conclusion of the North American Free Trade Agreement (NAFTA) and the WTO agreements which regulate—to varying degrees—investment matters (Vandevelde (2005), p. 177). Another significant development related to the proliferation of IIAs in the post-1980s is the emergence of 'model' BITs—that is, template agreements that are used as the basis for the negotiation of BITs (Schill (2009), p. 90). Although, historically, capital exporting countries have been the main exponents of this practice, developing countries are also increasingly using such texts. The objective of Model BITS is, first, to promote consistency in the language and interpretation of BITs so as to facilitate the management of multiple BITs by states and ensure predictability of the treatment accorded to foreign investors (Newcombe (2013a), p. 21). It also confers to the authors of the Model BIT a strategic advantage in the context of negotiations as they can impose their positions on counterparts (Ibid).

### 5.2.2 From neo-liberalism to recalibration?

The rise of international investment law during the twentieth century seems to be characterized by an ever-increasing push for further liberalization and enhancement of the protection of foreign investment. Because IIAs were generally imposed by capital exporting countries on capital importing countries as a pre-condition for any foreign investment, they tended to reflect the liberalizing agenda of the former and the interests of foreign investors (Alvarez and Sauvant (2011c), p. 23). Since these agreements were designed to protect private investments in capital importing countries, no thought was given to how the rights of investors may impact on the right of host countries to regulate to pursue public interest objectives. This proved to be particularly problematic because IIAs, unlike traditional trade agreements, were not focused solely on non-discrimination but also imposed standards that would impact on the substance of non-discriminatory domestic regulation (Lester (2015), pp. 77–8). Moreover, it is contended that the advent of ISDS mechanisms based on arbitration led by *private* legal practitioners progressively created a body of case law that has, in the main, been biased towards the protection of the private and commercial interests (Muchlinsky (2013), pp. 217–18). Although the claim that the system is biased in favour of investors remains disputed (Alvarez (2011b), p. 384), the perceived lack of balance between commercial and public interest concerns in international investment law is a criticism that has been consistently levelled by developing countries and has been identified as the foremost reason behind the failure to adopt strong multilateral disciplines in this area (Ziegler (2013), pp. 203–4). Finally, a consequence of a fragmented legal system, such as that of international investment law, populated by a plethora of IIAs and subject to the jurisdictions of arbitral tribunals composed of arbitrators of varying legal backgrounds, is the development of an inconsistent and incoherent body of case law. The vagueness of treaty provisions, the variation in language used from one IIA to another and the reliance on ad hoc tribunals have all been identified as factors that lead to the proliferation of conflicting interpretations. The inconsistency of arbitral awards and the legal uncertainty that characterizes some of the major investment protection standards have exacerbated the concerns regarding the legitimacy of international investment law. Such criticisms relate directly to the functioning of the ISDS mechanism, and proposals for reform range from the development of more stringent rules on procedural transparency, the establishment of appellate mechanisms, and the outright removal of investor-arbitration from IIAs (Newcombe and Paradell (2009), p. 64).

The content of more recent IIAs suggests that this trend has seemingly been reversed as states increasingly seek to recalibrate (or rebalance) international investment law in a manner that ensures a better balance between the right of investors and the regulatory and policy autonomy of host states (Alvarez (2011a), p. 234; Hoffman, Schill, and Tams (2013), p. 11). The change in approach has come at a time when the increase of inward investment flows into developed countries (in part due to the rise of emerging economies) means that traditional capital exporting countries are increasingly exposed to the problems associated with the first generation of BITs (Sornarajah (2010), p. 25)—from the lack of balance between the protection of investors and host state's right to regulate to the vagaries of an inconsistent and unpredictable body of case law based on investment arbitration (Gagné and Morin (2006), p. 359). The recalibration trend can be seen in the evolution of the US Model BITs over the course of the past two decades. When the NAFTA was concluded in 1994, its chapter on investment was used as a model for subsequent BITs entered into by the US (Gagné and Morin (2006), pp. 357–82). These BITs secured a very high level of protection for investors, covering non-discrimination, prohibitions of regulatory expropriation, minimum standard treatment, and binding ISDS mechanisms. However, in 2004, the US revised its Model BIT, both to reduce investment protection and to add safeguards intended to protect regulatory autonomy of states—a shift towards a 'sovereignty-centred' approach which reflected to a large extent the US's experience in the ISDS litigation in the context of the NAFTA (Ibid, p. 359; Sornarajah (2010), p. 175). As explained by Alvarez, the 2004 US Model BIT has 'shrunk, sometimes dramatically, virtually every right accorded to foreign investors while at the same time increasing, sometimes vastly the discretion accorded to host states' (Alvarez (2011a), p. 235). This recalibration process has continued with the latest US Model BIT—the 2012 US Model BIT,[1] which contains additional safeguards protecting the regulatory autonomy of states (Simmons (2014), p. 43). What is more, the rebalanced US Model BITs have served as inspiration to both developed and developing countries, several of which have since revised their BITs in order to protect their ability to regulate to pursue public interest objectives (Alvarez (2011a), p. 238; Vandevelde (2012), p. 312). For example, the 2004 Canadian Model BIT—referred to as the 'Foreign Investment Promotion and Protection Agreements' (Canadian Model FIPA)[2]—built on the 2004 US Model BIT, as it concomitantly restricts investment protection rights (by limiting standards of fair and equitable treatment, expropriation and national treatment) and expands exceptions to such rights. Other countries have gone further. Australia, for one, announced in 2011 its intention to no longer include ISDS in BITs so that claims arising from a suspected violation of such agreements would be brought by foreign investors before domestic courts (Trakman (2014), p. 153). The reason given by Australia for this policy shift was the conviction that ISDS mechanisms conferred 'greater legal rights on foreign businesses than those available to domestic businesses'[3] and that this would undermine their ability to 'make laws on social, environmental and economic matters where those laws do not discriminate between domestic and foreign businesses'.[4] Further, there is a

[1] 2012 US Model Bilateral Investment Treaty. Available at: http://www.state.gov/e/eb/ifd/bit/.

[2] 2004 Canada Foreign Investment Promotion and Protection Agreement. Available at: http://www.international.gc.ca/trade-agreements-accords-commerciaux/agr-acc/fipa-apie/index.aspx?lang=eng.

[3] Australia Government, Department for Foreign Affairs and Trade, Gilliard Government Trade Policy Statement: Trading our Way to More Jobs and Prosperity, 14. Available at: http://www.acci.asn.au/getattachment/b9d3cfae-fc0c-4c2a-a3df-3f58228daf6d/Gillard-Government-Trade-Policy-Statement.aspx.

[4] Ibid.

growing trend among developing nations to remove themselves from the system altogether with some countries terminating their BITs (e.g. Ecuador and Venezuela) and/or withdrawing from the ICSID convention (e.g. Argentina, Bolivia, Ecuador, and Venezuela) (Alvarez (2011a), p. 239; Simmons (2014), p. 43).

## 5.3 EU Investment Protection Policy—Towards a Recalibrated EU Model BIT?

### 5.3.1 Past EU practice

The EU may have only recently acquired exclusive external competence with respect to investment policy, but its interest in incorporating investment protection within international trade law is longstanding. It was one of the key proponents of the inclusion of investment in the Singapore issues and, throughout the late 1990s and early 2000s, advocated the negotiation of investment rules at the multilateral level that would ensure the protection secured under the US Model BITs (Wolf (2008), p. 76). As with all the other Singapore issues (with the exception of trade facilitation), negotiations on the relationship between trade and investment were eventually removed from the Doha Round largely because of concerns from developing countries regarding the loss of regulatory autonomy and potential costs of implementing regulatory reforms, but also because of the muted support for such reforms from the US who favoured a plurilateral approach in the context of the OECD (Ibid; Woolcock (2003), p. 251). In the absence of an exclusive competence on the matter, it was left up to Member States to negotiate IIAs. Over 1,400 BITs signed by Member States are currently in force (European Commission (2015a), p. 1). These Member State BITs followed the template of modern IIAs in providing high standards of protection for European investors abroad, albeit with one minor difference; these BITs focused on regulating post-establishment standards—that is, substantive investment protection standards. This is in contrast to the EU practice of negotiating trade agreements that deal exclusively with market access and non-discriminatory treatment of foreign investors (Cardwell and French (2011), p. 203). This focus on pre-admission situations is certainly found in the vast majority of EU DCFTAs concluded to date. Because negotiations for the CEPA, the KOREU FTA, the Colombia–Peru FTA and the EU–CA FTA were initiated prior to the signing of the Lisbon Treaty, these agreements do not contain the type of far-reaching investment protection rules typically found in BITs. In fact, the limited external competence of the EU in this area meant that, in certain cases, the EU was forced to rebuff demands from some of its FTA counterparts for stronger FDI rules (Sauvé and Ward (2009), p. 15). There are, therefore, no provisions relating to standards on FET, full protection and security, expropriation and compensation, performance requirements, or investor–state dispute settlement. The more important rules on investment are located in the mode 3 'commercial presence' sections of the services chapters of the agreements and, in line with what is currently provided under GATS, focus on MFN, national treatment, and market access obligations (Wu (2012), p. 339). Surprisingly, given that it was concluded prior to the Treaty of Lisbon, the CEPA is the only Global FTA to include obligations that regulate post-entry situations, as it imposes certain restrictions on investor behaviour (Leal-Arcas (2012), p. 269). The parties of the CEPA are enjoined to take measures to prohibit the bribing and corruption of officials in order to secure favourable treatment, to act in accordance with ILO core labour standards, to ensure that investors do not circumvent international environmental or labour obligations arising from international agreements and to establish and maintain local community liaison processes.[5] Besides services chapters, EU DCFTAs also contain rules on capital movement, such as the prohibition on 'restrictions on the free movement of capital relating to direct investments made in accordance with the laws of the host country, to investments and other transactions [liberalized with regards to trade in services and electronic commerce]'[6] as well as restrictions on the ability of investors to liquidate or repatriate to the liquidation invested capital and of any profit generated from such investments.[7] It must be noted, however, that such provisions do not signal a foray into the field of portfolio investment, as free movement of capital is only provided for those investors who have established a commercial presence in the territory of the signatories of the concerned agreement.

## 5.3.2 A new approach to investment protection

Not long after the expansion of the EU's exclusive external competence in the area of investment protection under the Treaty of Lisbon, the European Commission issued a communication outlining a comprehensive international investment policy (Investment Policy Communication) (European Commission (2010b)). This policy document justified the EU's aim to include investment liberalization and protection issues in future trade and investment agreements and outlined certain features of the substantive rules that would be included in these agreements. The EU did not tie itself to a particular form of investment agreement, acknowledging the possibility of signing bilateral, regional, multilateral, or sectoral stand-alone investment agreements or, alternatively, including investment-related provisions in FTAs (European Commission (2010b), p. 7). The latter has been the EU's preferred option thus far, with investment chapters having been included in, or currently under negotiation in the context of, EU DCFTAs such as the EU–Singapore, the CETA and the TTIP. As far as stand-alone agreements are concerned, the only example currently available relates to the ongoing negotiations of the EU–China investment agreement launched on 21 November 2013 (European Commission (2014a)). With respect to the

[5] Article 72 CEPA. [6] Article 123 CEPA; Article 8.2 KOREU FTA.

[7] Article 123 CEPA; Article 8.2 KOREU FTA; Article 169 Colombia–Peru FTA; Article 206 EU–CA FTA.

possible content of these agreements, the EU has not strayed too far from the types of provisions typically included in modern IIAs (Reinisch (2013), p. 184). First, it is made clear that the EU intends to go beyond the standard Member State BIT format, which has focused on post-admission issues, by also regulating the market access issues and securing non-discriminatory treatment of investors (European Commission (2010b), p. 3). Secondly, in terms of the scope of investment protection provisions, the EU is seeking to regulate foreign direct investment as well as portfolio investment (Ibid, p. 8). Thirdly, with respect to the standards of investment protection, the EU envisages including provisions relating to FET, full protection and security treatment, and expropriation (Ibid, pp. 8–9). Finally, the communication also proposes including ISDS into its IIAs, arguing that it 'is such an established feature of investment agreements that its absence would in fact discourage investors and make a host economy less attractive than others' (Ibid, pp. 9–10).

The Investment Policy Communication also makes clear that the EU's approach to investment protection will include certain distinctive features that can be aligned with the general trend towards the rebalancing of IIAs. First, it seems to exclude the development of a Model BIT-type template that could be used in the context of negotiations with third countries. In line with its commitment to a differentiated approach to trade negotiations, the Commission argues that a 'one-size-fits-all model for investment agreements [...] would necessarily be neither feasible nor desirable' and that 'the level of development of [the EU's] partners should guide inter alia the standards the Union sets in a specific investment negotiation' (Ibid, p. 6). In other words, the Commission proposes flexibility in the negotiation of IIAs, particularly in connection with developing countries—that is, countries that have traditionally opposed the negotiation of such agreements on the grounds that they undermine their regulatory autonomy. In addition, the Commission provides that its investment policy 'should be guided by the principles and objectives of the Union's external action more generally, including the promotion of the rule of law, human right and sustainable development' (Ibid). Moreover, the need to achieve a balance between the right of foreign investors and the right of host states to regulate is presented as a general goal of all IIAs, not just those concluded with developing countries (Ibid, p. 9):

> [The] Union's trade and investment policy has to fit with the way the EU and its Member States regulate economic activity within the Union and across our borders. Investment agreements should be consistent with the other policies of the Union and its Member States, including policies on the protection of the environment, decent work, health and safety at work, consumer protection, cultural diversity, development policy and competition policy. Investment policy will continue to allow the Union, and the Member States to adopt and enforce measures necessary to pursue public policy objectives.

In other words, for the EU, IIAs must allow for the balancing of investment liberalization and investor protection imperatives against non-trade goals in a manner that reflects the EU's own approach to the internal market—that is, by ensuring that the agreements do not undermine the EU and its Member States' rights to pursue public interest objectives. The balancing exercise, which is to be accomplished by the EU's IIAs, has both an external and internal dimension. The EU's IIAs must be designed in a manner that ensures that they do not run counter to developmental goals of developing countries and that the EU is able to regulate to pursue public interest objectives.

Such statements have not sufficed to quell concerns from the public and Member States regarding the inclusion of investment protection and ISDS clauses in EU DCFTAs (Bishop (2015), pp. 7–8). On the contrary, the criticism of this practice only increased when the EU announced its intention to pursue this practice in the context of the contentious TTIP negotiations. The criticisms were partly due to the secrecy surrounding the negotiations but also centred to a large extent on the perceived democratic deficit and lack of legitimacy attached to ISDS mechanisms (Monbiot (2014); Jones (2014)). In response to mounting public scepticism, the Commission decided to suspend negotiations on the investment protection and ISDS chapter of the TTIP and launched an online public consultation on the topic ('TTIP Public Consultation') (Commission (2014c)). This public consultation presented the EU's proposed text for the investment protection and ISDS chapters of the TTIP (which was based on the text of the CETA), an explanation by the EU for the rationale for such provisions and the extent to which these would address the legitimacy, transparency and consistency problems typically associated with ISDS, and offered the public the opportunity to comment on the EU's proposals for the TTIP. Through the TTIP Public Consultation the EU expressed its objective to negotiate a text that would safeguard the Member States' right to regulate, limit the scope of the rights of foreign investors and reform the ISDS mechanism by enhancing transparency, setting out rules of conduct for arbitrators, and establishing an appellate mechanism (Cremona (2015), p. 357). Such promises did not convince detractors of investment protection and ISDS. The EU received nearly 15,000 responses to the TTIP Public Consultation, the majority of which took a negative view of the EU's proposals either because they: (i) rejected the TTIP in its totality; (ii) considered that the inclusion of an investment protection and ISDS clauses within the TTIP was unnecessary; or (iii) argued that the EU's reform proposals did not go far enough in terms of securing an adequate balance between the right of foreign investors and the right of Member States to regulate and in ensuring the establishment of legitimate and transparent ISDS mechanism (Commission (2015b), pp. 3–4). The latest development in this area is that, in response to the negative feedback received by the EU in the context of the TTIP Public Consultation, the EU has published a concept paper entitled 'Investment in TTIP and beyond, the path for reform' (Concept Paper) outlining in broad terms possible future areas of reform intended to enhance the right of states to regulate, improve the establishment and functioning of the ISDS system and develop an appellate mechanism system (Commission (2015c)).

## 5.4 Investment Protection Chapters in EU DCFTAs

### 5.4.1 Scope

#### *5.4.1.1 Concept of 'investment'*

In general, modern BITs have embraced a broad asset-based definition of the concept of investment, which covers any tangible or intangible asset owned by an investor in a host state (Ranjan (2008), p. 218). This is also the approach that has been followed by the EU in both the EU–Singapore FTA and the CETA, where investment is defined as 'every kind of asset that an investor owns or controls, directly or indirectly, that has the characteristics of an investment, which includes a certain duration and other characteristics such as the commitment of capital or other resources, the expectation of gain or profit or the assumption of risk'.[8] These EU DCFTAs also contain a non-exhaustive enumeration of 'forms of investment' that may come under the scope of the agreement, such as enterprises, equity participation, loans, debt securities on enterprises, interests arising from concessions, turnkey, construction, production or revenue-sharing counteracts, IP rights, and moveable property.[9]

The first thing to point out is that the language used in these agreements is almost entirely based on that of the 2012 US Model BIT. Indeed, both the definition of the term 'investment' as well as the list of examples provided under the EU DCFTAs replicate almost verbatim what is found in the 2012 US Model BIT.[10] The US's approach to the concept of investment is expansive in that it contrasts to other Model BITs—most notably the Canadian Model FIPAs (Levesque and Newcombe (2013), p. 69), as there is no attempt to limit the scope of the agreement to those assets that are expressly listed therein. The upshot is that, with respect to the EU DCFTAs, arbitration tribunals will be free to determine what constitutes an investment regardless of the form of the investment concerned. The only relevant considerations in a tribunal's assessment will be whether the asset is 'owned or controlled directly or indirectly by an investor' and 'has the characteristics of an investment'. The reference to indirectly controlled investments means that an investor will be covered by the agreement even if the asset is controlled via a subsidiary incorporated in a third party country. As for the 'characteristics of an investment', the EU DCFTAs provide some guidance by specifying that these include characteristics such as a 'commitment of capital or other resources, the expectation of gain or profit or the assumption of risk'.[11] The aim of this approach is to ensure that only investments that make a substantial contribution to the economy of the host state will be covered by the agreement. However, this definition of an investment arguably remains overly broad because, in addition to being

[8] Article X.3 Chapter 10 CETA; Article 9.1 EU–Singapore FTA.
[9] Ibid.
[10] Article 1 2012 US Model BIT.
[11] Article X.3 Chapter 10 CETA; Article 9.1 EU–Singapore FTA.

non-cumulative, the listed characteristics are not exhaustive. This means that it would perfectly be possible for an arbitration tribunal to determine that an asset presents the 'characteristics of an investment' on the basis of a sole criterion not identified in the agreement (Van Duzer, Simons, and Mayeda (2013), p. 52).

One area in which the CETA and the EU–Singapore FTA differ is that the former only covers investments made in accordance with the applicable laws in the host state at the time of the investment. This 'in accordance with host state law' formula is a standard feature of most modern BITs and is intended to ensure that only those investments that are legal benefit from investment protection provisions. There is no similar clause in the EU–Singapore FTA, although the absence of such clause is mitigated by the fact that the requirement for a protected investment to be made in accordance with the law is recognized a general principle of international investment law (Krajewski (2014), p. 9; Moloo and Khachaturian (2010), p. 1475).

#### *5.4.1.2 Concept of 'investor'*

With regard to the question of *who* can invoke investment protection provisions under the EU DCFTAs, these agreements follow the general practice in international investment law of defining the concept of investor as encompassing both natural persons and enterprises of a party. The criteria generally used to determine what constitutes an enterprise (or a 'corporation') of a party to an IIA are the incorporation and/or the registered seat of the business (Dolzer (2008), p. 49). In other words, the mere fact that a company is constituted under the laws of a party to an IIA allows it to fall under the definition of an investor covered by the agreement. This broad definition of 'investors' led to the problematic practice of 'treaty-shopping' where corporations with no substantial connection to a party establish shell companies (or mailbox companies) in the territory of one of the parties for the sole purpose of challenging measures adopted by another party to an agreement.[12]

The issue of treaty shopping is addressed in the CETA and the EU–Singapore FTA by requiring enterprises to satisfy various cumulative conditions in order to benefit from the investment protection provisions. First, the agreements set out the traditional incorporation test by providing that the term 'enterprise' or 'juridical person' covers 'any entity duly constituted or otherwise under applicable law'.[13] This applies to any legal person whether 'for profit or otherwise, and whether privately-owned or controlled or governmentally owned or controlled'.[14] However, in order to fall under the scope of the agreement, an enterprise (or juridical person) must also demonstrate the existence of an additional connecting factor with the home state. Under the CETA, an enterprise constituted under the laws of a party will only fall under the scope of the agreement if: (a) it has

[12] *Saluka v Czech Republic*, Partial Award, 17 March 2006, para 240.

[13] Article X.3 Chapter 10 CETA; Article 9.1(4) EU–Singapore FTA.

[14] Ibid.

'substantial business activities in the territory of that party'; or (b) is 'owned directly or indirectly or controlled by an natural person of a party or an enterprise mentioned under (a)'.[15] Therefore, an enterprise must satisfy two cumulative conditions under the CETA: it must be incorporated under the laws of the home state and have substantial business activities in that home state or be controlled by a natural person who is a national of a party. The regime under the EU–Singapore FTA is more complex. A 'juridical person' should have a registered office, central administration (that is, the head office where ultimate decision making takes place), or principal place of business in the territory of one of the parties.[16] Such language is taken directly from Article 54 TFEU, which grants companies or firms having their registered office, central administration, or principal place of business in a EU Member State the right to be treated on a non-discriminatory basis. However, in the event that the investor does not have its principal place of residence in the home state, it must demonstrate that it is engaged in 'substantive business operations' in the home state. In this way, the EU–Singapore FTA establishes a distinction between two types of foreign investors. First, legal persons that are either incorporated or have their central administration in the territory of one of the parties must also show that they have 'substantive business operations' in that party. On the other hand, even where a legal person is neither established nor has its central administration in the territory of one of the parties, that legal person can invoke investment protection rights under the EU–Singapore FTA if it has its 'principal place of business' in either Singapore or in the EU. Therefore, as in the CETA, the EU–Singapore FTA grants foreign investor status to legal persons that are incorporated and have substantial business activities in the territory of a party, but, unlike the CETA, such status is not extended to legal persons controlled by nationals of a party. Moreover, the EU–Singapore FTA also grants foreign investor status to legal persons on the sole basis that they have their 'principal place of business in the territory' of a party.[17]

Despite such variations, the additional links requirements included in both EU DCFTAs can be hailed as positive and welcome developments that will bar mailbox companies from invoking investment protection rights under the agreements (Bernasconi-Osterwalder (2014), p. 8). However, the operation of these criteria could prove problematic, as the concept of 'substantive business operations' is not clearly spelled out in the agreements. In the context of international investment law, the concept of 'substantive business operations' appears to be most closely related to the 'substantive business activities' term found in the denial of benefits clause in some of the US's BITs (Thorne and Doucleff (2010), p. 10). Although the US BITs do not define the term, the US Executive Office has stated that a legal person would be deemed to have its substantive business operations in the territory of a party if it maintains its 'central administration or principal place of business in the territory or has a real or continuous link' with the party (Ibid).

[15] Article 10.3 Chapter 10 CETA.

[16] Article 9.1(4) EU–Singapore FTA.

[17] Ibid.

This definition indicates that the test of substantive business operations/activities is satisfied, inter alia, when a legal person is shown to have its 'central administration' located within the territory of a party. This would be problematic from the perspective of the EU–Singapore FTA, as the agreement provides that a legal person having its central administration in the EU or Singapore must, *in addition*, demonstrate that it engages of substantive business operations in those territories. One must assume, therefore, that in the EU DCFTAs the concept of substantive business operations is wholly distinct from that of the central administration requirement. In fact, the concept of 'substantive business operations' seems to have been borrowed directly from Article XXVIII GATS defining juridical persons of a WTO Member (Hoffmeister and Alexandru (2014), p. 385). Although the GATS does not define 'substantive business operations', the EU–Singapore FTA attempts to provide some clarity on the matter as it contains a footnote specifying that the EU equates 'substantive business operation' to the EU law concept of 'effective and continuous link with the economy of a Member State'.[18] Although this concept is also broad, the existence of an effective link is typically derived from 'the amount of gross business done within the EU or by the permanent nature of the investments in the EU' (Xanthaki (2001), p. 4) and the continuity of the link from evidence of a 'history of commerce or production in one of the Member States' (Ibid). This clarification is limited as it denotes the EU's understanding of the concept, rather than an agreed-upon definition by the parties to the agreement. In practice, as the EU acknowledges in the EU–Singapore FTA, this means that the EU reserves the right to only extend investor protection rights to those persons that it considers to have engaged in substantive business operations in Singapore.

## 5.4.2 Non-discrimination

IIAs generally include non-discrimination requirements in the form of national treatment and MFN obligations. The language used in non-discrimination provisions tends to be homogenous across IIAs (Dolzer and Schreuer (2008), p. 179). The national treatment obligation typically requires each party to accord investors of the other party treatment no less favourable than that accorded to its own investors, whilst the MFN provisions state that parties must accord investors of the other party treatment no less favourable than that accorded in like circumstances to investors of a non-party. Most IIAs only apply such obligations to post-entry situations (Newcombe and Pradelli (2009), p. 158)—that is, the right of investors not to be discriminated against on the grounds of nationality only arises once the investor is lawfully established in the host state. Historically, BITs entered into by EU Member States have tended to conform with the norm by applying the non-discrimination obligations exclusively to post-entry situations (Dolzer and Schreuer (2008), p. 81). This contrast with other BITs, such as those concluded by

[18] Footnote 5 Investment Protection Chapter EU–Singapore FTA.

the US or Canada, which apply national treatment and MFN standards to both pre-entry and post-entry situations (Ibid). Another point of difference between European BITs and their US and Canadian counterparts relates to the fact that the former generally do not provide any clarification concerning the basis of comparison when applying national treatment. Whilst the US and Canadian BITs specify that the non-discrimination obligations only apply with respect to 'like situations' or 'like circumstances', Member State BITs provide for 'unqualified' national treatment and MFN clauses (Hoffmeister and Alexandru (2014), p. 385), meaning that there is no express guidance as to how to assess whether foreign and domestic investors are in comparable situations for arbitral tribunals. However, the absence of such qualification is not generally considered to be problematic to the extent that discrimination analyses on the grounds of nationality inherently require comparative assessments of investments and investors that are in similar or like situations (Newcombe and Paradell (2009), p. 161).

Currently, the EU's practice with respect to non-discrimination provisions included in its EU DCFTAs indicates that the EU intends to move away from the Member State approach and toward the Canadian Model FIPAs and US Model BITs by including obligations relating to both pre-entry and post-entry situations. In the EU–Singapore FTA, there is no MFN obligation, but national treatment in pre-entry situations is regulated under the establishment provisions of the Services chapter,[19] whilst post-entry situations are regulated in the Investment chapter.[20] The CETA follows the template set by Canadian FIPAs by providing that the non-discrimination obligations apply to 'the establishment, acquisition, expansion, management, conduct, operation and sale or other disposition of investments'.[21] The CETA therefore requires non-discrimination at both the pre-entry and post-entry stage of investments. The CETA also provides for qualified non-discrimination requirements in that they clarify that they entail a comparative assessment of foreign and domestic investors who are determined to be in 'like circumstances'.[22]

With respect to the MFN clause, the EU has stated that it will ensure that its EU DCFTAs remove the uncertainty affecting modern BITs on the 'importation of standards' issue (TTIP Consultation Document (2014), p. 3). The question here is whether the MFN clause entitles investors covered by an IIA to claim substantive and procedural rights granted in other IIAs, and, as a result, amend the legal regime negotiated under the former agreement. The case law suggests that MFN clauses do entitle investors to claim rights provided under IIAs concluded with third parties, although in general it seems that the importation of standards only occurs where the IIAs involved are broadly similar and compatible and where the discrepancy in treatment relates to a minor detail (Dolzer and Schreuer (2008), p. 191). The CETA specifies that its MFN clause does not cover ISDS procedures and substantive obligations provided for under other IIAs and

[19] Article 8.11 EU–Singapore FTA. [20] Article 9.3 EU–Singapore FTA.
[21] Article X.6 and X.7 Chapter 10 CETA. [22] Ibid.

trade agreements.[23] Similarly, in the TTIP Consultation Document, the EU has confirmed that it intends to ensure that the MFN clauses in that agreement will not 'allow procedural or substantive procedural or substantive provisions to be imported from other agreements' (European Commission (2014c), p. 3).

### 5.4.3 Fair and equitable treatment

The requirement to ensure the FET of foreign investors is the most important substantive standard under international investment law (Newcombe and Paradell (2009), p. 257). It is protected under most IIAs and is the most invoked standard in international investment litigation (Dolzer and Schreuer (2008), p. 119). However, because the formulation of this rule is broad and can vary from one IIA to another, there remains significant uncertainty regarding what constitutes FET. It is broadly thought to include 'inter alia, denial of justice (understood both in procedural and substantive terms), lack of due process (in the administration of justice as well as other forms of governmental decision making such as administrative proceedings) [...] arbitrariness (including at least unfair, unjust or idiosyncratic conduct and possibly unreasonable conduct too) [and] the protection of legitimate expectations' (Ortino (2013), p. 163). FET standards can be viewed as a residual category of rights intended to ensure that those acts of host states which are not caught by the other rules and standards of IIAs are nevertheless prohibited if these are found to be incompatible with the object of IIAs (Dolzer (2014), p. 12). The vagueness and broad reach of the FET standard means that there are few factual circumstances relating to the treatment of foreign investors by host states that would fall outside of its scope.

By far the most controversial component of FET standards relates to the protection of the investor's legitimate expectations—that is, the requirement on the host state not to adopt measures that affect the basic expectations that were taken into account by the investors at the time when the decision to invest was made (Choudhury (2005), p. 308). As explained in the context of a NAFTA arbitral ruling, the concept of legitimate expectations relates to a 'situation where a [party's] conduct creates reasonable and justifiable expectations on the part of the investor (or investment) to act in reliance on such conduct'.[24] These legitimate expectations can be grounded in the status of the host state's legal order at the time when the investment was made, contractual arrangements between the foreign investor and the host state or unilateral representations made by the host state to the foreign investor (Sornarajah (2010), p. 354). The expectations based on the overall regulatory framework of the host state are particularly controversial, as they have in the past been construed by arbitral tribunals as entailing an obligation not to alter a legal environment in a manner that would frustrate such expectations.

[23] Article X.7(4) Chapter 10 CETA.

[24] *International Thunderbird Gaming Corporation v The United Mexican States*, Award, 26 January 2006, para. 147.

For example, in *Tecmed S.A. v Mexico*, a NAFTA arbitration tribunal proclaimed that host states must act 'in a consistent manner free from ambiguity and totally transparently in its relations with the foreign investor, so that it may know beforehand any and all rules or regulations that will govern its investments [...]'.[25] This has led to concerns that IIAs can lead to 'regulatory chill', where host states decide against regulating in order to achieve public interest objectives for fear that such laws will be challenged by foreign investors (Tienhaara (2011), pp. 606–27). Increasingly, however, arbitration tribunals have taken a more nuanced approach to legitimate expectations based on the host state's general regulatory framework where the sovereign right of countries to regulate will only be brought into question under limited circumstances (e.g. where a legislative amendment is made specifically to cause harm to the investor or where there is a specific commitment from the state not to amend its laws) and taking into account the level of development of the country involved (Potesta (2013), pp. 27–34). Similarly, recent BITs have sought to limit the scope of the FET standard by providing guidance regarding its content. The 2012 US Model BIT, for example, states that FET 'includes the obligation not to deny justice in criminal, civil, or administrative adjudicatory proceedings in accordance with the principle of due process embodied in the principal legal systems of the world'.[26] However, this illustrative list of examples of FET obligations does not remove the lack of clarity surrounding the concept and allows arbitration tribunals a considerable amount of discretion in determining the content of the FET standard (Caplan and Sharpe (2013), p. 784).

In the TTIP Consultation Paper the EU outlines its intention to go further than the 2012 US Model BIT by curtailing the concept of the FET standard. It states that the TTIP shall include a closed list of rights encompassed by the FET standard, and that the legitimate expectations standard will be limited to cases where 'clear, specific representations have been made by a [p]arty' in order to ensure that investors are not able to 'expect that the general regulatory and legal regime will not change' (European Commission (2014c), p. 6). This is also the approach followed in the EU–Singapore FTA and the CETA. Both agreements provide an exhaustive list of acts that constitute violations of the FET standard. The parties are required not to adopt measures that constitute denial of justice in criminal, civil, or administrative proceedings, fundamental breach of due process, including a fundamental breach of transparency, in judicial and administrative proceedings, manifest arbitrariness, targeted discrimination on manifestly wrongful grounds, such as gender, race, or religious belief, and abusive treatment of investors, such as coercion, duress, and harassment.[27]

With respect to the protection of legitimate expectations, both agreements attempt to limit the circumstances where such rights can be invoked by foreign investors. In the EU–Singapore FTA, a breach of the legitimate expectations of

[25] *Tecmed S.A. v United Mexican States*, ICSID Case No. ARB/AF/00/2 para 154, 29 May 2003.
[26] Article 5.2(a) US 2012 Model BIT.
[27] Article 9.4 EU–Singapore FTA; Article X.9 Chapter 10 CETA.

an investor must arise either 'from specific or unambiguous representations from a [p]arty so as to induce the investment and which are reasonably relied upon by the investor'[28] or 'any specific and clearly spelt out commitment in a contractual written obligation'.[29] In addition, in relation to contractual commitments, the EU–Singapore FTA provides that such commitments may not be frustrated by a party either deliberately or 'in a way which substantially alters the balance of rights and obligations in the contractual written obligation unless the [p]arty provides reasonable compensation to restore the investor or investment to a position which it would have been in had the frustration or undermining not occurred'.[30] The CETA provides that when assessing a violation of one of the enumerated rights covered by the FET standard under the agreement, a tribunal may take into account whether a party 'made a specific representation to an investor to induce a covered investment, that created a legitimate expectation, and upon which the investor relied in deciding to make or maintain the covered investment'.[31] Therefore, CETA limits the ability of foreign investors to rely on legitimate expectations by stating that these must be based on specific representations made by the host state.[32] As the EU explains in the TTIP Consultation Document, the clarifications included in these agreements with respect to the concept of legitimate expectations aim to make clear that the legitimate expectations of investors are not frustrated as a consequence of a change on the host state's regulatory framework (European Commission (2014c), p. 5). The requirement that the representations be 'specific' or 'unambiguous' should mean that investors cannot rely on broad and vague representations made by the host state concerning its regulatory framework but only on express and deliberate commitments or assurances made by host states to induce investments.[33] In reality, such language does no more than reflect the current case law on legitimate expectations, which provides that such expectations only be triggered in response to state conduct that is specific and unambiguous. As explained by Newcombe and Paradell, IIA case law accepts that 'encouraging remarks from government officials do not themselves give rise to legitimate expectations', that 'there must be an unambiguous affirmation or definitive, unambiguous and repeated assurance' and that 'the conduct must be targeted at a specific person or identifiable category of persons' (Newcombe and Paradell (2009), pp. 281–2). Under this approach a change in the legislation in a Member State will not constitute a violation of the FET standard unless a specific and unambiguous representation was made by that Member State that no such changes would occur. However, the language used in these agreements still leaves scope for expansive jurisprudential interpretations. First, the specification need not be written and can therefore take any form. Secondly, it has been argued that the term 'specific' does not necessarily 'exclude legislation addressing a particular type of investment and promising a specific treatment like

[28] Article 9(4)(e) EU–Singapore FTA.
[29] Article 9(5) EU–Singapore FTA.
[30] Article 9(4)(b) EU–Singapore FTA.
[31] Article 10(9)(4) Chapter 10 CETA.
[32] Article X.9 CETA, Investment Protection Chapter.
[33] *Glamis Gold, Ltd v United States*, UNCITRAL, Award, 8 June 2009, para 766.

e.g. tax reductions or another preferential treatment' (Kriebaum (2014), p. 478). Thirdly, in both the CETA and the EU–Singapore FTA, arbitral tribunals may rely on specifications made by the host state in general. As Krajewski points out, it would have been preferable for the agreements to only cover representations made by 'competent authorities' as it is not uncommon for organs of the state to make promises to attract foreign investors in areas where they have no competence to act (Krajewski (2014), pp. 12–13).

Another area where the EU restricts the scope of the concept of fair and equitable treatment is with regard to the requirement to ensure the full protection and security of foreign investors and their investments. This standard complements FET by requiring host states to 'adopt all reasonable measures to protect assets and property from threats or attacks which may particularly target foreigners or certain groups of foreigners'.[34] It is generally agreed that it entails an obligation on the part of host states to act proactively to protect the physical integrity of foreign investments against acts from private and state organs (e.g. demonstrators, employees, and army forces) (Schreuer (2010), p. 2). However, some arbitral awards have taken a more expansive approach to the concept, where it is not limited to instances of physical interferences but also extends to any measures, including legislative amendments and administrative acts, which would have the effect of depriving the security and protection of the investment[35] (Herdegen (2013), p. 405; Baetens (2013), pp. 43–5). This interpretation views the full security and protection standard as providing a guarantee of legal stability and security to foreign investors, an approach which has been criticized for blurring the line with the FET standard (Newcombe and Paradell (2009), p. 311). The EU removes any uncertainty regarding the scope of the full security and protection standard in its EU DCFTAs by specifying that the standard refers exclusively to the Party's obligations relating to physical security of investors and covered investments.[36]

### 5.4.4 Expropriation

Customary international law recognizes the right of sovereign states to expropriate the property of foreign investors. The right to expropriate is, however, not absolute and must comply with the following four cumulative requirements: (i) the expropriation must seek to achieve a public interest objective; (ii) the expropriation must not be discriminatory; (iii) the expropriation must comply with the principles of due process; and (iv) the investor must be compensated for the interference with its property (Dolzer and Schreuer (2008), p. 91; Fortier and Drymer (2004), p. 295). Whilst the conditions for the legality of an expropriation are well established, the concept of expropriation remains itself subject to much debate.

[34] *Saluka Investments BV v Czech Republic* (2006) IIC 211 para 484.

[35] *CME Czech Republic BV (The Netherlands) v The Czech Republic* (Final Award) para 163; *Compania de Aguas del Aconquija SA and Vivendi Universal v Argentina Republic* (2007) para 7.4.15.

[36] Article X.9 Chapter 10 CETA; Article 9.4(4) EU–Singapore FTA.

Historically, most expropriations took the form of direct expropriations—that is, 'compulsory transfers of titles to property to the state or a third party or the outright seizure of the property by the state' (Fortier and Drymer (2004), p. 297) such as nationalizations, requisitions, and confiscations. Direct expropriations are rare occurrences today and modern international investment law is increasingly concerned with tackling indirect appropriation—that is, government measures which, whilst leaving the foreign investor's title intact, has the effect of depriving the foreign investor of the use and benefit of the property (Newcombe and Paradell (2009), p. 322). Examples of indirect expropriation include government measures such as 'exorbitant or arbitrary taxation, deprivation of profits, measures substantially interfering with the management or control of a business enterprise, annulment or cancellation of property rights, contractual rights, debts or licenses [and] the total prohibition on the sale and occupancy of a property' (Ibid, pp. 327–8).

In practice, arbitration tribunals have relied on a variety of factors to assess whether a governmental measure amounts to indirect expropriation. These include the effect of the measure on the investment (whether the measure amounts to a substantial deprivation of the property), the effect of the measure on the legitimate expectations of the foreign investor, the duration of the measure and the purpose of the measure (whether the measure seeks to achieve a public interest). The manner in which these criteria are applied will vary significantly on a case-by-case basis and from one tribunal to another. For example, when assessing the effect of the measures, tribunals have established various levels of property deprivations, ranging from 'unreasonable interferences' on property to the 'radical deprivation of the economical uses and enjoyment of an investment' (Fortier and Drymer (2004), pp. 305–6; Newcombe and Paradell (2009), p. 345). Similarly, the required duration of the deprivation will fluctuate depending on the facts of the case (Newcombe and Paradell (2009), p. 345). Another issue that has proved problematic relates to the ongoing uncertainty as to the distinction between indirect expropriation and non-compensable regulatory measures. Two contrasting approaches are generally distinguished in international investment case law with respect to the assessment of expropriation claims centred on regulatory activity (Vadi (2013), p. 75). Some tribunals have opted for the 'sole effects test', where the focus is placed on the extent to which the regulation adversely impacts on the investment or the legitimate expectations of the investor. The 'sole effects test' significantly undermines regulatory autonomy in that it considers that any regulation that causes an economic loss will constitute expropriation, regardless of the public purpose pursued by the measure. The most notable illustration of this approach is the *Metalclad v Mexico* ruling, delivered in the context of the NAFTA, where it was found that the 'motivation or intention'[37] of regulation pursuing environmental protection goals was irrelevant for the determination of indirect expropriation. Other tribunals have opted for the 'police powers doctrine' or 'purpose test' whereby regulatory measures are not generally found to

[37] *Metalclad Corp v United Mexican States* ICSID Case No. ARB(AF)97/1, para 111.

constitute compensable expropriation where it is established that they pursue public interest objectives (Ibid). An example of such case law is the *Feldman v Mexico* ruling where a NAFTA Tribunal determined that a measure could not be considered expropriatory because the public interest objectives pursued by the measure outweighed the economic disruption incurred by the investor.[38] In fact, few arbitration tribunal rulings have equated general regulatory measures to indirect expropriation, and recent arbitral jurisprudence generally tends to eschew the 'sole effects test' in favour of a more balanced approach where the adverse economic effect of the regulatory measure will be weighed against the public purpose of the measure (Fortier and Drymer (2004), p. 326). Still, as a consequence of criticisms that followed cases such as *Metalclad v Mexico* there is now a growing trend in IIAs to include detailed guidance on the factors that have to be taken into account by arbitration tribunals to determine whether a governmental measure amounts to indirect expropriation (Newcombe and Paradell (2009), p. 224). The US 2012 Model BIT, for example, contains an annex specifying that the determination of an indirect expropriation requires a case-by-case, fact-based enquiry that considers, among other factors: (i) the economic impact of the government action, although the fact that an action or series of actions by a Party has an adverse effect on the economic value of an investment, standing alone, does not establish that an indirect expropriation has occurred; (ii) the extent to which the government action interferes with distinct, reasonable investment-backed expectations; and (iii) the character of the government action.[39] Although the list is non-exhaustive and therefore leaves arbitrators with a degree of discretion in terms of how to conduct a determination of compensable expropriation, it rules out the application of a sole effects theory by making it clear that the economic impact of the measure cannot, on its own, lead to a finding of indirect expropriation (Ibid, p. 335). The third criteria—the 'character of the measure'—is also crucial as it means that the fact that the challenged measure is a regulatory measure pursuing a public interest will be a significant factor weighing against the determination of indirect discrimination (Caplan and Sharpe (2013), p. 791). Finally, the 2012 US Model BIT also clarifies that '[e]xcept in rare circumstances, non-discriminatory regulatory actions by a Party that are designed and applied to protect legitimate public welfare objectives, such as public health, safety, and the environment, do not constitute indirect expropriations'.[40] This provision has the dual purpose of confirming that although there is no 'blanket exception for regulatory measures', regulatory measures are not, in the majority of cases, expropriatory (Caplan and Sharpe (2013), p. 791).[41]

The EU's current practice indicates that it is intent on following the US's approach by drafting expropriation provisions that reflect the rules of customary international law and provide guidance on the criteria that should be taken

[38] *Marvin Roy Feldman Karvpa v Mexico,* ICSID Case No. ARB(AF)99/1, para 111.
[39] Annex B Para 4(a) US 2012 Model BIT.
[40] Annex B Para 4(b) US 2012 Model BIT.
[41] *SD Myers, Inc v Canada* (Separate Opinion of Bryan Schwartz of 12 November 2000, para 207.

into account by arbitrators when examining indirect expropriation claims. Both the CETA and the EU–Singapore FTA include texts that replicate the list of factors mentioned in the US 2012 BIT Model that must be taken into account by arbitral tribunals in their assessment of whether an action constitutes indirect discrimination.[42] Both agreements add that 'except in the rare circumstance *where the impact of a measure or series of measures is so severe in light of its purpose that it appears manifestly excessive*, non-discriminatory measures [or series of measures] by a [p]arty that are designed and applied to protect legitimate public policy objectives such as public health, safety and the environment, do not constitute indirect expropriation'.[43] Such language is also taken from the 2012 US Model BIT, but by adding that the impact of the measure must be severe and manifestly excessive, the EU DCFTAs further emphasize that regulatory measures are not in principle expropriatory. The EU's objective is to make clear that regulations pursuing public interest objectives may not be equated to expropriatory measures simply because they cause some form of economic prejudice to the investor. The TTIP Consultation Paper reflects these concerns by stating that the TTIP will include interpretative guidance so as 'to avoid claims against legitimate public policy measures' (TTIP Consultation Document (2014), p. 6). It further echoes the content of the EU–Singapore FTA and the CETA by stating that the EU wants to clarify that 'non-discriminatory measures taken for legitimate public purposes, such as to protect health or the environment cannot be considered equivalent to an expropriation, unless they are manifestly excessive in light of their purpose' and that 'the simple fact that a measure has an impact on the economic value of the investment does not justify a claim that an indirect expropriation has occurred' (Ibid).

### 5.4.5 Right to regulate and exceptions

The EU has repeatedly stressed that the protection of investor rights enshrined in EU DCFTAs should not come at the expense of the legitimate right of Member States to regulate. As discussed in the previous subsections, this objective is pursued in the EU DCFTAs by limiting the scope of the investment protection provisions and by clarifying the scope of key substantive standards of protection. In addition to this, the EU has also included further safeguards to protect the regulatory flexibility of the parties in its EU DCFTAs. First, the preambular language of the CETA recognizes the right of the parties 'to regulate within their territories'[44] and to preserve 'their flexibility to achieve legitimate policy objectives, such as public health, safety, environment, public morals and the promotion and protection of cultural diversity'.[45] However, as such language is found in a recital rather than an operational provision, it may not be considered legally

[42] Para 2 Annex 9-A of Investment Protection Section EU–Singapore FTA; Article X.11(2) Chapter 10 CETA.

[43] Para 2 Annex 9-A of Investment Protection Section EU–Singapore FTA; Article X.11(3) Chapter 10 CETA. Emphasis added by the author.

[44] Recital 10 Preamble CETA. [45] Ibid.

binding and, at best, can only be used to colour the interpretation of the agreement (Spears (2010), pp. 1068–9). Secondly, unlike most IIAs, the EU DCFTAs do not include an umbrella clause—that is, a provision stipulating that host states must observe unilateral and contractual commitments undertaken with respect to foreign investors. In practice, such provisions have the effect of elevating the contractual rights of investors to the level of rights enshrined under the IIAs. By forgoing an umbrella clause, the EU DCFTAs significantly reduce the scope of claims that can be brought against host states (Krajewski (2014), p. 15).

Thirdly, under the CETA, the EU extends the flexibilities typically included in trade agreements to investment protection chapters. This means that the general exceptions provision of the CETA (which reproduces Article XX GATT) and the prudential carve-out included in the GATS Financial Services Annex apply to the investment protection chapter. In the TTIP Consultation Document, the EU correctly points out that the inclusion of a general exception provision is a significant departure from standard BIT practice (European Commission (2014c), p. 7). In fact, although it is true that the Canadian Model FIPA is the only other example of a Model BIT incorporating an Article XX GATT-type clause (Levesque and Newcombe (2013), p. 77), the practice is not uncommon in the context of FTAs containing investment protection obligations (Newcombe and Paradell (2009), pp. 501–2). The general exception provision in the CETA is limited in one respect; it only applies to the non-discriminatory treatment provisions included in the investment chapter. This means that Member States may not justify derogations to problematic standards such as FET and the prohibition on expropriation by reference to the agreement's general exceptions provisions. However, this limitation may prove to be a blessing in disguise as the incorporation of a general exceptions provision actually reduces the regulatory autonomy of the parties. First, because the public interest objectives that may be invoked to justify derogations to investment protection obligations are limited to the exhaustive list of objectives listed under Article XX and therefore do not encompass the myriad of legitimate regulatory goals pursued by countries (Krajewski (2014), p. 14). This contrasts with the significant body of international investment case law that has accepted that non-discriminatory treatment obligations can be derogated from by invoking legitimate public interests other than those listed under Article XX GATT (Newcombe (2013b), p. 279). Secondly, the very presence of a 'general exceptions' provision creates a 'perception' that states' right to regulate must be subordinate to the protection of investors' rights (Schepel et al. (2013), p. 8). In particular, the general exceptions provision would lead an arbitral tribunal to undertake an assessment of the extent to which a public measure is 'necessary' to achieve a legitimate public interest objective. Again, this contrasts with the softer approach adopted by most arbitral tribunals in international investment law cases where the focus is on whether there is 'a "reasonable" or "rational" nexus between the measure and the policy pursued' (DiMascio and Pauwelyn (2008), p. 76).

The issue of the 'right to regulate' attracted a great deal of attention and criticism during the TTIP public consultation process. A significant portion of the submissions argued that the approach adopted by the EU was insufficient and would seriously undermine the regulatory autonomy of Member States. In response, the EU has proposed the inclusion in the TTIP of an operational provision (as opposed to preambular language) recognizing the right of Member States to adopt 'measures to achieve legitimate public policy objectives, on the basis of the level of protection that they deem appropriate' (European Commission (2014c), p. 16). How this provision will be applied in practice is not specified. At the very least, one can assume that the proposed language would go some way to ensuring that when balancing competing public interest goals, arbitral tribunals do not give added weight to investment protection compared to non-economic goals. In this regard, some have suggested that a general provision on the right to regulate would have the effect of shifting the burden of proof that currently applies in the context of the general exceptions provision from the host state to the claimant (Schepel et al. (2013), p. 9).

### 5.4.6 Investor–state dispute settlement

#### *5.4.6.1 Recalibrating ISDS*

The inclusion of ISDS in the EU DCFTAs is arguably the most controversial aspect of the EU's deep trade agenda. No other feature of the EU's EU DCFTAs has attracted the same level of attention or caused the same degree of consternation from the media, politicians and civil society actors. The nature of these criticisms touches the very heart of the misgivings concerning the mixing of trade with regulatory issues: in essence, that trade agreements are being used to undermine regulatory autonomy and the democratic process. More specifically, the concern is that ISDS will lead to a barrage of claims being brought by private investors (mostly multinational corporations) against any regulatory initiative that would somehow adversely impact their economic interests and that, inevitably, the threat of litigation would come to represent an inhibiting factor in the policy-makers' decisions to adopt regulatory measures in the public interest. These views on ISDS also reflect wider concerns about the evolution of international investment law. It is the proliferation of arbitral awards that has led to the development of expansive and problematic interpretations of investment protection standards. As explained by Sornarajah, much of the excess associated with international investment law can be attributed to the role played by lawyers and arbitrators involved in ISDS in promoting neo-liberalist interpretations of treaties (Sornarajah (2011), p. 633). It is argued that these ideological inclinations have naturally led to arbitral awards that are skewed in favour of open market imperatives and tend to reduce the role of the state (Ibid). As a consequence, the push for the recalibration of IIAs also comprises attempts by states to reclaim ownership of international investment law by addressing the lack of transparency of arbitral proceedings, the perceived impartiality of arbitrators and the inconstancy of arbitral awards. Moreover, there are calls to completely remove ISDS clauses from IIAs (The Economist (2014)). This is particularly relevant with regard to IIAs concluded between developed countries, whose legal and judicial systems already offer high levels of investment protection. In such cases, the argument is made that allowing foreign investors to bypass domestic courts and submit claims directly before an ad hoc arbitration tribunal is not necessary. This is the approach followed by Australia in its BITs, as exemplified for example in the Australia–US BIT which provides that claims based on the provisions of said treaty should be directly applicable and invoked before domestic courts (Kleinheisterkamp and Poulsen (2014), p. 3).

In its EU DCFTAs, the EU has sought to maintain ISDS whilst addressing some of its systemic flaws. In other words, the EU's approach towards ISDS is one focused on recalibration rather than outright rejection. The systemic flaws associated with ISDS mechanisms typically concern the lack of transparency of the procedures, the profusion of claims designed to challenge measures adopted in the public interest, the need for safeguards to ensure the independence and impartiality of arbitrators appointed on an ad hoc basis, the inconsistency in the interpretation of investment protection provisions, and the unpredictability of arbitral decisions resulting from the absence of an appeals system. Recent ISDS reform proposals have thus tended to enhance transparency, limit investor access to ISDS, and, in some instances, establish appeals mechanisms. For example, in IIAs such as the US Model BITs and the Canadian Model FIPAs, increased transparency is achieved by requiring that all documents relating to the dispute be made public, by allowing the public to access hearings, and by allowing third parties to participate in proceedings through amicus curiae submissions.[46] The enhancement of the legitimacy of the procedure is pursued by establishing procedural safeguards against frivolous or spurious claims or including gate-keeping provisions that delineate the conditions under which claims to arbitration can be initiated (Fortier (2009), p. 540). Finally, in order to ensure consistency of interpretation of investment protection provisions, IIAs are increasingly including provisions that allow parties to issue interpretations of provisions that bind the arbitrators (OECD (2006), p. 178). Another solution to the issue of inconsistency that is increasingly gaining traction is the introduction of an appellate mechanism in the context of ISDS. Since 2004, the US has called for the establishment of a multilateral appellate body to provide consistency in the interpretation of international investment law and typically includes rendez-vous clauses in its BITs whereby parties commit to subjecting the agreement to the jurisdiction of such appellate body, should it ever come into being (Gagné and Morin (2006), p. 378). In line with the general trends outlined above, the EU has identified three priority areas where it believes that ISDS must be improved (European Commission (2014c), p. 10). First, the EU DCFTAs should ensure that ISDS mechanisms are fully transparent so as to increase the legitimacy and accountancy of proceedings. This, the EU argues can be achieved by allowing stakeholders to participate in proceedings and by ensuring that all documents are made publicly available (Ibid). Secondly, the EU DCFTAs aim to clearly define the parameters of the arbitrators' remit by setting out rules of conduct designed to ensure that they remain independent

[46] Article 29 2012 US Model BIT; Articles 38 and 39 Canadian Model FIPA.

and impartial (Ibid). Thirdly, in order to further promote the consistency of the interpretation of investment protection provisions, the EU proposes allowing the parties to issue binding interpretations on the issues of law resulting from the agreements and establishing appellate mechanism at the bilateral and multilateral levels (Ibid). The following three subsections examine some of the steps taken by the EU in its EU DCFTAs to achieve the aforementioned objectives.

### *5.4.6.2 Transparency*

As regards the objective of transparency, the EU has proposed the inclusion of the UNCITRAL Rules on Transparency in Treaty-based Investor–State Arbitration[47]—an instrument that regulates the openness of ISDS proceedings, disclosure requirements and participation of non-disputing parties—in its EU DCFTAs. In both the CETA and the EU–Singapore FTA, the EU has negotiated provisions that are based on the text of the UNCITRAL Transparency Rules. Both agreements replicate rules that apply to the disclosure of information to the public concerning ISDS disputes. As a result, these EU DCFTAs provide, for example, that documents, such as requests for consultations, pleadings, minutes and transcripts of hearings and orders of awards must be made available to the public.[48] Moreover, the arbitral tribunal may on its own initiative or upon the request from any person decide whether and how to make available exhibits other than documents.[49] Confidential information cannot be disclosed to the public and is defined as 'confidential business information, information protected against being made public in accordance with the agreement and information that is protected against being made public under the laws of the respondent or any law or rule determined to be applicable by the arbitral tribunal'.[50] Furthermore, in accordance with the UNCITRAL Transparency Rules both agreements provide that hearings for the presentation of evidence or oral arguments should be made public.[51] Finally, the agreements replicate the entire text of Article 4 of the UNCITRAL Rules on Transparency, which states that parties to the agreement may, after consultation, allow third persons to file written submissions.[52] Therefore, as the EU–Singapore FTA and the CETA currently stand, the parties have a discretionary power but not an obligation to allow amicus curiae to file submissions in the context of investment protection-related disputes. In the

[47] UNCITRAL Rules on Transparency in Treaty-based Investor–State Arbitration, 1 April 2014. Available at: http://www.uncitral.org/uncitral/uncitral_texts/arbitration/2014Transparency.html.

[48] Article 1.1 Annex 9-C Investment Protection Section EU–Singapore FTA; Article X.33 Chapter 10 CETA; Article 3.1 UNCITRAL Rules on Transparency.

[49] Article 1.2 Annex 9-C Investment Protection Section EU–Singapore FTA; Article X.33 Chapter 10 CETA; Article 3.3 UNCITRAL Rules on Transparency.

[50] Article 4.2 Annex 9-C Investment Protection Section EU–Singapore FTA.

[51] Article 2 Annex 9-C EU–Singapore FTA; Article X.3(5) Chapter 10 CETA.

[52] Paragraph 44 Annex I Investment Protection Chapter CETA; Article 3 Annex 9-C EU–Singapore FTA.

context of the TTIP Public Consultation, the absence of a legally binding obligation to permit amicus curiae submissions was criticized and has led the EU to propose the inclusion of a provision in the TTIP 'conferring a right to intervene to third parties with a direct and existing interest in the outcome of a dispute' (Concept Paper (2015), p. 8).

### *5.4.6.3 Impartiality of arbitrators*

In order to address the concerns regarding the lack of impartiality and, in particular, the perceived pro-market bias of arbitrators, the EU DCFTAs all include provisions which regulate the selection and conduct of arbitrators. In the TTIP Consultation Document, the EU recognized that such rules were at least in part justified by the need to ensure that arbitrators do not adopt rulings that are skewed in favour of the interest of foreign investors, but rather are able to balance investment protection and liberalization objectives with conflicting public interest objectives (European Commission (2014c), p. 10). Thus, the EU declares that ISDS arbitrators should preferably be 'retired judges who generally have experience in ruling issues that touch on both trade and investment and societal and public policy issues' (Ibid, p. 34). This approach is already reflected in the CETA and the EU–Singapore FTA, which follow the lead of the Canadian Model FIPAs, by providing that arbitrators must also be independent and 'not affiliated with or take instructions from a disputing party or the government of a [party] with regard to trade and investment matters'.[53] Moreover, arbitrators must have 'expertise in public international law, in particular international investment law'[54] and it is 'desirable for them to have expertise and experience in international trade law and the resolution of disputes arising under international investment and international trade agreements'. The requirement that arbitrators must have experience in public international law is noteworthy, in that it ensures that lawyers who practise solely in the areas of private commercial law may not be appointed as arbitrators.

The EU also wants to establish codes of conduct in its EU DCFTAs regulating conflicts of interest of arbitrators. The EU–Singapore FTA includes—in an Annex 15-B to the agreement—a 'Code of Conduct for Arbitrators and Mediators' which seems to replicate in large parts the code of conduct applicable to arbitrators sitting in NAFTA panels. In accordance with paragraph 2 of Annex 9-B, arbitrators are instructed to, inter alia, avoid 'impropriety and the appearance of impropriety',[55] 'direct and indirect conflicts of interests'[56] and to 'observe high standards of conduct so that the integrity and impartiality of the dispute settlement mechanism is preserved'.[57] The duty of impartiality is further spelled

[53] Article 6.26 CETA Investment Protection Chapter; Article 9.21(7) EU–Singapore FTA; Article 29(2) Model FIPA.

[54] Article 6.26 CETA Investment Protection Chapter; Article 9.21(6) EU–Singapore FTA; Article 29(2) Model FIPA.

[55] Para 2 Annex 15-B EU–Singapore FTA. [56] Ibid. [57] Ibid.

out under paragraph 10 of Annex 9-B which provides that an arbitrator must 'avoid creating an appearance of bias or impropriety and shall not be influenced by self-interest, outside pressure, political considerations, public clamour, loyalty to a disputing party or a non-disputing party or fear of criticism'.[58] By following the NAFTA's lead, the EU–Singapore FTA sets out broad principles of ethical behaviour which must be followed by arbitrators and can be used by the parties to challenge the appointment of arbitrators (see Gibson (2012), pp. 1201–2). The approach followed in the CETA is far more ambitious as it requires arbitrators to comply with International Bar Association Guidelines on Conflicts of Interest in International Arbitration and allows the 'Committee on Services' established by the agreement to negotiate a code of conduct that will either replace or complement applicable rules pertaining to disclosure obligations, independence and impartiality of arbitrators, and confidentiality.[59] The incorporation of IBA Guidelines on conflict of interest is significant because it goes beyond the generalities of the EU–Singapore FTA's code of conduct and provides detailed guidance for arbitrators and parties to determine where the impartiality or independence of the former may be jeopardized.

#### 5.4.6.4 *Consistency and legitimacy of arbitral awards*

The fact that disputes relating to IIAs can be brought before different tribunals composed of different arbitrators presents the possibility of inconsistent, and sometimes conflicting, interpretations of similar or identical standards (Frank (2005); Steger (2013), p. 250). Such inconsistency is often identified as an important threat to the legitimacy of the international investment law system, and the EU has been keen to stress its desire to address this particular flaw. In order to avoid rulings that do not conform to the parties' understandings of the meaning of investment protection provisions and to remove confusion concerning the interpretation of such provisions, the CETA and the EU–Singapore FTA provide that the parties can provide interpretations of the investment protection provisions that will be binding on arbitral tribunals established under the agreement. In accordance with both agreements, if serious concerns arise regarding matters of interpretation that may affect investment, the services committees established by the agreements may recommend that the trade committees of the respective agreements adopt interpretations.[60]

In order to further the consistency and predictability of arbitral awards, the EU has proposed limiting the number of arbitrators that may be used in the context of ISDS proceedings by establishing a closed roster of arbitrators. By ensuring that only a small group of persons can be called upon to deliver arbitral awards, the EU hopes to not only promote the development of a consistent body of jurisprudence, but also reduce the chance of conflicts of interest arising in the context of ISDS

[58] Para 10 Annex 15-B EU–Singapore FTA. [59] Article X.25 Chapter 10 CETA.
[60] Article X.27 CETA Investment Protection Chapter; Article 9.22 EU–Singapore FTA.

proceedings. However, the roster system currently established under the CETA and the EU–Singapore FTA has certain limitations. Arbitral tribunals under these two agreements must be composed of three arbitrators: one appointed by each disputing party, and the presiding arbitrator by agreement between the disputing parties.[61] It is only where the parties fail to agree on a presiding arbitrator (or a sole arbitrator) within 90 days from the submission of the claim that a disputing party may request the Secretary General of the ICSID to appoint an arbitrator from the roster.[62] In other words, the roster only comes into play if the parties cannot agree on the appointment of a presiding arbitrator and, even then, there is no legally binding obligation on the parties to resort to the roster. However, with respect to the TTIP, the EU has recently proposed going further by requiring that all arbitrators be sourced from a pre-established roster (European Commission (2015c), p. 7). The EU has also repeatedly stated the case for the creation of an appellate mechanism in its EU DCFTAs. As discussed, the US Model BITs have included rendez-vous clauses whereby the parties agree to sign up to any future multilateral agreement establishing an appellate mechanism in the area of international investment law. The CETA and the EU–Singapore FTA differ slightly in that whilst they also include rendez-vous clauses, these relate specifically to the possibility of including an appellate mechanism within the agreements themselves.[63] In both cases, however, there is still no legally binding commitment to establish an appellate mechanism, only to carry out consultations exploring the feasibility and parameters of any such mechanism. Recently, the EU has proposed going further. In the Concept Paper, the Commission signalled the EU's intent to include an appellate mechanism for ISDS in the TTIP, the remit of which would be focused on the review of errors of law and manifest errors, and would follow the institutional structure of the WTO Appellate Body (European Commission (2015c)). In addition to the objective of ensuring consistency of arbitral awards issued by any TTIP ISDS mechanism, DG Trade Commissioner Cecilia Malmström has asserted that the ultimate goal of any appellate mechanism included in the TTIP with respect to ISDS would be to set a template for a future multilateral permanent appellate court (Malmström (2015), p. 3). However, recent reports suggest that the US consider that this particular reform of the ISDS system is unnecessary and has rejected the EU's proposals for the establishment of an appellate mechanism within the TTIP (EUobserver (2015)).

## 5.5 Conclusion

Thus far, the EU has decided against developing an EU Model BIT text, instead favouring a flexible approach to negotiating investment protection issues. The

[61] Article X.25(1) CETA Investment Protection Chapter; Article 9.21(1) EU–Singapore FTA.
[62] Article X.25(2) CETA Investment Protection Chapter; Article 9.21(2) EU–Singapore FTA.
[63] Article 9.3 EU–Singapore FTA; Article X.42 Chapter 10 CETA.

content of the investment chapters included in the EU DCFTAs varies depending on the identity of the contracting party and the political environment surrounding the negotiations. However, it is clear, at this early stage, that such investment chapters broadly follow a similar template and, in particular, that they can all be categorized under the new generation of 're-calibrated' IIAs which attempt to rectify the perceived pro-investor bias associated with past IIAs and international investment case law. Evidence of this recalibration can be seen everywhere in the EU DCFTAs, from the limiting of the scope of the chapter, the circumscription of substantive standards (e.g. FET, full security and protection, and expropriation), the omission of problematic obligations typically included in IIAs (e.g. umbrella clause), and the development of new procedural safeguards in the context of the ISDS mechanism. These features all contribute, in different ways, to the overall objective of ensuring that the protection of investor rights do not come at the expense of the right of sovereign states to regulate in the public interest. It is also clear that in drafting the investment chapters of the EU DCFTAs, the EU has been hugely influenced by existing and predominant recalibrated Model BITs. Much of the language relating to substantive standards of treatment in the EU DCFTAs is taken directly from the text of the 2012 US Model BIT and, to a lesser extent, the Canadian Model FIPA. Where the EU departs from such models is with respect to the scope of application of the investment protection chapters and the procedural aspects, which have been reformed significantly in light of the colossal opposition to ISDS within the EU.

Therefore, in the EU DCFTAs, the EU has genuinely sought to pursue a more balanced approach to the regulation of investment protection. Furthermore, the EU has also shown itself to be receptive to domestic concerns regarding the content of the investment protection chapter, particularly in the context of the TTIP where, faced with an avalanche of criticism, it has proposed reforms to existing negotiating drafts. However, this chapter has shown that the current investment provisions in the EU DCFTAs still present a number of problematic features. For example, although there is an attempt to clarify what constitutes an investment or legitimate expectations under the agreements, the concepts remain vague and open to expansive interpretations. Also, it was explained how, by adding a GATT-type general exceptions provision that applies to non-discrimination obligations, the EU may unwittingly further reduce the ability of Member States to pursue public interest objectives. And whilst the EU has stressed its desire to reform the ISDS system, the existing agreements do not include any legally binding obligations to establish such mechanisms. At a fundamental level, it should also be questioned whether the EU's drive to recalibrate international investment law ultimately misses the point. Try as the EU may to refine substantive standards of investment protection and assert the right of states to regulate, as long as IIAs allow for the judicial review of non-discriminatory domestic measures, there will always be a danger that arbitrators will strike down regulatory measures pursuing legitimate purposes. This also means that there is always a possibility that states will be discouraged from regulating where they fear foreign investor challenges. Similarly, as long as the EU continues to endorse a system which accords privileged and direct judicial access to a specific category of actors (foreign investors), there will always be questions surrounding the legitimacy of rulings issued in relation to investment protection chapters. These concerns are all the more salient in relation to developed country IIAs. Strong investment protection and ISDS clauses may be justified in the context of IIAs with states where the rule of law is lacking, but it is harder to argue their necessity when the countries involved have well-functioning legal and judicial systems. As the growing opposition to the investment component of the TTIP illustrates, recalibration may not be enough for the EU to sell its investment protection chapters simply because it is the very existence and relevance of the international investment law system that is being challenged.

# 6

# Intellectual Property

## 6.1 Introduction

The EU, spurred on by the industry lobby, was one of the main proponents of TRIPS—an agreement which is generally considered to have protected the economic interests of developed countries to the detriment of those of developing countries (Deere (2009), p. 391). In the post-TRIPS era, this North–South divide has continued, with the former requesting an expansion of existing levels of IP protection and the latter the strengthening of flexibilities within TRIPS, allowing them to pursue national policy objectives. Another topical concern surrounding current demands for higher standards of IP protection and enforcement relates to the possibility that the implementation of such standards may lead to the violation of human rights (Yu (2012), p. 1045).

Until recently, the EU was said to have adopted a 'generalist' approach to the regulation of intellectual property (IP) rights protection in its FTAs, where it required contracting parties to ratify existing IP-related international agreements (Perez Pugatch (2007), pp. 7–12). This contrasted with the FTAs concluded by the US, which are littered with provisions requiring the implementation of extensive domestic regulatory reforms that mimic US legislation. The EU's approach, whilst in line with its stated intention of focusing on achieving multilateral consensus in international trade regulation, presented certain drawbacks. The EU's immediate economic interests would undoubtedly have been better secured by requiring trading partners to implement IP protection provisions equivalent to those existing within the EU. Moreover, the reliance on references to international agreements also meant that the IP protection secured in the EU's trade agreements was not as comprehensive as those entered into by the US, with key issues such as the civil and criminal enforcement of IP rights often completely absent. However, the Global Europe strategy signals the intent to switch from the hitherto generalist approach to the more prescriptive approach adopted in the US FTAs, as it encourages the negotiation of stronger IP provisions inspired by existing EU laws. The purpose of this chapter is to assess the EU's efforts to promote, through its FTAs, the adoption of high standards of IP protection and enforcement by third countries in line with the EU's own regulatory model. It finds that although the EU uses its EU DCFTAs to require signatories to comply with existing international agreements regulating IP (e.g. patents and copyrights), it is by no means averse to imposing EU standards of IP protection in areas where current international rules are deemed unsatisfactory. The chapter also examines how the divisive issues that are currently hindering the progress of negotiations at WTO level, including the demands from developing and developed country WTO Members to maintain a degree of autonomy in the area of IP regulation, as well as the need to balance IP protection with human rights protection, are being dealt with in recent EU FTAs.[1] To undertake such analyses, the chapter focuses on the two IP areas in which the EU's external trade policy has been the most active: the protection of geographical indications and the enhancement of existing international standards for the enforcement of IPRs. An examination of both issues is desirable not only because the EU has adopted a policy of exporting key aspects of its own internal legislation in its EU DCFTAs, but also because they illustrate very different challenges faced in the deep trade agenda. Whereas higher standards of IP rights enforcement is an issue that pits developed countries against developing countries and raises questions regarding the protection of fundamental human rights, that of the protection of geographical indications does not fit with the classic North–South divide that we have come to expect in the context of multilateral trade negotiations (Das (2010), p. 448). The major opponents to further negotiations on geographical indications in the WTO are developed countries such as the US and Australia. Here, the divergence between negotiators does not result from the varying levels of economic development but rather from historical differences that have led to the existence of contrasting regulatory ideologies.

The chapter is divided into three sections. Section 6.2 provides an overview of IP regulation in the context of the WTO and covers some of the major issues inhibiting further reform at this level, particularly the refusal of developing countries to acquiesce to further removal of flexibilities incorporated within TRIPS. Section 6.3 describes how the EU has reacted to the current stalemate and describes the legal tools and mechanisms that are currently being used to promote this policy. Sections 6.4 and 6.5 address, respectively, the EU's regulation of geographical indications and the enforcement of IP rights in its EU DCFTAs.

## 6.2 Global IP Regulation, TRIPS, and the Struggle for Policy Space

The main purpose of TRIPS is to propagate the adoption of minimum standards of IP protection and enforcement worldwide. The agreement contains three major sets of rules, the first relating to minimum standards of protection for a diverse range of IP rights, including copyright and related rights, trademarks, geographical indications, industrial designs, and patents. The second set of rules comprises a number of horizontal rules on the enforcement of IP rights, and the third set subjects violations of WTO Member obligations under TRIPS to the WTO dispute settlement procedure. Although the MFN and national treatment

[1] Article 207(1) TFEU.

principles are included in TRIPS, the innovative element of the agreement lies not in the fact that it curtails WTO Members' ability to adopt discriminatory measures but rather the fact that it requires them to alter their domestic regulatory framework where necessary, in order to ensure that the minimum standards of protection and enforcement are met (Otto and Wager (1994), p. 391; Deere (2009), p. 113). The EU counted amongst the main proponents of the agreement, all of which were net exporters of IP rights seeking to expand the regulatory protection of such rights in order to stop other nations from 'free riding' by procuring products that were developed as a result of expensive and protracted research and development processes and to combat the increasing manufacture of counterfeited and pirated products in developing countries (Gervais (2007), pp. 53–4; Reichman (2007), p. 923). For developing countries, predominantly consumers of IP rights, the benefits from TRIPS were harder to identify. Monopoly rights, typically associated with the granting of an IP right, enable the holders of such rights to drive up prices and, consequently, restrict public access to technologies (Lindstrom (2010), p. 992). This is particularly problematic where access to essential medicines is at stake (Scherer and Watal (2001), p. 913; Abbott (2002), p. 15). High levels of IP protection can also hinder economic development insofar as they impede the transfer of technologies (Lindstrom (2010), p. 922). For these reasons, the developing world had little interest in signing TRIPS, but eventually did so in exchange for commitments on increased market access in areas such as textiles, where their immediate economic interests lay (Yu (2006), p. 369; Young and Peterson (2006), p. 802).

If one issue demonstrates the North–South divide that has hampered the progress of negotiations at WTO level, it is that of IP. Despite assurances that increased levels of IP rights protection in developing nations resulting from the implementation of TRIPS would foster economic development by encouraging foreign direct investment, the agreement has been criticized for being heavily stacked in favour of developed countries (Deere (2008), pp. 113–42). The agreement aims to ensure the protection of intellectual property which is, for the most part, produced by developed countries. Therefore, while TRIPS generates revenues for the latter, it represents a cost for developing nations who have to pay to access technologies developed elsewhere (Sell (2003), p. 9; Das (2005), p. 33). There are, however, so-called 'flexibilities' included in TRIPS that leave some 'wiggle room' for WTO members to pursue national policy interests. For example, Article 1.1 TRIPS allows WTO Members to determine the appropriate manner in which to ensure the minimum standards of IP protection mandated by the agreement. Articles 7 and 8 TRIPS both identify a number of policy objectives which, in accordance with the WTO jurisprudence,[2] should guide WTO Members when interpreting and implementing the agreement (e.g. promotion of technological innovation, the transfer and dissemination of technology, and the balancing of interests of producers and users of technological knowledge, protection of

[2] Panel Report, *Canada—Patent Protection of Pharmaceutical Products*, WT/DS114/R, 2000, adopted 7 April 2000.

public health, etc.) (Yu (2009), pp. 797–1046). Likewise, there are a number of provisions—such as Article 41.2 TRIPS, according to which IP enforcement provisions must be fair and equitable—which afford WTO Members a certain margin of discretion when determining how best to implement TRIPS, as well as TRIPS provisions that allow WTO Members to establish exceptions to specific IP rights under certain restrictive circumstances.[3]

It bears noting, however, that there is no equivalent under TRIPS to the general exceptions under Article XX GATT and Article XIV GATS which would allow WTO Members to adopt measures which would otherwise be deemed illegal in order to pursue certain non-trade objectives. Therefore, under TRIPS, developing countries are left with relatively few options to set aside the agreement in order to pursue critical development objectives. The lack of a margin of discretion afforded to WTO Members when pursuing national policy objectives has become a highly contentious issue, particularly in the context of public health, an area where developing counties are keen to maintain full regulatory autonomy. The clash between TRIPS and public health is an issue that has received much attention and that has come to symbolize the tensions that have led to the paralysis in the Doha Round negotiations. Following the entry into force of TRIPS and, more specifically, the end of the transitional period for the implementation of patent protection in developing countries in 2005,[4] developing countries continued the practice of issuing compulsory licences allowing the copying of patented pharmaceutical products in order to produce low-cost generic drugs. The right of WTO Members to issue such compulsory licences would be asserted in the Doha WTO Ministerial Declaration on the TRIPS Agreement and Public Health (Public Health Declaration) which recognized that TRIPS 'should be interpreted and implemented in a manner supportive of WTO members' right to protect public health and, in particular, to promote access to medicines for all' (WTO (2011e)) and listed a number of flexibilities including, inter alia, that TRIPS should be read in light of 'the object and purpose of the Agreement as expressed, in particular, in its objectives and principles' and the 'right to grant compulsory licences and the freedom to determine the grounds upon which such licences are granted'. The Public Health Declaration would thereafter be complemented by an amendment of TRIPS in the form of a new Article 31bis TRIPS which allows generic drugs produced under compulsory licences to be exported to countries lacking production capacity (WTO (2005d))—but which is yet to take effect.[5] The debate concerning the conflict between IP protection

[3] Articles 13, 16, 26.2 and 30 TRIPS.

[4] Article 65.4 TRIPS. The deadline for the transitional period for LDCs has been extended to 1 July 2013 (Extension of the Transition period Under Article 66.1 for Least-Developed Country Members, Decision of the Council for TRIPS of 29 November 2005. See http://www.wto.org/english/news_e/pres05_e/pr424_e.htm).

[5] The EU accepted the Protocol [Council Decision of 19 November 2007 on the acceptance, on behalf of the European Community, of the Protocol amending the TRIPS Agreement, done at Geneva on 6 December 2005 (2007/768/EC)]. However, the amendment must be accepted by two-thirds of the WTO's Members before it can take effect.

and public health is but one example of the more fundamental issue of ascertaining the extent to which WTO Members can sacrifice IP protection in order to pursue other policy objectives. The issue becomes all the more relevant as negotiations shift from the multilateral setting of the WTO to the bilateral and regional settings of FTAs, where it is to be expected that major players such as the EU will use their superior bargaining power to further erode existing flexibilities.

## 6.3 EU External Trade Policy in IP

### 6.3.1 Plurality of IP rule-making venues

The EU is not particularly selective in the methods used to pursue the objectives of its external IP policy, envisaging both legislative and non-legislative initiatives (De Gucht (2011)). Non-legislative initiatives include the granting of technical and financial assistance to priority countries to support the establishment of fully operational IP rights protection and enforcement systems (Matthews and Munoz Tellez (2006), p. 629), and engagement in so-called 'IP dialogues' with certain countries in order to facilitate the exchange of information and share expertise on a variety of IP-related issues.[6] With regard to legislative initiatives, the EU's external policy does not exclude any existing or future bilateral or multilateral fora where the international regulation of IP is a topic of relevance. The Commission's 2005 Strategy for the Enforcement of Intellectual Property Rights in Third Countries (the 'Enforcement Strategy') (European Commission (2005b)), which sought to reduce the number of IPR violations in third countries states that the institutional structures created by 'multilateral and bilateral agreements (TRIPs Council, Association Councils, the World Intellectual Property Organization—WIPO, etc.) can be used to monitor and discuss legislation and enforcement problems from a very early stage' and further adds that they 'can act as fora to submit new initiatives or to act as "early warning" for arising problems, before there is a need to adopt stricter measures' (Ibid, p. 5). More generally, the IP Single Market Communication adds that '[t]he Commission will pursue its objective to enhance the respect of IPR standards at an international level through enhancing effective cooperation and engagement with third countries in international fora, in particular through its work in the context of WIPO, WTO and UPOV, aimed at improving protection and enforcement of IPR at global level' (European Commission (2011c), p. 20).

The intermittent use of bilateral, inter-regional and multilateral venues to further strengthen IP protection and enforcement is, of course, nothing new. The US—and to a lesser extent the EU—used the tactic in the lead-up to the signing of the TRIPS and a similar approach has been followed in the aftermath of the collapse of the Doha Development Round. This follows a global historical

[6] The EU is currently conducting IP dialogues with China, Russia, Ukraine, Thailand, and Turkey. See Commission website: http://ec.europa.eu/trade/creating-opportunities/trade-topics/intellectual-property/dialogues/.

trend towards forum-shifting in the context of external IP policy. Mercurio has noted in this regard that the recent push for the extension and enhancement of IP rights in bilateral agreements was but a manifestation of a 'never-ending cycle of multilateral standard setting which lead to increased standards via bilateralism/regionalism followed by consolidation in the form of more multilateralism' (Mercurio (2006), p. 235). It is what Drahos calls the 'global intellectual property ratchet' (Drahos (2003), p. 2). Developed countries use forum-shifting techniques to impose the desired standard for IP protection in the venue where they will encounter the least resistance. Typically, bilateral agreements offer the path of least resistance, since developed countries are able to use their higher bargaining power to impose the adoption of TRIPS-plus rules. When multilateral venues are not receptive to the strengthening or extension of levels of IP protection, bilateral agreements are used to ratchet up IP protection standards and tie the signatories of these agreements to the multilateral process. As we have seen, this strategy is currently being used in the EU DCFTAs.

### 6.3.2 The link between internal and external IP policy and law

Failure to force through higher standards of IP protection and enforcement at WTO level led to a renewed emphasis on signing bilateral and regional agreements that included TRIPS-plus provisions with a distinctly European flavour. One of the first examples of this policy shift can be found in the Enforcement Strategy, where the Commission acknowledges that the policy is a 'logical consequence' of recently enacted TRIPS-plus enforcement legislation at EU level. The assertion reflects an understanding that the EU's own legislation would not suffice to combat IP infringements at the border, since cross-border IP infringements do not only occur in the country of importation. Remedies and sanctions available under EU law are of little use when the violation occurs in third countries and the infringing goods were either consumed domestically or exported to third countries.

The link between internal market rules and external policy becomes manifest when perusing the recommended action points suggested by the Commission in order to address the problem. It proposes that the approach towards the negotiation of IP chapters within bilateral agreements be revisited to clarify and strengthen enforcement clauses by using the EU's own internal legislation as 'an important source of inspiration and a useful benchmark' (European Commission (2005b)). The narrative adopted in the Enforcement Strategy is that of the external projection of the EU's own internal market rules in the context of FTAs concluded with third countries, and the negotiation of IPR provisions replicating existing EU rules is not a policy that would be limited to the area of IP rights enforcement. Under the Global Europe strategy, the Commission has advocated the negotiation of stronger rules covering both the protection and enforcement of IP rights (European Commission (2006a)). The internal and external IP policies of the EU have become so interwoven that, in more recent times, even policy statements relating to specific internal market proposals discuss at length the issue of the external dimension of IP rights. In a Communication dated

24 May 2011 concerning the development of a single market for IP rights ('IP Single Market Communication'), the Commission stresses the need to 'put the spotlight on the international dimension of IP rights' and states that '[i]n negotiating FTAs, the IPR clauses should as far as possible offer identical levels of protection to that existing in the EU' (European Commission (2011c)).

How does this new approach to the EU's IP-related trade policy manifest itself in recently concluded EU DCFTAs? Until as recently as 2007, the EU had been said to have adopted a 'generalist' approach (Meier Pugatch (2007), pp. 7–12). IP provisions in EU FTAs would not oblige signatories to adopt specific standards of protection and enforcement but rather to sign up to existing international treaties (Ibid; Horn, Mavroidis, and Sapir (2009)). This contrasted with the 'nanny' approach pursued by the US whose FTAs contain detailed provisions intended to secure the adoption of TRIPS-plus commitments (Meier Pugatch (2007), pp. 7–12). The EU's policy statements described above seem to indicate a willingness from the EU to combine the 'generalist' approach with the US' prescriptive 'nanny'-like approach, cajoling its counterparts to adopt TRIPS-plus commitments replicating existing IPR standards within the EU. In general, it can be said that the EU DCFTAs concluded to date follow a similar path. They all contain comprehensive IP chapters covering a variety of areas: patents, trademarks, copyright and related rights, geographical indications, design rights, utility models, plant varieties, genetic resources, traditional knowledge and folklore, and the enforcement of IP rights.

The 'nanny' approach is most evident in the fields which hold a particular strategic interest for the EU, namely geographical indications and, as will be assessed later, the enforcement of IP property rights. Regardless of whether the EU's counterpart is a developed or a developing nation, the provisions relating to these areas in the EU DCFTAs are extensive and detailed and export to a large extent the EU's current regulatory framework. More often than not, the exact wording used in EU law is replicated in the provisions of these agreements, and in doing so secures a level of protection that is far higher than that currently provided under TRIPS. With respect to other IP rights addressed in these agreements, the picture is mixed. In certain areas, such as trademarks, the EU has retained a 'generalist' approach. The EU's trading partners are generally required to maintain a legal framework for the protection of trademarks and comply or accede to certain international agreements concerning the protection of trademarks such as the 1989 Protocol Relating to the Madrid Agreement Concerning the International Registration of Marks (Madrid Protocol),[7] the 1994 Trademark Law Treaty[8] and the Singapore Treaty on the Law of Trademarks.[9] Most such obligations

[7] Article 144.E CEPA; Article 202(b) Colombia–Peru FTA; Article 238(a) EU–CA FTA.

[8] Article 10.16 KOREU FTA; Article 202(3) Colombia–Peru FTA; Article 239(b) EU–CA FTA; Article 11.12 EU–Singapore FTA.

[9] Article 144.E CEPA; Article 10.16 KOREU FTA; Article 11.12 EU–Singapore FTA; Article 6 Chapter 22 CETA.

to ratify and/or comply with international agreements are best endeavour requirements, with the exceptions of the KOREU FTA and the Colombia–Peru FTA which establish binding obligations on the parties to accede to the 1994 Trademark Law Treaty[10] and the 1989 Madrid Protocol.[11] With regard to other IP rights, the EU has opted for a 'third way', through which the obligation to sign up to existing international agreements is complemented, where possible, with TRIPS-plus obligations inspired by EU law. Taking copyrights as an example, alongside provisions enjoining the parties to comply with certain international agreements (1881 Berne Convention for the Protection of Literary and Artistic Works, 1961 Rome Convention for the Protection of Performers, Producers of Phonograms and Broadcasting Organizations, 1996 WIPO Copyright Treaty and 1996 WIPO Performances and Phonograms Treaty),[12] there are also provisions on the duration of author's rights,[13] moral rights,[14] broadcasting organizations,[15] broadcasting and communication to the public,[16] protection of technological measures, and the protection of rights management information.[17] The same pattern is present in the sections relating to patents, which require some trading partners to accede to certain international agreements (e.g. 1970 Patent Cooperation Treaty and 1977 Budapest Treaty on the International Recognition of the Deposit of Micro-organisms for the Purposes of Patent Procedure)[18] and contain TRIPS-plus obligations on the extension of the duration of rights conferred by patent protection,[19] on the protection of test or other data related to the safety and efficacy of pharmaceutical products and chemical agricultural products,[20] and the protection of data relating to market authorization applications for plant protection products.[21] There has been a significant change in the EU's approach to negotiating IP provisions in FTAs. While the EU DCFTAs still require parties to sign up to and comply with existing IP-related multilateral agreements, there is also an increasing emphasis on the inclusion of specific obligations to strengthen IP rights standards beyond those currently existing in the framework of TRIPS. The level of protection secured under EU law is increasingly being used as the benchmark to which the EU's counterparts in its EU DCFTAs must aspire.

[10] Article 10.16 KOREU FTA.
[11] Article 202(2) Colombia–Peru FTA.
[12] Article 143.A(1) CEPA; Article 10.2 KOREU FTA; Article 215(2) Colombia–Peru FTA; Article 233 EU–CA FTA; Article 11.4 EU–Singapore FTA; Article 5.1 Chapter 22 CETA.
[13] Article 10.6 KOREU FTA; Article 218 Colombia–Peru FTA.
[14] Article 216 Colombia–Peru FTA.
[15] Article 10.7 KOREU FTA.
[16] Article 10.9 KOREU FTA; Article 220 Colombia–Peru FTA; Article 5.2 Chapter 22 CETA.
[17] Articles 10.12 and 10.13 KOREU FTA; Article 11.9–10 EU–Singapore FTA; Article 5.3 Chapter 22 CETA.
[18] Article 147.A(2) CEPA; Article 230(1) Colombia–Peru FTA; Article 258(1) EU–CA FTA.
[19] Article 10.35 KOREU FTA; Article 11.31 EU–Singapore FTA; Article 9.2 Chapter 22 CETA.
[20] Article 10.36 and 10.37 KOREU FTA; Article 231 Colombia–Peru FTA; Article 10 Chapter 22 CETA.
[21] Article 11 Chapter 22 CETA.

## 6.4 Geographical Indications

### 6.4.1 Significance of geographical indications for the EU

Geographical indications are perhaps the most 'European' of all IP rights. First recognized in the nineteenth century under French law in order to protect wine producers from competitors free riding on the name and reputation of the wines produced in certain locations, geographical indications have been subject to a sophisticated legal framework at EU level since 1992.[22] Geographical indications are generally understood as terms that identify a product as originating from a particular geographical area to which certain characteristics and qualities are associated either as a result of the area's natural characteristics (e.g. climate and soil type) or of the production processes developed in that area (Fink and Maskus (2006), p. 201). Indications of geographical origin, whether going under the name of geographical indications, indications of source, or appellations of origins, tend to be collectively owned, typically by associations composed of producers who agree to manufacture the product covered by the geographical indication in accordance with certain rules designed to ensure the achievement of specific attributes and characteristics (Creditt (2009), pp. 436–8).

Geographical indications also occupy a special place in the EU's external trade policy. The EU was—along with Switzerland—the major proponent of the inclusion of provisions on geographical indications in TRIPS and has since then called for enhanced levels of protection (Goldberg (2001), pp. 107–11). The EU's particular interest in geographical indications is related to the economic values attached to European geographical indications. The global recognition and protection of geographical indications would allow the EU to differentiate the myriad of agricultural products (wines, spirits, and foodstuffs) developed in Europe over time from those produced by competitors and would stop other countries from usurping their regional names and free riding on the reputation and quality of their products (Das (2010), p. 455). The underlying concern is that in the absence of legal protection, geographical indications will lose their economic value: their reputations will be undermined, become generic, and create consumer confusion on the nature and characteristics of the product. The topic of geographical indications also occupies a strategic importance in the context of the Doha Round because of its linkages with the crucial issue of agricultural subsidies. The EU argues that the higher levels of protection for geographical indications which would secure exclusive rights on the registered indication of origin are necessary to compensate for the adverse impact that would be caused to its agricultural industry by the removal of the subsidies granted to EU farmers under the Common Agricultural Policy (CAP) that is being demanded by segments of the WTO Membership (European Commission (2003)).

[22] Council Regulation (EEC) No 2081/92 OJ [1992] L 208, replaced by Council Regulation (EC) No 510/2006 OJ [2006] L 93.

The EU's affinity for geographical indications is not shared by all WTO Members. Whereas the EU was able to rely on the support of industrialized countries to force the adoption of high levels of IP protection in TRIPS, the issue of geographical indications highlighted the fault line between developed countries. WTO Members such as the US, Australia, and Canada, whose legal systems had traditionally protected indications of origins through a mixture of consumer protection laws and trademark law, and as producers of goods whose manufacturing practices and know-how had been imported from Europe, did not look kindly upon the recognition of geographical indications in the context of the WTO (Creditt (2009), p. 445). In fact, it is not uncommon in many such countries to find that geographical indications protected under EU law are terms that are either covered by registered trademarks or are considered to be generic terms (e.g. Champagne, Chablis, and Feta cheese). These countries tend to view geographical indications as a disguised form of protectionism barring market entrance for goods that may traditionally have been produced in specific geographical locations but that currently can and have been produced elsewhere (Evans and Blakeney (2006), p. 575; Beresford (2007), p. 970; Vivas-Egui and Oliva (2010), p. 123). These conflicting economic interests and differing legal traditions of WTO Members explain why TRIPS does not impose a particular regulatory system of protection for geographical indications. Although TRIPS recognizes geographical indications as a separate category of IP right and imposes a minimum level of protection for geographical indications, WTO Members retain the ability to decide how to ensure such protection. This has resulted in a regulatory diversity amongst WTO Members which does little to enhance a geographical indication holder's ability to secure the protection of its rights abroad. The requirements to be met in order to be granted the protection of a geographical indication and the level of protection accorded to it may differ widely from one jurisdiction to another. From the EU's perspective, this is a major flaw and it has therefore consistently sought (and failed) to reform TRIPS provisions on geographical indications by, on the one hand, proposing legal mechanisms that can be used to ensure the automatic protection of geographical indications across the WTO's membership and, on the other hand, to increase the level of protection of geographical indications in a manner that replicates to the furthest extent the regulatory framework implemented within the EU. The EU's failed attempts to push through its proposals at WTO level has led to an increased focus on the promotion of the EU's own standards of protection of geographical indications in the context of its bilateral agreements.

## 6.4.2 Regulatory framework for geographical indications

### *6.4.2.1 Geographical indications under TRIPS—an area of regulatory diversity*

Prior to TRIPS, a number of international agreements regulating geographical indications were negotiated under the auspices of the WIPO, all counting EU

Member States among their main proponents (Murphy (2003), pp. 1200–4). However, these agreements are affected by two principal flaws; either the membership is limited or the level of protection too feeble. First, there is the Paris Convention on the Protection of Industrial Property[23] (Paris Convention) which contains a large membership, but its protection is limited to the prohibition of false or misleading uses of indications of source or appellations of origin. Other international agreements provide a higher level of protection but, conversely, have few contracting parties. The Madrid Agreement for the Repression of False or Deceptive Indications of Source on Goods[24] (Madrid Agreement), in addition to prohibiting false and deceptive geographical indicators, proscribes the use of false representations on the product itself as well as in advertising or other forms of public announcements, and the use of existing geographical indications for wines as generic terms. Likewise, the Lisbon Agreement for the Protection of Appellations of Origin and their International Registration[25] (Lisbon Agreement), which mandates the adoption of specific legislation protecting geographical indication at national level,[26] prohibits usurpations or imitations of existing indications by the use of terms such as 'kind', 'type', 'make', 'imitation',[27] and establishes an international registration system whereby any registered geographical indication is automatically protected in the jurisdictions of all contracting parties.[28]

From the EU's perspective, TRIPS represented a step in the right direction insofar as it is a multilateral agreement incorporating numerous features of the aforementioned international agreements. Articles 22 and 23 TRIPS establish a two-tier system of protection for geographical indications: a basic level of protection that applies for geographical indications for all goods and an additional level of protection for geographical indications for wines and spirits. The general protection accorded to geographical indications for goods creates two major substantive standards which, to a large extent, codify the aforementioned international agreements. Article 22.2(a) TRIPS replicates Article 1.1 of the Madrid Agreement by prohibiting the use of 'means in any designation or presentation of a good that indicates or suggests that a good originates in a geographical area other than the true place of origin in a manner misleading the public as to the geographical indication of the good'. TRIPS also clarifies that this prohibition extends to the uses of geographical indications 'which, although literally true as to the territory, region or locality in which the goods originate, falsely represents to the public

[23] Paris Convention for the Protection of Industrial Property of 20 March 1883. Available at WIPO Database of Intellectual Property: http://www.wipo.int/treaties/en/ip/paris/trtdocs_wo020.html.

[24] Madrid Agreement for the Repression of False or Deceptive Indications of Source on Goods of 14 April 1891. Available at WIPO Database of Intellectual Property: http://www.wipo.int/treaties/en/ip/madrid/trtdocs_wo032.html.

[25] Lisbon Agreement for the Protection of Appellations of Origin and their International Registration of 31 October 1958. Available at WIPO Database of Intellectual Property: http://www.wipo.int/lisbon/en/legal_texts/lisbon_agreement.html.

[26] Article 1.2 Lisbon Agreement. [27] Article 3 Lisbon Agreement.

[28] Article 5 Lisbon Agreement.

that the goods originate in another territory'.[29] The second prohibition, in Article 22.2(b) TRIPS, relates to uses constituting an act of unfair competition within the meaning of Article 10 *bis* of the Paris Convention.

An enhanced level of protection is provided with respect to geographical indications for wines and spirits. In addition to requirements set out with regard to geographical indications for all products, WTO members must ensure that legal means are provided to prevent the use of geographical indications for wines and spirits that do not originate from the place indicated by the geographical indication, even where the true origin of the goods is indicated, where the geographical indication is used in translation, or where it is accompanied by expressions such as 'kind', 'type', 'style', 'imitation', or the 'like'.

The increased protection of geographical indications under TRIPS was compensated by the introduction of certain flexibilities. At a fundamental level, there is no requirement under TRIPS for WTO Members to adopt a *sui generis* geographical indication national protection system. Both Articles 22.2 and 23.1 TRIPS state in this regard that WTO Members must provide 'legal means' to ensure the protection of geographical indications but since there is no clarification as to what these 'legal means' are, WTO Members retain the ability to determine how best to protect indications of origin. TRIPS provisions are therefore intended to accommodate the coexistence of legal systems protecting indications of origin, particularly trademark law and *sui generis* geographical indications protection systems (Vivas-Egui and Oliva (2010), p. 123). In addition to the regulatory flexibility afforded to WTO Members when devising a national regulatory framework for the protection of geographical indications, TRIPS provides a number of exceptions to the obligation to ensure the level of protection mandated under Articles 22 and 23 TRIPS. The application of TRIPS rules on geographical indications is waived with regard to generic products,[30] to indications of origin which are not or cease to be protected in their country of origin or which have fallen into disuse in that country,[31] or in circumstances where a person uses, in the course of trade, that person's name or the name of that person's predecessor in business unless the name is used in such a manner to mislead the public.[32] Another important flexibility relates to the relationship between geographical indications and trademarks. In principle, both such rights grant their owners the exclusive rights of use. However, TRIPS sets out certain limits to the exclusivity of geographical indications in relation to trademarks. For wines and spirits the rule is that the registration of a trademark must be refused or invalidated where it contains or consists of a geographical indication identifying wines or spirits.[33] For products other than wines or spirits the refusal or invalidation of a trademark need only occur if the use of the conflicting trademark is of such nature as to mislead the public as to the true place of origin of the product.[34]

[29] Article 22.4 TRIPS.
[30] Article 24.6 TRIPS.
[31] Article 24.9 TRIPS.
[32] Article 24.8 TRIPS.
[33] Article 23.2 TRIPS.
[34] Article 22.3 TRIPS.

### *6.4.2.2 EU law on geographical indications*

#### 6.4.2.2.1 TRIPS-plus level of protection

The protection of geographical indications under EU law is ensured via a *sui generis* legal regime. The major legal instrument governing geographical indications in the EU is Regulation No. 510/206 (GI Regulation) which applies to agricultural products and foodstuffs (wines and spirits are subject to a separate regime). The regime of protection of geographical indications in the EU is achieved by means of a centralized registration system managed by the Commission. Applications originating from within the EU may only be filed by a 'group'[35]—that is, any association of producers and processors working with the same product—via the concerned national government[36] whilst applications originating from outside the EU are to be filed directly with the Commission.[37]

The protection accorded to registered names is extensive. Article 13.1(a) of the GI Regulation prohibits all references of a commercial nature to a registered geographical indication in a comparable product (e.g. commercial information such as labelling, packaging and advertising). In addition, the prohibition also applies with regards to dissimilar products if the use of the geographical indication is intended to exploit the reputation attached to the name. Article 13.1(b) of the GI Regulation prohibits the 'misuse, imitation or evocations of the indication' and this applies regardless of whether the true origin of the product is included or the protected name translated or qualified by expressions such as 'style', 'type', 'method', and the like.

#### 6.4.2.2.2 Co-existence of geographical indications and trademarks

EU law is stacked in favour of geographical indications, according them a much higher level of protection than trademarks. The unequal treatment accorded to trademarks and geographical indications can be seen at the level of registration. In accordance with Article 14.1 of the GI Regulation, an application for the registration of a trademark that conflicts with a geographical indication must be rejected if the application is submitted after the date of application of the geographical indication. There are no circumstances under which a trademark could be registered where it contains a signal that is similar or identical to an earlier geographical indication. On the other hand, prior registration of a trademark does not necessarily preclude the registration of a conflicting geographical indication. Under Article 3.4 of the GI Regulation, registration of a geographical indication which conflicts with an existing trademark shall be refused only in cases where, because of the trademark's reputation and renown and the length of time it has been used, registration is liable to mislead the consumer as to the true identity of the product. Similarly, Article 7.4(c) of the GI Regulation provides that an objection to the registration of a geographical indication is admissible if it 'shows

[35] Article 5.1 GI Regulation.
[36] Article 5(4) GI regulation.
[37] Article 5.9 GI Regulation.

that the registration of the name proposed would jeopardise the existence of an entirely or partly identical name or of a trademark'. In short, whereas the registration of a geographical indication provides the collective owners with exclusive rights over the use of the concerned indication, trademark owners cannot preclude the registration and use of geographical indications unless certain specific circumstances are fulfilled. This means that, barring exceptional circumstances, EU law permits coexistence between a prior registered trademark and a later conflicting geographical indication, a point that is conclusively asserted under Article 14.2 of the GI Regulation which stipulates that a trademark that has been 'applied for, registered, or established by use, in good faith before either the date of protection of the geographical indication in the country of origin or before 1 January 1996, may continue to be used notwithstanding the registration of the geographical indication', provided that there are no grounds for its invalidity or revocation. The pre-eminence of geographical indications over trademarks under EU law is a view that conflicts with the rule of exclusivity of prior rights (first in time, first in right) which is applied in most countries that protect geographical indications through trademark law and has been challenged by the US and Australia before the WTO Dispute Settlement Panel.[38] It was claimed that Article 14.2 of the EU Regulation was inconsistent with Article 16.1 TRIPS, which recognizes the exclusive right of a trademark owner to prevent third parties from using identical or similar signs for goods or services where such use would result in a likelihood of confusion. The EU countered that the co-existence of geographical indications and pre-existing trademarks was authorized by two TRIPS provisions. First, Article 17 TRIPS allows WTO members to provide limited exceptions to the rights conferred by a trademark and, secondly, Article 24.5 of the GI Regulation provides that measures adopted to implement the minimum standards of protection of geographical indications under TRIPS 'shall not prejudice eligibility for or the validity of the registration of a trademark, or the right to use a trademark, on the basis that such a trademark is identical with, or similar to, a geographical indication'.

The Panel found that the EU's regime of coexistence was justified under Article 17 TRIPS as a limited exception; 'limited' in the sense that the rights of trademark owners were only curtailed with respect to those goods covered by the geographical indication, third parties using the concerned geographical indication, and the use of the registered indication (Evans and Blakeney (2006), pp. 610–12). The Panel also agreed with the EU that the trademark owner's legitimate interest in preserving the distinctiveness, or capacity to distinguish, of its trademark was taken into account by both Articles 3.4 and 7.4 of the EU Regulation. The Panel's ruling confirmed the neutrality of WTO law with respect to the relationship between the different and sometimes conflicting regulatory models for the protection of geographical indications adopted by WTO Members.

[38] Report of the Panel, *European Communities—Protection of Trademarks and Geographical Indications for Agricultural Products and Foodstuffs—Complaint by the United States*, WT/DS174/R.

### 6.4.3 EU external trade policy in the area of geographical indications

#### *6.4.3.1 EU proposals for TRIPS reform*

TRIPS did not go as far as the EU would have initially wished it to in the area of geographical indications. Although the agreement mandates a minimum level of protection for geographical indications, the regulatory diversity which prevails among WTO members does not assist the EU's aim of ensuring that geographical indications registered under EU law are not usurped elsewhere. EU geographical indication holders wishing to secure the protection of their rights abroad still have to apply for the registration and protection of their geographical indications in every third country where such protection is sought. The domestic procedures can be lengthy and expensive affairs. In addition, because of the varying degrees of protection available in different jurisdictions, there is no guarantee that an application for protection will be successful. A study commissioned by the Commission provides a lengthy account of the difficulties encountered by holders of EU geographical indications seeking to protect their rights in third countries where indications of sources are protected via trademark laws (European Commission (2010d)). Amongst the most important legal obstacles is the fact that holders of EU geographical indications have to contend with the possibility that a similar or identical name may already be protected by a prior existing trademark. In this case, it is more than likely that the registration of the geographical indication will be refused on the basis of the 'first in time, first in right' rule typically applied in such legal systems. It is also not uncommon for trademark law systems to reject the registration of geographical indications because such names are considered to have become generic in the concerned third country or because they are considered purely descriptive of the product.

In light of these difficulties, the EU has sought to: (i) establish a legal mechanism that would allow geographical indications protected under national law to be granted automatic protection at the multilateral level, thus obviating the need to go through cumbersome domestic procedures; (ii) ensure that all WTO Members extend the protection provided under Article 23 TRIPS to all products; and (iii) secure the automatic protection of an exhaustive list of EU geographical indications which have either become generic or are covered by trademarks in the jurisdiction of other WTO Members (so-called 'clawback proposal'). The first of these objectives resulted in a proposal for the establishment of a multilateral system of notification and registration for geographical indications.

To date, none of the EU's attempts for TRIPS reform have been successful. Countries favouring a trademark law-based system, such as the US, consider that such reforms would excessively impinge on their regulatory autonomy. With regard to the extension of the scope of protection under Article 23 TRIPS, the US has repeatedly stated that by removing the requirement that only uses of geographical indications that are liable to mislead consumers should be prohibited, the EU is effectively creating an absolute protection for all geographical indications insofar as holders of geographical indications would be granted exclusive rights regarding the use of the indications irrespective of whether the term is considered generic or even known in a given jurisdiction (GATT (1990a)). The EU was also forced to revise its initial proposals for a multilateral register, which would have had the legal effect of rendering all registered geographical indications fully and indefinitely protected—this would have applied to all WTO Members, with the exception of those having opposed the registration (WTO (1998a)). Subsequent proposals can be seen as an attempt to sweeten the pill by lessening the legal effects of registration, which no longer grants an automatic protection to registered geographical indications, but merely constitutes either a 'presumption of eligibility for protection' (WTO (2005c)) or a 'prima facie evidence' (Ibid) that the concerned geographical indication meets the definition as set out under Article 22.1 TRIPS (WTO (2008)). Critics have argued that such presumptions remain too intrusive as the registration of a geographical indication protected in one country would have a quasi extraterritorial effect to the extent that the registration would automatically create obligations in the legal systems of other WTO Members (Beresford (2007), p. 970).

### *6.4.3.2 EU approach to geographical indications in FTAs*

#### 6.4.3.2.1 From Wines and Spirits Agreements to comprehensive GI regulation

Article 24.1 TRIPS includes a provision acknowledging the right of WTO Members to bilaterally negotiate enhanced levels of protection for geographical indications. It states that the exceptions to the minimum levels of protections for geographical indications mandated in TRIPS 'shall not be used by a Member to refuse to conduct negotiations or to conclude bilateral or multilateral agreements'.[39] Therefore, WTO Members can enter into international agreements which remove existing exceptions under TRIPS (Das (2010), p. 471). This type of provision is an oddity in the context of WTO agreements, and may be seen as an open acknowledgement that, in light of the lack of progress in WTO-level negotiations, the unfinished business relating to geographical indications is unlikely to be resolved at the multilateral level. It is no surprise to see that the EU has used bilateral trade agreements as the main tool to further its interest in this domain. Initially, the EU sought to conclude agreements dealing specifically with geographical indications for wines and spirits (Wines and Spirits Agreements) with third countries, such as Australia, Chile, South Africa, and the US, that are important producers of these products and that typically classified terms protected under EU law as trademarks or generic terms at the time of the signing of TRIPS.[40] Generally speaking, the provisions contained therein reflect the general objectives of the EU pursued in the context of TRIPS. First, the agreements provide for mutual protection of geographical indications exhaustively listed in its

[39] Article 24.1 TRIPS.

[40] The first of such agreements was the EC–Australia Wine Agreement (Agreement between the European Community and Australia on trade in wine OJ [1994] L 86).

annexes. In doing so, the EU secures the automatic protection of key geographical indications for wines and spirits abroad. Secondly, with respect to the level of protection accorded to the concerned geographical indications, the agreements typically include a clause providing that the signatories will protect such geographical indications in accordance with the laws of the country of origin of the geographical indication. In other words, in its Wines and Spirits Agreements, the EU secures the extra-territorial application of its TRIPS-plus legislation on geographical indications.

The EU DCFTAs follow the lead of the Wines and Spirits Agreements to the extent that they provide for the mutual protection of specifically listed geographical indications. However, they also extend protection to other products, namely agricultural products and foodstuffs. In addition, these FTAs go further in terms of the level of protection. Rather than simply mandating the contracting parties to protect the listed geographical indications in accordance with the national law of the country of origin of the geographical indication, they contain provisions that oblige the contracting parties to adopt domestic legal frameworks for the protection of geographical indications. The one exception to this practice is the CETA. This is because Canada protects indications of origins via a firmly established trademark law system based on the rule of priority.

#### 6.4.3.2.2 Legal frameworks for geographical indications

The primary objective aim of the EU DCFTAs is to ensure the automatic protection of EU geographical indications in the jurisdictions of the co-signatories of the concerned agreements. Typically, the agreements include annexes which list those geographical indications that must be protected by the contracting parties.[41] Once listed in the annexes, a geographical indication benefits from an automatic protection in the jurisdiction of the other party without the requirement to register the geographical indication in accordance with the relevant domestic procedure. In the best of worlds, this is effectively the function that the EU would like the multilateral WTO register to fulfil.

Such mutual protection also requires the existence of a functioning regulatory system for the protection of geographical indications and the recognition that the other party's legislation and domestic procedures provide a sufficient level of protection. This is clearly not a problem for the EU which, as has been seen, has possibly the most developed protection system for geographical indications in the world. The same could not be said of the EU's counterparts. Korea and Singapore are required to amend their laws in order to enhance the level of protection afforded to geographical indications, whilst the EU's co-signatories in the CEPA and the EU–CA FTA did not have, at the time of signing, a comprehensive protection system for geographical indications.[42] In both these agreements, the EU requires its co-signatories to establish a system of protection that fulfils certain

[41] Articles 10.18.3 and 10.18.4 KOREU FTA.

[42] Article 10.18 KOREU; Article 11.17 EU–Singapore FTA.

minimum conditions. The conditions included in the EU–CA FTA mirror in broad terms the basic characteristics of the GI Regulation. There is, for example, an obligation to ensure that geographical indications must comply with product specifications,[43] that a registered name may be used by any operator marketing agricultural products or foodstuffs conforming to the corresponding specification[44] and that an objection procedure is put in place to allow prior users of names to protect their legitimate interests.[45] The CEPA, whilst not prescribing a particular regulatory system, provides certain clues that the legislation, once adopted, will have a distinctively European flavour. Article 145.B.2 CEPA states that the protection of geographical indication must be reserved for goods originating from the area concerned and protected in accordance with product specifications. To the extent that trademarks do not necessarily require product specifications, this provision can be viewed as an indication of a preference towards a system of registration, control and protection of geographical indications similar to that currently in place in the EU.[46] Moreover, there is a provision stating that the parties shall discuss issues concerning the implementation of the system of protection and exchange of information on legislative and policy developments on geographical indications. The CEPA therefore creates an institutional framework that ensures that the EU will have an impact on the development of geographical indication legislation in CARIFORUM States.

#### 6.4.3.2.3 Expansion of Article 23 TRIPS protection to agricultural products and foodstuffs

Through its EU DCFTAs, the EU has succeeded in extending the enhanced protection accorded to wines and spirits under Article 23 TRIPS to agricultural products and foodstuffs. In CEPA, EU–CA FTA and the EU–Singapore FTA, the level of protection afforded to wines and spirits and other products is identical.[47] These agreements provide that the use of a geographical designation identifying a good for either a 'like good' or a good 'in the same class' which does not originate in the area indicated is prohibited even where the geographical indication is used in translation or accompanied by terms such as 'kind', 'type', style', 'imitation', or other similar terms. Therefore, the objective protection of Article 23 TRIPS applies to all goods covered by the Global FTA. The CEPA goes further by also prohibiting the use of geographical indications accompanied by the term 'method', which is borrowed from Article 13.1(b) of the GI Regulation.

The KOREU FTA operates a distinction between wines and spirits and agricultural products and foodstuffs insofar as the former are governed by rules based on Article 23 TRIPS, whilst the latter are to be protected in accordance with the

[43] Article 244.2(c) EU–CA FTA; Article 4 Regulation No 510/2006.
[44] Article 244.2(e) EU–CA FTA; Article 8 Regulation No 510/2006.
[45] Article 244.2(f) EU–CA FTA; Recital 14 and Article 5.5 Regulation No 510/2006.
[46] Article 145.A(2) CEPA.
[47] Article 145.B CEPA; Article 246 EU–CA FTA; Article 11.19 EU–Singapore FTA.

relevant laws of the country of origin of the concerned geographical indication.[48] Such extra-territorial application of the domestic legislation law of the contracting parties follows the practice already pursued by the EU in its Wines and Spirits Agreements. It is a requirement that will be more burdensome for Korea than the EU given that, to date, Korea has only listed one spirit in the annexes of the FTA in comparison to the 105 wines and spirits listed by the EU.

The Colombia–Peru FTA differs from the agreements described above, as it maintains a lower level of protection for products other than wines and spirits. Article 210.1(b) of the Colombia–Peru FTA prohibits 'any unauthorised use of geographical indications other than those identifying wines, aromatized wines or spirits drinks that *creates confusion*, including even in cases where the name is accompanied by indications such as style, type, imitation or other similar uses that create confusion to the consumer'. The provision reflects the current legislation in Peru and Colombia, which replicates the two-tier level of protection under TRIPS. However, the same provision adds that should the internal legislation of either country be amended to provide a higher level of protection, the same protection must also be extended to geographical indications listed under the relevant Annex of the agreement. Another aspect of the increased protection of geographical indications in the EU DCFTAs is the conspicuous absence of provisions on exceptions to the protection of geographical indications under TRIPS. This is to be expected, since the objective pursued by the EU is to ensure the exclusivity of rights of EU holders of geographical indications. The exceptions concerning generic products, products of the vine, geographical indications that have been used in a continuous manner prior to the entry into force of the agreement, and the use of a person's name in the course of trade are absent from the Colombia–Peru FTA. The KOREU FTA does not lag far behind, as it only replicates Article 24.8 TRIPS permitting the use of a person's name in the course of trade. In the EU–CA FTA, the exception concerning generic products applies only to geographical indications other than wines and spirited drinks.[49] The CEPA and the EU–Singapore FTA replicate the exceptions pertaining to generic products and on products of the vine—which is extended to also cover plants or animals.[50] Summing up, the EU ensures a high level of protection of geographical indications by not only extending the Article 23 TRIPS protection to all agricultural products and foodstuffs but also, in some cases, by eliminating the exceptions under which such protection need not be applied.

#### 6.4.3.2.4 Relationship with trademarks

As regards the contentious issue of how to resolve potential conflicts between geographical indications and trademarks, the strategy adopted by the EU in its EU DCFTAs has been to replicate its own legal regime. In other words, the EU DCFTAs have opted for a system of co-existence of trademarks and geographical indications which favours the latter, as the registration of geographical indications

[48] Article 10.19 KOREU FTA.
[49] Article 246.4 EU–CA FTA.
[50] Article 145.C.3 CEPA; Article 11.22 EU–Singapore FTA.

that conflict with prior trademarks shall only be invalidated in a narrow set of circumstances—if at all.

In general, the EU DCFTAs require the refusal or invalidation of the registration of a trademark conflicting with a pre-existing geographical indication for identical or like goods.[51] For this rule to apply, the application for the registration of the trademark must be made after the date of entry of the agreement and the date of application for protection of the concerned geographical indications. The Global FTA provisions go further than TRIPS in so far as, contrary to Article 22.3 TRIPS, the prohibition to register new trademarks is not limited to cases where the use of the indication in the trademark is of such a nature as to mislead the public as to the true place of origin. In line with the extension of the enhanced level of protection under Article 23 TRIPS for wines and spirits to agricultural goods and foodstuffs, the mere pre-existence of a geographical indication is enough to preclude the registration of a new conflicting trademark, irrespective of whether or not the new trademark will cause consumer confusion.

Where a trademark has been applied for or registered prior to an application of a geographical indication, the general approach adopted in the EU DCFTAs is that such trademark may continue to be used unless there are grounds for its invalidation or revocation. This approach is an application of the grandfather clause included in TRIPS (Article 24.5 TRIPS)—that is, that the protection accorded to geographical indications under TRIPS shall not prejudice eligibility for or the validity of the registration of a trademark, or the right to use a pre-existing trademark. However, there are some certain deviations in some cases. Under Article 24.5 TRIPS, the trademark may only continue to be used if it was registered in 'good faith'. The same requirement can be found in the CEPA[52] and the EU–Singapore FTA[53] but not in the KOREU FTA, the Colombia–Peru FTA, and the EU–CA FTA. By eliminating the good faith requirement, the three latter agreements provide a stronger protection for trademarks than is currently available under both TRIPS and the GI Regulation.

The prior existence of a trademark is not a barrier to the registration of a geographical indication. From this perspective, the EU has successfully exported the principle of coexistence between geographical indications and trademarks in the context of its FTAs and, in some cases, its co-signatories were forced to amend existing domestic legislation (O'Connor and Richardson (2012), p. 13). As stated above, the only circumstance under which the registration of a geographical indication conflicting with a prior trademark is prohibited under EU law is where the registration of geographical indication is liable to mislead the consumer as to the true identity of the product in the light of a trademark's reputation and renown and the length of time it has been used. This provision can be found in both the CEPA[54] and the Colombia–Peru FTA[55] and the EU–CA FTA.[56]

[51] Article 145.D.2 and 3 CEPA; Article 10.23 KOREU FTA; Article 11.21 EU–Singapore FTA.

[52] Article 145.D.4 CEPA.

[53] Article 11.22.3 EU–Singapore FTA.

[54] Article 145.D.1 CEPA.

[55] Article 211.2 Colombia–Peru FTA.

[56] Article 258 EU–CA FTA.

No such consideration is at stake in the KOREU FTA which is even less considerate towards trademarks than the EU law itself, as the agreement does not identify any circumstances under which the geographical indication may be refused in light of the prior existence of a registered trademark.

The EU–Singapore FTA is the one exception to this rule, as it does not incorporate the EU's principle of coexistence. This can be explained by the fact that under the US–Singapore FTA concluded in 2003,[57] Singapore was required to adopt a 'first-in-time, first-in-right' principle[58] which would make it impossible to allow the registration of geographical indications that conflict with pre-existing trademarks. Instead, the EU–Singapore FTA provides that it is acknowledged 'that the existence of a prior conflicting trademark in a Party would not completely preclude the registration of a subsequent geographical indication for like goods in that Party'.[59] It is then clarified in a footnote that '[i]n the case of Singapore, a geographical indication which conflicts with a prior existing trademark is capable of being registered with the consent of the prior existing trademarks holder'.[60] In other words, contrary to EU law, the protection of geographical indications under Singapore law does not undermine the exclusivity of rights accorded to trademark holders.

### 6.4.4 Limits of the EU's trade policy on geographical indications

The EU's inability to secure higher levels of protection for its geographical indications at the WTO level has led it to resort to bilateral trade agreements to achieve its objectives. It is clear, however, that in the recent EU DCFTAs, the EU's demands far exceed those that were proposed before the TRIPS Council. Not only do the EU DCFTAs ensure the exclusivity of specifically identified EU geographical indications, but they also replicate important features of EU law for geographical indications, notably the rules governing the relationship between geographical indications and trademarks. By successfully exporting the principle of coexistence between geographical indications and trademarks, the EU is chipping away at the regulatory diversity in the area of geographical indications which was allowed to persist under TRIPS and provides some legal certainty to EU holders of geographical indications.

The EU's approach to the negotiation of provisions on geographical indications in the EU DCFTAs shows no real consideration towards the issues that may arise as a result of the clashes with diverging regulatory systems. However, it is in this respect that the success of the EU's exportation of its regulatory system must be qualified. The EU DCFTAs have either been concluded with countries that already have functioning regulatory systems protecting geographical indications

[57] Free Trade Agreement signed between the United States and South Korea on 30 June 2007. Available at: http://www.ustr.gov/trade-agreements/free-trade-agreements/korus-fta/final-text.

[58] Article 16.2(2) US–Singapore FTA.

[59] Article 11.22(2) EU–Singapore FTA.

[60] Footnote 19 EU–Singapore FTA.

(Korea, Colombia, and Peru) or developing countries (CARICOM and Central American States), which have traditionally not had defensive interests in the area. The EU DCFTAs cannot be held as examples of how geographical indications may come to be regulated at the WTO.

The EU is not alone in using FTAs to promote its regulatory approach to the protection of geographical indications. While the FTAs concluded by the EU promote its *sui generis* system of protection, those concluded by the US require the adoption of trademark law systems based on the priority rule. The EU and the US seem to be engaged in a race to expand their respective regulatory spaces and these conflicting approaches to the protection of geographical indications have already shown the potential for regulatory clashes. For example, the signing of the KOREU FTA led the US dairy industry to raise concerns that their rights under the Korea–US FTA, which entered into force on 15 March 2012 and provides, inter alia, for the protection of trademarks based on the rule of priority, would be violated (Cooper (2011), p. 15). In this regard, it has been claimed that Korea will not be able to comply with the diverging requirements of both these FTAs (O'Connor (2013), p. 2). Likewise, with regard to the CETA, a major sticking point in the negotiations related to concerns that the adoption of the EU's system of protection may infringe market access rights enjoyed by US trademark holders under the NAFTA (Viju, Yeung, and Kerr (2013), pp. 409–37). The upshot is that, unlike most other EU DCFTAs, the CETA makes no mention of the need for the parties to implement an effective system of protection for geographical indications, does not include a provision requiring compliance with the principle of co-existence between trademarks and geographical indications, and is limited to extending the high level of protection accorded under Article 23 TRIPS to an exhaustive range of products listed in the agreement.[61] Similar issues have predictably arisen with the US in the framework of the TTIP negotiations (Hall (2014)). Therefore, it is in the context of ongoing and future negotiations with larger economies that have adopted a trademark-based system for the protection of geographical indications that the limits of the EU's current approach is being tested. Since it is unlikely that developed countries favouring trademark law-based systems would agree to protect EU geographical indications on the EU's terms, it may well transpire that the negotiation of EU DCFTAs concluded with such countries will be limited to seeing whether the parties can agree to grant each other exclusive rights on a few key indications of origin. A more ambitious approach would be to explore solutions that accommodate the diverging interests of its own regulatory system with that of trademark law-based systems. One possible solution could be to implement a true principle of coexistence between trademarks and geographical indications where both types of IP rights can be registered concomitantly as long as they do not lead to consumer deception (Stern (2001), p. 221; Doster (2006), p. 872; Gangjee (2007), pp. 1290–1), This may, however, prove too challenging an enterprise—first, because the assessment of

[61] Article 7.4 Chapter 22 CETA.

whether a designation is intended to deceive or mislead the public undermines the EU's quest to secure legal certainty for holders of geographical indications, since such assessments may be subject to varying interpretations from different courts. Secondly, it would entail a significant rethink of the national legal systems of the parties involved. For trademark-based law systems it would mean abandoning the application of the 'first in time, first in right' principle, whilst for the EU it would mean accepting that geographical indications may not be treated more favourably than trademarks. Therefore, the protection of geographical indications is one area where regulatory diversity is likely to persist among developed countries, meaning that the latter will continue to disseminate their contrasting regulatory approaches through bilateral trade agreements, which will in turn increase the probability that the countries importing such rules will be subject to conflicting obligations (Viju, Yeung, and Kerr (2013), pp. 432–6).

## 6.5 IP Enforcement

### 6.5.1 Regulatory framework for the enforcement of IPRs

#### *6.5.1.1 Enforcement of IP rights under TRIPS*

TRIPS provided the first multilateral set of rules pertaining to the domestic procedures, rights and remedies for the enforcement of IP rights. The agreement operates a distinction between general infringements of IP rights and the more particular infringements of trademark counterfeiting[62] or copyright piracy.[63] With regard to general infringements of the IP rights covered by TRIPS, civil judicial and administrative procedures are to be made available by WTO Members. IP right holders have the right to fair and equitable proceedings; a requirement which entails, inter alia, the right to timely and sufficiently detailed written notice, to be allowed to be represented by independent legal counsel and to substantiate one's claims and to present all relevant evidence.[64] WTO Members are also enjoined to provide remedies to prevent infringements (injunctions to desist from an infringement)[65] or rectify damages caused by infringements as well as remedies that can act as deterrents to further infringements (forfeiture and disposal of infringing goods).[66]

[62] Footnote 14(a) of Article 51 TRIPS defines counterfeit trademark goods as 'any goods, including packaging, bearing without authorization a trademark which is identical to the trademark validly registered in respect of such goods, or which cannot be distinguished in its essential aspects from such a trademark, and which thereby infringes the rights of the owner of the trademark in question under the law of the country of importation'.

[63] Footnote 14(b) of Article 51 TRIPS defines pirated copyright goods as 'any goods which are copies made without the consent of the right holder or person duly authorized by the right holder in the country of production and which are made directly or indirectly from an article where the making of that copy would have constituted an infringement of a copyright or a related right under the law of the country of importation'.

[64] Article 42 TRIPS. [65] Article 44 TRIPS. [66] Articles 45 and 46 TRIPS.

With regard to counterfeiting and piracy, TRIPS recognizes the need for border measures and criminal proceedings. Article 51 TRIPS requires WTO Members to enact procedures enabling right holders that suspect the importation of counterfeit trademark or pirated copyright goods to request the suspension by the customs authorities of the release into free circulation of such goods. The right holder must provide *prima facie* evidence of the infringement in accordance with the laws of the country of importation and, if granted, the customs authorities must be informed within ten working days that proceedings leading to a decision on the merits of the case have been initiated by a party other than the defendant, or that the duly empowered authority has taken provisional measures prolonging the suspension of the release of the goods.[67] Criminal procedures apply to cases of wilful trademark counterfeiting or copyright piracy on a commercial scale. Here, WTO Members must make available remedies such as imprisonment and/or monetary fines, seizure, forfeiture, and destruction of the infringing goods and of any materials and implements the predominant use of which has been in the commission of the offence.[68]

### *6.5.1.2 Enforcement of IPRs under EU law*

The EU has enacted two major legal instruments regulating the enforcement of IP rights: the EU Directive 2004/48 on the enforcement of Intellectual Property Rights (Enforcement Directive)[69] and the Regulation No 608/2013 concerning customs enforcement of intellectual property rights (Customs Enforcement regulation)[70] which replaced Regulation No 1383/2003 concerning customs action against goods suspected of infringing certain intellectual property (Customs Control Regulation).[71]

The Enforcement Directive was the first piece of EU legislation aimed at achieving the horizontal harmonization of measures, procedures, and remedies necessary to ensure the enforcement of IP rights—it applies to all IP rights covered by either EU law or national law of the Member States. In terms of the protection it affords, it certainly goes beyond what is currently provided for under TRIPS. The remedies available to combat IP rights infringement range, as in the context of TRIPS, from provisional and precautionary measures[72] to measures resulting from a decision on the merits of the case.[73] The former measures look to ensure the immediate cessation of infringements, especially in those circumstances where waiting for a final decision on the merits could cause irreparable damage. Under Article 9 of the Enforcement Directive, Member States are obliged to ensure that judicial authorities are authorized to issue interlocutory injunctions

[67] Article 52 TRIPS. [68] Article 61 TRIPS.

[69] Directive 2004/48/EC, OJ [2004] L 157.

[70] Council Regulation (EU) No 608/2013 OJ [2013] L 181. Replacing Council Regulation (SC) No 1383/2003 OJ [2003] L 196.

[71] Council Regulation (EC) No 1383/2003, OJ [2003] L 196.

[72] Article 9 Enforcement Directive. [73] Articles 10 to 12 Enforcement Directive.

intended to prevent imminent infringements of IP rights and order seizures or delivery up of goods suspected of such infringements. As for measures resulting from the merits, judicial authorities can order corrective measures such as ordering the recall or definite removal from the channels of commerce, and destruction of the infringing goods. Injunctions may be issued against the infringer of an IP right so as to prohibit the continuation of an infringement. Courts may also award damages to compensate for the prejudice incurred by the IP right holder as a result of the infringement and order the reimbursement of legal costs incurred by the successful party.[74] The Enforcement Directive is complemented by the Customs Control Regulation, which sought to provide tools for the fight against cross-border infringements of IP rights. Like the Enforcement Directive, the Customs Control Regulation differed from previous EU-level legislation on customs controls, as it operates across the board (Bonadio (2008), p. 320). It applies to counterfeit goods, pirated goods and goods that infringe patents, supplementary protection certificates, national plant variety rights, designations of origins or geographical indications covering counterfeit goods, pirated goods and associated rights, designs, models, and patents.[75] Moreover, it permits customs authorities of Member States inter alia, to suspend the release or detain goods suspected of infringing an intellectual property right that are either declared for release for free circulation, export or re-export, entering or leaving the customs territory of the Union or placed under suspensive procedure or in a free zone or warehouse'.[76] Unlike Article 51 TRIPS, which only covers situations where goods are being imported, the Customs Control Regulation covers most conceivable circumstances under which goods may be passing through customs.

The EU is yet to regulate the issue of criminal enforcement of IP infringements. This is not through want of trying. In 2005 (and then in 2006),[77] the Commission proposed the adoption of a criminal enforcement directive which required the criminalization of all IP infringements committed on a commercial scale, prohibited aiding and abetting of such criminal offences and listed the criminal sanctions to be imposed (e.g. imprisonment, fines, confiscation, bans from establishing commercial activities, etc.). The EU's competence to regulate criminal enforcement was disputed at the time, as was the necessity of a harmonizing directive, given that many of the issues covered were already regulated at national level. Furthermore, the content of the proposals was also highly problematic. The European Parliament approved the draft only after making significant amendments intended to ensure that a balance was reached between the protection of the interests of IP rights holders and the protection of fundamental human rights (Seville (2009), p. 413). Nevertheless, the proposal remained controversial and was eventually scrapped by the Commission in 2010.[78]

[74] Article 13 Enforcement Directive. [75] Article 2 Customs Control Regulation.

[76] Article 1(a) and (b) Customs Control Regulation.

[77] Amended proposal for a Directive of the European Parliament and of the Council on criminal measures aimed at ensuring the enforcement of intellectual property rights COM(2006) 0168 final.

[78] Withdrawal of Obsolete Commission Proposals OJ 2010/C 252/04.

## 6.5.2 EU external trade policy in IP enforcement

### 6.5.2.1 *The EU's TRIPS-plus policy in IP enforcement*

The paradox presented by TRIPS is that while it has led to the strengthening of the level of IP infringement enforcement worldwide, the transnational circulation of goods infringing IP rights has steadily increased over the course of the last 20 years. In 2008, the OECD published a study entitled *The Economic Impact of Counterfeiting and Piracy* which estimated the value of international trade in counterfeit and pirated products to be as high as USD 200 billion (OECD (2008b)). This amount only tells part of the story, as the study is only concerned with infringements of a select number of IP rights, namely copyrights, patents, trademarks, and design rights, and does not take into account domestic IP infringements nor pirated products distributed by means of the Internet. The findings of the OECD merely reasserted what was already public knowledge as successive G8 summits have reaffirmed the need to promote and uphold the laws, regulations, and procedures to strengthen effective enforcement of IP rights as far back as 2005 (G8 Gleneagles (2008)).

The EU, for its part, followed the enactment of both the Enforcement Directive and the Customs Control Regulation by setting out a policy framework with the purpose of addressing the continuous increase of IP rights violations in third countries—the 2005 Enforcement Strategy. The Enforcement Strategy identifies a number of mechanisms that should be put in place in order to pursue this objective. These include, inter alia, the identification and targeting of those countries and regions where the issue of enforcement is most problematic, the enhancement of IPR enforcement in multilateral and bilateral agreements, the launch of political dialogues, the granting of financial and technical assistance, and the increased use of EU trade sanctions and dispute settlement mechanisms under the auspices of the WTO (European Commission (2005), p. 3). In addition to calls for the improvement in the level of implementation of TRIPS enforcement rules (WTO (2005b)), the EU—along with other major developed nations (Li (2010), p. 638; Von Braun and Munyi (2010), p. 238)—has demanded the adoption of higher standards of IP enforcement under TRIPS. In particular, the EU circulated a communication in the TRIPS Council identifying the issue of border measures as a priority area for any future discussion regarding TRIPS enforcement (WTO (2005b)). Of particular importance was the issue of the narrow scope of Article 51 TRIPS on suspension of release by customs authorities, which is limited in terms of IP rights covered (to copyright and trademark infringements), and which seemingly only covered importation of goods as opposed to transhipment, export, and transit of goods. The Communication was then followed by a 'Communication on a Customs response to the latest trends in counterfeiting and piracy' (European Commission (2005d)), which notably suggested the enhancement of TRIPS provisions relating to border measures and inclusion of provisions on customs controls in future bilateral agreements entered by the EU.

### *6.5.2.2 Concerns relating to higher levels of IP enforcement*

#### **6.5.2.2.1 Loss of TRIPS flexibilities**

Although the EU has received some support for its endeavours (WTO (2006)), there is little appetite from most developing WTO Members to further remove existing flexibilities under TRIPS (Emert (2006)), especially in the context of a negotiation round focusing on development issues. Two cases illustrate how demands for higher standards of IP enforcement can reduce policy space available to WTO Members and, as a result, undermine their ability to pursue legitimate policy objectives: the expansion of the scope of border measures and criminal procedures required under TRIPS.

One aspect of the Customs Control Regulation that came under scrutiny was that it allowed customs authorities to suspend the release of or detain goods suspected of IP infringements even where the concerned goods originated from a third country and were in transit to another third country[79] (Daele (2004), p. 215). This remains the case in the context of the Customs Enforcement Regulation. In other words, the EU rules go beyond Article 51 TRIPS insofar as the adoption of border measures is not limited to cases of suspected counterfeit trademark and pirated copyright, but also extend to goods in transit (Heath (2010), p. 881). The TRIPS-plus nature of the Customs Control Regulation proved controversial when it was used by the Dutch customs authorities to seize generic pharmaceutical goods in transit which originated from India and were destined to Latin America on the grounds that such drugs were suspected of infringing patents registered in the Netherlands (Mercurio (2012), p. 389). This led Brazil and India to lodge a complaint at the WTO against the EU customs measures,[80] arguing, inter alia, that they violated Article 41.1 TRIPS by creating barriers to legitimate trade in generic pharmaceuticals and Article 52 TRIPS which provides that WTO Members initiating customs procedures must 'provide adequate evidence [...] that under the laws of the country of importation, there is a prima facie an infringement of the right holder's intellectual property right'. Since TRIPS does not provide any guidance as to what constitutes a country of importation, it was unclear whether the term could be construed widely enough to encompass the laws of the countries of transit, and the Dutch authorities were able to make the seizures on the basis of evidence of IP infringement based on domestic law rather than that of the country from which the goods originated from. In doing so, they were applying the so-called 'manufacturing fiction' whereby goods are considered to have been manufactured in the country where they are transiting for the purposes of establishing an IP infringement (Kumar (2010), pp. 512–13). However, no clarity was provided on the issue, since the dispute failed to reach the Panel stage. The EU settled the case diplomatically and it is now unlikely that Brazil's complaint

[79] Article 1.1 Customs Control Regulation.

[80] *European Union and a Member State—Seizure of Generic Drugs in Transit*—Request for Consultations by India, DS408.

will be taken further, given that the Court of Justice has subsequently rejected the manufacturing fiction by confirming that, barring exceptional circumstances, no border measures may be adopted against third country in-transit goods which are not intended to be released onto the EU internal market on the mere basis that they are suspected to infringe EU IP rights.[81] Moreover, the Commission has since issued guidelines for the application of the Customs Control Regulation (and now applicable in relation to the Customs Enforcement Regulation[82]) in light of the concerns raised by Brazil and India, as well as the recent case law, which stress that the 'mere fact that medicines are in transit through the EU territory, does not itself constitute enough grounds for customs authorities in any Member State to suspect that the medicines infringe patent rights'.[83]

The expansion of the scope of IP infringements that must be subject to criminal enforcement under TRIPS is also a highly controversial issue. Under Article 61 TRIPS, Members are required to provide for criminal procedures and penalties to be applied at least in cases of wilful trademark counterfeiting or copyright piracy on a commercial scale. Since there is no definition as to what is to be understood by IP infringements on a 'commercial scale', Article 61 TRIPS provides a significant margin of discretion for WTO Members in terms of limiting the types of infringements that may be subject to criminal enforcement. The flexibility ingrained in Article 61 TRIPS was confirmed in *China—Measures Affecting the Protection and Enforcement of IPRs*, which assessed the legality of a Chinese law which provided that criminal prosecution would only be undertaken if the value of the infringing goods exceeded certain minimum thresholds. The US claimed, inter alia, that the Chinese law violated Article 61 TRIPS because the term 'commercial scale' should be understood to cover any infringement whose underlying purpose is to secure a financial gain. The Panel disagreed, considering that there is a quantitative criterion underlying the term but that the thresholds could not be pre-determined but assessed on a case-by-case basis taking into account the product and the market in question.[84] This approach to the construction of 'commercial scale' ensures a degree of flexibility, as it allows WTO Members to determine whether to introduce criminal provisions depending on the size of their domestic markets. A good example of problems caused by agreements that provide TRIPS-plus obligations in the area of IP criminal enforcement can be found in the context of ACTA which builds on the Article 61 TRIPS reference to commercial acts by specifying that such acts 'include at least those carried out as commercial activities for direct or indirect economic or commercial advantage'.[85] What

[81] Joined Cases C-446/09 *Koninklijke Philips Electronics NV v Lucheng Meijing Industrial Company Ltd and Others* and C-495/09 *Nokia Corporation v Her Majesty's Commissioners of Revenue and Customs*.

[82] See Recital 11 of Customs Enforcement Regulation.

[83] Commission, Guidelines of the European Commission concerning the enforcement by the EU customs authorities of intellectual property rights with regard to goods, in particular medicines, in transit through the EU, 1 February 2012.

[84] WTO Panel Report in the *China—Measures Affecting the Protection and Enforcement of Intellectual Property Rights* (WTO, 2009), para 7.577.

[85] Article 23.1 ACTA.

is meant by 'direct or indirect economic or commercial advantage' is unclear. Misgivings were voiced as to how such language has the potential to reduce the flexibility offered by TRIPS and, in particular, that it 'might cover internet users downloading copyrighted files without right holder authorization and so receiving an (indirect) economic advantage of not having to pay the retail price' (Grosse Ruse-Khan (2010b), p. 16).

### *6.5.2.3 Protection of fundamental human rights*

Related to the issue of flexibilities is the concern that increasingly high levels of IP enforcement demanded by developed countries in trade agreements can lead to violations of fundamental human rights such as the freedom of expression, the right to property, the right to privacy and data protection, and the right to a remedy and a fair trial. This is because whereas most national regulatory systems have long recognized the need to balance the protection of IP rights with other valid public interests, trade agreements tend to approach IP rights regulation from the perspective of property holders, giving 'broad rights to producers and exceptional rights to the public' (Abbott (2006), pp. 301–20).

The uneasy relationship between IP protection and human rights in trade agreements was brought to the fore in the context of ACTA—which, as referred to previously, was rejected by the European Parliament because of its perceived potential to adversely impact on the protection of fundamental human rights within the EU. Recent studies have explained how the areas of conflict between ACTA and human rights law follow directly from the fact that the increased levels of enforcement of IP rights infringements are not complemented by the exemptions, limits, and safeguards that are typically included in advanced IP law systems in order to ensure the adequate protection of human rights (Brown and Korff (2011); Opinion of European Academics (2011)). As an illustration, the criminalization of wilful trademark counterfeiting or copyright on a commercial basis could be problematic, since it does contain certain exemptions provided under US law or by the European Convention on Human Rights case law to ensure the freedom of expression (Brown and Korff (2011), p. 22). The question raised by ACTA is whether it requires parties to expand the scope of criminal enforcement of IP rights infringements in a manner that would undermine the aforementioned safeguards. The same reflection is made with regard to the requirements to enact legislation providing for *inaudita altera parte* proceedings without specifying the very exceptional nature of such proceedings and including the safeguards ensuring that the persons targeted by such measures are able to challenge them (Ibid, p. 47).

It should be noted that the text of ACTA includes general flexibilities (e.g. requirement that IP enforcement procedures must be applied in a fair, equitable, and proportionate manner[86]) which arguably provide its signatories enough

[86] Article 6(2) and (3) ACTA.

leeway to implement the IP enforcement obligations in a manner that would not undermine the protection of human rights recognized under national or international law. However, the fact that ACTA's detailed and extensive rules on IP enforcement are only offset by very general and vague safeguards on human rights engendered concerns that the agreement might be implemented in a manner that would compromise the protection of human rights (Brown and Korff (2011), p. 59). Again, the problem lies with the skewed approach to IP regulation in trade agreements, which focus primarily on the protection of the IP rights holders' interests to the detriment of other conflicting rights.

### 6.5.3 EU's approach to enforcement of IP rights in EU DCFTAs

#### *6.5.3.1 Scope of provisions*

The IP rights chapters of the EU DCFTAs all contain a section concerning the enforcement of intellectual property rights. Typically, the provisions contained therein can be subdivided into three categories: those pertaining to civil proceedings, border measures, and the liability of online service providers. The main source of inspiration for the regulation of these fields can be found in EU law. The EU DCFTAs signed with developed countries (Korea FTA and EU–Singapore FTA) differ slightly in that they reproduce certain provisions sourced from ACTA. This approach can be explained by the fact that the EU, Korea, and Singapore were negotiating ACTA and their respective FTAs at the same time (both Korea and Singapore have ratified ACTA). The KOREU FTA presents an added peculiarity in that it contains provisions on criminal enforcement of IP rights—also inspired by ACTA. It is peculiar not only because it is the only Global FTA to address this area in detail, but also because this is an area that remains unregulated under EU law. It has been argued in this respect that the EU's apparent eagerness to negotiate provisions in a field where regulatory harmonization at EU level has been rejected in the past may not necessarily reflect an external trade policy objective, but rather reveals more surreptitious designs to circumvent difficulties encountered in the context of its internal legislative process (so-called 'policy laundering') (Blakeney (2012), p. 333). These concerns must be tempered by the fact that these are mixed agreements, meaning that the rules included therein must be ratified by both the EU and the Member States. In fact, the provisions on criminal enforcement of IP rights were (along with the Protocol on Cultural Cooperation) the only provisions which did not apply on a provisional basis pending the completion of the national ratification procedures of the EU Member States. However, the practice remains a controversial one. Despite the fact that the European Parliament rejected the Commission's attempts to introduce internal legislation on criminal enforcement and refused to give its assent to ACTA, the EU still finds itself bound by a good number of the TRIPS-plus criminal enforcement provisions included in that agreement through the KOREU FTA. And the inclusion of such provisions in the KOREU FTA is not just a flash in a pan—an accidental by-product of concomitant negotiations of ACTA—but an established policy practice of the EU in its EU DCFTAs. Leaked drafts of the IP rights chapter in the CETA negotiated between the EU and Canada contained similarly ambitious provisions on criminal enforcement[87]—although following the rejection of ACTA by the European Parliament, the EU has clarified that ACTA criminal enforcement provisions were removed from CETA (Commission (2013d), p. 2). Moreover, the EU is not averse to including comparable provisions in trade agreements with developing countries. For example, even though the EU–CA FTA only contains a provision that mainly replicates the current content of Article 61 TRIPS, the initial proposals presented by the EU sought to expand criminal liability to infringements of patents (Drexl (2009), p. 11).

### *6.5.3.2 Flexibilities*

In accordance with the EU's current policy, the IP enforcement provisions of the EU DCFTAs are generally TRIPS-plus in nature. Whether concluded with developed or developing countries, they impose high standards of enforcement in line with what is currently provided under EU law. This raises the question of whether IP provisions contained in the EU DCFTAs attempt to find a balance between its policy of exporting internal market rules and the concern of WTO Members to maintain a degree of regulatory authority to achieve national policy objectives. The EU DCFTAs do not contain 'general exceptions' provisions that would allow parties to derogate from their IP-related obligations in order to pursue a pre-determined set of national policy objectives. Rather, there are a number of provisions reasserting the parties' commitment to uphold existing TRIPS flexibilities (Grosse Ruse-Khan (2011)). The impact of such provisions is limited where they merely acknowledge the already existing obligation of the parties to comply with TRIPS. This includes commitments to 'ensure an adequate and effective implementation of the international treaties dealing with intellectual property to which they are party including [TRIPS]',[88] or in the case of the Colombia–Peru FTA, affirm their 'rights and obligations under WTO Agreements and any other multilateral agreement under the auspices of the WIPO'.[89] These general provisions are of a declaratory nature and cannot be construed as entitling a country to derogate from TRIPS-plus obligations to which they have willingly signed in the context of an FTA.

Besides general references, there are also provisions replicating specific flexibilities under TRIPS. These include provisions that allow signatories to exceptionally derogate from the requirement to ensure the level of protection provided for under the EU DCFTAs with regard to a specific IP right but also provisions recognizing the right of parties to determine an appropriate method to ensure the

[87] Draft of IP rights chapter Comprehensive Economic and Trade Agreement, February 2012. Available at: www.bilaterals.org.

[88] Article 10.1 KOREU FTA; Article 229 EU–CA FTA.

[89] Article 196.1 Colombia–Peru FTA.

levels of IP protection required by the FTA under their respective national legal systems,[90] the commitment of the parties to implement and interpret the provisions of the EU DCFTAs in a manner that is consistent with the Public Health Declaration,[91] and more general references to TRIPS flexibilities, such as the principles set out in Article 8 TRIPS.[92] Further, the EU DCFTAs reproduce language from the Enforcement Directive that is intended to provide flexibility in the implementation of the IP enforcement obligations in domestic law. They provide that IP enforcement measures must 'be fair and equitable'[93] as well as 'effective, proportionate and dissuasive and [...] applied in such a manner as to avoid the creation of barriers to legitimate trade and to provide for safeguards against their abuse'.[94] The extent to which such flexibilities can provide a margin of discretion for FTA parties varies in accordance with the level of IP protection predicated by the agreement. This can be seen clearly with regard to references to Article 8 TRIPS and the Public Health Declaration. Because these flexibilities have an interpretative value, the extent to which they can impact on the implementation of TRIPS-plus obligations in FTAs will depend on whether a specific obligation leaves room for interpretation. In other words, the more ambiguous the obligation, the more discretion the parties have to implement the obligation in a manner that seeks to ensure the promotion of the concerned policy objectives (Ibid, p. 40). One exception may be found in Article 139(2) CEPA which provides, inter alia, that nothing in the agreement 'shall be construed as to impair the capacity of the [p]arties and the [s]ignatory CARIFORUM States to promote access to medicines'. Although phrased as an interpretative tool, this provision erects the promotion of access to medicines as an objective overriding any IP-related obligation resulting from CEPA. Here, CARIFORUM States could reasonably argue that they have a legal basis to disregard the application of an IP-related obligation that is clear and unambiguous, if such application were to undermine the promotion of access to medicines.

It would be remiss not to mention those provisions in EU DCFTAs that acknowledge the existence of other policy objectives, against which the protection of IP rights should be balanced. Article 196.3 of the Colombia–Peru FTA recognizes 'the need to maintain a balance between the rights of IP holders and the interest of the public, particularly regarding education, culture, research, public health, food security, environment, access to information and technology transfer'. The provision is noteworthy as it adds policy considerations that are not included in TRIPS (e.g. education, culture, research, food security) but remains subject to the same limitations that apply to those provisions

[90] Article 140 CEPA (replicating Article 1.1 TRIPS); See also Article 234(4) Colombia–Peru FTA.

[91] Article 148 CEPA; Article 10.34 KOREU FTA; Article 10.34(b) and (c) Colombia–Peru FTA; Artcle 229.2(b) EU–CA FTA; Article 11.30 EU–Singapore FTA; Article 3 Chapter 22 CETA.

[92] Article 139 CEPA; Article 197(1) Colombia–Peru FTA; Article 11.2 EU–Singapore FTA.

[93] Article 2(1) Enforcement Directive. Article 151.1 CEPA; Article 10.41.2(b) KOREU FTA; Article 260.1(2) EU–CA FTA; Article 13 Chapter 22 CETA.

[94] Article 2(2) Enforcement Directive. Article 151.2 CEPA; Article 10.41.2(d) KOREU FTA; Article 260.3 EU–CA FTA; Article 13 Chapter 22 CETA.

replicating Articles 7 and 8 TRIPS, insofar as—at best—it can only purport to have an interpretative value.

In short, the EU DCFTAs recognize the continued validity of all flexibilities embedded in TRIPS and emphasize the importance of certain key flexibilities, namely the need to protect public health. However, as TRIPS-plus agreements, the EU DCFTAs will always necessarily result in the erosion of existing flexibilities. The more stringent and detailed IP protection and enforcement are, the harder it becomes for countries to disregard such obligations in order to pursue national policy objectives. In the case of the EU DCFTAs, generally speaking, the proliferation of TRIPS-plus obligations in such agreements—and in particular the exportation of specific standards of IP protection under EU law—means that they include less room for manoeuvre than that currently provided under TRIPS.

#### *6.5.3.3 Civil enforcement*

The provisions of the EU DCFTAs on enforcement of IP rights replicate to a large extent the structure and content of the EU's Enforcement Directive. Like the Enforcement Directive, the EU DCFTAs regulate a number of issues such as the definition of the persons entitled to seek enforcement of their IP rights, evidence, the right of information of claimants, and the power of judicial authorities to issue provisional and precautionary measures and order the payment of damages. The language of some of these provisions borrows heavily from that used in the Enforcement Directive (e.g. presumption of authorship or ownership,[95] provisional and precautionary measures,[96] corrective measures[97]), and in some cases effectively transpose verbatim the content of the Enforcement Directive (e.g. evidence,[98] right of information,[99] injunctions,[100] alternative measures,[101] damages,[102] legal costs,[103] and publication of

[95] Article 5 Enforcement Directive; Article 10.52 KOREU FTA; Article 21 EU–CA FTA; Article 23 CETA; Article 23 Chapter 22 CETA.

[96] Article 9 Enforcement Directive; Article 156 CEPA; Article 10.46 KOREU FTA; Article 240 Colombia–Peru FTA; Article 18 CETA; Article 18 Chapter 22 CETA.

[97] Article 10 Enforcement Directive; Article 157 CEPA; Article 10.47 KOREU FTA; Article 241 Colombia–Peru FTA.

[98] Article 6.2 Enforcement Directive; Article 153 CEPA; Article 10.44(1) KOREU FTA; Article 237 Colombia–Peru FTA; Article 12 EU–CA FTA; Articles 15(2) and 16 Chapter 22 CETA.

[99] Article 8 Enforcement Directive; Article 155 CEPA; Article 10.45 KOREU FTA; Article 239 Colombia–Peru FTA.

[100] Article 11 Enforcement Directive; Article 158 CEPA; 10.48 KOREU FTA; Article 11.42 EU–Singapore FTA.

[101] Article 12 Enforcement Directive; Article 159 CEPA; Article 10.49 KOREU FTA; Article 243 Colombia–Peru FTA; Article 11.43 EU–Singapore FTA.

[102] Article 13 Enforcement Directive; Article 169 CEPA; Article 10.50 KOREU FTA; Article 244 Colombia–Peru FTA.

[103] Article 14 Enforcement Directive; Article 161 CEPA; Article 10.51 KOREU FTA; Article 245 Colombia–Peru FTA; Article 19 EU–CA FTA; Article 11.45 EU–Singapore FTA; Article 22 CETA.

judicial decisions[104]). Finally, all agreements provide an exhaustive list of persons entitled to seek application of the enforcement measures identified in each agreement, which is identical to that provided under Article 4 of the Enforcement Directive. The EU–Singapore FTA and the CETA stand out with regard to the issue of civil enforcement insofar as they also include civil enforcement provisions sourced from ACTA, such as rules relating to measures for preservation of evidence,[105] right of information,[106] injunctions,[107] and damages.[108]

The imposition of high standards of civil enforcement in the context of FTAs does not generate the sort of headlines that are usually associated with more contentious issues of border measures and criminal enforcement. However, the inclusion in the EU–Singapore FTA of civil enforcement provisions of the ACTA—including Article 11.2 ACTA allowing the imposition of provisional measures in the context of *inaudita altera parte* proceedings, which was widely criticized for undermining fair trial guarantees—shows that such provisions can raise certain concerns from a human rights law perspective. Further, the exportation of EU legislation abroad can be problematic where it is done selectively, and to be more precise, where the agreements replicate enforcement standards provided under EU law without the accompanying safeguards. A case in point is CEPA, where the EU successfully transposed large segments of its Enforcement Directive but omitted, in some instances, provisions seeking to ensure that the enforcement of IP rights is applied in a manner that ensures proportionality and the respect of rights of defence. For example, while CEPA mandates the availability of provisional and precautionary measures intended to prevent suspected imminent infringements of IP rights as provided under Article 9 of the Enforcement Directive (interlocutory injunctions intended to prevent imminent infringements, seizures of delivery up of goods suspected of infringement, and precautionary seizures of movable and immovable property), it does not replicate any of the provisions of the Enforcement Directive intended to ward off potential abuses of such procedures by right holders (e.g. requirement to revoke a provisional measure where the applicant fails to 'institute, within a reasonable period, proceedings leading to a decision on the merits'[109]).

It can be argued that the general flexibilities included in the Enforcement Directive and replicated in the EU DCFTAs (e.g. requirement to ensure that IP enforcement measures are fair, equitable, and proportionate) provide enough leeway to enact safeguards against abuses of human rights in domestic law. Nevertheless, the very fact that the EU Enforcement Directive complements these general flexibilities with more specific safeguards suggests that, in the absence of

[104] Article 15 Enforcement Directive; Article 162 CEPA; Article 10.52 KOREU FTA; Article 246 Colombia–Peru FTA.

[105] Article 10 ACTA; Article 11.39 EU–Singapore FTA; Article 17 Chapter 22 CETA.

[106] Article 11 ACTA; Article 11.40 EU–Singapore FTA.

[107] Article 8 ACTA; Article 20 CETA; Article 20 Chapter 22 CETA.

[108] Article 9(1) ACTA; Article 11.44 EU–Singapore FTA; Article 21(b) CETA.

[109] Article 9(6) Enforcement Directive.

the latter, the EU DCFTAs do not sufficiently guard against implementations that violate fundamental human rights. The selective exportation of the Enforcement Directive means that it is possible to envisage a situation in which the EU's trading partners would enact laws that reproduce the EU standards of IP enforcement without the adequate human rights safeguards. The danger is acute with regard to those trade agreements concluded with developing countries with nascent IP regulatory frameworks (Deere (2008), p. 224). In order to fulfil its obligation to protect human rights in its external relations, the EU must be mindful that the exportation of its internal market rules in the area of IP does not lead to the implementation of regulatory frameworks that may lead to infringements of fundamental human rights. This could be done by ensuring that where EU standards are imposed in EU DCFTAs, these are accompanied by the corresponding safeguards included under EU law. Further, the EU should also take care to emphasize the importance of such safeguards in the context of technical assistance given to developing countries enacting TRIPS-plus obligations.

#### *6.5.3.4 Border measures*

The Global FTA provisions on border measures are, like those on civil enforcement, inspired by existing EU internal rules, namely the Customs Control Regulation (now replaced by the Customs Enforcement Regulation). However, whereas the civil enforcement rules are detailed and tend to reproduce the bulk of the rules included in the Enforcement Directive, the border measure rules contained in the Global FTA are not extensive. In part, this reflects the fact that IP civil enforcement requirements are typically already incorporated into the general enforcement rules of a national legal system. Therefore, such rules do not always entail significantly onerous legislative and institutional reforms. Rules relating to enforcement by customs authorities, especially those applied in the EU, require the mobilization of considerable financial resources as well as the availability of expertise, which is often lacking in some of the EU's trading partners. There are, therefore, no references to rights of applicants in the context of proceedings before customs authorities, nor are there any provisions governing actions by customs authorities and other authorities competent to decide on cases concerning border measures.

Instead, all of the focus is placed on one of the EU's main strategic interests in the context of TRIPS reform—that of the expansion of the scope of border measures as currently provided under Article 51 TRIPS to cover trade activities other than the mere importation of goods (e.g. by covering in-transit goods), but also to cover infringement of IP rights other than pirated copyrights and counterfeited trademarks. The EU DCFTAs generally provide that parties must adopt procedures that enable right holders to apply for the suspension by the customs authorities of the release into free circulation or detention of goods for which there are valid grounds for suspecting that goods infringe certain IP rights. Border measures will generally apply to a range of IP right infringements and situations that go beyond those listed under Article 51 TRIPS. This raises the question of whether the border measure provisions require the type of TRIPS-plus legislation that may potentially be used—in the same way as the Customs Control Regulation had in the past—as a barrier to legitimate trade in in-transit generic pharmaceuticals.

Under CEPA, border measures can be applied in the case of suspected infringements of counterfeit and pirated goods as well as infringements of designs and geographical indications.[110] This goes further than TRIPS in two respects. First, because Article 51 TRIPS does not cover designs and geographical indications and, secondly, the definition of what constitutes counterfeit goods is wider than that provided under Article 51 TRIPS, as in addition to covering goods bearing without authorization a trademark registered in respect of the same goods or which cannot be distinguished from such trademark, it also concerns counterfeit trademark symbols and packaging materials. However, there is no requirement to take action against suspected infringements of patents, nor is there a requirement to take action against goods that are in-transit. Therefore, the provisions of CEPA alone do not impose a requirement to enact legislation that may lead to situations where customs authorities may detain in-transit generic pharmaceuticals. The same reflection can be made with regard to the Colombia–Peru FTA which, whilst permitting action against goods that are in-transit, is limited in terms of its scope of application to counterfeit and pirated goods.[111] The approach pursued in these EU DCFTAs is in line with their strong emphasis on the need to ensure that IP protection is not used in such a way as to undermine public health objectives and impair access to medicines. In fact, the flexibilities included in these agreements mean that even if patent holders were allowed to lodge applications with regard to goods in-transit suspected of infringing such rights, national authorities would still have sufficient legal grounds to reject such applications. The CETA and the EU–Singapore FTA follow suit, as they expand the IP rights covered by Article 51 TRIPS (counterfeit trademark goods, pirated copyright goods, counterfeit geographical indications, and pirated designed goods[112]) but do not require parties to adopt or maintain e border measures to goods in transit.[113]

However, not all EU DCFTAs are as circumspect with regard to the issue of the expansion of the scope of border measures under TRIPS. The EU–CA FTA adopts a similar approach to EU law by allowing the application of border measures in situations other than the importation of goods suspected of infringing IP rights, including to goods in-transit. The agreement requires signatories to: (i) enable IP rights holders to request the application of border measures when they have 'valid grounds for suspecting that the importation, exportation, re-exportation, entry or exit of the customs territory, placement under a suspensive procedure or placement under a free zone or a free warehouse of goods infringing trademarks, or copyrights may take place';[114] and (ii) provide that 'competent authorities may initiate border measures ex officio in the cases of import, export and transit'.[115] The scope of IP infringements covered is also more

[110] Article 164 footnote 2 CEPA. [111] Article 249 Colombia–Peru FTA footnote 75.
[112] Article 11.49 EU–Singapore FTA; Article 24 Chapter 22 CETA.
[113] Article 11.50.3 EU–Singapore FTA. [114] Article 273 (2) EU–CA FTA.
[115] Article 273(4) EU–CA FTA.

extensive than in TRIPS, as customs authorities may apply border measures against all suspected infringements of trademarks and copyrights, not just counterfeit trademarks of pirated goods. Although there is no obligation to apply such measures in cases of patent infringement—which reduces the potential for these provisions to be used as barriers to the trade of in-transit generic pharmaceuticals—the fact that customs authorities are empowered to act against any suspected trademark infringement could prove problematic. Counterfeit trademarks, as defined in TRIPS, only concern cases where goods bear without authorization a trademark which is identical to a validly registered trademark. Under the EU–CA FTA, however, since border measures are permitted against all types of trademark infringements, customs authorities may take action against generic drugs whose names, labels or packaging are merely confusingly similar to those of patented drugs protected by trademarks (Grosse Ruse-Khan (2010c), pp. 673–77).

In the KOREU FTA, border measures can be applied in case of suspected infringements of the following IP rights: counterfeit trademark goods, pirated copyright goods, patents, plant variety rights, registered designs, or geographical indications.[116] As for the circumstances under which border measures may be applied, the KOREU FTA covers the importation, exportation, and transit of goods.[117] The KOREU FTA goes beyond even what is provided in ACTA, which does not require border measures against patent infringements, but only recognizes the right of the signatories to adopt such measures (Ibid, p. 646). Further, as a consequence of the KOREU FTA, Korea has amended its legislation, which previously only covered trademark and copyright infringements, to provide for the possibility of border measures against patents (Lim and Choi (2009); Nahm (2011)). The KOREU FTA has therefore created a situation where the EU has induced national regulatory reform in a third country whose application could lead to the application of border measures against in-transit generic pharmaceuticals. Finally, the CETA differs from other EU DCFTAs in that its provisions are largely taken from the text of the ACTA. This includes provisions regulating applications from right holders for the imposition of border measures,[118] determinations of infringement,[119] and availability of remedies where an infringement has been found.[120] The scope of border measure provisions is, however, wider than that of ACTA as such measures may be applied not only with respect to pirated copyright goods and counterfeit goods but also counterfeit geographical indication goods.[121] Moreover, the suspension of release of or detainment of such goods may be envisaged in cases of import and export shipment, transhipments and shipment in customs transit.[122] However, unlike the KOREU FTA, the CETA parties retain full discretion to decide whether or not to require the imposition border measures in the above-mentioned circumstances.

[116] Article 10.67, footnote 76 KOREU FTA.
[117] Article 10.67(1) KOREU FTA; Article 249 Colombia–Peru FTA.
[118] Articles 24.2, 24.3 and 24.4 CETA; Articles 17 and 18 ACTA.
[119] Article 25.5 CETA; Article 19 ACTA.
[120] Article 24.6 CETA; Article 20 ACTA.
[121] Article 24.1(1) CETA.
[122] Articles 24.1, 24.2 and 24.3 CETA.

### 6.5.3.5 Criminal enforcement

Only two EU DCFTAs regulate on criminal enforcement of IP infringements. EU–CA FTA contains a provision which merely reproduces Article 61 TRIPS on criminal procedures, and the KOREU FTA goes beyond TRIPS on this topic, using ACTA as its major source of inspiration. Of all the criminal enforcement provisions found in the latter agreement, only Article 23.3 ACTA permitting criminal enforcement regarding cinematographic works and Article 26 ACTA on ex officio criminal enforcement are omitted in the KOREU FTA. Some provisions (e.g. liability of legal persons, aiding and abetting) are almost word for word reproductions, whilst others (e.g. criminal penalties and seizures, forfeitures, and destruction) are watered down versions of the corresponding provisions under ACTA.

The KOREU FTA, however, does not seek to define the concept of commercial scale in the same manner as ACTA. It provides that '[e]ach Party shall provide for criminal procedures and penalties to be applied at least in cases of wilful trademark counterfeiting and copyright and related rights piracy on a commercial scale'.[123] The only substantive difference compared to Article 61 TRIPS is the additional reference to 'related rights piracy', which in any event seems to be covered by footnote 14 of Article 51 TRIPS (Grosse Ruse-Khan (2010b), p. 15). In other words, despite having used the text of ACTA as a source of inspiration, the parties to the KOREU FTA were not willing to incorporate the controversial TRIPS-plus language regarding the scope of criminal offences as defined under ACTA.

The KOREU FTA proves problematic when one considers that many of the obligations contained therein were actually also put forward in the Commission's ill-fated proposals for a criminal enforcement directive. The KOREU FTA is in this way imposing criminal enforcement obligations that the Commission could not push through domestically, reinforcing the claims from those who argue that the Commission is using trade agreements to force internal regulatory reform by stealth (Drexl (2009), p. 11). To add insult to injury, the text of the KOREU FTA fails to include amendments to the proposed criminal enforcement directive that have been put forward by the European Parliament in order to provide safeguards against abuses by IP rights holders and to protect human rights.[124]. For example, the European Parliament had suggested that the inclusion of the proposed directive should specify that 'infringements on a commercial scale' should not be understood as excluding 'acts carried out by private users for personal and not-for-profit purposes'.[125] It also included an obligation to ensure that the

[123] Article 10.54 KOREU FTA.

[124] European Parliament legislative resolution of 25 April 2007 (COM(2006)0168–C6-0233/2005–2005/0127(COD)) (Amended Criminal Enforcement Proposal). See also Report on the amended proposal for a directive of the European Parliament and of the Council on criminal measures aimed at ensuring the enforcement of intellectual property rights, 27 March 2007, A6-0073/2007 (COM(2006)0168–C6-0233/2005–2005/0127(COD)).

[125] Article 2(b) Amended Criminal Enforcement Proposal.

'fair use of a protected work, [...] for purposes such as criticism, comment, news reporting, teaching (including multiple copies for classroom use), scholarship or research, does not constitute a criminal offence',[126] to ensure that misuse of criminal sanctions is prohibited,[127] as well as safeguards aimed at ensuring the rights of defence[128] and the right to privacy.[129] The fact that the human rights safeguards proposed by the EU Parliament in relation to the proposed criminal enforcement directive are absent from the EU DCFTAs (along with the recent rejection of the ACTA by the European Parliament) confirms that this is one area where the EU's deep trade agenda has failed to fully take into account non-trade goals. It seems that the EU is not just falling short of its obligation to promote human rights abroad, but also its own expectations regarding the protection of human rights.

The inclusion of criminal enforcement provisions in EU DCFTAs also highlights a novel feature of the EU's deep trade agenda. Here, the EU is not merely content to impose existing international rules or even to export its own norms. It is participating in the development of rules, for which there is no corresponding legislation with the EU, and incorporating them into trade agreements. It may be questioned why the EU is seeking to address issues that have proved so controversial internally in its EU DCFTAs. On the surface, the regulation of IP criminal enforcement in trade agreements, such as the EU DCFTAs, appears to give credence to accusations that the EU is engaged in policy laundering. The EU DCFTAs must be ratified by the European Parliament and the parliaments of Member States, but the ratification process is much less flexible than the legislative process that would be applied for the adoption of internal legislation. Whereas, parliaments take an active role in the shaping of laws in internal legislative processes, ratification leaves parliaments with a decision to either approve or reject the trade agreements as a whole. The upshot is that, in the case of the KOREU FTA, the European Parliament could not (as it had done on the context of proposals for the adoption of internal legislation on criminal enforcement in the area of IP) propose amendments designed to safeguard the protection of human rights. In fact, the criminal enforcement provisions of the KOREU FTA passed almost unnoticed, notably because they did not seem to require any amendments to the domestic laws of Member States.[130]

However, another criticism levelled at the inclusion of criminal enforcement provisions in EU DCFTAs is that these provisions strengthen the case for the adoption of internal rules on criminal enforcement, because the EU remains liable for any violation of the obligations included therein and must therefore ensure

[126] Article 3 Amended Criminal Enforcement Proposal.
[127] Article 7 Amended Criminal Enforcement Proposal.
[128] Article 8 Amended Criminal Enforcement Proposal.
[129] Article 9.3 Amended Criminal Enforcement Proposal.
[130] See for example France (Projet de Loi autorisant la ratification de l'accord de libre-échange entre l'Union européenne et ses États membres, d'une part, et la République de Corée, d'autre part; 19 Juin 2013 NOR: MAEJ1236777L/Bleue-1) and Belgium (Projet de loi portant assentiment à l'Accord de libre-échange entre l'Union européenne et ses Etats membres, d'une part, et la République de Corée, d'autre part, fait à Bruxelles le 6 octobre 2010 DOC 53 2576/002).

their uniform implementation by all Member States (Drexl (2011), pp. 11–12; Cremona (2012), p. 173). In other words, whilst it would not be wholly accurate to claim that the EU uses its FTAs to harmonize EU law by stealth (given that the criminal enforcement provisions are all subject to ratification by Member States), it may be that such agreements are being used to progressively erode opposition to such legislation.

## 6.6 Conclusion

The EU's current external trade policy in the area of IP shows that it is increasingly veering towards the more aggressive and prescriptive approach adopted by the US in its FTAs. Although the EU has maintained its policy of requiring signatories to sign up to international IP agreements that go beyond TRIPS, it is certainly not averse to complementing these with provisions which contain standards of IP protection sourced from EU law (e.g. copyrights and patents). Moreover, in those areas where existing international agreements are not perceived to go far enough (geographical indications and enforcement of IP rights), the EU has transposed significant parts of its own legislation into the EU DCFTAs. IP is therefore one area where the EU certainly lives up to its reputation as an exporter of norms. The EU has used the EU DCFTAs to promote the adoption by third countries of TRIPS-plus standards of IP protection that replicate as much as possible those applicable within the EU's internal market.

The prescriptive stance adopted in EU DCFTAs is reflective of the strong offensive interests of the EU regarding the protection and enforcement of IP rights. There can be no doubting that the EU uses its higher bargaining power in the bilateral context to push through TRIPS-plus regulatory reforms whose inclusion at WTO level remains controversial. This can be seen from the two case studies addressed in the present chapter. The EU's policy concerning geographical indications is primarily motivated by self-interest rather than a belief that its regulatory model is necessarily superior to other models applied elsewhere. Through the EU DCFTAs, the EU not only seeks to secure the protection of its geographical indications in third countries, but also to ensure that such countries adopt legislation which—like that of the EU—prioritizes geographical indications over trademarks. The exportation of the EU's regulatory model abroad gives EU producers a significant advantage over foreign competitors and increases the support for its own reform proposals on this matter at WTO level. However, the EU is not alone in pursuing this policy, as the US is also using its FTAs to promote its own regulatory model, which conflicts with that of the EU. With every new FTA signed, the EU and the US are further entrenching their regulatory positions and diminishing the chances of a multilateral consensus ever being formed. The case study on IP enforcement also shows that the EU's prescriptive approach can undermine its commitment to further human rights protection abroad and to take into account the level of development of its trade partners. This results in part from the fact that in its eagerness to export higher standards of IP protection and enforcement, the EU sometimes omits to include adequate flexibilities and safeguards. The EU DCFTAs generally reassert many of the flexibilities provided under TRIPS and are particularly mindful, in the agreements concluded with developing countries, of the need to ensure that signatories maintain the right to pursue public health imperatives. However, these general TRIPS flexibilities and safeguards can, in certain cases, be insufficient to ensure that the more detailed and stringent TRIPS-plus standards of the EU DCFTAs are not implemented in a manner that favours IP rights holders disproportionately relative to legitimate competitors and consumers, and that may lead to infringements of fundamental human rights. In the context of the provisions regulating civil and criminal enforcement provisions as well as those relating to border measures that may be applied by customs authorities, this chapter has shown that the EU DCFTAs could lead to the enactment of domestic laws that violate fundamental human rights or even undermine the right of states to pursue public health objectives by creating barriers to legitimate trade of drugs in-transit.

Finally, the examination of IP enforcement provisions in the KOREU FTA has highlighted a problem that comes from the inclusion of regulatory issues in trade agreements—that of how such agreements can be used to bypass internal legislative difficulties. Although the European Parliament can try to shape the content of trade agreements during the negotiation process, it cannot propose amendments—as it did to the proposed criminal enforcement directive—to the final text of the agreement. The decision to approve the KOREU FTA was, in practice, facilitated by the fact that it was not considered to require any amendments to existing domestic laws. However, one cannot exclude the possibility that future EU DCFTAs including more stringent requirements may place the European Parliament and national parliaments in the unenviable position of having to consider whether to reject an entire agreement in light of the inclusion of regulatory issues which would have either been dismissed or regulated differently in the context of the internal legislative process.

# 7

# Competition

## 7.1 Introduction

Competition law concerns the 'set of legal instruments created and maintained by governments to regulate the behaviour of firms that restrict competition in the market' (Dawar and Holmes (2012), p. 228) such as anti-competitive agreements, abuses by firms in a dominant position within a reference market, and mergers and acquisitions that adversely impact on competition. The purpose of introducing disciplines on competition laws in the context of international trade regulation is to ensure that once state-made barriers to trade are removed, private economic operators are not allowed to erect similar barriers (Odudu (2006), p. 13; Jones (2011), p. 262). It is a policy that is intrinsically linked with the EU's own identity, which has historically apprehended competition law from a market access perspective (Nicolaidis and Vernon (1997), pp. 271–312). The EU has thus exported its competition laws abroad through the enlargement process or by signing bilateral agreements with third countries, and has steadfastly supported the idea of including rules on competition at the WTO level.

Numerous explanations have been advanced to explain the EU's attachment to the dissemination of competition laws. In addition to the aim of enhancing market contestability (Wigger (2008), pp. 181–202) it has, for example, been argued that the promotion of EU competition rules is a policy pursued by the Commission to 'build an international identity' (Aydin (2012), p. 669) and assert its pre-eminence relative to other Member States in the area of competition law (Damro (2001), pp. 208–26). Others claim that the EU's singular approach towards competition policy as a market access issue has more to do with ideological self-projection than it has to do with a solid economic liberalization rationale (Poletti (2012), p. 64).

Yet, the EU's external policy in the area of competition law has had mixed results. The EU's attempts to externalize its competition laws through trade can be traced back to the 1990s when it started negotiating bilateral agreements with third countries, providing for minimum competition law standards and frameworks for cooperation between national competition authorities. The policy was so successful that the EU's approach to the regulation of competition issues soon became the most widespread regulatory model in the world (Fox (2000), pp. 1791–3). This, along with the success of the Uruguay Round, gave the EU confidence to propose, as one of the 1996 Singapore issues, the adoption of a stand-alone WTO agreement on competition. The proposal was, however, met with strong opposition and was eventually removed from the Doha Round. The opposition came from both developed countries concerned by the possibility that multilateral rules on competition could require them to amend their existing national regimes and developing countries concerned equally by the loss of policy space and the onerous burden resulting from the obligation to comply with such rules.

Since the rejection of its proposals at the WTO level, the EU has continued to push through competition policy disciplines in bilateral FTAs and cooperation agreements, as well as other multilateral fora such as the OECD and International Competition Network (ICN). This chapter aims to describe the EU's efforts to promote adoption of competition policies through its EU DCFTAs and asks, in particular, whether and in what ways the EU has sought to advance the disciplines on competition proposed in the context of the Singapore issues in the aftermath of the collapse of the Doha Round. It is found that although the EU DCFTAs include language inspired from the TFEU competition rules, most provisions contain general and unenforceable obligations. There is, in fact, an apparent gap between the EU's rhetoric, which emphasizes the importance of linking trade and competition policy, and the reality of the EU's external trade practice in the EU DCFTAs. It must be noted that the present chapter does not deal with the issue of state aid (or subsidies)—which although regulated by EU competition law, is typically absent from most other competition law systems, which focus exclusively on the conduct of private enterprises. Moreover, state aid was not one of the new trade issues covered under the Singapore issues (as the WTO already regulates subsidies under the Agreement on Subsidies and Countervailing Measures (SCM)), and the EU DCFTAs generally include but a few disciplines that go further than those currently provided by the SCM (Jarosz-Friis, Pesaresi, and Kerle (2010), pp. 79–80). The last point can be explained by the fact that these other EU DCFTAs have been concluded with developing countries that do not have state aid regimes in place (European Commission (2008b)).

Section 7.2 goes into more detail on the various issues and diverging positions concerning the relationship between competition and trade liberalization. This section highlights in particular that in the debate concerning the desirability of establishing international competition rules, the focus is as much on its potential adverse impact on the policy space of national governments as it is on what conception of competition law should be favoured. Section 7.3 provides a descriptive overview of the current international regulatory framework for competition issues. It looks at the existing rules at WTO level and the EU's proposals for a multilateral agreement on competition. Section 7.4 analyses the EU's current external trade policy in this area. It focuses in particular on the content of the Global FTA provisions dedicated to the issue of competition and examines to what extent these impose binding disciplines on competition policy.

## 7.2 Trade Liberalization and Competition Policy

### 7.2.1 Political economy of the trade/competition interface

Demands for international rules on competition are a natural consequence of the gradual integration of global markets. As corporations expand their activities beyond the limits of national frontiers, national governments are increasingly called upon to tackle the conduct of foreign corporations that undermine domestic competition. In order to address this, major economies, such as the EU and the US, have resorted to the extra-territorial application of their national competition laws in cases where the conduct of foreign companies produce, or is intended to produce, anti-competitive effects within their territories (Fox (2003), pp. 916–17). This 'effects doctrine' is, however, subject to a number of limitations. To the extent that it requires the mobilization of substantial resources, it remains very much a developed country luxury. Poorer developing countries, on the other hand, rarely have the means to protect themselves against the anti-competitive consequences of the activities of foreign corporations (Hamilton and Whalley (1996), pp. 3–94). In addition, even developed countries with strong institutional capabilities face significant difficulties in carrying out investigations and gathering evidence of anti-competitive behaviour when the alleged anti-competitive behaviour is conducted abroad (Hoekman and Holmes (1999), p. 8). Finally, under the effects doctrine, jurisdiction may only be applied with regard to anti-competitive practices which produce effects domestically. As a result, jurisdictions such as the EU and the US cannot prohibit practices which produce effects exclusively outside of their respective jurisdictions, even if such practices harm the interests of their firms doing business abroad (Bourgeois (2013), p. 384). Another issue arising from global economic integration comes from the increasing number of international mergers. As competition law is generally dealt with at the national level, multinational corporations wishing to merge may be required to obtain the prior approval of multiple national competition authorities, and as a result incur considerable transactional costs (Bradford (2007), p. 392). Moreover, because of the substantial analysis for merger controls, the outcomes can vary significantly from one jurisdiction to another and lead to political conflicts (Hoekman and Holmes (1999), p. 5).

Competition law also has clear links with trade policy. Trade agreements focus on the removal of tariff and non-tariff barriers to trade created by governments. However, the anti-competitive conduct of private economic operators, such as vertical market restraints, import cartels, and monopolies, can impede market access. In the absence of international rules on competition applied on a non-discriminatory basis, there is always an incentive for national governments to favour domestic industry by under-enforcing competition laws (if these exist) with regard to local enterprises and over-enforcing the same rules against foreign market entrants (Guzman (2001), pp. 1156–8; Hoekman and Kostecki (2001), p. 427). For example, the Chinese antitrust enforcement authorities have recently been accused of applying competition law in a discriminatory manner (by targeting foreign investors in investigations on anti-competitive practices and routinely blocking acquisitions of Chinese companies) in order to protect domestic industries (Sakoui and Politi (2013)). It is also argued that competition policy would help to maximize the benefits from trade liberalization. The standard economic theory underpinning competition policy contends that competitive markets result in allocative efficiency (firms cannot limit output in order to increase prices and must instead produce goods until the price of sale corresponds to the marginal costs) and productive efficiency (all firms must produce at the lowest possible cost in order to avoid losses of market shares) (Dewey (1964), p. 434). Therefore, by enhancing market contestability, competition rules foster economic efficiency and consumer welfare and contribute to the overall aim of trade liberalization (Anderson and Holmes (2002), p. 532).

### 7.2.2 Objectives of competition policy and law in the context of trade liberalization: Market access versus economic efficiency

EU competition rules are set out under Articles 101 to 109 TFEU. Article 101 TFEU prohibits concerted practices (e.g. vertical and horizontal agreements) which may 'affect trade between Member States and which have as their object or effect the prevention, restriction or distortion of competition within the common market'. The provision also includes an illustrative list of the types of concerted practices that can be deemed illegal, including price fixing, supply restrictions, and market sharing agreements. Article 102 TFEU prohibits 'the abuse of a dominant position within the common market or a substantial part of it'. Like Article 101 TFEU, Article 102 TFEU also includes a list of the conducts that may constitute such abuses (e.g. imposition of unfair prices and limiting production to the prejudice of consumers). Another distinctive feature of EU competition law is that in addition to regulating the conduct of private enterprises, it also covers the conduct of public authorities that may hinder competition and, more specifically, it prohibits state aid. The prohibition of EU state aid (or subsidies) was incorporated into EU competition law in the post-war period to address the prevalence of state monopolies in Member States as well as to emphasize the EEC's free market credentials in opposition to the Communist bloc (Papadopulous (2010), pp. 161–2). Article 107(1) TFEU prohibits 'aid granted by a Member State or through State resources in any form whatsoever which distorts or threatens to distort competition by favouring certain undertakings or the production of certain goods [...] in so far as it affects trade between Member States'.[1] As in the case of restrictive agreements and abuse of dominant position, the TFEU identifies certain state aids that are compatible with the internal market (e.g. those with a social character or granted to individual consumers, provided that such aid is granted without

[1] Article 107(1) TFEU.

discrimination related to the origin of the products concerned or aid to make good the damage caused by natural disasters or exceptional occurrences)[2] and state aid that *may* be deemed compatible with the internal market (e.g. aid to promote the economic development of areas where the standard of living is abnormally low or where there is serious underemployment, aid to promote the execution of an important project of common European interest, or aid to promote culture and heritage conservation, etc.).[3]

Finally, Article 106 TFEU clarifies that with regard to 'public undertakings and undertakings to which Member States grant special or exclusive rights', Member States may not enact or maintain measures that are contrary to the provisions of the Treaty, particularly the provisions on competition. Article 106(2) TFEU further adds that EU competition law applies to 'undertakings entrusted with the operation of services of general economic interest or having the character of a revenue-producing monopoly', provided that such application does not obstruct the performance of their tasks.

In the EU, competition policy was identified as an important tool for the promotion of market integration within the EU (Fox (1997), p. 6; Elhauge and Gerardin (2007), p. 36). Article 3(1)(g) TFEU states that the EU should establish a system that ensures that 'competition in the internal market is not distorted'. Whereas jurisdictions such as the US have developed their competition systems incrementally on the basis of economic efficiency concerns, the EU has also envisaged competition law and policy as a complement to the fundamental economic freedoms enshrined in its treaties (Motta (2004), p. 13). It ensures that the dismantling of barriers to trade created by national governments is not undermined by barriers erected by private undertakings through, for example, arrangements designed to delimitate markets within specific jurisdictions (Korah (2004), p. 20). This characteristic of EU law on competition is reflected in the outright prohibitions by EU law of price discrimination across Member State borders (Motta (2004), p. 41), as well as arrangements segmenting geographical markets or prohibiting parallel trade (Monti (2007), p. 15), in addition to EU case law which has, for example, historically adopted a zero tolerance approach to vertical restraints despite evidence that such arrangements may create distribution efficiencies because of their potential to undermine market integration (Hawk (1995), p. 974). The market access focus of EU competition law has, furthermore, resulted in determinations of the legality of business practices being traditionally carried out through a forms-based analysis (where a finding of illegality depends on the determination of the existence of a particular type of conduct) rather than the US Post-Chicago School of economics-oriented effects-based analysis (where the focus is on the effect of the conduct on consumer welfare and the efficient allocation of resources, irrespective of whether the conduct of enterprises constitutes barriers to entry) (Fox (2000), pp. 1789–93). It should be noted, however, that there is evidence that the EU is progressively

[2] Article 107(2) TFEU. [3] Article 107(3) TFEU.

moving towards the US-style system of antitrust regulation. From the mid-1990s onwards, in response to calls from EU officials, academics, and legal professionals who were increasingly influenced by Chicago School ideas (which, at the time, seemed to be validated by the fact that the EU's economy was struggling in comparison to that of the US), the EU has shifted from a forms-based approach to an effects-based analysis of competition law infringements (Gerber (2010), pp. 195–8). The shift can be seen in the enactment of regulations and the publication of Commission guidelines identifying the effect of vertical and horizontal constraints as the primary considerations in the assessment of their legality.[4] Similar attempts to emphasize the primacy of effects-based analysis with respect to abuses of dominant position failed because such reforms would have required a major overhaul of the extensive EU case law on Article 102 TFEU (Jones and Sufrin (2010), pp. 296–7).

Despite its own attempts to move towards a US-type competition regulation focused on allocative efficiency, the EU has pushed hard for the conclusion of a multilateral agreement on competition in the context of the WTO as a means to remove barriers to market access. Such agreement would include minimum competition rules and core principles and would regulate enforcement cooperation between national competition authorities. These efforts, however, have been rebuffed by a significant portion of the WTO Membership. The US, in particular, has opposed the idea, mainly because it sees such an agreement as a threat to its own regulatory system. Unlike EU competition law, modern US antitrust law is not concerned with market access issues but rather with the effects of anti-competitive behaviour on consumer welfare. The US had the obvious concern that the introduction of competition policy within the context of a multilateral agreement focused on trade liberalization would force it to change its approach to antitrust to take into account market access issues. The US's reservations were by no means fanciful and were in fact shared by officials within the Commission itself—namely those at DG Competition, who saw their counterparts at DG Trade as ill-equipped to fully apprehend the complexities surrounding competition issues (Damro (2006), p. 878). This concern was reinforced by the fact that EU competition law has proved to be a far more attractive regulatory model than that of the US, with developing countries in particular being more comfortable with the EU system, which is based on ex ante codification of competition rules where the emphasis is placed on the illegality of specific types of conduct which restrict market contestability, rather than the US system where the law is determined on a case-by-case basis by the courts and which relies on complex economic analyses (Bradford (2007), p. 407). In short, the US's main fear was that a WTO agreement on competition policy would lead to the global harmonization of competition rules and that, because of the WTO's focus on trade liberalization

[4] Regulation 2790/99 OJ [1999] L336/21 and guidelines explaining Commission's interpretation of Regulation 2790/99 OJ [1999] L291/1; Commission Guidelines on the Application of Article 81 EC to Horizontal Cooperation Agreements, OJ [2001] L3/2 (2001).

and the popularity of the EU competition regime, these rules would inevitably be based on the EU model (Ibid, p. 408).

### 7.2.3 Developing country concerns

For developing countries, the case for a WTO agreement imposing disciplines on competition is also far from clear cut. On the one hand, these countries are both the worst affected by and the least equipped to combat the anti-competitive practices of foreign multinationals, particularly the developed country practice of exempting export cartels from competition laws which adversely impact the interests of importing (and primarily developing) countries (Hamilton and Whalley (1996), pp. 93–4). On the other hand, it is argued that applying competition law primarily with export interests in mind, instead of other concerns such as economic efficiency, may lead to 'outcomes that are detrimental from a welfare point of view' (Hoekman and Holmes (1999), p. 16) for developing countries. However, in Geneva, developing country opposition to competition was motivated first by concerns about the costs—both regulatory and political—that they would incur if required to implement and enforce national competition law systems. Not only would developing countries have to make significant expenditures to put in place an effective competition regime, but in the likely event that such countries proved unable to comply with the agreement, they would also find themselves subject to the WTO Dispute Settlement Mechanism (Bhattacharjea (2006), p. 297). Secondly, developing countries were reluctant to subscribe to international rules that would require them to discontinue politically popular policies favouring domestic industries (Bradford (2007), p. 412). The developing country objections to WTO rules on competition reflect their own difficult experience in the implementation of national competition regimes. Although there is growing recognition of the importance of fostering competition in domestic markets, many have failed to enact and enforce competition laws because of the lack of institutional capacity as well as of the political and ideological backing required in order to effectively implement such rules (Dawar and Holmes (2012), pp. 234–5).

## 7.3 Competition Law in the WTO

### 7.3.1 Current legal framework

The non-discrimination obligations that are the central theme of the WTO Agreements are in fact heavily imbued with competition-related concerns. The MFN and national treatment obligations are intended to ensure the equality of competitive conditions between foreign and domestic suppliers (Jones and Sufrin (2010), p. 132). However, these rules only relate to restrictions imposed by the state, not those that result from the behaviour of private enterprises. The deficiencies of the existing WTO legal framework in dealing with private restraints on international trade were demonstrated in the *Photographic Film* case,[5] where the US argued that the Japanese government had violated GATT rules by deliberately failing to properly enforce its competition laws against the film manufacturer Fuji Film Company, allowing the latter to maintain its exclusive distribution agreements and, in doing so, precluding its American rivals from entering the Japanese market. The WTO Panel found, however, that GATT rules had not been breached since the competition laws of Japan did not discriminate against firms. Even if the exclusive distribution agreements did indeed restrict market access, such restrictions equally affected both domestic and foreign firms. The problem that the US encountered in this particular case was that the discrimination was being carried out by Fuji Film Company, a private enterprise whose anti-competitive practices remained outside the scope of WTO law (Matsushita (2004), p. 370; Fox (2006), p. 276).

However, there are a few provisions specifically regulating anti-competitive practices. Under GATS, monopoly suppliers of a service are prohibited from acting in a manner that is inconsistent with the national treatment obligation[6] and from abusing the monopoly position in areas where the WTO Member has made specific liberalization commitments[7] (Bigdeli and Reichner (2008), p. 205). These GATS provisions are then complemented with more detailed competition disciplines included in the Reference Paper which, as previously discussed, is not only limited to the telecommunications sector but is also a plurilateral instrument that is only binding on WTO Members on a voluntary basis. Under TRIPS, there is an acknowledgement that IP rights holders may abuse the market power conferred by such rights in a manner that harms competition and undermines trade.[8] As such, TRIPS recognizes that the protection of IP rights may be limited where the exercise of such rights undermines competition in the market of a WTO Member. Furthermore, an enforcement cooperation mechanism is established whereby WTO Members must, upon request, enter into consultations with another WTO Member where it is believed that an IP rights holder that is a national of the latter is abusing its rights in violation of the laws of the WTO Member requesting the consultations.[9]

### 7.3.2 EU proposals for a WTO agreement on competition

The EU has been the main driver for the inclusion of competition policy within the realm of the WTO since the early 1990s. Even before the conclusion of the Uruguay Round, EU officials were openly discussing the possibility of negotiating a multilateral agreement on competition which would not only regulate

[5] Panel Report, *Japan—Measures Affecting Consumer Photographic Film and Paper*, report of the Panel, WT/DS44/R, adopted 22 April 1998.

[6] Article VIII.1 GATS.

[7] Article VIII:2 GATS.

[8] Article 40(1) TRIPS.

[9] Article 40(3) TRIPS.

enforcement cooperation and exchange of information proceedings but also contain rules impacting on the content of national competition laws (Fox (1997), pp. 9–10). The idea eventually made its way to Geneva, and a WTO Working Group on Trade and Competition Policy (Working Group) was established in the 1996 WTO Ministerial conference held in Singapore, which was given the task of exploring the interaction between trade and competition policy, including anticompetitive practices, 'in order to identify the areas that may merit further consideration in the WTO framework' (WTO (1996)).

The EU's position regarding the place of competition policy in the WTO was spelled out in 1999 by Leon Brittan, the EU Trade Commissioner, in a speech delivered at the World Competition Forum in Davos, Switzerland (Brittan (1999)). This position was that a multilateral agreement on competition should be negotiated under the auspices of the WTO and should address a number of issues. First, the agreement should include a commitment for WTO Members to gradually introduce competition laws, complemented by strong enforcement procedures. Secondly, the agreement should include core principles of competition law, including, inter alia, the prohibition of hard core cartels, which must be based on non-discrimination and transparency. Thirdly, the agreement should establish cooperation mechanisms between national competition authorities and fourthly, the commitments included in the agreement should be subject to the WTO dispute settlement mechanism. Therefore, the EU's initial plans were ambitious in that they entailed the negotiation of a legally-binding multilateral agreement requiring all WTO members to adopt comprehensive regulatory systems on competition in compliance with a number of core principles and in that they subjected such agreement to the WTO dispute settlement mechanism. Among some of the most controversial issues discussed in the Working Group was the application of a non-discrimination obligation, which would require the competition laws of WTO Members not to discriminate on the basis of the nationality of the economic operator. As previously discussed, there were concerns that this would cause WTO Members to adopt competition laws that would be overly focused on market access issues to the detriment of other objectives typically pursued by national competition systems. Moreover, it was unclear whether the non-discrimination obligation would only apply de jure—that is, with regard to the content of the legislation and its implementation, or whether it would also apply de facto—that is, with regard to the actual practice of national competition authorities (Holmes (2003), pp. 152–3). The fear here was that the WTO Courts would be empowered to undermine the 'exercise of prosecutorial discretion and other decisions of national competition authorities and courts' (Anderson and Holmes (2002), p. 533). Even though the EU had stressed from the outset that a WTO agreement on competition should not 'result in panels second-guessing individual decisions taken by competition authorities or by national courts' (Brittan (1999), p. 6) and should focus exclusively on 'whether a Member's legislation and enforcement structure are in accordance with their WTO commitments'

(Ibid) and in cases where a 'pattern of non-enforcement' was established, there remained considerable doubts (especially from the US) about the potential for such an agreement to dictate the content and application of domestic competition laws (Holmes (2003), p. 252).

The outright opposition of the US to the introduction of competition rules beyond the establishment of voluntary cooperation mechanisms within the WTO and the ambivalence of developing countries towards an issue they regarded as unimportant led the EU to revise its ambitions. An EU proposal tabled at the Working Party suggested the adoption of core principles in competition law and policy, the establishment of cooperation mechanisms between WTO Members and technical assistance for developing countries in their implementation and enforcement of competition policy (WTO (2000)). The core principles included the requirement to put in place competition authorities with effective enforcement powers, the application of the principle of non-discrimination and transparency to competition law, guarantees of due process, and an obligation to prohibit 'hard-core' cartels (including restrictive agreements relating to price fixing, bid rigging, output restriction, or customer allocation) (Matsushita (2004), p. 376). Significantly, the proposal omitted any references to the WTO dispute settlement mechanism and it was clarified that non-discrimination should be ensured as 'de jure discrimination in the domestic competition law framework' (WTO (2012), p. 4). Subsequently, the EU also put forward the idea of allowing developing countries to opt out from the agreement and for WTO Members in general to exclude sectors from the scope of application of the core principles (Holmes (2002), p. 453). This culminated in the 2001 Doha Declaration, which included competition in multilateral negotiations under the following terms (WTO (2001c)):

> In the period until the Fifth Session, further work in the Working Group on the Interaction between Trade and Competition Policy will focus on the clarification of: core principles, including transparency, non-discrimination and procedural fairness, and provisions on hardcore cartels; modalities for voluntary cooperation; and support for progressive reinforcement of competition institutions in developing countries through capacity building. Full account shall be taken of the needs of developing and least-developed country participants and appropriate flexibility provided to address them.

Although competition was still being envisaged in the context of multilateral negotiations, there would be no role to be played by the WTO dispute settlement mechanism. Still, despite the fact that the EU made considerable compromises on its initial vision by agreeing to a reduced mandate, which effectively ruled out the prospect of a binding agreement on competition, WTO Members proved unable to make any substantial progress in the negotiations and, following continued opposition from developing countries, competition was removed from the Doha Agenda at the 2003 Cancun Ministerial Conference (Hufbauer and Kim (2008)).

### 7.3.3 International cooperation in non-binding venues

As the attempts to introduce competition policy within the realm of the WTO legal framework floundered, the international community has increasingly looked towards other international fora, such as the Organisation for Economic Co-operation and Development (OECD), the United Nations Conference on Trade and Development (UNCTAD) and the International Competition Network (ICN), to address problems created by regulatory diversity and the lack of coordination in enforcement of competition laws. A characteristic shared by these organizations is that harmonization of competition laws and procedures are all pursued through soft law mechanisms (e.g. sharing of best practices, peer review mechanisms, voluntary recommendation, and model regulatory frameworks), which suits the demands of countries for regulatory flexibility in adapting any international norms to the specific goals.

The work of the OECD and UNCTAD in the development of competition law predates the establishment of the WTO. However, the success encountered by these organizations in pushing through regulatory convergence has been mixed. This is not only due to the fact that competition policy is but one of the many issues addressed by these organizations, but also because of their very specific agenda. The OECD is an organization for developed countries, which means that its membership is limited, and its work is focused on issues that are of interest to such countries (Sokol (2007), pp. 111–12). On the flipside, UNCTAD promotes the interests of developing countries. While it has produced a model competition regulatory framework that has been used as the basis for the development of the competition laws of a number of developing countries, its work has largely been shunned by developed countries.[10]

Although the ICN was only established in 2001, it has rapidly become the 'go-to' international organization for issues pertaining to international competition policy. The ICN is the brainchild of the International Competition Policy and Advisory Committee—a US-sponsored body created in 1997 and tasked with the assignment of assessing the possibility of promoting international competition policy and regulatory convergence. As such, the conception of the ICN was intended to provide an alternative to the legally binding regulatory convergence associated with the WTO (Ibid). It is a transnational regulatory network focusing exclusively on competition law, comprising officials from national competition authorities, NGOs, academics, lawyers, and businesses, and which provides a forum for discussion on international competition policy issues. It operates through working committees that focus on specific areas of law and seeks to promote international regulatory harmonization by consolidating best practices. Two novel features distinguish the ICN from the OECD and UNCTAD (Sokol (2007), pp. 108–9) and explain its relative success. First, it is a virtual

[10] Gerber (2010), p. 111.

network: with no headquarters and no permanent staff, most discussions occur via email or teleconferencing (Ibid, p. 115). This feature not only facilitates the participation of a wide pool of countries but also means that participants are able to react to and address current issues as they arise. Secondly, the ICN is an action-driven (Ibid) organization insofar as it focuses on issues where there is a pressing demand for international action and for which practical solutions can reasonably be envisaged by the international community. In fact, a large part of the ICN's success can be explained by the fact that its work has tended to focus on a specific set of issues—essentially on the reduction of transactional costs associated with merger and anti-cartel enforcement (Gerber (2010), p. 116). It has thus developed 'recommended practices' for merger controls and provided guidance for anti-cartel investigation and enforcement techniques which have influenced national legislations.

## 7.4 Post-Doha EU External Trade Policy in Competition

### 7.4.1 Shift towards bilateralism

Despite the rejection of its proposals to conclude a multilateral agreement on competition, the EU has maintained its policy of promoting competition policy and law as a tool to enhance trade liberalization. In the Global Europe strategy, the Commission clearly frames the issue of competition as a market access issue. The rationale remains the same: 'competition rules' are viewed as necessary to ensure that the benefits of the removal of tariff and non-tariff barriers are not undermined by the raising of non-traditional barriers such as private restraints (European Commission (2010a), p. 8).

However, the Commission accepts that its desire for such rules to be agreed under the auspices of the WTO may not be fulfilled, and indicates that bilateral trade agreements offer a suitable setting to address some competition issues (European Commission (2010c), p. 13):

> Absent or ineffective competition and state aid rules in third countries limit market access for EU exporters. The EU therefore has a strategic interest in developing international rules to ensure that European firms do not suffer in third countries from unfair subsidisation of local companies or anti-competitive practices. A multilateral set of rules adopted in the WTO framework would be the best outcome. However, many key issues can also be addressed through bilateral agreements.

The inclusion of competition law issues in bilateral agreements is far from a radical move on the part of the EU, as most modern bilateral and regional trade agreements concluded by developed countries contain provisions on this topic (Geboye Desta and Barnes (2006), pp. 239–64). Historically, the EU has tended to conclude two types of bilateral agreements. First, bilateral cooperation agreements concluded with developed countries that already have sophisticated competition regulatory systems in place (e.g. Canada,[11] Japan,[12] and US[13]) provide for cooperation and coordination between competition authorities in order to avoid conflicts in the application and enforcement of competition laws. These agreements include extensive provisions relating to positive comity, exchange of information and consultations in cases of mutual interest and obligations ensuring the confidentiality of information transferred between the parties' competition authorities (Geboye Desta and Barnes (2006), pp. 248–56). Secondly, where the EU is dealing with neighbouring and developing countries, it has concluded trade agreements (association agreements or FTAs), which include less detailed cooperative arrangements but require to varying degrees the substantive harmonization of competition laws. This differs from the US practice of concluding trade agreements that—whilst requiring the enactment and effective enforcement of competition laws—remain primarily concerned with the establishment of cooperation mechanisms between national competition authorities. On the other hand, the EU trade agreements generally replicate the major competition rules included in the TFEU (prohibition of anti-competitive agreements, abuse of dominant position, and state aids where these may affect trade between the parties), which are then complemented by technical assistance and capacity building programmes to assist the concerned developing country in the implementation of competition laws. Therefore, unlike the US, the EU uses bilateral trade agreements not solely to address cross-border enforcement issues or to promote fair competition, but also to disseminate its regulatory model abroad (Wigger (2008), pp. 186–9).

### 7.4.2 Substantive obligations on competition law in EU trade agreements

A comprehensive study of the substantive competition provisions included in bilateral trade agreements distinguishes three types of agreements (Papadopoulos (2008), pp. 105–37): (i) association agreements concluded with potential candidates for accession; (ii) association agreements concluded with countries covered by the European Neighbourhood Policy (ENP); and (iii) agreements concluded with other third countries.

The agreements with candidates for EU accession contain far-reaching obligations on co-signatories to conform to EU competition laws. The standard language used in such agreement provides that the anti-competitive practices covered under Articles 101, 102 and 107 TFEU are 'incompatible with the proper functioning

[11] Agreement between the European Communities and the Government of Canada regarding the application of their competition laws OJ [1999] L175.

[12] Agreement between the European Community and the Government of Japan concerning cooperation on anti-competitive activities OJ [2003] L183.

[13] Agreement between the European Communities and the Government of the United States of America on the application of positive comity principles in the enforcement of their competition laws OJ [1998] L173.

of the agreement insofar as they may affect trade between the [parties]'.[14] These provisions differ from the TFEU in two major aspects. First, the anti-competitive conduct is only deemed 'incompatible with the proper functioning of the agreement', whereas in the TFEU, such conduct is '*prohibited* as incompatible with the internal market'.[15] Secondly, these agreements do not provide a list of examples of conducts covered by restrictive agreements, abuses of dominant position, or state aids. However, despite the absence of an outright prohibition on anti-competitive conduct (Holmes (2010, p. 6) and of detailed guidance as to what constitutes such conduct, there can be no doubt that these agreements require the EU's partners to adopt and maintain competition laws that replicate the EU's model. There is an obligation on countries to approximate their legislation to that of the EU—which is monitored over time by the EU—and it is specified that anti-competitive practices covered by the agreements 'shall be assessed on the basis of criteria arising out of the application of the competition rules applicable in the [EU]'.[16]

The association agreements concluded with ENP countries include those concluded with Southern Mediterranean (Euro-Med), Eastern European, and Central Asian countries. From the EU's perspective, the ENP is primarily motivated by political and security concerns rather than pure economic considerations: the trade arrangements included in association agreements concluded with ENP countries are but one of the many tools used to promote stability and prosperity in the EU's neighbourhood. The Euro-Med agreements contain similar substantive provisions to those included in agreements with accession candidates—that is, they consider 'incompatible with the proper functioning of the agreement'[17] certain anti-competitive practices, namely restrictive agreements and abuses of dominant position. However, they make no references to the prohibition of state aid, nor do they require the EU's partners to apply such prohibitions on the basis of the criteria applied under EU law. The agreements concluded with Eastern European and Central Asian countries are even less ambitious in that they only include a general obligation 'to remedy or remove through the application of their competition laws or otherwise, restrictions on competition by enterprises or caused by state intervention insofar as they may affect trade between the [parties]'.[18] There is no clarification as to what types of practices are actually prohibited, although the parties agree that competition law is one of the areas where approximation

[14] Article 73(1) Stabilisation and Association Agreement between the European Communities and the Republic of Montenegro; OJ [2010] L 108; Article 73(1) Stabilisation and Association Agreement between the European Communities and the Republic of Serbia, OJ [2013] L 278.

[15] Articles 102 and 103 TFEU. Italics added by author.

[16] Article 73(2) Stabilisation and Association Agreement between the European Communities and the Republic of Montenegro; Article 73(2) Stabilisation and Association Agreement between the European Communities and the Republic of Serbia.

[17] Article 36 EU–Israel Association Agreement, OJ [2000] L 147; Article 53 EU–Jordan Association Agreement, OJ [2002] L 129; Article 41 EU–Algeria Association Agreement, OJ [2005] L 265.

[18] Article 49 Partnership and Cooperation Agreement between the EU and Ukraine OJ [1998] L 49; Article 48 Partnership and Cooperation Agreement between the EU and Moldova OJ [1998] L 181.

should be pursued. ENP countries are typically only required to cooperate and make best efforts to approximate their domestic laws to those of the EU. However, the EU then plays a key role in guiding and monitoring the ensuing regulatory reforms through the publication of bilateral action plans and annual progress reports as well as by funding technical assistance programmes. In this way, the soft process of legal approximation has allowed the EU to play a significant role in the shaping of competition regimes in ENP (Papadopoulos (2008), p. 113; Aydin (2012), p. 671). One recent development with regard to this third category of bilateral agreements concerns the EU–Ukraine deep and comprehensive free trade agreement (Ukraine DCFTA),[19] which contains an obligation to approximate its competition laws and enforcement practices with the EU acquis within specific deadlines.[20]

The competition provisions of the trade agreements concluded outside of the context of the ENP and prior to the launch of the Global Europe strategy are less demanding. The bilateral agreements concluded with Mexico and Chile contain no substantive obligations beyond the obligation on the parties to adopt and maintain competition law systems, whilst the Trade, Development and Cooperation Agreement signed with South Africa (TDCA) only provides that the restrictive agreements and abuses of dominant position 'are incompatible with the proper functioning of [the agreement]'[21] if they affect trade between the parties.

To summarize, the EU's bilateral agreements have generally included provisions on competition law. Those concluded with accession countries contain substantive obligations with regard to anti-competitive practices to the extent that these affect trade between the parties and provide for legislative approximation. Similar provisions are found in a number of agreements concluded with ENP countries, with the caveat that legal approximation is only envisaged with ENP countries on a voluntary basis. However, agreements that have been concluded with countries not within its periphery in the past do not—with the exception of the TDCA which focuses on market access implications of competition law—include any binding substantive obligations impacting on the content of the parties' respective competition laws and, to the extent that the only notable legally binding provision relates to a general obligation to maintain competition laws and enforcement systems, it can be argued that this latter category of EU trade agreements does not bring more to the table than the current US FTAs.

## 7.4.3 Competition chapters in EU DCFTAs

### *7.4.3.1 Rules on private restraints of competition*

The competition chapters of the EU DCFTAs are generally concerned with three types of anti-competitive practices: anti-competitive agreements and concerted practices, abuses of dominant position between one or more enterprises and

[19] Article 256 DCFTA. [20] Article 256 Ukraine DCFTA.
[21] Article 53 TDCA.

mergers that significantly impede effective competition.[22] For example, Article 11.1(3) of the KOREU FTA states:

> The Parties agree that the following activities restricting competition are incompatible with the proper functioning of this Agreement, in so far as they may affect trade between them: (a) agreements between enterprises, decisions by associations of enterprises and concerted practices, which have as their object or effect the prevention, restriction or distortion of competition in the territory of either Party as a whole or in a substantial part thereof; (b) any abuse by one or more enterprises of a dominant position in the territory of either Party as a whole or in a substantial part thereof; or (c) concentrations between enterprises, which significantly impede effective competition, in particular as a result of the creation or strengthening of a dominant position in the territory of either Party as a whole or in a substantial part thereof.

These provisions replicate the three basic prohibitions on private restraints addressed by EU competition law, and the language used to describe them either replicates or closely resembles that of the texts of Articles 101 and 102 of the TFEU and Article 3 of the EC Merger Regulation.[23] The agreements also replicate Article 106 TFEU by asserting that competition rules apply to public enterprises and enterprises entrusted with special or exclusive rights in so far as the application of such rules does not obstruct the performance, in law or in fact, of the particular tasks assigned to them.[24] A notable exception to this approach can be found in the CETA, which draws inspiration from the light touch approach to competition policy adopted in the NAFTA rather than the more prescriptive stance typically found in EU FTAs. It requires the parties to take appropriate measures to prescribe anti-competitive business conduct[25] and that such rules apply to economic operators of the other party to the extent required by their respective laws.[26]

The foregoing supports the notion that the EU generally tends to transpose its regulatory model on competition policy in trade agreements to further enhance market access. In addition to exporting the language used in the EU's own legal instruments, which are only concerned with anti-competitive practices to the extent that they may affect trade between the parties, the EU DCFTAs also recognize that the primary purpose of the provisions relating to competition is to ensure that market access is not undermined by the conduct of private economic operators. The agreements recognize the importance of free and undistorted competition in the parties' trade relations and require the application of national competition laws in order to ensure that the benefits of liberalization are not inhibited.[27] Market access is identified as the primary purpose of competition

[22] Article 126 CEPA; Article 11.1(3) KOREU FTA; Article 259(2) Colombia–Peru FTA; Article 278 EU–CA FTA; Article 12.2 EU–Singapore FTA.

[23] Council Regulation (EC) No 139/2004 OJ [2004] L 24.

[24] Article 129(2) CEPA; Article 11.4 KOREU FTA; Article 263 Colombia–Peru FTA; Article 280 EU–CA FTA; Article 12.3(2) EU–Singapore FTA.

[25] Article X.01(2) Chapter 19 CETA.

[26] Article X.02(1) Chapter 19 CETA.

[27] Article 125 (1) CEPA; Article 11.1(1) KOREU FTA; Article 259(1) Colombia–Peru FTA; Article 278(1) EU–CA FTA; Article 12.1(1) EU–Singapore FTA.

policy and law. In this regard, the Colombia–Peru FTA is slightly different to other agreements, as it recognizes other goals underpinning competition policy besides the issue of market access, including the fostering of economic and social development as well as economic efficiency and consumer welfare.[28] However, the EU DCFTAs do not establish a legally binding obligation to prohibit any anti-competitive practices or activities that restrict market access. Unlike the TFEU provisions, the EU DCFTAs do not expressly prohibit anti-competitive practices, but merely provide that the parties 'agree that the [...] activities restricting competition are incompatible with the proper functioning of the [agreement], insofar as they may affect trade between them'.[29] The EU–Singapore FTA differs in that, whilst not prohibiting anti-competitive practices restricting market access, it does enjoin parties to maintain laws that 'address' anti-competitive agreements, concerted practices, abuses of dominant position, and concentrations significantly impeding effective competition which affect trade between them.[30] However, no guidance is provided as to the types of anti-competitive conduct that are covered, or not covered, by very general concepts such as 'concerted practices' or 'abuses of dominant position'. This potentially leaves national competition authorities with a considerable degree of flexibility in determining what practices affect or do not affect international trade between the parties. More significantly, the EU DCFTAs remain rather limited in comparison with what the EU had wished to achieve in the context of the WTO. Only the EU–Singapore FTA and the CETA establish a binding obligation on the parties to apply their respective competition laws in a non-discriminatory and transparent manner.[31] There is no non-discrimination or transparency requirement in CEPA or EU–CA FTA, whilst in the KOREU FTA and the Colombia–Peru FTA, the parties only '*recognise* the importance'[32] of applying such laws in 'a transparent, timely and non-discriminatory manner'.[33] Therefore, at best, the parties are subject to a best endeavours obligation to not discriminate in the implementation and enforcement of their respective competition laws.

The impact of the EU DCFTAs on the domestic legal systems of its trading partners is also limited. The agreements state that each party must maintain competition laws that address certain anti-competitive practices as well as competition authorities appropriately equipped for the implementation or enforcement of such competition laws.[34] The type of anti-competitive practices covered varies depending on the Global FTA. CEPA provides that the parties must ensure that they have laws 'addressing restrictions on competition'. Neither CEPA nor EU–CA FTA, however, expand on what types of conducts are covered by the

[28] Article 259(1) Colombia–Peru FTA. [29] Supra footnote 23.

[30] Article 12.1(2) EU–Singapore FTA.

[31] Article 12.2(2) EU–Singapore FTA; Article 19.01(4) CETA.

[32] Article 11.3(2) KOREU FTA; Article 260(3) Colombia–Peru FTA. Emphasis added by author.

[33] Ibid.

[34] Article 127 CEPA; Article 11.3(1) KOREU FTA; Article 260 (1) and (2) Colombia–Peru FTA; Article 279 EU–CA FTA.

notion of 'restrictions on competition'. The KOREU FTA provides more detail by specifying that the competition laws of the parties must address 'restrictive agreements, concerted practices and the abuse of dominance [...] and which provide for effective control of concentrations between enterprises'.[35] Similarly the Colombia–Peru FTA refers to the prohibition of anti-competitive agreements and concerted practices, abuse of dominant position, and concentrations which significantly impede effective competition.[36] The EU–Singapore FTA goes furthest by requiring the horizontal and vertical agreements between undertakings, decisions by associations of undertakings and concerted practices which have as their object or effect the prevention, restriction, or distortion of competition, abuses by one or more undertakings of a dominant position, and concentrations between undertakings which result in a substantial lessening of competition or which significantly impede effective competition.[37] However, such provisions will not entail the harmonization of competition laws, since the broadly-termed anti-competitive practices mentioned are already addressed by most national competition laws, including those of the parties to the EU DCFTAs. In particular, the competition rules for the CARICOM States set out under the Treaty of Chaguaramas, those provided in the Andean Community Commission decision 608, which applies to both Colombia and Peru, as well as Singaporean competition laws are largely inspired by EU law (Papadopoulos (2008), p. 182; Miranda Lodono (2012), p. 5; Ong (2006), p. 280). CEPA does provide a transitional period of five years for CARIFORUM States to put in place national competition laws prohibiting restrictions on competition but, as the EU acknowledged, this was only done because the implementation of the Treaty of Chaguaramas was still in progress at the time of signing (European Commission (2008b)). Therefore, the EU DCFTAs are at best being used to lock in and reinforce domestic reforms in the area of competition law. The 'hands off' approach adopted in the EU DCFTAs can be contrasted with that adopted in the context of the ENP, which places greater emphasis on the process of legal approximation. The argument that the EU is exporting its legislation to expand its sphere of influence may be valid with regard to its neighbouring countries where trade relations are interwoven with wider political concerns and, in some instances, seen as a prelude to accession, but there is little evidence of this in its trade relations with the wider world. In its EU DCFTAs, the EU is exporting EU competition law stripped to its bare bones, and as the EU's own competition law evolves from a conduct-based approach towards an effects-based approach system, these basic provisions are in no way sufficient to determine the orientation of domestic legal systems. Far more important is how legislators and competition authorities implement, and how the judiciary interprets, these obligations. In this respect, the EU's co-signatories retain full autonomy.

[35] Article 11.1(2) KOREU FTA. [36] Article 260(2) Colombia–Peru FTA.
[37] Article 12.1(2) EU–Singapore FTA.

### 7.4.3.2 Dispute settlement

Despite the EU's pronouncements regarding the importance of competition policy in the context of its trade relations, the competition chapters of the EU DCFTAs are generally rather weak. There is no obligation to apply national competition rules in a non-discriminatory manner, and the obligation to prohibit anti-competitive conduct affecting market access is expressed in very broad terms. The parties are asked to maintain domestic laws which address certain restrictive practices, but these are already covered by most modern competition regimes, including those of the EU's co-signatories. The limited impact of the few binding commitments included in these competition chapters is further reduced by the fact that, barring CEPA, such provisions are expressly excluded from the dispute settlement mechanism of the EU DCFTAs.[38] Instead, most agreements provide that the parties may enter into consultations to resolve any matters that arise with regard to such provisions.[39] The exclusion is not surprising, given that the vast majority of competition law provisions have no legal force, and demonstrates the disinclination of the parties to subject national competition policy to market access concerns. It is telling in this respect that even in the essentially political context of consultations procedure, the Colombia–Peru FTA stresses that the parties shall maintain their 'full autonomy as regards the final decision on the issues subject to consultations'.[40] Moreover, the EU itself is keen to ensure that competition law remains outside the scope of the dispute settlement mechanisms provided under its EU DCFTAs. This is evident from the negotiating drafts of these agreements, which show that it is the EU's policy to subject disagreements relating to competition law provisions to non-binding consultation procedures. This is the case even in the context of those agreements being negotiated with larger economies, such as the CETA. Here, despite Canada's desire to allow the parties to have recourse to the dispute settlement procedure under the agreement for matters arising under the competition chapter, the EU has stressed that competition law and policy should only be subject to consultations.[41] The final text of the CETA not only exempts competition policy from the agreement's dispute settlement mechanism but also from any form of consultation process.[42]

In other words, it is the EU that is demanding non-enforceable rules on competition in its EU DCFTAs. The exemption of competition law provisions from the scope of the dispute settlement mechanisms included in EU

[38] Article 11.8 KOREU FTA; Article 266 Colombia–Peru FTA; Article 283 EU–CA FTA; Article 12.14 EU–Singapore FTA.

[39] Article 11.7 KOREU FTA; Article 265 Colombia–Peru FTA; Article 12.13 EU–Singapore FTA.

[40] Article 265(1) Colombia–Peru FTA.

[41] Article X-04 Consolidated Draft of the Comprehensive Economic and Trade Agreement of 13 January 2010. Available at: www.bilaterals.org.

[42] Article X.03 Chapter 19 CETA.

DCFTAs—especially with larger economies such as Korea and Canada—perhaps reflects a belief that most anti-competitive practices conducted abroad which significantly undermine the interests of EU firms will be caught by the broad reach of the effects doctrine. Generally speaking, such practice also suggests that the EU is perhaps more interested in encouraging countries to develop effective competition law systems rather than ensuring that such laws are used as means to complement market access commitments. This aversion towards binding rules on competition in FTAs is in line with many modern FTAs which include competition law chapters. According to Sokol, compliance with binding and enforceable provisions in the area of competition creates difficulties that are not present in other regulatory areas covered by FTAs (Sokol (2008), pp. 231–92). The assessment of competition law violations can often be a complex affair and, in the context of cross-border anti-competitive conduct, evidence-gathering may prove a significant stumbling block. Moreover, in the absence of significant regulatory harmonization, enforcement may be undermined by disagreements between the FTA parties concerning what constitutes a violation (Ibid). As a result, many of the competition provisions included in FTAs have a symbolic rather than normative value (Sokol (2008), pp. 138–9; Bourgeois (2013), p. 396). Their primary aim is not to coerce parties into removing private restraints on competition, but to send out a signal to foreign investors and domestic constituents regarding the parties' commitment to open markets and pro-competitive reforms.

### *7.4.3.3 Cooperation in enforcement of competition laws and technical assistance*

The EU DCFTAs include provisions regulating the cooperation between competition authorities regarding the enforcement of competition laws. The two exceptions are the KOREU FTA and the CETA, which simply refers to the existing cooperation agreements with the EU concerning cooperation and anti-competitive practices.[43] For the other agreements, the provisions—which relate mostly to confidentiality, exchange of information, and positive comity[44]—are considerably less detailed than the cooperation agreements entered into by the EU, and are generally phrased in best endeavour language.[45] The focus on trade explains to a certain extent the lack of emphasis on inter-agency cooperation mechanisms (Demedst (2007), pp. 245–6). It can also be explained by the absence of any real incentive for the EU to push for far-reaching cooperation commitments with developing countries. Since the national economies are relatively small, it is unlikely that many conflicts will arise from the enforcement or

[43] Article 11.06 (2) KOREU FTA; Article 19.01(3) CETA.

[44] Article 123 CEPA; Article 261 Colombia–Peru FTA; Article 281 EU–CA FTA; Article 12.12 EU–Singapore FTA.

[45] Article 12.11 EU–Singapore FTA.

under-enforcement of competition laws or that the EU will have to enforce its competition laws against operators from such countries. Moreover, there is the fact that the Commission's resources may be stretched too thinly, were it tasked with the job of monitoring the implementation and compliance of the competition law components of its multiple bilateral agreements (Cunningham (2011), p. 134). In fact, in some cases, the demand for the inclusion of cooperation mechanism originates from the developing countries themselves, keen to tap into the experience and knowledge of EU competition authorities (Ibid).

However, all EU DCFTAs concluded with developing countries provide for technical assistance. In the Colombia–Peru FTA and EU–CA FTA, the parties acknowledge the importance of technical assistance and undertake to promote initiatives to promote a competition culture.[46] Such initiatives include 'strengthening technical and institutional capacities as regards implementation of competition policy and enforcement of competition laws, training of human resources and exchange of experiences'.[47] In CEPA, technical assistance and capacity building are also provided to 'facilitate the implementation of the commitments and the objectives of [the] Chapter and in particular to ensure effective and sound competition policies and rule enforcement'.[48] CEPA also provides more detail as to the type of technical assistance envisaged. These include cooperation to promote the efficient functioning of CARIFORUM Competition authorities, assistance on drafting guidelines, manuals and legislation, the provision of independent experts, and training for key personnel involved in the implementation and enforcement of competition policy.[49]

## 7.5 Conclusion

The EU policy of linking trade and competition is typically presented as one of the most striking examples of its deep trade agenda. Competition law is seen as a crucial complement to trade liberalization, as it removes market access barriers by private economic operators and maximizes the benefits of liberalization by creating a regulatory environment which fosters economic efficiency and consumer welfare. Yet, the evidence suggests that the EU's desire to introduce competition policy in the context of trade negotiations may no longer be as strong as was once thought. The EU DCFTAs include competition chapters which list anticompetitive practices that are unquestionably based on the text of EU competition law. And like EU law, the emphasis is placed on the potential for these practices to cause market access issues. However, there is a vast chasm which separates the competition law component of the EU DCFTAs and the initial EU proposals for a multilateral WTO agreement which foresaw the negotiation of substantive competition rules backed up by the WTO dispute settlement mechanism. Most

[46] Article 264(1) Colombia–Peru FTA. [47] Article 264(2) Colombia–Peru FTA.
[48] Article 130(1) CEPA. [49] Article 130(2) CEPA.

provisions of the competition law chapters are phrased in very broad terms and some only create best endeavour obligations. In general, there is an obligation to maintain competition laws prohibiting certain anti-competitive practices and to ensure that they are effectively enforced, but no legal obligation on the parties to prohibit anti-competitive practices that impede market access. The importance of the non-discrimination and transparency principles is acknowledged, but there is—in all but one of the EU DCFTAs—no legal obligation on the parties to comply with such principles, nor any guidance as to how these principles could be applied in the area of competition law and policy. Any lingering doubts concerning the 'soft law' nature of the commitments included in the competition chapter are finally quashed by the exclusion of the dispute settlement in this area.

The EU DCFTAs do go further than previous trade agreements signed by the EU with third countries not located in its periphery, but the EU is not using them to push through the strong disciplines on competition that it wished to introduce in the context of the WTO. The disconnect between the EU's narrative concerning the links between trade and competition policy and the actual practice of its EU DCFTAs is all the more baffling because there is no evidence that the type of resistance encountered to the EU's proposals for disciplines on competition at the WTO has also factored into the FTA negotiations. On the contrary, the negotiating drafts of the EU DCFTAs show that the final texts of the competition drafts do not stray far from the EU's proposals. Moreover, the EU appears to have rejected overtures from large trading partners, such as Canada, who are willing to negotiate more ambitious and enforceable rules on competition. Therefore, the recent policy statements asserting the EU's designs to use competition rules to further market access in the context of bilateral trade agreements are not verified in practice. On the contrary, the competition chapters included in EU DCFTAs seem to be in line with the vast majority of modern bilateral FTAs in that they are not enforceable, that their value is largely symbolic and that any ensuing pro-competitive regulatory reforms are most likely to come from regulatory and enforcement cooperation as well as technical assistance programmes. It is tempting to draw the obvious parallels between the evolution of EU competition law and that of its external trade practice in this area. Just as the EU's competition rules have evolved from a regime focused on market integration to a US-type regime focused on efficiency, so is the EU's current FTA practice suggesting that the EU is increasingly coming round to the US's idea that competition law and trade are not necessarily ideal bedfellows. Moreover, one may question whether the EU's commitment to link competition and trade was ever that strong. It was a policy which divided the European Commission—with DG Competition particularly unimpressed by the prospect of losing jurisdictional autonomy over competition matters. The EU's reluctance to subject competition provisions to a binding dispute settlement mechanism—a feature found in the vast majority of modern FTAs—is consistent with the general mistrust felt by national competition authorities towards external interference (Sahu and Gupta (2007), pp. 70–1). Finally, there is also the realization that the successful dissemination of competition rules included in the TFEU has not led to the establishment of global common ground on competition law. Again, as the EU's experience of competition law shows, the meaning and purpose attributed to competition rules can be changed by competition authorities. The manner in which competition rules are applied and enforced matters just as much as the actual wording of these rules. In this sense, the DG Competition is also taking an increasingly prominent role in the work of the ICN—an organization promoted by the US in response to the EU's demands for the introduction of competition disciplines in the WTO—and leading calls for further efforts to promote, but also to 'improve the framework for cooperation on individual cases; and make progress with the practical, day-to-day guidance to competition authorities' (Almunia (2013), p. 4) in light of the importance of '[o]pen markets, vibrant competition, and a global level playing' (Ibid).

# 8

# Public Procurement

## 8.1 Introduction

Public (or government) procurement relates to the 'purchase by governments and state-owned enterprises of goods, services and works' (OECD (2011b), p. 148). Its importance to the global economy is not to be underrated, representing 17 per cent of the world's GDP (European Commission (2012d)). Its contribution to the EU's economy is even greater, making up 19 per cent of the region's GDP (The Economist (2010)). Predictably, the EU has historically been an ardent supporter of the liberalization of public procurement rules at the multilateral level (Meunier (2005), pp. 125–43). However, liberalization at multilateral level remains deficient. Public procurement has largely been left outside the scope of the rules of the GATT and GATS (Arrowsmith and Anderson (2011), pp. 6–7) due to WTO Members' concerns that this would inhibit their ability to use public procurement as a policy tool to promote domestic industries (Hoekman (1998), p. 253). The concern is particularly prevalent among developing countries, which fear that any commitment to not discriminate between domestic and foreign suppliers in this area would remove a valuable economic development tool. To counter these concerns, the EU famously proposed the signing of a multilateral transparency agreement whereby developing countries would be bound by transparency and procedural requirements but not by a non-discrimination obligation (Reich (2009), p. 993). The proposal was part of the Singapore issues which would later be rejected by developing countries and removed from the Doha Development Agenda (Woolcock (2012b), p. 14). Faced with stiff opposition, proponents of public procurement liberalization have resorted to signing plurilateral procurement-related agreements, first under the auspices of GATT 1947 and then under that of the WTO's Government Procurement Agreement (GPA). The successive versions of the GPA—of which the latest was adopted in 2012—go beyond the mere requirement of non-discrimination, providing an over-arching regulatory framework for public procurement which covers the principal aspects of the procurement bidding process and the enforcement of procurement rules. However, the impact of the GPA is also undermined by significant deficiencies. Its membership remains limited and, because coverage is negotiated bilaterally, market opening commitments can vary greatly from one signatory to another.

The EU's recent trade policy, as formulated in the Global Europe strategy and subsequent policy statements, aims to open procurement markets in the EU's strongest-performing sectors (e.g. public transport, medical devices, pharmaceuticals, and green technologies) (European Commission (2010c), p. 6) and specifically targets 'developed and large emerging economies' (Ibid). To achieve this, and in light of the GPA's limitations, the EU has adopted a two-pronged strategy: externally, the EU is to complement its ongoing efforts to liberalize public procurement at the WTO level by negotiating ambitious public procurement chapters in its FTAs; and internally, keen to rectify what it perceives to be an asymmetry in terms of the level of openness compared to its trading partners, the EU is now looking to complement its multilateral and bilateral efforts with a regulatory instrument that would allow it to preclude market access to third country suppliers where reciprocal market access is not provided. This chapter aims to examine how the EU is currently conducting its deep trade agenda in the area of public procurement and attempts to determine the extent to which the EU's current drive to open procurement markets abroad is informed (or not) by the issues that have undermined attempts to thrash out a multilateral trade agreement on procurement—particularly the concerns voiced by developing countries regarding the loss of policy space.

Section 8.2 discusses the parameters of the current debate regarding the interface between international trade liberalization and public procurement regulation. It describes the two main areas through which liberalization of public procurement markets is being sought—market access through non-discrimination and national regulatory reforms aimed at ensuring transparency and good governance—and explores some of the main reasons why the WTO membership has so far proved reluctant to push for multilateral liberalization in this area. Section 8.3 briefly describes the regulatory frameworks for public procurement established at WTO and EU level. Section 8.4 then analyses the EU's current external trade policy in the area of public procurement. It assesses how the EU has sought to expand the reach of the GPA rules through the EU DCFTAs, and how through new proposals published by the Commission the EU is looking to grant market access only on the basis of the principle of reciprocity.

## 8.2 Liberalization of Public Procurement

### 8.2.1 Market access and 'framework rules'

The very nature of public procurement—a government-led economic sector whose primary aims are not driven by profit, but rather focused on the promotion of the public interest (Trepte (2004), p. 27)—means that it is a sector where non-tariff barriers are pervasive. A wide variety of objectives are advanced by governments to justify restrictions on market access for foreign contractors. For instance, countries may wish to restrict the award of procurement contracts to domestic suppliers if the sector is politically sensitive (Arrowsmith (2003), p. 15). Governments have also resorted to the increasingly discredited argument that such restrictions are necessary to allow an infant domestic industry in a particular sector to develop and create economies of scale before exposing it to international competition (Ssennoga (2006), pp. 218–49). Measures providing a competitive advantage to the domestic industry either explicitly provide preferential treatment for domestic suppliers (e.g. exclusion of foreign suppliers in certain areas, price preference policies, offering domestic suppliers the possibility of matching offers from foreign suppliers) (Trepte (2004), pp. 235–40; Arrowsmith (2003), p. 14) or adopt rules which, whilst non-discriminatory, intend to favour domestic suppliers (e.g. drawing up technical specifications that exclude foreign products) (Trepte (2004), pp. 240–1). The efficient management of administration processes may also require the adoption of restrictive measures. This is the case, for example, where contracting authorities decide to limit the tendering process to a limited number of participants in order to keep administration costs in check (Ibid).

Other structural factors may also impede the ability of foreign firms to participate in tenders for procurement contracts. Administrative inefficiencies, such as a lack of resources to implement a transparent procurement regulatory system, excessive bureaucracy, badly drafted specifications and inadequate publicity measures may undermine competition in the procurement tendering process. Such barriers can, in certain instances, be the result of a deliberate decision from governmental authorities to restrict access to the concerned market (McLachlan (1984), p. 357). The lack of transparent procedures can be a tool to conceal illegitimate practices such as 'corruption, nepotism and patronage' (Arrowsmith (2003), p. 17) or unofficial discriminatory practices in favour of domestic contractors (Ibid).

The diversity of behind-the-border barriers to trade in public procurement means that besides non-discrimination obligations, trade agreements also tend to include so-called 'framework rules' (Woolcock (2008b), pp. 4–6)—that is, rules that together establish an overall regulatory framework that aims to ensure open, transparent and competitive public procurement regulatory frameworks. Such rules usually relate to transparency requirements, eligibility of tenderers, contract award procedures and judicial and administrative enforcement.

Framework rules essentially reflect the key features of developed countries' domestic regulatory frameworks for public procurement, which themselves were the result of neo-liberal reforms carried out in the 1980s. Along the lines of the Washington consensus, 'a policy framework built around the pillars of market liberalisation, privatisation and tight macroeconomic policy' (Sudgen and Wilson (2002), pp. 11–134), such reforms were fuelled by the conviction that the role of the state in the economic sector needed to be reduced, not only to curtail public spending but also in the belief that public services would either be more efficiently delivered by the private sector or, where this was not deemed possible, by the public sector operating under private market rules (McCrudden (2007), p. 10). The result was the development of public procurement rules focused on cost reduction and efficiency, namely through an emphasis on the need to obtain 'value for money'—that is, to 'acquire systems, works or services on best possible terms' (McCrudden (2007), p. 11). In liberal public procurement regimes, value for money is the overarching regulatory objective which permeates all other objectives (Beviglia-Zampetti (1997). pp. 274–5):

> The basic objective—acquiring the items needed on the best possible terms—is generally common to both the public and the private sector. [...] [C]ompetition is increasingly recognised as the most effective tool to achieve this result and the objective of fostering competition in the procurement process is gaining wider acceptance. This trend is of paramount importance from a 'liberal' trade policy perspective because it represents the best path towards ensuring that national procurement markets are internationally 'contestable'. While competition often is not mentioned as such in domestic regulations, related policy objectives that have the effect of increasing competition include 'economy and efficiency', non-discrimination and transparency, integrity and accountability.

The regulatory objective pursued in national public procurement systems can be observed in trade agreements such as the GPA, whose rules requiring transparency, competitive bidding procedures, and publicity for award criteria all contribute to the attainment of value for money and enhancement of the efficiency of domestic procurement market as well as the increased accountability of the public sector (Hoekman and Mavroidis (1997), p. 297; Arrowsmith (2002), p. 766).

### 8.2.2 Opposition to liberalization of public procurement markets

Although the liberalization of public procurement is often portrayed as a legitimate developmental policy tool (European Commission (2005e)), the extent to which the increased contestability of markets can actually engender welfare gains is not clear. For many developing countries, the loss of the ability to favour domestic firms or products in the context of public procurement would inhibit attempts to promote the development of industry and pursue important non-economic objectives (e.g. integration of disadvantaged communities or minorities in the economy) (Stiglitz and Charlton (2005), p. 69). The problem is further exacerbated by the fact that procurement suppliers from developed countries benefit from a number of competitive advantages compared to their counterparts in developing countries, such as their higher supply capacity for the type of products that governments wish to purchase (services and manufactures) and lower average costs—which mean that developing country suppliers would likely not reap many gains from market openness (Trionfetti (2000), p. 57; Khorana and Subramanian (2012), pp. 16–18). Besides, the inability to promote industrial, environmental, social, or other policy objectives through discriminatory procurement practices is not a concern that is exclusive to developing countries. While much has been made of the 'buy national' policies introduced by emerging economies such as Brazil (The Economist (2011)) and China (Wang (2011), pp. 98–102), developed countries have also often struggled to square free market rhetoric with less than open domestic policies in the area of procurement. This can be seen in Canada's historical reluctance to make GPA commitments in relation to its sub-central government entities (Collins (2011). p. 175) or in the recent enactment by the US of the American Recovery and Reinvestment Act of 2009—a response from the Obama administration to the financial and economic crisis—which prohibits the use of government funds for the 'construction, alteration or repair of public buildings or public works unless all of the iron, steel and manufactured goods used in the project are produced in the United States' (Linarelli (2011), p. 773).

Baldwin and Richardson have argued that the positive impact on national welfare that can be expected from disciplining public procurement depends heavily on the particular circumstances of the concerned market (Baldwin and Richardson (1972), pp. 243–63). In particular, they posit that discriminatory practices will not lead to welfare losses if demand from contracting authorities is 'too small' (Evenett and Hoekman (2004), p. 19)—something which is likely to be the case in many developing countries. Evenett and Hoekman added that, even where government demand increases, the long-term effects of discriminatory practices favouring domestic over foreign contractors will vary depending on other factors such as 'the extent of barriers to entry or exit' (Ibid, pp. 9–10), which in turn depend on other aspects of the national regulatory environment, such as the level of sophistication of competition policy and law (Ibid, pp. 17–19). In other words, the welfare effects of liberalization must be assessed on a case-by-case basis (e.g. size of the economy and government demand) (Ibid), and will only yield tangible benefits if complemented by the necessary regulatory reforms. Hence, whilst the benefits of national treatment in public procurement remain questionable—at least with regard to small developing economies—the adoption of framework rules need not be too controversial. From a market access perspective, it appears that public procurement rules on transparency enhance contestability of a domestic market and consequently incite firms to invest in the concerned market (Ibid):

> Opaque tendering procedures and poor governance tend to discourage potential bids from domestic and foreign firms; often leaving governments dependent on bids from a smaller group of 'insider' firms. Contract prices tend to be higher, quality lower and delays and costs over-runs common. Outright bans on procuring from foreign sources—or more subtle forms of preferences for national firms–reduce competition from abroad. Needlessly stringent pre-qualification requirements shut out bidders too; all to the detriment of the taxpayer who ends up paying more for less. (Evenett (2003), p. 2)

In addition, it is also argued that rules promoting transparency in public procurement can entail good governance-related benefits by encouraging sound management of expenditures and addressing corruption and rent-seeking. The perceived benefits of rules promoting transparency and good governance mean that many developing countries have embarked on attempts to reform public procurement systems (Rege (2001), p. 490). Such reforms are typically in line with the type of framework rules provided in trade agreements, as they tend to include requirements on: '(i) effective and wide advertising of upcoming procurement opportunities; (ii) public opening of bids; (iii) pre-disclosure of all relevant information including transparent and clear bid evaluation procedures;

(iv) clear accountabilities for decision making; and (v) enforceable review for bidders when public entities breach the rules' (Hunja (2003), p. 15). The main difficulty encountered by developing countries with regard to framework rules can be linked to compliance costs (Rege (2011), p. 512) and resistance from those with a vested interest in the status quo (e.g. political class benefiting from lack of transparency), the lack of expertise and capacity, and the complexity of the reform process (Hunja (2003), pp. 17–21).

Despite their supposed benefits, there remains developing country opposition to the adoption of multilateral framework rules in the area of procurement, stemming from the difficulty of dissociating such rules from the traditional non-discrimination principle (Woolcock (2008b), p. 8). In principle, the positives of framework rules should make the prospect of an international agreement requiring the adoption of minimum standards of transparency and good governance in national procurement systems more palatable than one entailing market opening commitments. The EU subscribed to this theory when, as part of the Singapore issues, it proposed the signing of a multilateral transparency agreement on public procurement, under which developing countries would be bound by transparency and procedural requirements but not by a national treatment obligation (Reich (2009), p. 993). This agreement was sold by its proponents as a tool to foster good governance by enhancing value for money and integrity in procurement systems (European Commission (2005e)). However, despite the EU's assurances that the proposed agreement 'will be limited to transparency, will not open up new markets or increase existing ones' (WTO (2003a)), developing countries questioned the need for regulatory harmonization at WTO level (some suggesting instead the conclusion of a non-binding agreement with a more limited scope) (Arrowsmith (2002), p. 764) and feared that such agreement was merely a Trojan horse through which non-discrimination would eventually be introduced (Anderson and Arrowsmith (2011), p. 10).

## 8.3 Regulatory Framework for Government Procurement

### 8.3.1 WTO Government Procurement Agreement

#### *8.3.1.1 Background*

The WTO Government Procurement Agreement, adopted on 22 March 2012 (Revised GPA),[1] is the result of a long and tortuous process that has spanned over forty years (Blank and Marceau (1996), p. 77). Public procurement was originally excluded from the scope of GATT 1947, and it was only in the context of the Tokyo Round of negotiations that a number of developed WTO Members signed a voluntary and plurilateral agreement on government procurement (Tokyo

[1] See http://www.wto.org/english/tratop_e/gproc_e/gp_gpa_e.htm. The Revised GPA will enter into force once ratified by two-thirds of the GPA parties.

Round Government Procurement Code or 'Tokyo Code'), which contained a non-discrimination obligation as well as procedural standards and transparency requirements. It was, however, limited in two respects. First, it was a plurilateral agreement which only applied to those GATT Members that decided to accede to it and, secondly, its scope was limited insofar as it only covered goods (not services) and central or federal entities (not sub-federal or local authorities). With the advent of the Uruguay Round came the opportunity to negotiate a new agreement that would expand the scope of market opening commitments relating to government procurement. The Agreement on Government Procurement concluded in 1994 (1994 GPA) delivered on this front, covering services and works and applying to procurement for sub-national (federal) authorities and public undertakings. It also added significant new procedural rules on transparency and procedures, such as requirements regulating technical specifications, tendering processes, conditions for the participation of suppliers, selection procedures and negotiation of procurement contracts, and the availability of legal mechanisms allowing suppliers to challenge violations of the 1994 GPA before an independent review body.

Despite these additions, the 1994 GPA still fell short of its proponents' expectations. Its membership remained modest (Guimaraes de Lima e Silva (2008), p. 68) and even those WTO Members that had acceded to it were permitted to ascribe limits (e.g. public entities subject to the agreement and minimum value of procurement contracts covered) and derogations to their market opening commitments. In fact, in many cases, such commitments were not made available on an MFN basis, as 1994 GPA signatories only extended their concessions to other signatories on a reciprocal basis (Anderson and Arrowsmith (2011), p. 20). Finally, by this time there was also a need to recognize the growing importance of information technology in relation to procurement, which was not covered in the agreement. These ongoing concerns were reflected in the 'built-in-agenda' for further negotiation which had been incorporated into the 1994 GPA.[2]

### 8.3.1.2 *The Revised GPA*

The Singapore issues having been rejected by developing countries, the most recent incarnation of the GPA (the Revised GPA) is still very much a plurilateral agreement, and currently has 15 signatories, most of which are developed countries.[3] As with its previous incarnations, the purpose of the Revised GPA is to ensure the contestability of national public procurement markets by providing for an obligation of non-discrimination between foreign and domestic suppliers and by establishing framework rules that seek to ensure the transparency, fairness, and efficiency of procedures relating to public procurement.

[2] Article XXIV.7(b) GPA 1994.

[3] Armenia, Aruba, Canada, Chinese Taipei, EU, Hong Kong, Iceland, Israel, Japan, Korea, Liechtenstein, Norway, Singapore, Switzerland, and USA.

The scope of the GPA remains subject to the same ailment that afflicted the 1994 GPA, in that parties are still able to specify derogations and limitations to their commitments. As such, the scope of the GPA continues to require an assessment of the individual annexes of each of its members, who are able to negotiate the applicable thresholds, and which entities and contracts are subject to the liberalization commitments contained in the agreement. However, the GPA minimizes the lack of uniformity in coverage by providing general definitions of what is actually covered by the agreement. The GPA covers procurement of goods and services for governmental purposes, although goods or services 'procured with a view to commercial sale or resale, or for use in the production or supply of goods or services for commercial sale or resale'[4] are excluded. In terms of what is covered by the concept of procurement defined in Article II GPA, there is an ongoing debate as to whether the GPA covers public–private partnerships, particularly concession contracts such as Build-Operate and Transfer (B.O.T.) projects, whereby private sector operators undertake the task of operating public infrastructures in exchange for remuneration from public users (Reich (2009), p. 1007).

The GPA also provides additional transparency and procedural requirements. Some such rules are intended to avoid the use of government procurement procedures for protectionist purposes. Thus, the conditions for participation in a tendering process must be limited to those 'that are essential to ensure that a supplier has the legal, commercial, technical and financial abilities to undertake the relevant procurement'.[5] Where the tendering process is selective—that is, open to only a limited set of bidders—countries may not arbitrarily select such bidders but must limit participation to those suppliers that satisfy the pre-determined restrictive conditions for participation.[6] Other provisions welcome the GPA to the twenty-first century by regulating the use of information technology in government procurement. The GPA provides, for example, that government procurement procedures relying on information technology may be subject to lower minimum timescales, must use generally available technology and must ensure interoperability with other generally available technology. Finally, in an attempt to placate concerns voiced by developing WTO Members, the agreement borrows from the proposed multilateral transparency agreement by including special and differential treatment provisions which permit acceding developing countries to apply the discriminatory measures. The flexibility afforded to developing countries is, however, limited in two significant ways. First, the ability to favour domestic firms and products is time-limited, as these may only be applied during a transitional period: three years for developing countries and five years for least developed countries.[7] Secondly, only certain discriminatory measures may be applied: price preferences, offsets, phased-in addition of specific entities or sectors; and thresholds higher than the permanent thresholds.[8]

[4] Article II:2(ii) Revised GPA. [5] Article VIII:1 Revised GPA.
[6] Article IX:4 Revised GPA. [7] Article V:4 GPA. [8] Article V:3 GPA.

### 8.3.2 EU legal framework

Under EU law, there is a general obligation not to discriminate between domestic and foreign suppliers as a result of the various treaty provisions aimed at prohibiting obstacles to intra-EU trade (Fernandez Martin (1996), pp. 16–20; Bovis (2007), pp. 4–5), including the provisions on non-discrimination on the grounds of nationality,[9] free movement of goods[10] and services, and the freedom of establishment.[11] The obligation for Member States not to impede market access was, however, considered inadequate to ensure a fully functioning internal market in light of the different regulatory systems adopted by Member States with regard to government procurement (Arrowsmith and Treumer (2012), p. 8). The general Treaty provisions have thus been complemented by a number of directives that harmonize the regulation of government procurement—the manner in which contracts are awarded, the objectives pursued by regulation and the remedies available in case of infringements of rules (Fernandez Martin (1996), p. 285)—across the EU in relation to supply contracts, public works contracts, utilities sectors, and public services contracts. In 2004, the various directives that once covered these sectors were consolidated into two directives: (i) Directive 2004/17 governing procurement procedures relating to the water, energy, transport and postal services sectors (Utilities Directive); and (ii) Directive 2004/18 on public works contracts, public supply contracts and public services contracts (Public Sector Directive) (together 'Procurement Directives'). The distinct legal treatment of public sector and utilities procurement is explained by the fact that contrary to public sector procurement, network industries had already undergone significant liberalization under EU law (Bovis (2012), p. 291). As a consequence, it was considered best not to extend the strict rules applicable to public sector procurement to the utilities sector (Ibid). Further, there are existing directives providing remedies for tenderers[12] in case of violation of the Procurement Directives and, more recently, the EU adopted Directive 2009/91 regulating procurement in the politically sensitive areas of defence and security (Defence and Security Directive).[13]

There are numerous similarities between the EU and WTO regimes for public procurement. This can be partially explained by the fact that the Tokyo Code was largely inspired by the text of the 1976 OECD Instrument on Government Purchasing Policies, which in turn borrowed heavily from the EU's own regulatory system (Blank and Marceau (1997), pp. 37–40). Ever since, the EU has both influenced and been influenced by the content of the subsequent WTO rules on public procurement (Woolcock (1993), p. 539; Didier (1997), p. 125). The EU regulatory system for public procurement follows generally the same principles as those set out under the GPA, in that they are both geared towards ensuring equality of treatment and transparency throughout the tendering process (Steinicke

[9] Article 18 TFEU. [10] Article 34 TFEU. [11] Articles 49 and 56 TFEU.

[12] Directive 89/665 OJ [1989] L 395; Directive 92/13 OJ [1992] L 76.

[13] Directive 2009/91/EC OJ [2009] L216/76.

(2012), p. 365). However, as is to be expected from a more mature and detailed regulatory system, EU law goes further in a number of aspects.

The main piece of EU legislation, the Public Sector Directive, applies to all works, supply, and services contracts, provided that they exceed minimum value thresholds. Within this large scope of application there are, however, a few caveats that are worth mentioning. First of all, certain sensitive service sectors which are not viewed as raising cross-border issues, such as legal and social services, are only subject to a limited set of rules included in the Public Sector Directive (technical specifications and requirement to send notice of results of award procedure).[14] Secondly, works concession contracts—which are not covered by the GPA—are also only subject to a separate set of rules governing the award of contracts to and by concessionaires,[15] whilst services concession contracts are excluded from the scope of application of the Public Sector Directive altogether.[16]

The Public Sector Directive regulates all aspects of the public procurement tendering process and aims to ensure that the procurement markets of Member States are regulated in a non-discriminatory, transparent, and objective manner.[17] These principles permeate the entire body of EU law and case law on public procurement (Arrowsmith and Treumer (2012), p. 10). Included in the Directive is the requirement for contracting authorities to notify and publish their intention to initiate a bidding process for a procurement contract. The Directive also includes rules regulating the qualifications requirements to be fulfilled by suppliers (e.g. technical specifications, contract performance conditions etc.), in order to ensure that such requirements are not used as means to hinder market access. Thus, technical specifications must afford equal access for tenderers and not have the effect of creating unjustified obstacles to the opening of public procurement to competition'.[18] In addition, suppliers may not be excluded from the tendering process where they can demonstrate compliance with technical specifications that are equivalent to those identified by the contracting authorities.[19] There are also rules on the criteria that must be used when awarding procurement contracts. Generally, the contract must be awarded to the bidder that has either submitted the lowest price or the 'most economically advantageous offer' (Bovis (2012), p. 270). The latter category requires an assessment of various factors by the awarding authority such as the price, quality, technical merit of the bids, environmental factors, security of supply etc. (Bovis (2007), p. 67). In certain sectors, there is a requirement for contracting authorities to provide a weighing scale to assess the relative importance of each award criteria.

As far as contract award procedures are concerned, the Public Sector Directive establishes a preference towards tendering processes that are open to all suppliers.[20] Contracting authorities are required to award procurement contracts either on the basis of an 'open procedure'[21] (where any interested contractor or supplier

[14] Article 21 Public Sector Directive.
[15] Articles 56 to 65 Public Sector Directive.
[16] Article 17 Public Sector Directive.
[17] Article 2 Public Sector Directive.
[18] Article 23 Directive 2004/18.
[19] Article 23.3 Directive 2004/18.
[20] Article 28 Public Sector Directive.
[21] Article 1.11(a) Public Sector Directive.

can submit a bid) or 'restricted procedure'[22] (where any interested contractor or supplier may request to participate but where the contracting authority can choose to invite the contractors or suppliers that may submit tenders). Exceptionally, in a specified set of circumstances, the contracting authorities may choose to apply a contract award procedure that is not open to all. This is the case of the 'negotiated procedure',[23] where contracting authorities contact the contractors and suppliers of their choice and negotiate terms with one or more of these, and the 'competitive dialogue',[24] a procedure that applies for complex contracts and allows contracting authorities to open dialogue with a select group of contractors or suppliers in order to discuss the best way in which to achieve the stated aim of the procurement contract. The Public Procurement Directives also tend to better reflect advances in IT and procedural innovations in the area of public procurement by recognizing and regulating public procurement tools and procedures such as electronic auctions,[25] framework agreements,[26] dynamic purchasing systems,[27] and the above-mentioned competitive dialogues.[28]

## 8.4 EU External Trade Policy and Law in Public Procurement

### 8.4.1 External policy and legislative reform

The EU has traditionally been one of the main proponents of further international liberalization in the area of public procurement. It was one of the original signatories of the Tokyo Code and one of the main advocates for the conclusion of a multilateral WTO Transparency Agreement, and has since sought to increase market access commitments in the context of the successive GPAs (Smith, (2010), p. 949). The work at WTO level has also been complemented by bilateral FTAs with the EU stating that its EU DCFTAs should 'systematically provide for the substantial liberalisation of public procurement markets' (European Commission (2006b), p. 18), and '[...] in particular fight against discriminatory practices' (European Commission (2010c), p. 6). However, the EU's ability to obtain market opening commitments from third countries has been called into question. Few countries have signed up to the GPA, and even where commitments are secured, these tend to be subject to limitations. GPA Members have tended to exclude a number of key sectors (e.g. railways) and procurement contracts (regional and sectoral procurement) from the scope of the agreement and, with regard to FTAs, commitments can be somewhat limited. Noting the general reluctance of countries to commit to market openings as well as the rise of protectionism in the area of public procurement, the EU is now looking to complement its policy of liberalizing foreign public procurement markets by equipping itself with a legal instrument

[22] Article 1.11(b) Public Sector Directive. [23] Article 1.11(d) Public Sector Directive.
[24] Article 1.11(c) Public Sector Directive. [25] Article 54 Public Sector Directive.
[26] Article 32 Public Sector Directive. [27] Article 33 Public Sector Directive.
[28] Article 1(11) Public Sector Directive. Not provided for under the Utilities Directive.

that would allow it to bar third country access to its own procurement market in the absence of reciprocity.

## 8.4.2 Proposal on third country market access to the EU public procurement market

### *8.4.2.1 Rationale and content of proposal*

In the run-up to the 2012 French Presidential election, the then-President Nicolas Sarkozy made a pledge to the French electorate to push for the adoption of a 'Buy European Act' requiring contracting authorities of the Member States to purchase goods and services sourced from the EU and imposing a rule of reciprocity in the EU's relations with third countries that would enable it to restrict access to its procurement markets where reciprocal access was not secured for EU suppliers (Laurent and Picard (2012)). The pledge was also accompanied by a threat that if no action was taken at EU level within 12 months from Sarkozy's re-election, France would go it alone by enacting legislation protecting French suppliers. The promise may have been an empty one—it was not the first time a French politician had asked for protectionist measures in this area only to encounter considerable opposition in Brussels—and the threat may have lacked credibility, given the EU's exclusive competent in trade relations, but the suspicion is that Sarkozy's words gifted the EU with an opportunity to explore an issue which had been an ongoing concern for some time: how to pry open China's procurement markets. Although China submitted an application to accede to the GPA in 2007 (Wang (2009), pp. 663–706), its subsequent offers have all fallen short of the expectations of the current GPA parties. In the meantime, EU firms have consistently pointed to China's protectionist policies to explain their inability to make an impression on the hugely important Chinese procurement market (Simon (2012)). The spectre of China loomed large over the Proposal for a Regulation on the access of third country goods and services to the Union's internal market in public procurement (Proposal)[29] in March 2012 which, as Commission officials were keen to stress, should not be viewed as a protectionist measure but rather as a tool to improve the EU's negotiating position in trade negotiations relating to public procurement in order to gain access to public procurement markets of trading partners (European Commission (2011b)). According to the Commission, the open nature of the EU's public procurement markets compared to its competitors means that the EU lacks leverage in the context of trade negotiations and has therefore struggled to secure meaningful market access commitments in this area. The supposed 'openness' of the EU public procurement market to third countries is, according to the EU, due to two factors. First, in the context of the GPA, the EU has made more market opening commitments than any other major trading nation (e.g. Canada, Japan, and US). Secondly, most emerging economies have refused to liberalize their domestic procurement

[29] Proposal for a Regulation on COM(2012) 124 final.

markets either through the GPA or through FTAs. Where no market access commitments are made, countries—whether GPA signatories or not—have tended to impose protectionist measures in the form of domestic barriers such as price preferences, offsets, local establishment and content requirement, and 'buy national' policies (European Commission (2012a)). The Commission claims, however, that the EU's approach has been different insofar as it has tended to open its procurement markets even where it has made no binding international commitment. This is explained by the fact that, with the exception of the utilities sector,[30] there are no rules regulating the treatment of third country procurement suppliers. Faced with a legal void, it is claimed that a general preference towards openness has led Member States to not impose access restrictions on access to third country suppliers in most public procurement markets. The upshot is that the current regime leaves the EU exposed to free-riding from third countries, as non-EU procurement suppliers can exploit the lucrative internal market even though EU suppliers are not given reciprocal access to foreign markets. The EU is therefore unable to use access to the EU markets as a carrot to entice further liberalization from third countries. To redress the alleged asymmetry in terms of market access, the Proposal creates a right to refuse access to the internal market to suppliers from third countries that do not provide market access to EU contractors.[31] The Proposal states that, for procurement contracts with a value equal to or exceeding EUR 5 million, Member States' contracting authorities can opt to exclude tenders comprising goods or services originating from a third country, where the value of such products or goods exceeds 50 per cent of the total value of the procurement contract. Such exclusion will only be valid if it receives the approval of the Commission, which will only be given if one of the following conditions is met:[32] (i) if, where an international agreement exists between the EU and the third party containing commitments on public procurement, a reservation has been made with regard to the goods and services covered by the concerned procurement contract; or (ii) if, in the absence of an international agreement between the EU and the third country, it is determined that the third country has maintained restrictive procurement measures leading to a lack of substantial reciprocity.

A supplementary tool provided by the Proposal is that the Commission may, upon the request of an interested stakeholder or of its own initiative, investigate the application of trade-restrictive practices by third countries when it considers this to be in the interests of the EU.[33] Where restrictions to market access for EU contractors are found, the Commission may invite the third country for consultations to address the possibility of removing such restrictions and, if no action is taken, the Commission may temporarily restrict market access to the internal market for contractors of the third country[34] by either excluding tenders of which more than 50 per cent are made up of goods or services originating from the concerned

[30] Articles 58 and 59 Utilities Directive. [31] Article 10 Proposal.
[32] Article 6(4) Proposal. [33] Article 9(1) Proposal. [34] Article 10 Proposal.

third country, or by imposing a mandatory price penalty on the part of the tender consisting of goods or services originating from the third country.

The policy is aimed at securing more than just national treatment. In assessing whether there is a 'substantial lack of reciprocity' the Commission must examine, inter alia, 'to what degree public procurement laws of the country concerned ensure transparency in line with international standards in the field of public procurement'.[35] Part of the EU's assessment focuses on the domestic procurement rules and the manner in which they are applied by the local authorities, which may lead one to the conclusion that the regulatory framework of the third country concerned may also be the subject of any subsequent negotiations on market access. This presumption appears to be borne out by the fact that the Proposal provides that consultations with the third party may be terminated if international commitments are made in any one of the following contexts: accession to the GPA; conclusion of a bilateral agreement with the EU which includes market access commitments in the field of public procurement; and the expansion of market access commitments under the GPA or an existing bilateral agreement.[36]

#### *8.4.2.2 Shortfalls of the proposal*

From a policy perspective, the Proposal has received a considerable amount of criticism, not least from liberal-minded Member States such as Germany and the United Kingdom, who have bemoaned that even if the intention was to create an instrument that would force third countries to reconsider protectionist policies, the Proposal in its current state is more likely to reinforce current protectionist tendencies (Barker, Chaffin, and Pignal (2012); The Economist (2012)). First of all, by closing off its own market, the EU would lose the moral high ground when advocating the liberalization of public procurement (Financial Times (2012)) and may even spark retaliatory measures from key trading partners.[37] Secondly, in a rather embarrassing turn of events for the EU, it seems that the claim that the EU's public procurement markets are more open than those of its main trading partners is somewhat off the mark. A study conducted by Messerlin and Mirodout has shown that whilst it is true that the EU has made comparatively more de jure market opening commitments, its Member States have considerably undermined such commitments, restricting the de facto openness of the internal market. In fact, some of the countries targeted by the Proposal (e.g. Japan, China) have levels of de facto openness that are comparable to that of the EU (Messerlin (2012c), pp. 6–7). The very rationale of the Proposal appears flawed and raises questions regarding the necessity and effectiveness of adopting a reciprocity requirement

[35] Article 6.5(a) Proposal. [36] Article 9.5 Proposal.

[37] Procurement Policy Note—European legislative proposals on third country access to the EU public procurement market, Information Note 03/12, 5 April 2012.

under EU law: major economies are hardly likely to take the threat of seeing their access to EU markets restricted if their own markets are already similarly or more open than that of the EU (Messerlin (2012a), p. 13).

Another controversial aspect of the Proposal concerns the fact that restrictive measures may be adopted against developing countries (least developed countries are excluded[38]). While this makes sense to the extent that the main targets of the EU's drive for reciprocity are large emerging markets such as China, India, and Brazil, it also raises the possibility that the EU could bar market access to firms from developing countries whose own domestic markets hold no particular strategic importance for the EU. Commission officials have attempted to downplay the potential impact of the Proposal on developing countries, arguing that the Commission will only initiate investigations against restrictions applied by third countries where this is in the interests of the EU (European Commission (2011b), pp. 2–3). However, where national contracting authorities decide to exclude third country bidders, the Commission's only consideration when deciding whether to approve the exclusion is to determine whether there is a substantial lack of reciprocity. It is therefore not inconceivable that the Proposal may be used by contracting authorities to preclude bids even where the EU has no significant offensive interest in gaining access to the procurement market of the third country involved. If claims that the Proposal is unlikely to strengthen the EU's leverage in negotiations with larger economies are true, then there is a danger that, if adopted in its current format, the main legacy of the Proposal would be to have enabled Member States to exclude smaller developing third countries—which already suffer from competitive disadvantages—from competing in the EU's internal market.

### *8.4.2.3 Legality of Proposal*

#### 8.4.2.3.1 GPA

The scope of the Proposal does not exclude goods or services that originate from countries that have signed international agreements covering public procurement, which raises the question of the legality of excluding procurement suppliers from GPA or FTA parties. With regard to the GPA, several arguments have been advanced to justify the Proposal's illegality. It is argued that the Proposal violates the national treatment obligation under Article III.1 GPA and is contrary to the objectives of the GPA—in particular, the commitment of its signatories in the Preamble to recognize 'the need for an effective multilateral framework for government procurement, with a view to achieving greater liberalization and expansion of, and improving the framework for, the conduct of international trade'[39] and 'that measures regarding government procurement should not be prepared, adopted or applied so as to afford protection to domestic suppliers,

[38] Article 4 Proposal. [39] Recital 1 Proposal.

goods or services, or to discriminate among foreign suppliers, goods or services'.[40] This position is, however, based on the false premise that the Proposal 'seeks to re-negotiate or alter the GPA Parties' existing coverage outside of the forum of the WTO GPA, with the aim of getting the Parties to expand their schedules to "match" EU coverage' (Dawar (2012), p. 95), and where reciprocity is not secured, that the EU will 'contract its own coverage' under the GPA. Nowhere in the Proposal is it suggested that the EU should reduce its commitments under the GPA (or for that matter under existing FTAs) where reciprocal market access is not provided. In fact, the Proposal specifically provides that the Commission may not approve the exclusion of third country bidders where such exclusion would violate market access commitments entered into in its international agreements.[41] In other words, where the EU has made a binding commitment to accord to a GPA or FTA party national treatment no less favourable than that accorded to domestic goods or services, the EU may not revisit this commitment just because the GPA or FTA party concerned does not offer reciprocal market access. Under the Proposal, the EU is only permitted to envisage the exclusion of third country goods or services from its domestic procurement markets in circumstances where it has opened its markets despite either not having made an international commitment or having taken an explicit market reservation. The Proposal therefore complies with existing international agreements covering public procurement, to the extent that it does not affect procurement for which market opening commitments have been made.

#### 8.4.2.3.2 EU law

Qualms concerning the Proposal's legality are on much firmer ground when one assesses it in light of EU law and, in particular, the free movement of goods rules provided for under Articles 28 et seq. TFEU. The right to free movement of goods applies to both goods originating from Member States and goods originating from third countries that are in free circulation in the EU.[42] A good is considered to be in free circulation 'if the import formalities have been complied with and any customs duties or charges having equivalent effect which are payable have been levied in that Member State'.[43] The Proposal allows restrictive measures against 'non-covered goods', which are defined as goods not originating from the EU or from least developed countries. The origin of goods is in turn determined in accordance with Articles 22 to 26 of Regulation (EC) No 2913/1992, which provide that in order to be considered a good originating from the EU, the good must either have been 'wholly obtained or produced' in the EU or, where the production of goods has involved one or more third countries, the last substantial transformation of the good must have taken place within the EU. By allowing contracting authorities to reject bids comprising 'goods or services originating outside the Union' without taking into account the possibility that

[40] Recital 2 Proposal. [41] Article 6(4) Proposal.
[42] Article 28(2) TFEU. [43] Article 29 TFEU.

such goods may already be in free circulation in the EU, the Proposal violates the free movement of goods rules.[44] Under the current text, one may well envisage the possibility of a contracting authority rejecting a bid from an EU supplier even if the non-covered goods—that is, the goods not originating from the EU—were legally imported into the EU.

The Proposal has also been criticized for distorting the conditions of competition within the EU by allowing restrictions of market access to be applied individually by contracting authorities of Member States (Dawar (2012), p. 93). Such criticism is to a certain extent unfair, given that such distortions already exist under the current regime. As pointed out by the Commission, the absence of clear rules concerning the treatment of third countries in the area of procurement has led to a situation where a number of Member States have taken it upon themselves to regulate the market access of foreign procurement suppliers, in some cases even applying protectionist measures that are incompatible with the EU's existing international commitments (European Commission (2012a), p. 15). The Proposal has at the very least the merit of being mindful of the need to maintain the EU's exclusive competence with regard to external trade policy in the area of public procurement by requiring that any restriction be approved by the Commission and, in doing so, ensures that Member States are no longer able to apply illegal market access restrictions. The Proposal can, however, be criticized for not going far enough in its attempts to reduce distortions of competition within the EU—by allowing restrictions to be applied on a national basis, it maintains the diverging treatment of foreign procurement suppliers across the EU. This flaw exposes the fact that, despite the Commission's protestations to the contrary, the Proposal is not solely about ensuring reciprocity but also panders to the protectionist impulses of (some) Member States. If the aim is to encourage third countries to offer reciprocal market access, there is no reason why a uniform restriction should not be applied across the EU, since this would both increase the EU's leverage in trade negotiations and avoid distortions of competition. The fact that uniformity has not been sought suggests that the drafters of the Proposal were attempting to accommodate, on the one hand, the interests of those Member States who wish to use it for protectionist purposes and, on the other hand, those Member States who do not wish to close their markets to foreign procurement suppliers.

### 8.4.3 EU DCFTAs

#### *8.4.3.1 Expansion of GPA rules*

A survey of public procurement rules included in FTAs has shown that these may be divided into three categories: (i) FTAs with no provisions on public procurement; (ii) FTAs with some 'soft' provisions on public procurement; and (iii)

[44] A similar analysis was made with regard to the Utilities Directive. See Eeckhout (1994), pp. 314–16.

FTAs with detailed regulatory frameworks on public procurement (Anderson, Muller, Osei-Lah, Pardo de Leon, and Pelletier (2011), pp. 561–6). Since the turn of the century, the EU has signed a number of FTAs that promote the adoption of rules on public procurement. The content and scope of such rules has varied significantly on a case-by-case basis (Schnitzer (2005), p. 15). Certain FTAs only provided for non-binding commitments to liberalize procurement markets, whilst others provided legally binding obligations based on the text of the GPA, or replicated the regulatory systems of the respective signatories (e.g. EU Mexico Agreement referred to existing NAFTA provisions) (Ibid, pp. 65–89). However, since the Global Europe strategy, the EU's approach to public procurement regulation in the context of EU DCFTAs is to require compliance with standards set by the GPA (Woolcock (2012b), pp. 15–17).

The public procurement chapters of the EU DCFTAs are based on the text of the GPA, and differences between these agreements reflect either the timing of the signature (CEPA and the KOREU FTA were signed prior to the adoption of the Revised GPA) or the level of economic development of the EU's counterparts. Since Korea is already a signatory of the GPA, the KOREU FTA merely reaffirms the parties' rights and obligations under that agreement. In fact, even though the conclusion of the KOREU FTA pre-dates that of the Revised GPA, the eventual amendments of the Revised GPA were included in the KOREU FTA (WTO (2012b), p. 3). Since Singapore is a signatory of the GPA and because the EU–Singapore FTA was signed after the adoption of the Revised GPA, the EU–Singapore FTA transposes the vast majority of provisions of the Revised GPA.[45] Furthermore, like the KOREU FTA, the EU–Singapore FTA also provides that if the Revised GPA is amended or superseded by another agreement, the parties must amend the provisions of the agreement in accordance.[46] Finally, the most recent Global FTA—the CETA—replicates verbatim the entire text of the Revised GPA with the exceptions of the provisions on dispute settlement and mechanisms for the amendment of the public procurement-related provisions.[47]

Those EU DCFTAs signed with countries that are not signatories of the GPA tend to replicate the text of the GPA as much as possible. The Colombia–Peru FTA provisions on public procurement have been largely copy-pasted from the text of the Revised GPA, and CEPA contains provisions—inspired from the 1994 GPA (CEPA was concluded prior to the signing of the Revised GPA)—regulating conditions of participation, qualification of suppliers, technical specifications, time periods, contract negotiations, awarding of contracts, transparency, and notice obligations as well as the availability of procedural challenges. By and large, the language of such provisions is either identical or similar to that of the 1994 GPA. However, the EU DCFTAs go further than the GPA in one important respect. Both the KOREU FTA and the Colombia–Peru FTA do away with the debate on whether procurement provisions apply to concession contracts. The KOREU

[45] Article 10.1–10.20 EU–Singapore FTA.
[46] Article 10.20 EU–Singapore FTA.
[47] Chapter 21 CETA.

FTA follows a similar approach to that applied under EU law by subjecting such contracts to a specific set of rules, separate from the general provisions on public procurement.[48] It provides for a non-discrimination and national treatment obligation,[49] as well as general requirements to publish notices on intended contracts[50] and contract award decisions[51] and to provide effective review mechanisms.[52] The Colombia–Peru FTA, on the other hand, includes public works concession and B.O.T. contracts within the general definition of procurement, and in doing so, subjects those to the more far-reaching obligations found in the GPA.[53] Evidently, the EU sees the GPA as providing a more than adequate regulatory framework for public procurement liberalization and sees no need to export specific aspects of its own legislation. The policy is to require compliance with GPA rules or GPA-like rules, whilst securing additional commitments in terms of the scope of entities (central, federal, federated authorities, etc.) and contracts (e.g. B.O.T. and public works concession) covered by such rules.

#### *8.4.3.2 EU DCFTAs and developing countries*

The EU DCFTAs concluded with developing countries deviate from the GPA in certain areas. In CEPA, the non-discrimination obligation is transformed into a best endeavours requirement,[54] the scope of coverage is limited to central government procurement contracts[55] and there is no prohibition to apply offsets (Anderson, Muller, Osei-Lah, Pardo de Leon, and Pelletier (2011), p. 607). Moreover, there are numerous GPA provisions that have been watered down to take into account the reduced capacity of developing countries. Thus, the detailed GPA rules on valuation methods are omitted,[56] as are references to numerous obligations relating to the awarding of contracts (e.g. obligation not to penalize late bids if the delay is due solely to mishandling on the part of procuring entity,[57] and the right to verify that the supplier satisfies conditions for participation and is capable of fulfilling the terms of the contract where the price offered in the tender is abnormally low[58]), time limits (e.g. no reference for minimum deadlines for submission of bids[59]), and procedural challenges (e.g. no reference to detailed procedural standards[60] or requirement to provide corrective action or compensation[61]).

The approach adopted in CEPA has faced criticism for presuming that procurement regulatory reform is automatically antithetical to development objectives (Dawar and Evenett (2011), p. 657). The opposing view is that 'sound regulatory frameworks' in public procurement are crucial regardless of the level of economic

[48] Article 9.2 and Annex 9 KOREU FTA; Article 172 Colombia–Peru FTA.
[49] Article 2.1 Annex 9 KOREU FTA. [50] Article 2.3 Annex 9 KOREU FTA.
[51] Article 2.4 Annex 9 KOREU FTA. [52] Article 2.5 Annex 9 KOREU FTA.
[53] Article 173.2(b) Colombia–Peru FTA. [54] Article 167.2(b) CEPA.
[55] Article 167 CEPA. [56] Article 167B CEPA. [57] Article XV.2 GPA.
[58] Article XV.6 GPA. [59] Article XI.2 and 3 GATS.
[60] Article XVIII.2, 3, 6; Article 179 CEPA. [61] Article XVIII.7; Article 179 CEPA.

development (Ibid, p. 662), and that the omission of various GPA provisions intended to ensure non-discrimination, transparency and fairness in procurement processes and in the context of procedural challenges actually undermines economic development. Be that as it may, the GPA-minus content of CEPA reflects the essentially defensive interests of the CARICOM States in the area of procurement, and highlights the continuing misgivings held by developing countries in liberalizing this sector (Sauvé and Ward (2009), p. 17).

No such problems can be placed at the door of the Colombia–Peru FTA and EU–CA FTA, which do not stray too far from the text of the Revised GPA. The omissions reflecting the lack of resources and the absence of a sophisticated public procurement system infrastructure (e.g. the requirements to maintain supplier registration systems[62] and to maintain data to ensure the traceability of the conduct of procurement by electronic means[63]) are few and far between. Significantly, both the Colombia–Peru FTA and EU–CA FTA replicate the non-discrimination requirement provided under the GPA. This requirement includes a commitment to: (i) 'accord immediately and unconditionally' to the goods and services of [the other party] treatment no less favourable than the treatment accorded to its own goods, services, and suppliers and (ii) 'not treat a locally established supplier less favourably than another locally established supplier on the basis of the degree of foreign affiliation or ownership' or 'discriminate against a locally established supplier on the basis that the goods or services offered by that supplier for a particular procurement are goods or services of another [p]arty'. To the extent that these agreements do not contain a provision equivalent to the aforementioned Article V GPA, which extends certain flexibilities to developing countries, such as the right to apply discriminatory measures under certain conditions, the presence of a legally binding non-discrimination obligation means that developing country signatories in these agreements have undertaken obligations that are more burdensome than those currently found in the Revised GPA. The national treatment obligation included in the Colombia–Peru FTA and the EU–CA FTA has led to some criticism (CIFCA (2011), p. 8):

> Transparent procurement systems are important, not least to fight corruption. But to open up procurement markets for foreign actors means reducing the possibility of governments in Central America, Colombia and Peru to use government procurement as a critical economic tool to stimulate and promote the local economy and national industries. Considering the huge asymmetries in capacities, these have little chance of competing with European companies. An important policy instrument for industrialization, employment and macroeconomic stability would be lost.

The claim that economic development is necessarily impaired as a result of a requirement to not discriminate against foreign firms and products in the area of public procurement is debatable. As we have seen, studies have shown that the realization of welfare effects derived from liberalization depend on a wide range

[62] Article IX GPA. [63] Article XVI:3(a) GPA.

of factors, including the existence of the type of regulatory frameworks promoted by the Colombia–Peru FTA and EU–CA FTA. However, criticism may legitimately be aimed at the EU for not having included in the Colombia–Peru FTA and EU–CA FTA (as they did in CEPA) a binding commitment to provide its co-signatories with the technical assistance required to implement and enforce the public procurement regulatory system envisaged by the agreement.[64]

## 8.5 Conclusion

The liberalization of public procurement markets has proved an arduous task because of the importance of public procurement as a tool to pursue national policy objectives. This is particularly true for developing countries, which represent the biggest opposition towards a multilateral trade agreement in this area, but also applies to developed countries, which are not averse to pursuing protectionist practices to boost flagging economies. The EU, for its part, has consistently advocated market openness in the area of public procurement, a policy which can be seen from its consistent support for the GPA over the years, the proposals for a multilateral agreement on transparency for public procurement and increasingly through the conclusion of the EU DCFTAs.

The EU uses the EU DCFTAs as tools to spread the reach of the GPA rather than its own regulatory system. The reliance of the EU on the GPA is natural given that it has been, and remains, one of its main proponents. It is also logical in light of the fact that EU public procurement law and GPA rules are inexorably linked, both by a common origin and by the EU's subsequent contribution to the development of the GPA. The framework rules of the GPA thus provide the foundation for the implementation of an EU-type public procurement regime based on regulatory objectives such as transparency and good governance. The EU DCFTAs codify the provisions of the GPA and even build upon them in some instances by increasing the scope of these rules (e.g. public works concessions and B.O.T. contracts). However, the EU DCFTAs are not used as a laboratory for innovation of GPA-plus rules. There is certainly no attempt to address some of the unresolved issues of the GPA (e.g. contracts between public sector entities) (Wang, Carvallo Perin, and Casalini (2011), p. 197), or even to incorporate some of the novel public procurement tools and procedures developed under EU law. The promotion of GPA rules, rather than those of the EU, can be welcomed insofar as the former are still characterized by a level of generality which enables developing countries to maintain a great deal of flexibility when implementing the required regulatory reforms. Deviations from the GPA are present in agreements signed with non-GPA parties and can be largely explained by the lesser level of economic development of the parties concerned. Less stringent requirements than those provided under the GPA—particularly in CEPA—take into consideration

64 Article 193 Colombia–Peru FTA.

the not insignificant costs of complying with the GPA. However, more recent EU DCFTAs signed by the EU appear less concerned with the plight of developing countries, as not only do they faithfully reproduce most elements of the content of the GPA, but they also remove the flexibilities afforded by the GPA to developing countries. More damning is the absence of a binding commitment from the EU to provide technical assistance to some of its developing country co-signatories to implement the framework rules included in the EU DCFTAs. Given that the ability to reap the benefits of liberalization is known to be highly conditional on the effective application and enforcement of the applicable public procurement rules, the EU can be said to have missed an opportunity to expand market openness and further its commitment to promote economic development in tandem.

As for the EU's desire to introduce reciprocity in its external trade policy, it is difficult to imagine a more ill-conceived regulatory instrument than the Proposal put forward by the EU, whose dubious legality is compounded by the fact that it fails to meet any of its supposed objectives. First, with the claims of the openness of the EU procurement market having been discredited, it seems unlikely that reciprocity will assist the EU in its quest to secure market opening concessions from any third countries other than smaller developing economies. Secondly, whilst falling short of the sort of 'buy national' policies recently introduced by other major economies, there are certain elements of the Proposal—notably the ability of Member State contracting authorities to exclude third country bidders even where there is no tangible strategic offensive interest of the EU at stake—which betray the protectionist designs of its drafters. Thirdly, it fails to ensure a uniform trade policy in procurement by openly inviting Member State contracting authorities to preclude bids from third countries on an individual basis and, in doing so, effectively legitimizes the distortions of competition within the EU.

Viewed as a whole, the EU's current external trade policy in the area of procurement is possibly the best example of the EU's more aggressive trade policy in the aftermath of the Global Europe strategy, embracing competitive liberalization where access to the internal market is used as both carrot and stick to coerce third countries to liberalize domestic markets, rather than merely being held up as a model of openness to which to aspire. Without making any judgements as to the possible benefits or drawbacks of market opening in the area of public procurement—a topic that remains very much open to debate—the Proposal (which covers developing country goods and services), together with the EU DCFTAs, should only reinforce the suspicions long held by developing WTO Members that, in the context of procurement, opening national markets—rather than regulatory reforms aiming to establish transparent public procurement systems—remains very much the primary goal.

# 9

# Conclusion

This study has examined the EU's deep trade agenda by focusing on major regulatory issues, such as services, intellectual property, competition, and public procurement, included in its most recent deep FTAs. This concluding chapter seeks to shed some light on how the EU's deep trade agenda is being implemented in practice and how this agenda impacts on perceived notions of the EU as an international actor. Section 9.1 reviews the type of disciplines included in the EU DCFTAs and attempts to make sense of the EU's preference for the promotion of international rules and standards. Section 9.2 assesses how non-trade goals have been incorporated into the EU's deep trade agenda in light of both the EU's constitutional obligation to take into account non-trade goals when conducting trade policy and the developing country concerns relating to proposals for inclusion of deep disciplines at WTO level voiced during the Doha Round. Section 9.3 questions whether the prevailing characterizations of the EU as a distinctive actor in foreign policy can be maintained in light of the prescriptive approach adopted by the EU in its deep FTAs. Section 9.4 provides an interim assessment of the EU's overall trade policy, as materialized in EU DCFTAs, and considers how this agenda impacts on the multilateral process and the future development of the international trade regime.

## 9.1 The EU as a Promoter of Deep Disciplines

Generally speaking, the EU has sought to use EU DCFTAs to expand the reach of existing international rules—from plurilateral rules at WTO level to international rules and standards developed in other fora. The parties to these agreements are required to comply with such rules or to participate in ongoing negotiations of international agreements, or contribute to the work of international standard-setting bodies. All of the EU DCFTAs contain rules that apply to specific services sectors and impose a number of regulatory disciplines that go beyond the mere requirement of non-discrimination. These regulatory principles are, however, largely inspired by the rules included in WTO instruments. The rules on telecommunications services (e.g. prohibition of anti-competitive standards, universal service obligations, and rules on interconnection) are based on the GATS Reference Paper for Telecommunication Services, whilst the rules on financial services (e.g. prudential regulation) replicate the disciplines contained in the GATS Annex on

Financial Services. Both WTO legal instruments mentioned are only binding upon WTO Members if specific commitments are made to this effect. By incorporating these rules into the EU DCFTAs, the EU ensures that its counterparts are effectively bound by them, irrespective of whether or not commitments have been made at WTO level. Likewise, with respect to government procurement, the EU DCFTAs either codify a considerable number of the rules of the GPA or, where both parties are already signatories to the GPA, reaffirm their rights and obligations under such agreement. Harmonization is also sought in the area of intellectual property by requiring the parties to sign up to a number of existing international agreements, or to participate in the ongoing multilateral negotiations. A similar approach can be found in other areas. For example, in the area of goods, the KOREU FTA and the EU–Singapore FTA have sought to bridge the gaps between the regulatory approaches adopted by the parties with respect to technical regulations (safety and other standards) applicable in the manufacturing of motor vehicles and parts by using the standards developed by the World Forum for Harmonization of Vehicle Regulations (WP.29)—under the auspices of the United Nations Economic Commission for Europe (UNECE)—as a regulatory benchmark for the harmonization of motor vehicle standards.

An examination of the EU DCFTAs shows that there are but few examples of these agreements exporting EU-specific regulation. This occurs primarily in regulatory areas for which no international rules are currently in place or where existing international rules are not deemed sufficient to address the EU's offensive interests in the area. In some instances, the requirement to comply with existing international rules (e.g. Reference Paper on Telecommunication Services, WIPO conventions regulating on patents and copyrights) is complemented by provisions imposing obligations borrowed from EU law. In certain regulatory areas, however, the EU has opted to export norms sourced almost exclusively from its own acquis. In the case of geographical indications, the EU has made it clear that it believes that the level of protection afforded under existing TRIPS rules or international conventions concluded under the auspices of WIPO do not go far enough. Having failed to convince WTO Members to agree to its proposed TRIPS reform in this area, the EU has used its trade agreements (including the EU DCFTAs) to expand key features of its own legislation on geographical indications. Likewise, in the area of IP rights enforcement, the EU was left frustrated by the unwillingness of WTO Members to consider more stringent requirements, and has since used the EU DCFTAs to transpose sizeable portions of its internal legislation on IP enforcement. However, the EU's external trade policy in this area also demonstrates that, given the choice, the EU would rather disseminate international rather than domestic rules. The EU's endorsement of ACTA was an attempt to develop plurilateral rules which could then be held up as global standards. It is not fanciful to suggest that, had the EU managed to conclude ACTA, it would have used the EU DCFTAs to spread the reach of the enforcement standards included therein.

Competition law and investment are also areas for which there are no existing binding international rules and where the EU's attempts to introduce rules in the context of the WTO were famously rejected in the Doha Round. The EU DCFTAs included provisions inspired from the competition law provisions of the TFEU, prohibiting anti-competitive practices that affect trade between the parties and requiring the signatories to adopt and enforce domestic competition law systems. However, unlike the provisions on IP enforcement, those concerning competition law are phrased in very broad terms and are, in any event, unenforceable. It seems that in this area the EU is not overly concerned by the promotion of its regulatory model (in some cases the EU's trading parties have already enacted legislation inspired by EU competition law) and is content to simply use the EU DCFTAs to lock in domestic competition law systems. The approach followed in the area of investment is different, as the investment chapters included in the EU DCFTAs are modelled on the US Model BITs. In doing so, the EU is promoting what is already seen as the predominant BIT model in international investment treaty making and, therefore, further contributing to the harmonization of international investment law.

It turns out, then, that the EU does not utilize the EU DCFTAs to promote its own norms but to disseminate broad regulatory principles that underpin rule-based market economies, and which are themselves sourced from already existing international legal instruments. This focus of the EU DCFTAs on the promotion of international and plurilateral standards and rules contributes to the global harmonization of economic rules and can be viewed as facilitating multilateral liberalization. This approach adopted by the EU has the merit of reducing regulatory divergence in market regulation among states. It reduces the risk of trade diversion and, where plurilateral WTO trade agreements are incorporated into the EU DCFTAs, creates common ground for future negotiations at the multilateral level. Moreover, the 'internationalist' approach adopted in the EU DCFTAs presents benefits for the EU which extend beyond its commitment to multilateralism. In the past few years, the EU has developed (within the framework of its overall economic strategy), a policy which emphasizes the complementarity of internal regulatory reforms and external action. Proposals for new EU legislation must take into account the potential impact of such legislation on the competitiveness of EU economic operators abroad and, in particular, strive to ensure the compatibility of EU rules with existing international standards so as to minimize the regulatory barriers encountered by EU economic operators abroad. The promotion of international rules through the EU DCFTAs contributes to this general strategy: it requires third countries to comply with international rules that have been absorbed into the EU's regulatory framework. Therefore, the EU's promotion of deep disciplines abroad seems to be operating through a feedback loop system. It participates in the development of international rules, which are then incorporated into the EU regulatory framework and re-exported into its EU DCFTAs. Other examples of this particular dynamic can be seen in the EU's ill-fated attempt to conclude ACTA, as well as its most recent proposals to negotiate a plurilateral agreement on services, which would go beyond market access by developing 'new rules on trade in services, such as those applying to government procurement of services, licensing procedures or access to communication networks' (European

Commission (2013a)). By the EU's own admission, the intention is to set rules at a plurilateral level so that these may eventually be 'multilateralized'.

The picture which emerges of the EU's current external trade policy is one characterized by two seemingly opposing movements which are, in fact, a reflection of the increasing blurring of the divide between internal and external economic policy and law. On the one hand, the EU seeks to export rules to third countries, and on the other hand, the EU's own rules are influenced by negotiations occurring in external plurilateral and multilateral fora. This raises the question of whether the EU DCFTAs can also be used to influence regulatory reform within the EU. The EU has long made use of international standards as a means to trigger regulatory harmonization within the EU. This has, for example, been observed in the context of procurement, IP (TRIPS and WIPO conventions), and in the area of financial services, where recourse is often made to rules developed by international standard-setting bodies to overcome the divergent regulatory cultures of Member States. This study finds, however, that in the EU DCFTAs, the EU tends not to venture beyond regulatory areas where internal harmonization has been achieved and acts primarily as an exporter of norms. The one exception to this rule concerns the Global FTA provisions on IP criminal enforcement, which put the spotlight on a problematic feature of the EU's deep trade agenda in the context of trade agreements—namely how the inclusion of regulatory issues in such agreements can undermine internal legislative processes. The criminal enforcement of IP is one area where the EU has previously attempted and failed to achieve internal harmonization. By regulating subject matters hitherto untouched by EU law in trade agreements, the EU can harmonize the laws of Member States by circumventing the more cumbersome domestic decision-making rules (parliaments can only ratify or reject trade agreements en masse) or, at the very least, reinforce the argument for future harmonization (harmonization may be needed in order to ensure the uniformity required under the CCP). The controversy that has surrounded IP criminal enforcement provisions in the ACTA, and subsequently in EU DCFTAs, led the EU to envisage no longer including them in its agreements (Hoffmeister (2013), p. 22). This approach appears to have been followed in the more recent EU DCFTAs (CETA and the EU–Singapore) which contain no IP criminal enforcement provisions.

## 9.2 Deep Trade Disciplines and Non-trade Objectives

The EU's obligation and commitment to take into account the values and principles that must guide its external action in its trade policy is mainly materialized in the EU DCFTAs through human rights clauses and chapters on sustainable development, promoting social and environmental standards. Although the application of human rights clauses in FTAs is a long-held practice of the EU, the provisions on sustainable development are innovative both in terms of the comprehensive nature of the social and environmental rights included therein, and the fact that they remain by and large legally binding obligations. The one main distinction between these two sets of provisions is that the human rights clause permits the EU to adopt trade sanctions—in the shape of withdrawal of market concessions—against partners who commit human rights violations. However, in both cases, the primary aim pursued by the EU is to ensure that minimum international standards are adopted by its trade partners with little consideration given as to the interaction between trade and non-trade objectives. This is clearly the case with regard to human rights where, for example, no consideration is given as to the potential negative implications of the high standards of IP enforcement imposed in the EU DCFTAs. In the same vein, even though the EU DCFTAs are replete with reminders that these agreements should contribute to the promotion of sustainable development, there are no provisions that would allow parties to derogate from their obligations in order to pursue sustainable development principles and obligations other than those already provided under the general exception provision and, with the exception of CEPA, none of the provisions relating to sustainable development are subject to a dispute settlement mechanism. In fact, the only provisions which deal specifically with the relationship between trade and sustainable development relate to the parties' obligations not to reduce environmental or social standards for protectionist purposes or to increase such standards in order to attract investment, which suggests that behind the EU's commendable drive to promote non-trade values lies a certain degree of self-interest. The EU, through its EU DCFTAs, seeks to increase compliance with international social and environmental standards, and in doing so arguably removes one of the very few areas where developing countries retain a competitive advantage.

Unsurprisingly, given its pre-eminence in the Doha Round and its status as a Treaty-recognized objective of EU external action, the idea that trade liberalization must take into account developmental goals occupies a singularly important place in the EU's current trade policy. This commitment to promote development is increasingly reflected in the EU's stated intention to adopt a differentiated approach in the implementation of EU trade policy. However, beyond the vague assertion that EU DCFTAs must 'take into account the level of development of [...] partners, offering flexible approaches tailored to their needs and the capacities of each country', there is little in the way of guidance as to how differentiation is to be achieved in these agreements. The EU has adopted a flexible approach towards the negotiation of its EU DCFTAs with developing countries and, in this respect, must be distinguished from the US's competitive liberalization 'take it or leave it' policy towards FTA negotiations (Ajulu and Vickers (2008), p. 16). First, asymmetrical liberalization is an important feature of agreements with developing countries. Not only are the EU's commitments in the schedules relating to goods and services higher than those of its partners, but the EU also tends to include transitional periods during which the developing countries can progressively liberalize in economic sectors where commitments have been made. There can be no doubt that differentiation is a key feature of the EU DCFTAs negotiated with developing countries (Woolcock (2014)). Secondly, this study has shown that the EU DCFTAs do contain provisions intended to safeguard the policy space of the parties: in the area of trade in services, the agreements recognize the parties' right to regulate in order to meet legitimate policy objectives and include general exceptions and public services exemption provisions, whilst the IP chapter recognizes the need to maintain the flexibilities in the TRIPS agreement and emphasize the need to ensure that IP protection does not undermine public health concerns. By and large, however, these provisions do not add much to what is currently found in WTO law.

There is also evidence of differentiation with respect to the content of deep disciplines included in the EU DCFTAs. The mandates provided for the negotiation of these agreements are almost identical, and as we have seen, the content of the EU DCFTAs themselves follow the exact same template, covering trade in goods, trade in services, IP, public procurement, competition, sustainable development issues, and, more recently, investment protection. However, although the EU's starting negotiating position does not appear to 'differentiate' between trading partners based on the level of economic development, the EU is willing to deviate from its standard text depending on the demands and needs of its counterparts during the negotiation process. For example, although the final text of CEPA only requires the adoption of border measures for a limited set of IP infringements, the initial proposals submitted by the EU required border measures for all types of IP infringements (Santa-Cruz (2007), p. 30). The sector-specific disciplines on services included in agreements such as the CEPA, the Colombia–Peru FTA, and the EU–CA FTA are far less stringent than those included in developed country FTAs such as the KOREU FTA, the EU–Singapore FTA, and the CETA. Likewise, the removal of the non-discrimination requirement from the public procurement chapter of the CEPA was also made at the specific request of the CARIFORUM States (Dawar and Evenett (2011), p. 657).

Whilst the EU's brand of differentiation is a preferable option to the approach adopted by the US in the framework of its competitive liberalization strategy, it does come with certain pitfalls. Currently, the EU's policy is tantamount to throwing everything at the wall and seeing what sticks. It is an approach that is consistent with the EU's position in the Doha Round and the EU's managed globalization rhetoric where integrated regulatory frameworks are presented as important developmental tools but which, as the rejection of the Singapore issues show, are out of kilter with what many developing countries actually want from trade negotiations. The approach adopted by the EU is problematic on two fronts. First, the idea that the regulatory reforms required under the EU DCFTAs are always beneficial does not always stand up to scrutiny. The imposition of increasingly high standards of IP protection has been demonstrated, in some cases, to adversely affect the protection of human rights and the development needs of developing countries (Anderson and Wager (2006)). This study has addressed how the EU's calls for the expansion of border measures provided under TRIPS could undermine legitimate trade in generic drugs and, in doing so, undermine public health objectives in developing countries. It could also have asked how the EU's demands to introduce data exclusivity protection provisions (which allow pharmaceutical companies to retain exclusive rights over undisclosed test or other data related to the safety and efficacy of pharmaceutical products for up to 10 years) in EU DCFTAs concluded with developing countries can be justified as anything other than as a move intended to pander to the demands of the powerful pharmaceutical industry lobby (Dur and De Bievre (2007), p. 79). And it is not only in the area of IP that some of the regulatory disciplines proposed by the EU conflict with developing country interests. Part of the problem stems from the EU's assumption that the rationale for liberalization of trade in goods—that is, that free trade is welfare-inducing as it allows countries to better exploit their comparative advantages—holds for other sectors of economic activity. However, it is wrong to apply such reasoning to services markets which are heterogeneous and where trade liberalization does not necessarily lead to welfare gains (Whalley (2004), p. 1231). In fact, there is ample evidence to suggest that increased competition in services markets can in certain cases reduce welfare (Hay (2007), p. 39). Likewise, the rationale for the inclusion of investment protection and ISDS clauses in trade agreements signed with developing countries (e.g. ongoing FTA negotiations between EU and Vietnam) can be questioned. Not only do such provisions reduce the policy autonomy of states but there is also some evidence that they do little to attract FDI (Yackee (2008), pp. 827–8). By failing to recognize that not all disciplines it seeks to include in EU DCFTAs with developing countries are necessarily welfare enhancing for developing countries, the EU leaves itself open to accusations that it is simply attempting to pass off and package self-interested regulatory reforms as development-friendly policies. The EU may have shown itself to be willing to adapt its regulatory demands during the negotiation process of EU DCFTAs with developing countries, but given the power asymmetries that characterize such negotiations, it is quite possible that its counterparts may end up subscribing to disciplines whose implementation and enforcement are onerous and that do not further their developmental goals. In light of the above, the EU may wish to consider becoming more selective in the types of disciplines it puts on the negotiating table.

Secondly, even where there is ample evidence indicating that the disciplines proposed by the EU (e.g. transparency of public procurement procedures) are a must in order to maximize the benefits of trade liberalization, the welfare effects of such disciplines are highly contingent on the institutional and regulatory capacities of the developing countries involved. In light of this, the technical assistance and capacity building programmes offered by the EU in its EU DCFTAs take on a singular importance. However, these vary significantly from one EU DCFTA to another, with CEPA being by far the most ambitious—containing extensive provisions on the development cooperation segment of the agreement, it outlines not only an obligation to provide technical assistance and cooperation but also specifies the general objectives of development cooperation and identifies sources of EU funding—whilst the technical assistance commitments found under the Colombia–Peru FTA and EU–CA FTA are often couched in best endeavour language. An assessment of the effectiveness of the technical assistance and support for capacity programmes offered to the EU's trading partners in the EU DCFTAs has not been the object of the present study (not least because such agreements have only recently been concluded and in some cases are yet to be implemented); nevertheless it seems that if these agreements are truly to contribute to economic development, the EU must view the incorporation of capacity programmes in agreements with developing countries as a cornerstone of its trade policy rather than as an optional element that may be used or discarded on a case-by-case basis.

From the EU's perspective, the question of whether the deep disciplines included in the EU DCFTAs undermine its ability to regulate for public interest purposes did not garner much attention until quite recently. Indeed, as discussed, most of the EU DCFTAs concluded so far include very broad regulatory principles that are already fully integrated within the EU's own regulatory framework. But the recent negotiation of more ambitious trade deals with Canada, Singapore, and the US has brought this issue back to the fore. This is particularly the case with respect to the investment chapters envisaged in these agreements, which, it is claimed, will allow foreign investors to hold Member States to ransom and discourage regulators from adopting laws that may produce an adverse impact on their investment. The analysis conducted in this study has shown that although the EU has sought to address this by reducing the scope of these investment chapters and by proposing significant reforms to the ISDS mechanism included in its EU DCFTAs, these agreements still include elements that could undermine the regulatory autonomy of the parties. It is, at this stage, too early to make a final assessment of the EU's investment protection provisions in the EU DCFTAs. None of the EU DCFTAs including investment protection chapters have been ratified and the EU has expressed its readiness to revisit its approach in light of the many reform proposals put forward in the context of the TTIP debate. However, how far the EU can go in its attempts to remodel international investment law remains to be seen. In the TTIP, whilst the US may be happy to go along with investment protection chapters that are mostly based on its own model, it is unclear whether it will acquiesce to the EU's more radical proposals for reforms on ISDS. Domestically, there is also a growing sense that no reform will ever suffice to convince detractors of IIAs, and especially ISDS, that purported benefits of such agreements outweigh the potential threat to the regulatory autonomy of Member States. As has been noted elsewhere, there is a whiff of hypocrisy (Weiler (2015), pp. 961–7) surrounding much of the opposition to investment protection and ISDS in the EU DCFTAs. Indeed, the investment-related provisions included in the CETA and the EU–Singapore FTA—as well as those that are likely to be included in any incarnation of the TTIP—are far more balanced and protective of Member State regulatory autonomy than any of the many BITs concluded in the past by individual Member States. Yet the negotiations of Member State BITs have tended to pass without experiencing much in the way of opposition, namely because these agreements were signed with capital importing countries and their aim was to protect European investments abroad. But, as the EU enters into negotiations with significant economic powers, that are both importers and exporters of capital, the dangers associated with IIAs have, all of a sudden, become a highly relevant and politically sensitive issue. In other words, whilst the EU and its Member States were happy to promote the adoption of investment protection rules abroad, the prospect of being constricted by similar rules at home is much less appealing. Such double standards suggest that the true test of the EU's deep trade agenda will depend not on its ability to negotiate deep FTAs with developing nations (that famously opposed the Singapore issues) but rather on its ability to convince domestic constituencies of the merits of signing similar agreements with developed nations.

## 9.3 The EU—a Trade Power Like Any Other

A number of features of the various 'power narratives' typically associated with the EU are verified in the content of the EU DCFTAs. First, with respect to the normative power narrative, there is an emphasis on the diffusion of foundational values of the EU, such as principles of democracy, respect for human rights, the rule of law, and social justice. Secondly, the EU uses the EU DCFTAs to promote economic rules—whether sourced from international instruments or, occasionally, its own regulatory framework. These agreements therefore provide a clear example of what Ian Manners refers to as 'transference'—that is, the projection of norms and rules in the context of a relationship based on the exchange of goods, trade, or financial assistance. Trade partners agree to adopt norms and undertake regulatory reforms in exchange for increased market access to the internal market. Thirdly, the projection of norms through the establishment of procedural frameworks between the EU and its trade partners (known as 'procedural diffusion') is another distinctive feature of the EU DCFTAs. The latter requires trading partners to sign up to various international agreements and, in doing so, those countries become participants in the ongoing debates and negotiations being held in the concerned international organizations. The EU DCFTAs also establish institutional and regulatory cooperation mechanisms as tools to promote regulatory convergence in a number of areas. By enhancing regulatory transparency and establishing mechanisms that foster dialogues between national regulators these agreements allow the parties to iron out any market access issues that arise and promote a better understanding of each other's regulations, as well as providing an opportunity for the EU to influence the legislation of its trading partners.

Other conceptualizations of how the EU acts in external trade relations are also evident in the EU DCFTAs. The notion of EU as a 'market power' is based partly on the premise that the EU's sophisticated regulatory capacity allows it to better take into account the external dimension of internal market regulation. EU legislators are keen to align internal market rules with existing international regulatory standards so as not to undermine the competitiveness of EU firms. And where the regulatory standards imposed within the EU are more burdensome than those imposed at the international level, the EU tends to export its norms abroad to level the playing field. This process is manifest in the context of the EU DCFTAs which are used both to diffuse international rules adopted by the EU, and to impose EU rules where existing international rules are non-existent or deemed insufficient. Another feature of the EU as a market power can be observed from initiatives such as the recently proposed public procurement regulation, which would permit the EU to block access to its markets to third countries that do not provide reciprocal market access. In such cases, EU market access may be restored if, for example, the concerned third countries agree to enter into bilateral agreements which, like the EU DCFTAs, would require the adoption of public procurement rules sourced from the GPA. In other words, the EU is prepared to use the threat of blocking access to the internal market to force third countries to open up their own public procurement markets and undertake regulatory reforms in this area. Finally, the institutional and regulatory cooperation mechanisms included in the EU DCFTAs confirm the EU's tendency to externalize its modes of governance. By requiring that its trade partners sign up to various international agreements, the EU strengthens existing international institutions and regulatory frameworks. Moreover, EU DCFTAs include regulatory transparency and cooperation provisions which are inspired from the EU's experience and the difficulties it faced in establishing an internal market. These mechanisms provide a less prescriptive and less intrusive path towards the removal of regulatory barriers, whereby the regular interaction between regulatory authorities can act as a disincentive for countries to introduce domestic rules with protectionist purposes.

However, if one were to look at the manner in which the EU seeks to achieve the goals of its deep trade agenda, particularly in the context of the EU DCFTAs, it is hard to make a case for the distinctiveness of the EU as an external actor engaged in normative practices. On the whole, the EU appears to be failing to satisfy at least two of the three constitutive elements of procedural normative ethics identified by Manners. As discussed in the previous section of this concluding chapter, the EU does take into account the level of development of its counterparts in trade negotiations. Such differentiation, whilst not perfect, is very much in line with the consequential ethics requirement of Normative Power Europe to take into consideration the impact of the promotion of norms on its trade partners. However, as far as the 'virtue ethics' component is concerned, the EU can hardly be considered to be 'living by virtuous example' when its policies remain as conflicted (if not more) than in the context of the Doha Round. And serious doubts may also be cast regarding whether the EU DCFTAs represent the type of processes of engagement and dialogue envisaged in deontological ethics. The idea of the EU as a 'normative power' relies on the assumption that the supposedly self-evident benefits of its regulatory model—based on openness and the rule of law—will convince others to follow suit. The EU's commitment to rules-based international institutions such as the WTO is also a key aspect of this normative power because it emphasizes the distinctiveness of the EU as an international actor keen to regulate the behaviour of states, not through coercion, but through a mutually agreed set of rules. The EU's reluctance to engage in bilateral FTA negotiations during the Doha Round can be understood in that light. By forgoing the immediate economic benefits that would undoubtedly result from signing FTAs, instead focusing on the ongoing multilateral trade negotiations, the EU sent out an unequivocal message on its commitment to the multilateral trading system and set itself apart from other economic powers as an international actor willing to practice what it preached rather than one that would resort to power politics at the first sign of opposition. Needless to say, the strategy was also driven by self-interest—the EU had a lot riding on the Doha Round. By proposing the adoption of the type of deep disciplines that underpin its own experience of economic integration, the EU was seeking to usurp the US's place as a leader in international trade governance, and its agenda for reform could be rightly criticized on a number of fronts, from the excessively ambitious Singapore issues to unsatisfactory concessions in areas where it has defensive interests such as agricultural subsidies and the temporary movement of natural persons. However, at the very least, the EU's approach had the merit of ensuring that all WTO Members could have a say on the future shape of multilateral trade disciplines.

The content of the EU DCFTAs is consistent with the EU's position in the Doha Round, as it looks to promote deep integration by addressing a whole host of inter-related regulatory issues such as competition, investment, intellectual property, and social and environmental protection. However, this approach raises certain questions regarding the EU's credentials as a promoter of the multilateral trading system. It is clear that while the EU is still striving to promote multilateral rules, it has given up on the multilateral process itself. The EU may be using EU DCFTAs to promote the WTO, but not necessarily the WTO as we know it—as it currently exists—but rather as the EU would wish it to be: a WTO where TRIPS flexibilities are eroded, a WTO where geographical indications trump trademarks, a WTO imposing transparency and pro-competitive disciplines in all areas of economic activity, a WTO where all Members commit to opening their respective public procurement markets, and, finally, a WTO where foreign investors can use international arbitration tribunals to challenge state measures that adversely affect their investments abroad. There have been no attempts to address contentious and unresolved issues which have undermined the progress of negotiations in the Doha Round and the EU has so far been happy to merely impose its own positions. The approach is problematic because it supports the notion that the EU is using EU DCFTAs to force through the adoption of disciplines by countries that would have refused to do so in the context of the WTO. The Singapore issues were rejected by developing countries because they were seen as a distraction from more important issues (e.g. agricultural subsidies and standards and technical barriers), because of concerns regarding the ability of such countries to implement such reforms and because some of the reforms proposed—notably the demands for discussions on labour standards—were perceived to be aimed at removing some of the competitive advantages of developing countries over developed countries. Concomitantly, the EU is also increasingly contemplating whether the openness of the internal market on which it used to pride itself is something that needs to be reconsidered. Recent EU rhetoric puts much stock in the idea that increased competition from abroad will force EU firms to become more competitive and, as a result, create support for internal structural reforms that will enhance their competitiveness. If anything, early indications suggest that the opposite is occurring—that is, the EU is perfectly willing to sacrifice openness where there are concerns regarding the competitiveness of its own firms

(ODI (2012)). As we have seen, recent proposals to reform the EU's public procurement regime make access to the public procurement EU markets contingent on the reciprocal access being provided by third countries and even allow Member States to block market access to developing country suppliers. The arguments against protectionism in times of economic strife and doubts as to its effectiveness as a policy tool are already well rehearsed, but in the specific context of the EU, a protectionist trade policy puts paid to any notion that the EU wants to lead by example. In short, the EU advocates multilateral trade liberalization whilst actively contributing to the fragmentation of the international trading system and advocates market openness whilst considering protectionist policies.

The abandonment of the once lofty ideals guiding the EU's external trade policy in favour of a more pragmatic approach makes any pretence to the EU's uniqueness as international trade actor difficult to maintain. The EU may present its FTAs as instruments contributing to multilateral trade liberalization and taking into account the multiple concerns of various WTO Members but, ultimately, they also signal an acknowledgement that, for the time being, the EU is not averse to using its vast economic power to open markets abroad on its own terms. As FTAs become a central feature of EU trade policy, the EU's function as a normative power becomes less credible: the EU may be using these FTAs to spread the reach of international rules and standards, but it is only able to do so because of its increased leverage in bilateral negotiations. Economic coercion, rather than the ability to persuade others of the legitimacy of its own regulatory model, is the means through which the EU imposes its norms abroad. Therefore, in the context of the deep trade agenda, Zielonka's characterization of the EU as foreign policy actor engaged in 'imperial politics' makes more sense than the value-based conceptualizations of the EU as a normative power. By contrast, the notion of 'Market Power Europe' seems to provide a better conceptual framework to apprehend how the EU's deep trade agenda is actually being carried out in practice, namely because it accepts that access to the internal market—rather than non-coercive persuasion envisaged in the normative power literature, is the primary tool used by the EU to promote its regulatory positions abroad. The fact that there is little variation in terms of the rules included in the multiple EU DCFTAs, especially in areas which represent important offensive interests of the EU, suggests that the inclusion of these rules is not necessarily the consequence of a process of dialogue, more the result of an acceptance by the EU's trade partners that accepting such norms is one of the prices to pay for enhanced market access.

The shift to what some have called a less 'naive' trade policy (as some have called it) (Idrac (2011), p. 2; Barnier (2012), p. 7) is a natural response to the economic crisis and the changing face of the international order, namely the increasingly prominent role played by emerging economies. The EU's primary obligation is, after all, to protect the interests of its constituents, and the best way to achieve this in the short term is to explore all viable avenues to secure access to lucrative foreign markets. Nevertheless, it is a shift that raises fundamental questions regarding the EU's role in international trade governance. It would be wrong to claim that the EU is a trade actor of little or no significance. On the contrary, this book has shown that the EU remains a major player in the development and dissemination of global trade rules and disciplines. However, the current policy is a far cry from its original Doha Round designs to shape the international trading system in its own image. The EU has been brought down to earth, and now increasingly looks like just one economic power amongst others, jostling for position in international trade relations.

## 9.4 An Interim Assessment of the EU's Deep Trade Agenda in the Post-Doha Era: Promoting Multilateral Rules, but not the Multilateral Process

Eight years on since the launch of the Global Europe strategy, the EU appears to have fallen some way short of its original designs to sign a raft of deep and comprehensive FTAs with large and fast-growing emerging economies. Barring the KOREU FTA, the EU DCFTAs that have been concluded thus far do not concern the key economic players envisaged in its Global Europe strategy. The EU has successfully included deep disciplines in its EU DCFTAs, but these have mostly been concluded with either smaller economies who are grateful for the enhanced access to the internal market or partners that largely share the EU's trade liberalizing agenda. Meanwhile, ongoing trade negotiations with emerging economies, such as India and MERCOSUR, are beleaguered by difficulties, notably because of a number of irreconcilable differences on key areas of the EU's deep trade agenda. If the EU's experience in negotiating EU DCFTAs teaches us anything then, it is that developed and developing countries (at least those powerful enough to resist the EU's bargaining power) remain poles apart as far as the key issues of the Doha Round are concerned.

Viewed from this perspective it is hard to escape the conclusion that the Global Europe strategy has been failure. Undeterred by this setback, the EU has identified other means through which to push its agenda. Step forward the TTIP, an agreement which according to the EU 'offers a unique chance to give momentum to the development and implementation of international regulations and standards (multilateral or otherwise plurilateral)' (European Commission (2013e), p. 1). The aim is to shape the global rules of international trade for the twenty-first century or, as one US official bluntly put it, the TTIP is about setting 'the rules of world trade before others do it for us' (Vicenti (2014)). The disciplines developed in the TTIP—but also those included in other major trade agreements such as the TISA—would then be held as templates for other nations to follow, be transposed into other FTAs concluded by the EU and the US and in turn progressively become global standards. In short, the EU's current external trade practice confirms the view that bilateralism is used by trading powers to override the irksome developing country opposition in the multilateral context.

In all this, it is easy to forget that developing countries were not the only opponents to the EU's deep trade agenda during the Doha Round. The EU and other large developed nations may view themselves as 'like-minded' trade partners, but they also harbour significant differences of opinions and interests when it comes to addressing regulatory issues. The US, for example, was unconvinced by the need to introduce investment and competition disciplines within the WTO legal framework and steadfastly opposed the EU's proposals for the enhancement of the protection of geographical indications. And whilst regulatory issues have been billed as the centrepiece of the TTIP, the US's less than enthusiastic response to the EU's proposals for much-needed cooperation areas such as financial services suggests that there is still a considerable amount of mistrust between the parties that would inhibit moves towards regulatory approximation. Furthermore, multilateral trade liberalization also has its fair share of opponents within the EU. The EU seems to have been taken by surprise by the level of domestic opposition towards its deep trade agenda in the framework of FTA negotiations with large nations, in particular the TTIP. Because the EU had so far only concluded EU DCFTAs with smaller economies, it had not yet faced serious questions regarding the rules included in such agreements, which had not been the subject of much scrutiny beyond academic circles. However, as the EU pursues the negotiation of EU DCFTAs with large trading powers, the inherent tension between the deep trade agenda and regulatory autonomy and democratic accountability has been thrust into the limelight, with anti-globalization activists and Member States alike rushing to highlight the potential dangers lurking behind the EU's new generation of deep and comprehensive trade agreements. Some of these supposed dangers have been rightly dismissed as unfounded and belonging to the realm of the imaginary (Lamy (2014)). Others, as we have seen throughout this study (e.g. ISDS and IP regulation), represent legitimate and very real concerns. In response to such criticisms, the EU has made much of its attempts to improve access to information on the progress of TTIP negotiations to both the European Parliament and the public, in particular by organizing public consultations and by releasing multiple negotiating drafts prior to the finalization of the agreement. The level of transparency afforded by the EU with respect to the TTIP negotiations is unprecedented in the history of trade negotiations. The EU has also proved itself receptive to criticism by considering the revision of its initial negotiating stance on issues such as ISDS, in order to address misgivings voiced by its constituents. However, these measures have done little to alleviate fears that, amongst other things, these agreements will lead to the lowering of regulatory standards and the loss of regulatory autonomy. Politically, the regulatory component of the EU DCFTAs has become an exceptionally tough sell, to the extent that it may now be worth asking whether persisting with many of the key regulatory issues may ultimately cost the EU the opportunity of concluding trade deals with important economic and geopolitical implications. Curiously, and perhaps counter-intuitively, it would seem that it is in the context of trade agreements with 'like-minded countries' that the limitations of the EU's ambitious deep trade agenda may, once more, be exposed.

# Bibliography


Abbott, F. (2002), 'The TRIPS Agreement, Access to Medicines and the WTO Doha Ministerial Conference' 5(1) *Journal of World Intellectual Property* 15–52.

Abbott, F. (2005), 'Toward a New Era of Objective Assessment in the Field of TRIPS and Variable Geometry for the Preservation of Multilateralism' 8(1) *Journal of International Economic Law* 77–100.

Abbott, F. (2006), 'TRIPS and Human Rights: Preliminary Reflections', in F. Abbott, C. Kaufmann, and T. Cottier (eds.), *International Trade and Human Rights: Foundations and Conceptual Issues* Vol. 5, University of Michigan Press.

Abbott, F. (2007), 'A New Dominant Trade Species Emerges: Is Bilateralism a Threat?' 10(3) *Journal of International Economic Law* 571–83.

Abbott, F. and Reichman, J. (2007) 'The Doha Round's Public Health Legacy' 10(4) *Journal of International Economic Law* 921–87.

Adlung, R. and Matto, A. (2008) 'The GATS', in A. Mattoo, R. M. Stern, and G. Zanini (eds.), *A Handbook of International Trade in Services*, Oxford: Oxford University Press, 48–85.

Ajulu, C. and Vickers, B. (2008), 'South Africa's economic diplomacy: trade and investment promotion, Report prepared for The Presidency's Fifteen Year Review', Institute for Global Dialogue. Available at: http://dev.absol.co.za/Presidency/docs/reports/15year_review/irps/economic_diplomacy.pdf.

Akyuz, Y. (2010), 'Multilateral Disciplines and the Question of Policy Space' in J. Faundez and C. Tan (eds.), *International Economic Law, Globalization and Developing Countries*, Cheltenham: Edward Elgar, 34–66.

Allen, D. and Smith, M. (2001), 'External Policy Developments' 39(1) *Journal of Common Market Studies* 87 97–114.

Almunia, J. (2013), 'The Evolutionary Pressure of Globalisation on Competition Control', International Competition Network 12th Annual Conference, Speech/13/360, 24 April 2013. Available at: http://europa.eu/rapid/press-release_SPEECH-13-360_en.htm.

Alston, P. (ed.) (2003), *The EU and Human Rights*, New York: Oxford University Press.

Alvarez, J. (2010), 'Why Are we Re-Calibrating Our Investment Treaties?' 4(2) *World Arbitration & Mediation Review* 143–61.

Alvarez, J. (2011a), 'The Return of the State', 20 *Minnesota Journal of International Law* 223–64.

Alvarez, J. (2011b), *The Public International Law Regime Governing International Investment* Hague Academy of International Law: AllPocket.

Alvarez, J. and Sauvant, K. (2011c), *The Evolving International Investment Regime: Expectations, Realities, Options*, Oxford: Oxford University Press.

Anderson, R. and Holmes, P. (2002), 'Competition Policy and the Future of the Multilateral Trading System' 5(2) *Journal of International Economic Law* 531–63.

Anderson, R., Muller, A., Osei-Lah, K., Pardo de Leon, J., and Pelletier, P. (2011), 'Government Procurement Provisions in Regional Trade Agreements: a Stepping Stone to GPA Accession?' in S. Arrowsmith, and R. Anderson, (eds.), *The WTO Regime on Government Procurement: Recent Developments and Challenges Ahead*, Cambridge: Cambridge University Press, 561–656.

Anderson, R. and Wager, H. (2006), 'Human Rights, Development, and the WTO: The Cases of Intellectual Property and Competition Policy' 9(3) *Journal of International Economic Law*, 707–47.

Arbuthnott, H. and Edwards, G. (1989), *A Common Man's Guide to the Common Market*, London: Macmillan.

Arrowsmith, S. (2002), 'Reviewing the GPA: The Role and Development of the Plurilateral Agreement after Doha' 5(4) *Journal of International Economic Law* 761–90.

Arrowsmith, S. (2003), *Government Procurement in the WTO*, Kluwer Law International Publishing.

Arrowsmith, S. (2009), 'EC Regulation of Public Procurement' in S. Arrowsmith and P. Kunzlik (eds.), *Social Environment Policies in EC Procurement Law*, Cambridge: Cambridge University Press, 56–81.

Arrowsmith, S. and Anderson, R. (2011), 'The WTO Regime on Government Procurement: Past, Present and Future', in S. Arrowsmith, and R. Anderson (eds.), *The WTO Regime on Government Procurement: Challenge and Reform*, Cambridge: Cambridge University Press, 3–58.

Arrowsmith, S. and Treumer, S. (2012), 'Competitive Dialogue in EU Law: a Critical Review', in S. Arrowsmith and S. Treumer (eds.), *Competitive Dialogue in EU Procurement*, Cambridge: Cambridge University Press, 3–143.

Aydin, U. (2012), 'Promoting Competition: European Union and the Global Competition Order' 34(6) *Journal of European Integration* 663–81.

Baldwin, M. (2006), 'EU Trade Politics Heaven or Hell?' 13(6) *Journal of European Public Policy* 926–42.

Baldwin, R. (2004), 'Key Challenges facing the WTO', in M. Moore (ed.), *Doha and Beyond, The Future of the Multilateral Trading System*, Cambridge: Cambridge University Press, 46–67.

Baldwin, R. (2011), '21st Century Regionalism: Filling the Gap between 21st Century Trade and 20th Century Trade Rules', No. 2011-08, Staff Working Paper ERSD-2011-08. Available at: http://www.nber.org/papers/w17716.

Baldwin, R. (2012), 'WTO 2.0: Global Governance of supply chain trade' CEPR, Policy Insight No. 64. Available at: http://www.cepr.org/sites/default/files/policy_insights/PolicyInsight64.pdf.

Baldwin, R. and Richardson, J. (1972), 'Government Purchasing Policies, Other NTBs and the International Monetary Crisis' in H. Hay (ed.), *Obstacles to Trade in the Pacific Area*, Ottawa: Carleton School of International Affairs.

Baldwin, R., Evenett, S., and Low, P. (2009), 'Beyond Tariffs: Multilateralising Non-Tariff RTA Commitments', in R. Baldwin and P. Low (eds.), *Multilateralizing Regionalism Challenges for the Global Trading System*, Cambridge: Cambridge University Press, 79–141.

Barker, A., Chaffin, J., and Pignal, S. (2012), 'Germany warns on keeping EU market open', *Financial Times*, 21 March 2012.

Barnard, C. (2008), 'Unravelling the Services Directive' 45(2) *Common Market Law Review* 323–94.

Barnier, M. (2012), 'Competitiveness—the key to growth in a strong Europe, Europe Ceremony to award the Charlemagne Prize to Wolfgang Schäuble Aachen', 16 May 2012. Available at: http://europa.eu/rapid/press-release_SPEECH-12-361_en.htm.

Bartels, L. (2007), 'The Trade and Development Policy of the European Union' 18(4) *European Journal of International Law* 715–56.

Bartels, L. (2008), 'Social Issues: Labour, Environment and Human Rights', in S. Lester and B. Mercurio (eds.), *Bilateral and Regional Trade Agreements, Commentary and Analysis*, Cambridge: Cambridge University Press, 342–66.

Bartels, L. (2013), 'Human Rights and Sustainable Development Obligations in EU Free Trade Agreements' 40(4) *Legal Issues of Economic Integration*, 297–314.

Bartels, L. and Ortino, F. (eds.) (2006) *Regional Trade Agreements and the WTO System*, Oxford: Oxford University Press.

Bartels, L., Stevens, C., and Woolcock, S. (2012), 'EU: Trade Agreement with Colombia and Peru', Directorate-General for External Policies of the Union (European Union, Brussels, 2012). Available at: http://www.europarl.europa.eu/thinktank/en/document.html?reference=EXPO-INTA_ET(2012)433865.

Beat Graber, C. (2006), 'The New UNESCO Convention on Cultural Diversity: A Counterbalance to the WTO?' 9(3) *Journal of International Economic Law* 553–74.

Beresford, L. (2007), 'Geographical Indications: The Current Landscape' 17(4) *Fordham Intellectual Property Media & Entertainment Law Journal* 979–97.

Bernasconi-Osterwalder, N. (2014), 'The International Institute for Sustainable Development Commentary to the Draft Investment Chapter of the Canada–EU Comprehensive Economic and Trade Agreement', International Institute for Sustainable Development, 5 February 2014. Available at: https://www.iisd.org/publications/commentary-draft-investment-chapter-canada-eu-comprehensive-economic-and-trade.

Bernstein, W. (2008), *A Splendid Exchange. How trade changed the world*, New York: Grove Press.

Beviglia-Zampetti, A. (1997), 'The UNCITRAL Model Law on Procurement of Goods, Construction and Services', in B. Hoekman and P. Mavroidis (eds.), *Law and Policy in Public Purchasing, The WTO Agreement on Government Procurement*, Studies in International Trade Policy, The University of Michigan Press.

Bhagwati, J. and Hudec, R. (eds.) (1996), *Fair Trade and Harmonization: Pre-requisites for Free Trade?* Cambridge, MA: Massachusetts Institute of Technology Press.

Bhattacharjea, A. (2006), 'The Case for a Multilateral Agreement on Competition Policy: A Developing Country Perspective' 9(2) *Journal of International Economic Law* 293–323.

Bickerton, C. (2011), *European Union Foreign Policy, From Effectiveness to Functionality*, New York: Palgrave Macmillan.

Bieler, A. (2012), 'The Internal and External Dimensions of Neo-Liberal Restructuring', in P. Nouisis, H. Overbeek, and A. Tsolakis (eds.), *Globalisation and European Integration: Critical Appraisal*, New York: Routledge, 197–217.

Bigdeli, S. and Rechsteiner, S. (2008), 'Article VIII GATS', in R. Wolfrum, and P. Stoll (eds.), *WTO—Trade in Services*, Leiden: Martinus Nijhoff Publishers.

Biondi, A. and Eeckhout, P. (eds.) (2012), *European Union Law After the Treaty of Lisbon*, Oxford: Oxford University Press.

Bishop, D. (2015), 'Investor–State Dispute Settlement Under the Transatlantic Trade and Investment Partnership: Have the Negotiations Run Aground' 30(1) *ICSID Review* 1–9.

Blakeney, M. (2012), *Intellectual Property Enforcement: A Commentary on the Anti-counterfeiting Trade Agreement (ACTA)*, Cheltenham: Edward Elgar Publishing.

Blank, A. and Marceau, G. (1996), 'The History of Government Procurement Negotiations since 1945' 4 *Public Procurement Law Review* 77–147.

Bonadio, E. (2008), 'Remedies and Sanctions for the Infringement of Intellectual Property Rights under EC Law' 30 *European Intellectual Property Review* 320–5.

Bourgeois, J. (1987), 'The Common Commercial Policy', in E. Volcker (ed.), *Protectionism and the European Community*, Deventer: Kluwer Law and Taxation Publishers.

Bourgeois, J. (2013), 'Competition Policy: the Poor Relation in the European Union Free Trade Agreements', in I. Govaere, E. Lannon, P. van Elsuwege, and S. Adam (eds.), *The European Union in the World*, Leiden: Brill Publishers, 381–98.

Bovis, C. (2007), *Public Procurement in the EU: A Practitioner's Guide*, Oxford: Oxford University Press.

Bovis, C. (2012), 'Public Procurement in the EU: Jurisprudence and Conceptual Directions' 49(1) *Common Market Law Review* 247–89.

Bradford, A. (2007), 'International Antitrust Negotiations and the False Hope of the WTO' 48(2) *Harvard International Law Journal* 383–439.

Bradford, A. (2012), 'The Brussels Effect' 107(1) *Northwestern University Law Review* 1–65.

Brandt, L. (2012), 'Life Beyond Reciprocity: Why Competition in Public Procurement is in the EU's Own Interest', ECIPE Bulletin No. 10/2012. Available at: http://www.ecipe.org/publications/life-beyond-reciprocity-why-competition-public-procurement-eus-own-interest/.

Brenton, P. (2003), Rules of Origin in Free Trade Agreements, Trade Note 4, 29 May, World Bank. Available at: http://siteresources.worldbank.org/INTRANETTRADE/Resources/TradeNote4.pdf.

Brittan, L. (1999), 'Trade and competition: The need for a multilateral framework of competition rules', OECD Conference on Trade and Competition, Paris, 29 June 1999.

Brown, I. and Korff, D. (2011), 'Opinion on the compatibility of the Anti-Counterfeiting Trade Agreement (ACTA) with the European Convention on Human Rights & the EU Charter of Fundamental Rights'. Available at: http://www.greens-efa.eu/fileadmin/dam/Documents/Studies/ACTA_fundamental_rights_assessment.pdf.

Brulahrt, M. and Matthews, A. (2007), 'EU External Trade Policy', in A. El-Agraa (ed.), *The European Union: Economics and Policies*, Cambridge: Cambridge University Press, 473–91.

Bull, H. (1982), 'Civilian Power Europe: A Contradiction in Terms' 21(2) *Journal of Common Market Studies* 149–70.

Bungenberg, M. (2010), 'Going Global: The EU Common Commercial Policy After Lisbon', 1 *European Yearbook of International Economic Law* 123–51.

Bungenberg, M. (2011), 'The Division of Competences Between the EU and its Member States in the Area of Investment Policies', *European Yearbook of International Economic Law* 29–43.

Burri-Nenova, M. (2008) 'Trade versus Culture in the Digital Environment: An Old Conflict in Need of a New Definition' (2008) 12(1) *Journal of International Economic Law* 17–62.

Burtless, G., Lawrence, R., Litan, R., and Shapiro, R. (1998), *Globaphobia: Confronting Fears about Open Trade*, The Brookings Institution, Washington DC.

Caplan, S. and Sharpe, J. (2013), 'United States', in C. Brown (ed.), *Commentaries on Selected Model Investment Treaties*, Oxford: Oxford University Press, 755–852.

Cardwell, P. and French, D. (2011), 'The European Union as a Global Investment Partner: Law, policy and rhetoric in the attainment of development assistance and market liberalisation?' in C. Brown and K. Miles (eds.), *Evolution in Investment Treaty Law and Arbitration*, Cambridge: Cambridge University Press, 201–22.

Cartou, L. (1959), *Le Marché Commun et le Droit Public*, Paris: Sirey.

Catz, M. and Shapiro, C. (1986), 'Technology Adoption in the Presence of Network Externalities' 94(4) *Journal of Political Economy* 822–41.

Ceyssens, J. (2004), 'Towards a Common Foreign Investment Policy?—Foreign investment in the European Constitution' 32(3) *Legal Issues of Economic Integration* 259–92.

Chaitoo, R. (2008), 'Mode 4 in the Cariforum–EU Economic Partnership Agreement', PowerPoint Presentation, WTO, Geneva. September 22–23, 2008. Available at: www.wto.org/english/tratop_e/serv_e/mouvement.../chaitoo_e.ppt.

Chalmers, D., Davies, G., and Monti, G. (2011), *European Union Law*, Second Edition, Cambridge University Press.

Charlton, A. and Stiglitz, J. (2004), 'A Development-Friendly Prioritisation of Doha Round Proposals' 28(3) *The World Economy* 293–312.

Charnovitz, S. (2002), *Trade Law and Global Governance*, Folkstone: Cameron May.

Charnovitz, S. (2005), 'An Analysis of Pascal Lamy's Proposal on Collective Preferences' 8(2) *Journal of International Economic Law* 449–72.

Cho, S. (2004), 'A Bridge Too Far: The Fall of the Fifth WTO Ministerial Conference in Cancun and the Future of Trade Constitution' 7(2) *Journal of International Economic Law* 219–44.

Choudhury, B. (2005), 'Evolution or Devolution: Defining Fair and Equitable Treatment in International Investment Law' 6 *Journal of World Investment and Trade* 953–72.

Choynowski, P. (2004), 'Restructuring and Regulatory Reform in the Power Sector: Review of Experience and Issues', ERD Working Paper No. 52. Available at: http://www.adb.org/publications/restructuring-and-regulatory-reform-power-sector-review-experience-and-issues.

CIFCA (2011), 'EU Trade Agreements with Central America, Colombia and Peru: Roadblocks for sustainable development', Briefing for MEPs—July 2011. Available at: http://www.fta-eu-latinamerica.org/wp-content/uploads/2012/01/Brief-com-TLC-ING.pdf.

Cohn, T. (2001), 'Securing Multilateral Trade Liberalisation: International Institutions in Conflict and Convergence', in J. Kirton and M. Von Furstenberg, *New Directions in Global Economic Governance: managing globalisation in the twenty-first century*, Aldershot: Ashgate, 205–7.

Collins, D. (2011), 'Canada's Sub-central Government Entities and the Agreement on Government Procurement: past and present', in S. Arrowsmith and R. Anderson (eds.), *The WTO Regime on Government Procurement: Challenge and Reform*, Cambridge: Cambridge University Press, 175–96.

Copeland, B. and Mattoo, A. (2008), 'The Basics of Services Trade', in A. Mattoo, R. M. Stern, and G. Zanini (eds.), *A Handbook of International Trade in Services*, Oxford University Press, 84–129.

Correa, C. and Yusuf, A. (eds.) (1998), *Intellectual Property and International Trade: The TRIPS Agreement*, Kluwer Law International.

Cook, T. (2010), *EU Intellectual Property Law*, Oxford: Oxford University Press.

Cooper, W. (2011) 'The EU–South Korea Free Trade Agreement and Its Implications for the United States', Congressional Research Service 7-5700. Available at: https://www.fas.org/sgp/crs/row/R41534.pdf.

Cornford, A. (2004), 'Variable Geometry for the WTO: concept and precedents', UNCTAD Discussion Papers No. 171. Available at: http://unctad.org/en/docs/osgdp20045_en.pdf.

Cottier, T. and Delimatsis, P. (eds.) (2011), *The Prospects of International Trade Regulation, From Fragmentation to Coherence*, Cambridge: Cambridge University Press.

Craig, P. and De Búrca, G. (2011), *EU Law: Texts, Cases and Materials*, Fifth Edition, Oxford: Oxford University Press.

Creditt, E. (2009), 'Terroir vs. Trademarks: The Debate over Geographical Indications and Expansions to the TRIPS Agreement' 11(2) *Vand. Journal of Entertainment & Technology Law*, 425–59.

Cremona, M. (2000), 'EC External Competence after Amsterdam', in J. Weiler (ed.), *The EU, the WTO and the NAFTA, Towards a common law of international trade?*, Oxford: Oxford University Press, 5–34.

Cremona, M. (2003), 'The Draft Constitutional Treaty: External Relations and External Action' 40(6) *Common Market Law Review* 1347–66.

Cremona, M. (2007), 'A Constitutional Basis for External Action? An Assessment of the Provisions on EU External Action in the Constitutional Treaty', EUI Working Paper Law No. 2007/30. Available at: http://papers.ssrn.com/sol3/papers.cfm?abstract_id=963368.

Cremona, M. (ed.) (2008), *Developments in EU External Relations Law*, Oxford: Oxford University Press.

Cremona, M. (2011a), 'Coherence in EU Foreign Relations Law', in P. Koutrakos (ed.), *European Foreign Policy: Legal and Political Perspectives*, Cheltenham: Edward Elgar Publishing, 55–96.

Cremona, M. (2011b), 'Values in EU Foreign Policy', in P. Koutrakos and M. Shaw (eds.), *Beyond the Established Orders: Policy Interconnections between the EU and the Rest of the World*, Oxford: Hart Publishing, 275–313.

Cremona, M. (2012), 'Expanding the Internal Market: An External Regulatory Policy for the EU?' in S. Blockmans, B. Van Vooren, and J. Wouters (eds.), *The EU's Role in Global Governance*, Oxford: Hart Publishing, 162–77.

Cremona, M. (2015), 'Negotiating the Transatlantic Trade and Investment Partnership (TTIP)' 52 *Common Market Law Review* 351–62.

Crowley, P. and Klimenko, M. (2002), 'Telecommunications Reform in Developing Countries after the WTO Agreement on Basic Telecommunications Services' 12(2) *Journal of International Development* 265–81.

Cunningham, A. (2011), 'Competition Policy' in A. Beviglia-Zampetti and J. Lodge (eds.), *The CARIFORUM–EC Economic Partnership Agreement: A Practitioner's Analysis*, Alphen aan den Rijn: Kluwer Law International, 129–36.

Curzon, G. (1965), *Multilateral Commercial Diplomacy*, London, Michael Joseph Publishing.

Daele, K. (2004), 'Regulation 1383/2003: a new step in the fight against counterfeit and pirated goods at the borders of the European Union' 26 *European Intellectual Property Review* 214–25.

Damro, C. (2001), 'Building an International Identity: the EU and extra-territorial competition policy' 8(2) *Journal of European Public Policy* 208–26.

Damro, C. (2006), 'The New Trade Politics and EU Competition Policy: shopping for convergence and cooperation' 13(6) *Journal of European Public Policy* 867–86.

Damro, C. (2012), 'Market Power Europe' 19(5) *Journal of European Public Policy* 682–99.

Das, D. (2005), 'Intellectual Property Rights and the Doha Round' 8(1) *Journal of World Intellectual Property* 33–52.

Das, D. (2010), 'Unresolved Issues on Geographical Indications in the WTO', in C.M. Correa (ed.), *Research Handbook on the Protection of IP under WTO Rules*, Cheltenham: Edward Elgar Publishing, 448–554.

Dashwood, A. and Maresceau, M. (eds.) (2008), *Law and Practice of EU External Relations: salient features of a changing landscape*, Cambridge: Cambridge University Press.

Dashwood, A. and Wyett, D. (2011), *Dashwood's European Union Law Sixth Edition*, Oxford: Oxford University Press.

Davies, G. (2012), 'Trust and Mutual Recognition in the Services Directive', in I. Lianos and O. Odudu (eds.), *Regulating Trade in Services in the EU and the WTO*, Cambridge: Cambridge University Press, 99–119.

Dawar, K. (2012), 'The Proposed Buy European Procurement Regulation: An Analysis', in S. J. Evenett, Debacle the 11th GTA report on protectionism, CEPR, 89–97. Available at: http://www.globaltradealert.org/gta-analysis/proposed-%E2%80%98buy-european%E2%80%99-procurement-regulation-analysis.

Dawar, K. and Evenett, S. (2011), 'A Case Study in Regionalism: the EC–CARIFORUM Economic Partnership', in R.D. Anderson and S. Arrowsmith (eds.), *The WTO Regime on Government Procurement: Recent Developments and Challenges Ahead*, Cambridge: Cambridge University Press, 657–78.

Dawar, K. and Holmes, P. (2012), 'Trade and Competition Policy', in K. Heydon and P. Holmes (eds.), *Ashgate Research Companion to International Trade Policy*, Farnham: Ashgate, 225–44.

Dawson, L. (2012), 'Labour Mobility and the WTO: The Limits of GATS Mode 4' 51(1) *International Migration*1–23.

De Baere, G. (2008), *Constitutional Principles of EU External Relations*, Oxford: Oxford University Press.

De Baere, G. (2012), 'The Framework of EU External Competences for Developing the External Dimensions of EU Asylum and Migration Policy', Leuven Cenre for Global Governance Studies, Working Paper No. 50—May 2012. Available at: https://ghum.kuleuven.be/ggs/publications/working_papers/new_series/wp41-50/wp50.pdf.

De Bievre, D. (2006), 'The EU Regulatory Trade Agenda and the Quest for WTO Enforcement' 13(6) *Journal of European Public Policy* 851–66.

De Búrca, G. (2012), 'EU External Relations: The Governance Mode of Foreign Policy' in B. Van Vooren, S. Blockmans, and J. Wouters (eds.), *The EU's Role in Global Governance: The Legal Dimension* (Oxford: Oxford University Press), 39–58.

De Gucht, K. (2010), 'Strengthening the EU–Canada ties', Brussels, 9 December 2010. Available at: http://trade.ec.europa.eu/doclib/docs/2010/december/tradoc_147099.pdf.

De Gucht, K. (2011), 'International Trade and Intellectual Property Rights, Speech at the Conference on Intellectual Property Captured—Which Course to Take against Counterfeiters?' Brussels, 7 September 2011.

De Gucht, K. (2012a) 'Statement on the Anti-Counterfeiting Trade Agreement', Brussels, 22 February 2012.

De Gucht, K. (2012b), 'ACTA—State of Play 1st Exchange of Views with the Committee for International Trade of the European Parliament', Brussels 29 February 2012.

De Gucht, K. (2013a), 'Challenge and Opportunity: Starting the negotiations for Free Trade Agreement between the EU and Japan', 25 March 2013.

De Gucht, K. (2013b), 'On the EU-China investment agreement', 8 October 2013. Available at: http://europa.eu/rapid/press-release_SPEECH-13-793_en.htm.

De Gucht, K. (2014), 'Making the most of Europe—the EU's common commercial policy as a driver for growth', 21 February 2014. Available at: http://europa.eu/rapid/press-release_SPEECH-14-149_en.htm.

De Meester, B. (2008), 'Testing European Prudential Conditions for Banking Mergers in Light of the Most Favoured Nation in the GATS' 11(3) *Journal of International Economic Law* 609–47.

De Mestral, A. (2013), 'The Evolving Role of the European Union in IIA treaty-making' in A. de Mestral and C. Levesque (eds.), *Improving International Investment Agreements*, Abingdon: Routledge, 25–58.

De Ville, F., Orbie, J., and Van den Putte, L. (2014), The European Parliament's new role in trade policy: turning power into impact, CEPS Special report. Available at: http://hdl.handle.net/1854/LU-5672821.

De Witte, B. (2007), 'Setting the Scene: How did Services get to Bolkstein and Why?', Mitchell Working Paper Series, 3/2007. Available at: http://cadmus.eui.eu/handle/1814/6929.

Dee, P. and Sidorenko, A. (2006), 'The Rise of Services Trade: regional initiatives and challenges for the WTO', in C. Findlay and H. Soesastro (eds.), *Reshaping the Asia Pacific Economic Order*, Abingdon: Routledge.

Deere, C. (2008), *The Implementation Game: The TRIPS Agreement and the Global Politics of Intellectual Property Reform in Developing Countries*, Oxford: Oxford University Press.

Deere, C. (2009), *EU Intellectual Property Law and Policy*, Cheltenham: Edward Elgar European Law.

Delimatsis, P. (2007), 'Due Process and "Good" Regulation Embedded in the GATS—Disciplining Regulatory Behaviour in Services Through Article VI of the GATS' 10(1) *Journal of International Economic Law* 13–50.

Delimatsis, P. (2009), 'Concluding the WTO Services Negotiations on Domestic Regulation: hopes and fears' 9(4) *World Trade Review* 643–73.

Delimatsis, P. (2012), 'The EU Services Directive and Codes of Conduct', in I. Lianos and O. Odudu (eds.), *Regulating Trade in Services in the EU and the WTO*, Cambridge: Cambridge University Press, 317–44.

Demedts, V. (2012), 'International Competition Law Enforcement: Different Means, One Goal?' 8(3) *The Competition Law Review* 223–46.

Derclaye, E. (2009), 'Copyright without Frontiers: the problem of territoriality in European copyright law', in E. Derclaye (ed.), *Research Handbook on the Future of Copyright*, Cheltenham: Edward Elgar Publishing.

Deutsch, K. and Speyer, B. (2011), 'The EU: Contending for Leadership', in K. Deutsch (ed.), *The World Trade Organization Millennium Round: Freer Trade in the Twenty-First Century*, London: Routledge, 34–47.

Devuyst, Y. and Sedarevic, A. (2007), 'The World Trade Organisation and Regional Trade Agreements: Bridging the Constitutional Gap' 18(1) *Duke Journal of Comparative and International Law* 1–75.

Dewey, D. (1964), 'Theory of Antitrust: Science or Religion?' 50(3) *Virginia Law Review* 413–34.

DiMascio, N. and Pauwelyn, J. (2008), 'Non-Discrimination in Trade and Investment Treaties: Worlds Apart or Two Sides of the Same Coin?' 102 *American Journal of International Law* 48.

Di Matteo, L., Dosanijh, K., Frantz, P., and Bowal, P. (2003), 'The Doha Declaration and Beyond: Giving a Voice to Non-Trade Concerns within the WTO Regime', 36(94) *Vanderbilt Journal of Transnational Law* 95–160.

Didier, P. (1997), 'The Uruguay Round Government Procurement Agreement: Implementation in the European Union', in B. Hoekman and P. Mavroidis (eds.), *Law and Policy in Public Purchasing, The WTO Agreement on Government Procurement*, The University of Michigan Press, 125–48.

Diebold, N. (2010), *Non-discrimination in International Trade in Services—Likeness in WTO/GATS*, New York: Cambridge University Press.

Dillon, S. (2002), *International Trade and Economic Law and the European Union*, Oxford: Hart Publishing.

Dimopoulos, A. (2007), 'The Common Commercial Policy After Lisbon: Establishing Parallelism Between Internal and External Powers', 4 *Croatian Yearbook of European Law* 102–31.

Dimopoulos, A. (2011), 'The Effects of the Lisbon Treaty on the Principles and Objectives of the Common Commercial Policy' 15 *European Foreign Affairs Review* 153–70.

Dimopoulos, A. (2012) 'Creating an EU Investment Policy: Challenges for the Post-Lisbon Era of External Relations', in P. Cardwell (ed.), *EU External Relations Law and Policy in the Post-Lisbon Era*, The Hague: Springer Asser Press, 401–23.

Dimopoulos, A. (2014), 'The Involvement of the EU in Investor–State Dispute Settlement: A question of Responsibilities' 51 *Common Market Law Review* 1671–720.

Dolzer, R. and Schreuer, C. (2008), *Principles of International Investment Law*, Oxford: Oxford University Press.

Donnan, S. (2014a), 'WTO asks if Bali deal was a big commitment or just a tropical fling', 23 January 2014, Financial Times.

Donnan, S. (2014b), 'EU–US trade talks hit roadblock over financial services', 16 June 2014, Financial Times.

Donnan, S. and Chaffin, J. (2013), 'Green and consumer groups voice fears over EU–US trade agreement', 13 October 2013, Financial Times.

Dornbusch, R. (1992), 'The Case for Trade Liberalization in Developing Countries' 6(1) *The Journal of Economic Perspectives* 69–85.

Doster, I. (2006), 'A Cheese by Any Other Name: A Palatable Compromise to the Conflict over Geographical Indications' 59(3) *Vanderbilt Law Review* 873–904.

Drahos, P. (2003), 'Expanding Intellectual Property's Empire: the Role of FTAs' (2003). Available at http://ictsd.org/downloads/2008/08/drahos-fta-2003-en.pdf.

Drexl, J. (2009), 'Intellectual Property and Implementation of Recent Bilateral Trade Agreements in the EU', Max Planck Institute for Intellectual Property and Competition Law Research Paper No. 12-09. Available at: http://www.ip.mpg.de.

Drijber, J. and Stergiou, H. (2009), 'Public Procurement Law and Internal Market Law' 46(3) *Common Market Law Review* 804–45.

Duchene, F. (1973), 'The European Community and the Uncertainties of Interdependence', in M. Kollistamm and W. Hager (eds.), *Nation Writ Large: Foreign Policy Problems before the European Communities*, London, Macmillan, 1–21.

Dumberry, P. (2014) 'The Protection of Investors' Legitimate Expectations and the Fair and Equitable Treatment Standard under NAFTA Article 1105' 31(1) *Journal of International Arbitration* 47–74.

Dur, A. and De Bievre, D. (2007), 'Inclusion without Influence? NGOs in European Trade Policy' 27(1) *Journal of Public Policy* 79–101.

Dymond, W. and Hart, M. (2000), 'Post-Modern Trade Policy, Reflections on the Challenges to Multilateral Trade Negotiations After Seattle' 34(3) *Journal of World Trade* 21–38.

The Economist (2010), Government consumption of the world, The World in figures. Available at: http://www.economist.com/theworldin/2010.

The Economist (2011), 'Protectionism in Brazil: A self-made siege', 24 September 2011.

The Economist (2012), 'Trade Policy in the EU: Protect Trade or Protect Sarkozy?', 22 March 2012.

The Economist (2014), 'The Arbitration Game' 18 October 2014. Available at: http://www.economist.com/news/finance-and-economics/21623756-governments-are-souring-treaties-protect-foreign-investors-arbitration.

Eeckhout, P. (1994), *The European Internal Market and International Trade—A Legal Analysis*, Oxford: Oxford University Press.

Eeckhout, P. (2010), 'The Scales of Trade—Reflections on the Growth and Functions of the WTO Adjudicative Branch' 13(1) *Journal of International Economic Law* 3–26.

Eeckhout, P. (2011), *EU External Relations Law, Second Edition*, Oxford: Oxford University Press.

Eeckhout, P. and Ortino, F. (2012), 'Towards an EU Policy on Foreign Direct Investment', in A. Biondi, P. Eeckhout, and S. Ripley (eds.), *EU Law After Lisbon*, Oxford: Oxford University Press, 312–30.

Eilmansberger, T. (2009), 'Bilateral Investment Treaties and EU Law' 46 *Common Market Law Review* 383–429.

El-Agraa, A. (ed.) (2007), *The European Union: economics and policies*, Cambridge: Cambridge University Press.

Elhauge, E. and Gerardin, D. (2007), *Global Competition Law and Economics*, Oxford: Hart Publishing.

Ellis, R. (2011), 'Conflicts at the Intersection of ACTA & Human Rights: How the Anti-Counterfeiting Trade Agreement violates the right to take part in cultural life' 2(3) *Intellectual Property Brief* 64–71.

Elsig, M. and Dupont, C. (2010), 'European Union Meets South Korea: Bureaucratic Interests, Exporter Discrimination and the Negotiations of Trade Agreements' 3(5) *Journal of Common Market Studies* 492–507.

Enlazando Alternativas (2013), 'Background note for EU Member States on the EU-Peru-Colombia Trade Agreement'. Available at: http://www.enlazandoalternativas.org.

Ermert, M. (2006), 'EU IP Enforcement Directive Questioned on Procedure', *Intellectual Property Watch*, 11 July 2006. Available at: http://www.ip-watch.org/2006/07/11/eu-ip-enforcement-directive-questioned-on-procedure.

Estevadeordal, A., Suominen, K., and Teh, R. (2010), *Regional Rules in the Global Trading System*, Cambridge: Cambridge University Press.

Eurostat (2014), 'International trade in services', July 2014. Available at:http://ec.europa.eu/eurostat/statistics explained/index.php/International_trade_in_services.

EUobserver (2005), US rejects EU proposal on free trade tribunal, 11 May 2015. Available at: https://euobserver.com/tickers/128662.

Evans, G. and Blakeney, M. (2006), 'The Protection of GIs after Doha: Quo Vadis?' 9(3) *Journal of International Economic Law* 575–614.

Evans, J. (1971), *The Kennedy Round in American Trade Policy, The Twilight of the GATT?* Harvard University Press.

Evenett, S. (2003), 'Can Developing Countries Benefit from Negotiations on Transparency in Government Procurement in the Doha Round?'. Available at: www.evenett.com/reports/evenettgpanddoharound.pdf.

Evenett, S. (2007), 'Five Hypotheses concerning the failure of the Singapore issues in the Doha Round' 23(3) *Oxford Review of Economic Policy* 392–414.

Evenett, S. and Hoekman, B. (2004), 'Government Procurement: Market Access, Transparency and Multilateral Trade Rules', World Bank Policy Research Working Paper 3195. Available at: http://elibrary.worldbank.org/doi/pdf/10.1596/1813-9450-3195.

Evenett, S. and Meier, M. (2007), 'An Interim Assessment of the U.S. Trade Policy of "Competitive Liberalization"', Universitat St. Gallen, Discussion Paper no. 2007-18

Faber, G. and Orbie, J. (eds.) (2007) *European Trade Politics and Development, Everything But Arms Unravelled*, London: Routledge.

Faes-Cannito, F., Gambini, G., and Istatkov, R. (2012), 'Intra EU share of EU-27 trade in goods, services and foreign direct investments remains more than 50% in 2010', EUROSTAT, Statistics in Focus, 3/2012. Available at: http://epp.eurostat.ec.europa.eu/cache/ITY_OFFPUB/KS-SF-12-003/EN/KS-SF-12-003-EN.PDF.

Fernandez Martin, J. (1996), *The EC Public Procurement Rules: A Critical Analysis*, Oxford: Oxford University Press.

Ferran, E. (2011), 'Capital Market Openness after Financial Turmoil', in M. Evans and P. Koutrakos (eds.), *Beyond the Established Legal Orders: Policy Interconnections Between the EU and the Rest of the World*, Oxford: Hart Publishing, 47–80.

The Financial Times (2012), 'A tactical retreat on free trade—EU's goal must be "sell European", not "buy European"', 21 March 2012.

Findlay, C. and Soesastro, H. (eds.) (2006), *Reshaping the Asia Pacific Economic Order*, London: Routledge.

Finger, J. (2007), 'Implementation and Imbalance: dealing with the hangover from the Uruguay Round' 23(3) *Oxford Review of Economic Policy* 440–60.

Finger, J. and Nogues, J. (2002), 'The Unbalanced Uruguay Round Negotiations: The New Areas in Future WTO Negotiations' 25 *World Economy* 321–40.

Fink, C. and Maskus, C. (2006), 'The Debate on Geographical Indications in the WTO', in R. Newfarmer (ed.), *Trade, Doha, and Development—A Window into the Issues*, The International Bank for Reconstruction and Development/The World Bank.

Fink, C. and Jansen, M. (2009), 'Services Provisions in Regional Trade Agreements: stumbling or building blocks for multilateral liberalisation?', in R. Baldwin and P. Low (eds.), *Multilateralizing Regionalism Challenges for the Global Trading System*, Cambridge: Cambridge University Press.

Fink, C., Mattoo, A., and Neagu, I. (2002), 'Trade in International Maritime Services: How Much Does Policy Matter?' 16(1) *The World Economic Review* 81–107.

Flaesch-Mougin, C. (1980), *Les accords externes de la CEE, essai d'une typologie*, Bruxelles: Institut d'Etudes Européennes, Université Libre de Bruxelles.

Fortier, L. (2009), 'The Canadian Approach to Investment Protection: How Far Have We Come!', in C. Binder, U. Kriebaum, A. Reinisch, and S. Wittich (eds.), *International Investment Law for the 21st Century: Essays in Honour of Christoph Schreuer*, Oxford: Oxford University Press, 526–43.

Fortier, L. and Drymer, S. (2004), 'Indirect Expropriation in the Law of International Investment: I Know It When I See It, or Caveat Investor' 19(2) *ICSID Review* 293–327.

Fox, E. (1997) 'Towards World Antitrust and Market Access' 91(1) *American Journal of International Law* 1–25.

Fox, E. (2000), 'Antitrust and Regulatory Federalism: Races Up, Down, And Sideways' 75 *New York University Law Review* 1781–807.

Fox, E. (2003), 'International Antitrust and the Doha Dome' 43(11) *Virginia Journal of International Law* 911–32.

Fox, E. (2006), 'The WTO's First Antitrust Case—Mexican Telecom: A Sleeping Victory for Trade and Competition' 9(2) *Journal of International Economic Law* 271–92.

Francois, J. and Hoekman, B. (2009), 'Services Trade and Policy', The Vienna Institute of International Economic Studies, Working Paper Series 60. Available at: http://www.econ.jku.at/.

Frank, I. (1961), *The European Common Market*, London: Stevens & Sons Ltd.

Freund, C. (2000), 'Multilateralism and Endogenous Formation of Preferential Trade Agreements' 52 *Journal of International Economics* 359–76.

Gagné, G. and Morin, J.F. (2006), 'The Evolving American Policy on Investment Protection: Evidence of recent FTAs and the 2004 Model BIT' 9(2) *Journal of International Economic Law* 257–382.

Gallagher, K. (2008), 'Understanding the Developing Country Resistance to the Doha Round' 15(1) *Review of International Political Economy* 62–85.

Gallagher, K. (2012), 'Challenging Opportunities for the Multilateral Trade Regime', in R. Meléndez-Ortiz, C. Bellmann, and R. Rodriguez Mendoza (eds.), *The Future and the WTO: Confronting the Challenges, A Collection of Short Essays*, ICTSD Programme on Global Economic Policy and Institutions.

Gangjee, D. (2007), 'Quibbling Siblings: Conflicts between Trademarks and Geographical Indications' 83(3) *Chicago Kent Law Review* 1253–91.

Garcia Bercero, I. (2006), 'Dispute Settlement in European Union Free Trade Agreements: Lessons Learned?', in L. Bartels and F. Ortino (eds.), *Regional Trade Agreements and the WTO Legal System*, Oxford: Oxford University Press, 384–406.

Garcia Molyneux, C. (2001), *Domestic Structures and International Trade*, Oxford: Hart Publishing.

Geboye Desta, M. and Barnes, N. (2007), 'Competition Law and Regional Trade Agreements', in L. Bartels and F. Ortino (eds.), *Regional Trade Agreements and the WTO Legal System*, Oxford: Oxford University Press, 239–64.

Geddes, A. (1997), *Public and Utility Procurement, A Practical Guide to the UK Regulations and Associated Community Rules*, London: Sweet & Maxwell.

Gerber, D. (2010), *Global Competition: Law, Market and Globalization*, Oxford: Oxford University Press.

Gervais, D. (2007), 'The Changing Landscape of International Intellectual Property', in C. Heath and A. Kamperman (eds.), *Intellectual Property and Free Trade Agreements*, Oxford: Hart Publishing.

Geuze, M. (2009) 'The Provisions on Geographical Indications in the TRIPS Agreement' 10(1) *The Estey Centre Journal of International Law and Trade Policy* 50–64.

Ginsburg, J. (2011) 'Toward Supranational Copyright Law? The WTO Panel Decision and the Tree-Step Test for Copyright Exceptions' *Revue International de Droit d'Auteur*. Available at http://papers.ssrn.com/sol3/papers.cfm?abstract_id=253867.

Gkoutzinis, A. (2005), 'International Trade in Banking Services and the Role of the WTO: Discussing the Legal Framework and Policy Objectives of the General Agreement on Trade in Services and the Current State of Play in the Doha Round of Trade Negotiations' 39(4) *International Lawyer* 877–914.

Goldberg, S. (2001) 'Who will Raise the White Flag? The Battle between the United States and European Union over Geographical Indications' 22(1) *University of Pennsylvania Journal of International Economic Law* 107–44.

Gootiiz, B. and Mattoo, A. (2009), 'Services in Doha—What's on the Table?', World Bank Policy Research Paper no 4903. Available at: http://elibrary.worldbank.org/doi/pdf/10.1596/1813-9450-4903.

Gosalbo Bono, R. (2011), 'The organization of the external relations of the European Union in the Treaty of Lisbon', in P. Koutrakos (ed.), *The European Union's external relations a year after Lisbon*, Centre for the EU Law of External Relations, T.M.C. Asser Instituut Inter-University Research Centre, 13–38. Available at: http://www.asser.nl.

Grosse Ruse-Khan, H. (2008), 'A Comparative Analysis of Policy Space in WTO Law', Max Planck Institute for Intellectual Property, Competition and Tax Law Research Paper No. 08-02. Available at: http://pubman.mpdl.mpg.de/pubman/faces/viewItemOverviewPage.jsp?itemId=escidoc:838171:4.

Grosse Ruse-Khan, H. (2010a), 'A Real Partnership for Development? Sustainable Development as Treaty Objective in European Economic Partnership Agreements and Beyond' 13(1) *Journal of International Economic Law* 139–80.

Grosse Ruse-Khan, H. (2010b), 'From TRIPS to ACTA: Towards a New Gold Standard in Criminal Enforcement', Max Planck Institute for Intellectual Property and

Competition Law Research Paper No. 10-06. Available at: http://pubman.mpdl.mpg.de/pubman/faces/viewItemFullPage.jsp;jsessionid=0BDF8F78CA85751571702D837A57DA99?itemId=escidoc%3A1189625%3A5&view=EXPORT.

Grosse Ruse-Khan, H. (2010c), 'A Trade Agreement Creating Barriers to International Trade?: ACTA Border Measures and Goods in Transit' 6 *American University International Law Review* 645–723.

Grosse Ruse-Khan, H. (2011), 'The International Law Relation Between TRIPS and Subsequent TRIPS-Plus Free Trade Agreements: Towards Safeguarding TRIPS Flexibilities?' 18(2) *Journal of Intellectual Property Law* 3–41.

Gruber, G., Gruber, T., Mille, A., and Sachs, M. (2009) (eds.), *Public Procurement in the European Union*, Antwerp: Intersentia Publishers.

Guimaraes de Lima e Silva, V. (2008), 'The Revision of the WTO Agreement on Government Procurement: to what extent might it contribute to the expansion of current membership' (2008) 2 *Public Procurement Law Review* 61–98.

Guzman, A. (2001), 'Antitrust and International Regulatory Federalism' 76 *New York University Law Review* 1142–63.

Haight, F. (1972), 'Customs Unions and Free-Trade Areas under GATT: A Reappraisal' 4 *Journal of World Trade* 391–404.

Hall, M. (2014), 'EU, US face food labelling spat in TTIP talks, Euractiv, 17 July 2014. Available at: http://www.euractiv.com/sections/agriculture-food/eu-us-face-food-labelling-spat-ttip-talks-302895.

Hamilton, C. and Whalley, C. (1996), *The Trading System after the Uruguay Round*, Washington DC: Peterson Institute for International Economics.

Hanson, B. (1998), 'What Happened to Fortress Europe? External Trade Policy Liberalization in the European Union' 52(1) *International Organization* 55–85.

Hansson, G. (2012), 'Trade and Labour Standards', in K. Heydon and P. Holmes (eds.), *Ashgate Research Companion to International Trade Policy*, Farnham: Ashgate, 279–90.

Harrison, J. (ed.) (2013), *The European Union And South Korea—The Legal Framework for Strengthening Economic and Political Relations*, Edinburgh: Edinburgh University Press.

Hatzopoulos, V. (2007a), 'Que reste-t-il de la directive sur les services?', Research Papers in Law 5/2007, Bruges, College of Europe. Available at: http://aei.pitt.edu/44298/.

Hatzopoulos, V. (2007b), 'Legal Aspects of Establishing the Internal Market for Services', College of Europe, European Legal Studies 6-2007. Available at: https://www.coleurope.eu/sites/default/files/research-paper/researchpaper_6_2007_hatzopoulos.pdf.

Hatzopoulos, V. (2012), *Regulating Services in the European Union*, Oxford: Oxford University Press.

Hawk, B. (1995), 'System Failure: Vertical Restraints and EC Competition Law' 32(4) *Common Market Law Review* 973–91.

Hay, C. (2007), 'Keynote Article: What Doesn't Kill You Can Only Make You Stronger: The Doha Development Round, the Services Directive and the EU's Conception of Competitiveness' 45 *Journal of Common Market Studies* 25–43.

Heath, C. (2010), 'Customs Seizures, Transit and Trade' 41(8) *International Review of Intellectual Property and Competition Law* 902–4.

Heiskanen, V. (2004), 'The Regulatory Philosophy of International Trade Law' 38(1) *Journal of World Trade* 1–36.

Herdegen, M. (2013), *Principles of International Economic Law*, Oxford: Oxford University Press.

Heron, T. and Silles-Brugge, G. (2012), 'Competitive Liberalization and the "Global Europe" Services and Investment Agenda: Locating the Commercial Drivers of the EU–ACP Economic Partnership Agreements' 50(2) *Journal of Common Market Studies* 250–66.

Herrmann, C. (2002), 'Common Commercial Policy After Nice: Sisyphus would have done a better job' 39(1) *Common Market Law Review* 7–29.

Heydon, K. and Woolcock, S. (2009), *The Rise of Bilateralism: Comparing American, European and Asian Approaches to Preferential Trade Agreements*, Geneva and New York: United Nations University Press.

Heydon, K. (2012), 'The Political Economy of International Trade', in K. Heydon and S. Woolcock (eds.), *The Ashgate Research Companion to International Trade Policy*, Farnham: Ashgate, 29–46.

Hilaire, A. and Yang, Y. (2005), 'The United States and the New Regionalism/Bilateralism' 38(4) *Journal of World Trade* 603–25.

Hillion, C. (2008), 'Tous Pour Un, Un Pour Tous: Coherence in the External Relations of the European Union', in M. Cremona (ed.), *Developments in EU External Relations*, Oxford: Oxford University Press, 11–36.

Hindley, B. (1999), 'New Institution for Transatlantic Trade?' 75(1) *International Affairs* 45–60.

Hindley, B. (2002), 'What Subjects are Suitable for WTO Agreements', in D. Kennedy and J.D. Southwick, *The Political Economy of International Trade Law*, Cambridge: Cambridge University Press, 157–70.

Ho Sung, J. (2013), 'Some Reflections on Competition and Subsidies under the EU–KOREA FTA', in J. Harrison (ed.), *The European Union and South Korea—The Legal Framework for Strengthening of Trade, Economic and Political Relations*, Edinburgh: Edinburgh University Press, 87–101.

Hoekman, B. (1996), 'Assessing the General Agreement on Trade in Services', in W. Martin and L.A. Winters (eds.), *The Uruguay Round and the Developing Countries*, Cambridge: Cambridge University Press, 88–124.

Hoekman, B. (1998), 'Using International Institutions to Improve Public Procurement' 13(2) *The World Bank Research Observer* 249–69. Available at: http://elibrary.worldbank.org/doi/abs/10.1093/wbro/13.2.249.

Hoekman, B. and Braga, P. (1997), 'Assessing the General Agreement on Trade in Services: A Survey', Washington DC, World Bank, Policy Research Working Paper 1747.

Hoekman, B. and Mavroidis, P. (1997), 'Multilateralizing the Agreement in Government Procurement', in B. Hoekman and P. Mavroidis (eds.), *Law and Policy in Public Purchasing, The WTO Agreement on Government Procurement*, The University of Michigan Press.

Hoekman, B. and Holmes, P. (1999), 'Competition Policy a, Developing Countries and the WTO', October 1999, World Bank Policy Research Working Papers. Available at: http://elibrary.worldbank.org/doi/book/10.1596/1813-9450-2211.

Hoekman, B. and Messerlin, P. (1999), 'Liberalising Trade in Services: Reciprocal Negotiations and Regulatory Reform' World Bank and CEPR, 5 July 1999. Available at: http://siteresources.worldbank.org/INTRANETTRADE/Resources/SER-brook-fin.pdf.

Hoekman, B. and Kostecki, M. (2001), 'Towards Deeper Integration? The "Trade and" Agenda', in B. Hoekman and M. Kostecki (eds.), *The Political Economy of the World Trading System: WTO and Beyond*, Oxford: Oxford University Press, 413–58.

Hoekman, B., Mattoo, A., and Sapir, A. (2007), 'The Political Economy of Services Trade Liberalization: a case for international cooperation?' 23(3) *Oxford Review of Economic Policy* 367–91.

Hoekman, B. and Mattoo, A. (2008), 'Services Trade and Growth', World Bank, Policy Research Working Paper 4461. Available at: http://elibrary.worldbank.org/doi/book/10.1596/1813-9450-4461.

Hoekman, B. and Mattoo, A. (2011), 'Services Trade Liberalization and Regulatory Reform, Re-invigorating International Cooperation', World Bank Policy Research Paper 5517. Available at: http://econ.worldbank.org/external/default/main?pagePK=64165259&theSitePK=469382&piPK=64165421&menuPK=64166093&entityID=000158349_20110103094557.

Hoffmeister, F. (2011), 'The European Union's Common Commercial Policy After Lisbon—Sea Change or Business as Usual?', in P. Koutrakos (ed.), *The European Union's external relations a year after Lisbon*, Centre for the EU Law of External Relations, T.M.C. Asser Instituut Inter-University Research Centre, 83–96. Available at: http://www.asser.nl.

Hoffmeister, F. (2013), 'The Deep and Comprehensive Free Trade Agreements of the European Union', in M. Cremona and T. Tamacs (eds.), 'Trade Liberalisation and Standardisation—new directions in the low politics of the EU foreign policy', CLEER Working Papers 2013/6. Available at: http://www.asser.nl.

Hoffmeister, F. (2014), 'A First Glimpse of Light on the Emerging Invisible EU Model BIT' 15 *The Journal of World Investment & Trade* 379–401.

Holmes, P. (1999), 'Competition Policy, Developing Countries and the WTO', FEEM Working Paper No. 66-99. Available at: http://www.feem.it/userfiles/attach/Publication/NDL1999/NDL1999-066.pdf.

Holmes, P. (2002), 'Trade, Competition and the WTO', in B. Hoekman, A. Mattoo, and P. English (eds.), *Development, Trade and the WTO*, Washington: World Bank, 447–55.

Holmes, P. (2003), 'The Singapore Issues in Cancun: A Failed Negotiation Ploy or a Litmus Test for Global Governance?' 38(5) *Intereconomics* 152–253.

Holmes, P. (2008), 'The External Dimension of the Internal Market. An Economic Perspective', in J. Pelkmans (ed.), *The EU Internal Market in Comparative Perspective, Economic, Political and Legal Analyses*, Brussels: P.I.E. Peter Lang, 191–207.

Holmes, P. (2010), 'Deep Integration in EU FTAs', University of Sussex Economic Department Working Paper Series, No.7/2010. Available at: https://www.sussex.ac.uk/webteam/gateway/file.php?name=wps7-2010-holmes.pdf&site=261

Horn, H., Mavroidis, P., and Sapir, A. (2009), 'Beyond the WTO? An anatomy of EU and US preferential trade agreements', *Bruegel Blueprint Series*, Vol. II. Available at www.bruegel.org/.

Howse, R. (2012), 'Importing regulatory standards and principles into WTO dispute settlement: the challenge of interpreting the GATS Arrangements on Telecommunications', in I. Lianos and O. Odudu (eds.), *Regulating Trade in Services in the EU and the WTO*, Cambridge: Cambridge University Press, 446–52.

Hudec, R. (1996), 'Introduction', in R. Hudec and J. Bhagwati (eds.), *Fair Trade and Harmonization: Pre-requisites for Free Trade?*, Cambridge, MA: MIT Press, 1–18.

Hufbauer, G. and Stephenson, S. (2007), 'Services Trade: Past Liberalization and Future Challenges' 10(3) *Journal of International Economic Law* 605–30.

Hufbauer, G. and Kim, J. (2008), 'International Competition Policy and the WTO', Paper presented at a conference titled One Year Later: The Antitrust Modernization Commission's Report and the Challenges that Await Antitrust, New York University, April 11, 2008.

Hunja, R. (2003), 'Obstacles to Public Procurement Reform in Developing Countries', in S. Arrowsmith and M. Trybus (eds.), *Public Procurement: The Continuing Revolution*, Kluwer Law International, 13–22.

Idrac, A.-M. (2011), 'The European Trade Policy: Moving Towards Less Naivety', Fondation Robert Schuman, European issues n°222, 13th December 2011. Available at: http://www.robert-schuman.eu/doc/questions_europe/qe-222-en.pdf.

IMF (2007), Balance of Payments Manual. International Monetary Fund. Washington, DC. Available at: https://www.imf.org/external/pubs/ft/bopman/bopman.pdf.

ITC (2009) 'Case study: Tourism Services Liberalization in the Caribbean-European EPA negotiations'. Available at: http://www.intracen.org/uploadedFiles/intracenorg/Content/Trade_Support_Institutions/Business_voice_in_policy_making/How_to_influence_trade_negotiations/tourism_services_liberalization.pdf.

Jackson, J. (1988), *International competition in services: a constitutional framework*, Washington DC: AEI Studies.

Jaeger, T. (2010), 'The EU Approach to IP Protection in Partnership Agreements', Max Planck Institute for Intellectual Property, Competition and Tax Law Research Series Paper No.10-01. Available at: http://papers.ssrn.com.

Jarosz-Friis, A., Pesaresi, N., and Kerle, C. (2010) 'EU–KOREA FTA: a stepping stone towards better subsidies control at the international level' 1 *Competition Policy Newsletter*. Available at: http://ec.europa.eu/competition/publications/cpn/2010_1_19.pdf.

Johnson, S. and Schott, J. (2013), Financial Services in the Transatlantic Trade and Investment Partnership (Peterson Institute for International Economics Policy Briefs PB13-26, 2013). Available at: www.iie.com/publications/pb/pb13-26.pdf.

Jones, A. and Sufrin, B. (2010), *EC Competition Law: Texts, Cases and Materials*, Oxford: Oxford University Press.

Jones, C. (2011), 'Penumbras of European Union competition law: External governance, extraterritoriality and the shifting of borderlands of the internal market', in J. Drexl, W. Grimes, C. Jones, R. Peritz, and E. Swaine (eds.), *More Common Ground for International Competition Law*, Cheltenham: Edward Elgar Publishing, 261–78.

Jones, O. (2014), 'The TTIP deal hands British sovereignty to multinationals', *The Guardian*, 14 September 2014. Available at: http://www.theguardian.com/commentisfree/2014/sep/14/ttip-deal-british-sovereignty-cameron-ukip-treaty.

Jovanovic, M. (1998), *International Economic Integration Second Edition*, London: Routledge.

Kamperman Sanders, A., Shabalala, D., Moerland. A., and Pugatch, M. (2011), 'The Anti-Counterfeiting Agreement (ACTA): An Assessment', European Union, EXPO/B/INTA/FWC/2009-01/Lot7/12. Available at: http://www.europarl.europa.eu/activities/committees/studies.do?language=EN.

Katrak, K. and. Strange, R. (eds.) (2004), *The WTO and Developing Countries*, New York: Palgrave.

Kelsey, J. (2010), 'Legal Analysis of Services and Investment in CARIFORUM–EC EPA: Lessons for Other Developing Countries', South Centre Research Paper 31 July 2010. Available at: http://www.iadb.org/intal/intalcdi/PE/2012/11206.pdf.

Khor, M. (2004), 'The WTO and the Developing World: do as we say not as we do', in L. Wallach and P. Woodall (eds.), *Whose Trade Organization?*, New York: The New Press.

Khorana, S. and Subramanian, S. (2012), 'Potential Accession to the WTO Government Procurement Agreement: A Case-Study on India' 15(1) *Journal of International Economic Law* 287–309.

Kleinheisterkamp, J. (2012), 'European Policy Space in International Investment Law' 27(2) *ICSID Review* 416–31.

Kleinheisterkamp, J. and Poulsen, L. (2014), 'Investment Protection in TTIP: Three Feasible Proposals', LSE Global Economic Governance Programme, Policy Brief December 2014. Available at: http://www.globaleconomicgovernance.org/policy-brief-investment-protection-ttip-three-feasible-proposals.

Kleinheisterkamp, J. and Woolcock, S. (2011), 'The EU approach to international investment policy after The Lisbon Treaty', European Parliament Directorate General for External Policies, Brussels 2011. Available at: http://www.europarl.europa.eu/RegData/etudes/etudes/join/2010/433854/EXPO-INTA_ET(2010)433854_EN.pdf

Klevoric, A. (1996), 'Reflection on the Race to the Bottom', in J. Bhagwati and R. Hudec (eds.), *Fair Trade and Harmonization: Pre-requisites for Free Trade?* Cambridge, MA: MIT Press, 449–61.

Korah, V. (2004), *An Introductory Guide to EC Competition Law and Practice*, Oxford: Hart Publishing.

Koutrakos, P. and Shaw, M. (eds.) (2011), *Beyond the Established Orders: Policy Interconnections between the EU and the Rest of the World*, Oxford: Hart Publishing.

Kox, H. and Lejour, A. (2007), 'Regulatory heterogeneity as an obstacle for international services trade' CPB Discussion Paper, No 49. Available at: http://www.cpb.nl/en/publication/regulatory-heterogeneity-obstacle-international-services-trade.

Kox, H. and Nordas, H. (2007), 'Services Trade and Domestic Regulation', OECD Trade Policy Working Papers, No. 49. Available at: http://ideas.repec.org/p/oec/traaab/49-en.html.

Krajewski, M. (2003), *National Regulation and Trade Liberalisation in Services*, Kluwer Law International.

Krajewski, M. (2005), 'External Trade Law and the Constitution Treaty: Towards a Federal and More Democratic Common Commercial Policy?' 42 *Common Market Law Review* 91–127.

Krajewski, M. (2006), 'Services Liberalization in Trade Agreements', in L. Bartels and F. Ortino (eds.), *Regional Trade Agreements and the WTO*, Oxford: Oxford University Press, 175–202.

Krajewski, M. (2013), 'The Reform of the Common Commercial Policy', in A. Biondi, P. Eeckhout, and S. Ripley, *EU Law After Lisbon*, Oxford: Oxford University Press, 292–311.

Krajewski, Markus (2014), 'Modalities for investment protection and Investor–State Dispute Settlement (ISDS) in TTIP from a trade union perspective'. Available at SSRN 2519995.

Krenzler, H. and Pitschas, C. (2001), 'Progress or Stagnation?: The Common Commercial Policy After Nice' (2001) 6(3) *European Foreign Affairs Review* 291–313.

Kumar, S. (2010), 'Border Enforcement of Intellectual Property Rights Against In-transit Generic Pharmaceuticals: an analysis of character and consistency' 32 *European Intellectual Property Review* 504–18.

Kur, A. (2008) 'Of Oceans, Islands, and Inland Water—How Much Room for Exceptions and Limitations under the Three-Step Test' 8(3) *Richmond Journal of Global Law & Business* 305–26.

Lamy, P. (2002a), 'Stepping Stones or Stumbling Blocks? The EU's Approach towards the Problem of Multilateralism vs Regionalism in Trade Policy' 25 *The World Economy* 1399–413.

Lamy, P. (2002b), 'Malta and the EU—How to make globalization work for the small', Brussels 31 May 2002. Available at: http://trade.ec.europa.eu/doclib/docs/2004/september/tradoc_118849.pdf.

Lamy, P. (2004a), 'The Emergence of Collective Preferences in International Trade: Implications for Regulating Globalisation', Brussels 15 September 2004. Available at: http://trade.ec.europa.eu/doclib/docs/2004/september/tradoc_118929.pdf.

Lamy, P. (2004b), 'TRIPS—Ten Years Later' 38(6) *Journal of World Trade* 923–34.

Lamy, P. (2014), Transatlantic trade negotiators should own up to their ambition, Financial Times, 27 October 2014.

Langhammer, R. (2005), 'The EU Offer of Service Trade Liberalisation in the Doha Round: Evidence of a Not-Yet-Perfect Customs Union' 43(2) *Journal of Common Market Studies* 311–25.

Langhammer, R. (2008), 'Why a Market Place Must Not Discriminate: The Case Against a US–EU Free Trade Agreement', Kiel Institute of World Economy Working Paper No. 1407. Available at: http://ideas.repec.org/p/kie/kieliw/1407.html.

Larik, J. (2011), 'Shaping the International Order as a Union Objective and the Dynamic Internationalisation of Constitutional Law', CLEER Working Papers 2011/5. Available at: http://papers.ssrn.com/sol3/papers.cfm?abstract_id=1963235.

Laurent, S. and Ricard, P. (2012), '"Buy European Act", réciprocité: des propositions déjà en gestation à Bruxelles', *Le Monde*, 12 March 2012.

Laursen, F. (ed.) (2008) *The Rise and Fall of the EU's Constitutional Treaty*, Leiden: Brill/ Nijhoff.

Lawrence, R. (1996a), *Regionalism, Multilateralism and deeper integration*, Washington DC: The Brookings Institution.

Lawrence, R., Bressand, A., and Ito, T. (1996b), *A Vision for the World Economy: Openness, Diversity and Cohesion*, The Brookings Institution, Washington DC.

Leal-Arcas, R. (2008), 'The EU Constitutional Treaty and International Trade', in F. Laursen (ed.), *The Rise and Fall of the EU's Constitutional Treaty*, Leiden: Brill/ Nijhoff, 25–50.

Leal-Arcas, R. (2011), 'The Fragmentation of International Trade Law: Is Now the Time for Variable Geometry?' 2(12) *Journal of World Investment and Trade* 145–95.

Leal-Arcas, R. (2012), 'The EU's New Common Commercial Policy after the Treaty of Lisbon', in L. Rubini and M. Trybus (eds.), *The Treaty of Lisbon and the Future of European Law and Policy*, Cheltenham: Edward Elgar, 262–85.

Leary, V. (1996), 'Workers' Rights and International Trade: The Social Clause (GATT, ILO, NAFTA, US Laws)', in R. Hudec and J. Bhagwati (eds.), *Fair Trade and Harmonization: Pre-requisites for Free Trade?*, Cambridge, MA: MIT Press, 177–231.

Lenaerts, K. (1986), 'Les répercussions des compétences de la Communauté Européenne sur les compétences externes des Etats Membres et la question de préemption', in P. Demaret (ed.), *Relations extérieures de la Communauté européenne et marche intérieur: aspects juridiques et fonctionnels*, Bruges: Collège d'Europe, Story Scientia.

Lester, S. (2015), 'Reforming the International Investment Law System' *Maryland Journal of International Law* 70 70–81.

Lester, S. and Mercurio, B. (2009), *Bilateral and Regional Trade Agreements, Commentary and Analysis*, Cambridge: Cambridge University Press.

Levesque, C. and Newcombe, A. (2013), 'Canada', in C. Brown (ed.), *Commentaries on Selected Model Investment Treaties*, Oxford: Oxford University Press, 53–129.

Li, X. (2010), 'The Agreement on Trade Related Aspects of Intellectual Property Rights Flexibilities on Intellectual Property Enforcement: The World Trade Organization Panel Interpretation of China—Intellectual Property Enforcement of Criminal Measures and Its Implications' 13(5) *Journal of World Intellectual Property* 639–59.

Lianos, I. and Le Blanc, J. (2012), 'The "Trust Theory of Integration"', in I. Lianos and O. Odudu (eds.), *Regulating Trade in Services in the EU and the WTO*, Cambridge: Cambridge University Press, 46–52.

Lim, K. and Choi, A. (2009) 'Korea–EU Free Trade Agreement regarding Intellectual Property Rights', Kim & Chang Intellectual Property Newsletter, 2009/10. Available at www.ip.kimchang.com.

Lim, H., Marchetti, J., and Roy, M. (2010), 'Services Liberalization in New Generation PTAs', in A. Estevadeordal, K. Suominen, and R. Teh, *Regional Rules in the Global Trading System*, Cambridge: Cambridge University Press, 316–64.

Linarelli, J. (2011), 'Global Procurement Law in Times of Crisis: Buy American Policies and Options in the WTO Legal System', in S. Arrowsmith and R. Anderson (eds.), *The WTO Regime on Government Procurement: Challenge and Reform*, Cambridge: Cambridge University Press, 773–802.

Lindstrom, B. (2010), 'Scaling back TRIPS-Plus: An Analysis of Intellectual Property Provisions in Trade Agreements and Implications for Asia and the Pacific' 42 *International Law and Politics* 918–78.

Lodge, J. (2011), 'A Trade Partnerssship for Sustainable Development', in A. Beviglia-Zampetti and J. Lodge (eds.), *The CARIFORUM–EU Economic Partnership Agreement: A Practitioners' Analysis*, Alphen aan den Rijn: Kluwer Law International, 35.

Loisen, J. and De Ville, F. (2011), 'The EU–Korea Protocol on Cultural Cooperation: Toward Cultural Diversity or Cultural Deficit?' 5 *International Journal of Communication* 254–71.

Low, P. and Mattoo, A. (2000), 'Alternative Approaches to Liberalization', in P. Sauvé and R. Stern (eds.), *GATS 2000—New Directions in Services Trade Liberalization*, Washington DC: Brookings Institution, 467–8.

Luyten, P. (1991), 'A View from a Fortress that never was', in T. Oppermann and J. Molsberger (eds.), *A New GATT for the Nineties and Europe 1992*, Nomos Verlagsgesellschaft.

Mandelson, P. (2005) 'Trade at the Service of Development', London School of Economics, 4 February 2005. Available at: http://www.lse.ac.uk/publicEvents/pdf/20050204-Mandelson.pdf.

Manners, I. (2002), 'Normative Power Europe: A Contradiction in Terms?' 40(2) *Journal of Common Market Studies* 235–58.

Manners, I. (2008), 'The Normative Ethics of the European Union' 84:I *International Affairs* 65–80.

Marangoni, A. (2012), 'One Hat Too Many for the High Representative—Vice President? The Coherence of the EU's External Policies After Lisbon' (2012) 2 *EU External Affairs Review* 4–17.

Marceau, G. and Trachtman, J. (2002), 'The Technical Barriers to Trade Agreement, the Sanitary and Phytosanitary Measures Agreement and the General Agreement on Tariffs and Trade—A Map of the WTO Law of the Domestic Regulation of Goods' 36(5) *Journal of World Trade* 811–82.

Marchetti, J. (2011), 'The GATS Prudential Carve-out', in P. Delimatsis and N. Herger (eds.), *Financial Regulation at the Crossroads*, Alphen aan den Rijn: Kluwer Law International.

Marchetti, J. and Mavroidis, P. (2004), 'What are the Main Challenges for the GATS Framework? Don't talk about revolution' 5(3) *European Business Organisation Law Review* 511–62.

Marchetti, J. and Mavroidis, P. (2011), 'The Genesis of the GATS' 22(3) *European Journal of International Law* 689–721.

Marchetti, J. and Roy, M. (eds.) (2009), 'Services Liberalization in the WTO and in PTAs', in J. Marchetti and M. Roy (eds.), *Opening Markets for Trade in Services—Countries and Sectors in Bilateral and WTO Negotiations*, Cambridge: Cambridge University Press, 61–112.

Marin-Duran, G. (2013), 'The Role of the EU in Shaping the Trade and Environment Regulatory Nexus: Multilateral and Regional Approaches'in S. Blockmans, B. Van Vooren, and J. Wouters (eds.), *The EU's Role in Global Governance*, Oxford: Hart Publishing, 225–40.

Martin, W. and Winters, L. (eds.) (1996), *The Uruguay Round and the Developing Countries*, Cambridge: Cambridge University Press.

Matsushita, M. (2004), 'Basic Principles of the WTO and the Role of Competition Policy' 3 *Washington University Global Studies Law Review* 363–85.

Matthews, D. and Munoz-Tellez, V. (2006), 'Bilateral Technical Assistance and TRIPS: The United States, Japan and the European Communities in Comparative Perspective' 9(6) *Journal of World Intellectual Property* 629–53.

Matthews, D. (2010), 'The Lisbon Treaty, Trade Agreements and the Enforcement of Intellectual Property Rights' 3 *European Intellectual Property Review* 104–12.

Mattoo, A. and Subramanian, A. (1998), 'Regulatory Autonomy and Multilateral Disciplines: The Dilemma and a Possible Resolution', Staff Working Paper TISD9802. WPF/January. Available at: https://www.wto.org/english/res_e/reser_e/ptis9802.pdf.

Maull, H. (1990), 'Germany and Japan: The New Civilian Powers' 69(5) *Foreign Affairs* 91–106.

Maur, J.-C. (2008), 'Regionalism and Trade Facilitation: A Primer', World Bank, Policy Research Working Paper No. 4464. Available at: http://elibrary.worldbank.org/doi/book/10.1596/1813-9450-4464.

Mavroidis, P. (2011), 'Always Look at the Bright Side of Non-Delivery: WTO and Preferential Trade Agreements, Yesterday and Today' 10(3) *World Trade Review* 375–87.

Mayer, J. (2009), 'Policy Space: What, for What, and Where?' 27(4) *Development Policy Review* 373–95.

McCrudden, C. (2007), *Buying Social Justice, Equality, Government Procurement & Legal Change*, Oxford: Oxford University Press.

McCulloch, R. (2012), 'The International Trading System and its Future', in M. Kreinin and M. Plummer (eds.), *Oxford Handbook on International Commercial Policy*, Oxford: Oxford University Press, 32–49.

McLachlan, D. (1984), 'Discriminatory Public Procurement, Economic Integration and the Role of Bureaucracy' 23(4) *Journal of Common Market Studies* 357–72.

Mehta, P. (2003), 'The Doha Development Agenda: The Road Ahead', Canadian Development Report 2003. Available at: http://www.nsi-ins.ca/wp-content/uploads/2012/11/2003-Canadian-Development-Report-2003-Chapter-2.pdf.

Melo Araujo, B. (2015), 'Regulating Services Through Trade Agreements—A Comparative Analysis of Regulatory Disciplines Included in EU and US Free Trade Agreements' (13 May 2015), *Trade Law & Development*—Forthcoming. Available at SSRN: http://ssrn.com/abstract=2605776.

Mercurio, B. (2006), 'TRIPS-Plus Provisions in FTAs: Recent Trends', in L. Bartelsand F. Ortino (eds.), *Regional Trade Agreements and the WTO Legal System*, Oxford: Oxford University Press, 215–37.

Mercurio, B. (2012), 'Seizing Pharmaceuticals in Transit: Analysing the WTO Dispute that Wasn't' 61(2) *International and Comparative Law Quarterly* 389–426.

Messerlin, P. (2004), 'The Impact of EC Enlargement on the WTO: the future of the multilateral trading system', in M. Moore (ed.), *Doha and Beyond*, Cambridge: Cambridge University Press, 146–78.

Messerlin, P. (2012a), 'EU Public Procurement Markets: How Open Are They?', G.E.M. Policy Brief, 10 August 2012. Available at: http://gem.sciences-po.fr/content/publications/pdf/Messerlin-Miroudot_EU_public_procurement072012.pdf.

Messerlin, P. (2012b), 'Openness in public procurement markets: A fair report of the results of the EU impact assessment', G.E.M. Policy Brief 9 October 2012. Available at: http://www.gem.sciences-po.fr/content/publications/pdf/Messerlin_openness%20in%20public%20procurement%20markets102012.pdf.

Messerlin, P. (2012c), 'The Much Needed EU Pivoting to East Asia' 10(2) *Asia-Pacific Journal of EU Studies* 1–18.

Messerlin, P. (2013), 'The MERCOSUR–EU Preferential Trade Agreement: A view from Europe', CEPS Working Document no 377 Available at: http://ceps.be/book/mercosur%E2%80%93eu-preferential-trade-agreement-view-europe.

Metzger, D. (1964), *Trade Agreements and the Kennedy Round*, Corner Publications Ltd.

Meunier, S. (2000), 'What Single Voice? European Institutions and EU–U.S. Trade Negotiations' 54(1) *International Organization* 103–35.

Meunier, S. (2005), *Trading Voices, The European Union in International Trading Negotiations*, Princeton, New Jersey: Princeton University Press.

Meunier, S. and Abdelal, R. (2007), 'The Paradox of Managed Globalization' *European Studies Forum* 37:2.

Meunier, S. and Abdelal, R. (2010), 'Managed Globalization: Doctrine, Practice and Promise' 17(3) *Journal of European Public Policy* 350–67.

Meunier, S. and Nicolaidis, K. (2006), 'The European Union as a Conflicted Trade Power' 13(6) *Journal of European Public Policy* 906–25.

Milstein, J. and Kaddar, M. (2006), 'Managing the Effect of TRIPS on Availability of Priority Vaccines' 84(5) *Bulletin of the World Health Organization* 360–5.

Ming Du, M. (2011), 'The Rise of National Regulatory Autonomy in the GATT/WTO Regime' 14(3) *Journal of International Economic Law* 639–75.

Miranda Lodono, A. (2012), 'Competition Law in Latin America: Main Features and Trends', Centro des Estudos de Competencia. Available at: http://centrocedec.files.wordpress.com/2010/06/cornell-lacompetition-20123.pdf.

Mirodout, S., 'Investment', in J.-P. Chauffour and J.-C. Maur (eds.), *Preferential Trade Agreement Policies for Development*, Washington DC: The World Bank, 307–26.

Mitchell, A. and Lockhart, N. (2005), 'Regional Trade Agreements Under GATT 1994: An Exception and its Limit', in A. Mitchell (ed.), *Challenges and Prospects for the WTO*, London: Cameron May Publishers, 217–52.

Modwel, S. and Singh, S. (2012), 'The EU–India FTA Negotiations: leading to an Agreement or Disagreement?' GEM Policy Brief, 30 January 2012. Available at: http://www.ecipe.org/publications/eu-india-fta-negotiations-leading-agreement-or-disagreement/.

Molinuevo, M. (2012), *Protecting Investment in Services, Investor–State Arbitration versus WTO Dispute Settlement*, Alphen aan den Rijn: Kluwer Law International.

Monbiot, G. (2013) This transatlantic trade deal is a full-frontal assault on democracy, The Guardian 4 November 2013. Available at: http://www.theguardian.com/commentisfree/2013/nov/04/us-trade-deal-full-frontal-assault-on-democracy.

Monti, G. (2007), *EC Competition Law*, Cambridge: Cambridge University Press.

Moore, M. (ed.) (2004), *Doha and Beyond, The Future of the Multilateral Trading System*, Cambridge: Cambridge University Press.

Motta, M. (2004), *Competition Policy Theory and Practice*, Cambridge: Cambridge University Press.

Muchlinski, P. (2013), 'The Role of Preferential Trade and Investment Agreements in International Investment Law: From Unforeseen Historical Developments to an Uncertain Future' in R. Hofmann, S. Schill, and C.J. Tams (eds.), *Preferential Trade and Investment Agreements: From Recalibration to Reintegration* (Baden-Baden: Nomos Verlagsgesellschaft), 211–27.

Muller-Graff, P. (2008), 'The Common Commercial Policy Enhanced by the Reform Treaty of Lisbon', in A. Dashwood and M. Maresceau (eds.), *Law and Practice of EU External Relations: salient features of a changing landscape*, Cambridge: Cambridge University Press, 188–201.

Murkherjee, A. and Goyal, T. (2013), 'Examining Mode 4 Commitments in India and the EU's Agreements: Implications fo the India–EU BTIA', CARIM-India Research Report 2013/16. Available at: http://www.iimb.ernet.in/research/working-papers/examining-mode-4-commitments-india-and-eu%E2%80%99s-agreements-implication-india-eu-btia-0.

Murphy, K. (2003), 'Conflict, Confusion, and Bias under TRIPs Articles 22–24' (2003) 19(5) *American University Intellectual Law Review* 1181–230.

Nahm, H. (2011), 'New Policy Amendments to Take Effect on July 1, 2011', July 2011. Available at: http://patentkorea.com/english/bbs_view.asp?boardid=6&num=62.

Natens, B. (2013), 'The Doha Round and the Future of the Multilateral Architecture Regulation of Trade in Services', Leuven Centre for Global Governance Studies, Working Paper No.110—March 2013. Available at: https://ghum.kuleuven.be/ggs/projects/steunpunt-internationaal-vlaanderen/documenten/3-bregt-natens-report-dda-final.pdf.

Nesterowicz, M. (2011) 'Freedom to Provide Maritime Transport Services in European Community Law' 34(4) *Journal of Maritime Law and Commerce* 81–108.

Newcombe, A. (2013a), 'Developments in IIA treaty-making' in A. De Mestral and C. Levesque (eds.), *Improving International Investment Agreements*, Abingdon: Routledge, 15–24.

Newcombe, A. (2013b), 'The Use of General Exceptions in IIAs: increasing legitimacy or uncertainty?' in A. De Mestral and C. Levesque (eds.), *Improving International Investment Agreements*, Abingdon: Routledge, 265–83.

Newcombe, P. and Paradell, L. (2009), *Law and Practice of Investment Treaties*, Alphen aan den Rijn: Kluwer Law International.

Newman, E., Thakur, R., and Tirman, J. (eds.) (2006), *Multilateralism under Challenge? Power, International Order and Structural Change*, Tokyo: United Nations University Press.

Nicolaidis, K. and Schaeffer, G. (2005), 'Transnational Mutual Recognition Regimes: Governance Without Global Government' 68 *Law and Contemporary Problems* 267–317.

Nicolaidis, K. and Schmidt, S. (2007), 'Mutual Recognition "On Trial": the long road to services liberalization' 14(5) *Journal of European Public Policy* 717–34.

Nicolaidis, K. and Howse, R. (2002), 'This is my EUtopia…"Narrative as Power"' 40(4) *Journal of Common Market Studies* 767–92.

Nicolaidis, K. and Vernon, R. (1997), 'Competition Policy and Trade Policy in the European Union', in E. Graham and J. Richardson (eds.), *Global Competition Policy* Washington D.C.: Institute for International Economics, 271–312.

Nouisis, P., Overbeek, H., and Tsolakis, A. (eds.) (2002), *Globalisation and European Integration: Critical Appraisal*, London/New York: Routledge.

Nunes Ferreira, I. (2011), 'Civilian, Normative and Ethical Power Europe: Roles, Claims and EU Discourses' 16(1) *European Foreign Affairs Review* 1–20.

O'Connor, B. (2012), 'The Legal Protection of Geographical Indications in the EU's Bilateral Trade Agreements: moving beyond TRIPS' VI(4) *Rivista di Dirrito Alimentare* 1–29.

O'Connor, B. (2013), 'The EU and the US: Conflicting Agendas on Geographical Indications—what's happening in Asia?' Available at: http://www.nctm.it/wp-content/uploads/2013/10/The-EU-and-the-US_What-is-happening-in-Asia_Global-Newsletter_2013.pdf.

Odudu, O. (2006), *The Boundaries of EC Competition Law*, Oxford: Oxford University Press.

Ong, B. (2006), The Origins, Objectives and Structure of Competition Law in Singapore 29(2) *World Competition* 269–84.

Oppermann, T. and Molsberger, J. (1992) (eds.), *A New GATT for the Nineties and Europe 1992*, Baden Baden: Nomos.

Orbie, J. (2006), 'Civilian Power Europe: Review of Original and Current Debates' 41 *Cooperation and Conflict* 123–8.

Orbie, J. (ed.) (2008), *Europe's Global Role: External Policies of the European Union*, Farnham: Ashgate.

Orbie, J., Gistelinck, M., and Kerremans, G. (2008), 'The Social Dimension of EU Trade Policies', in J. Orbie and L. Tortell (eds.), *The European Union and the Social Dimension of Globalization: How the EU Influences the World*, New York: Routledge, 148–65.

Ortino, F. (2004), *Basic Legal Instruments of the Liberalisation of Trade, A comparative analysis of EC and WTO Law*, Oxford: Hart Publishing.

Otten, A. and Wager, H. (1994), 'Compliance with TRIPS: The Emerging World View' (1994) 29 *Vanderbilt Journal of Transnational Law* 391–413.

Overseas Development Institute (2012), 'The next decade of EU trade policy: confronting global challenges?', June 2012. Available at: http://www.odi.org.uk/publications/6693-eu-trade-policy-international-development-global-challenges.

Panizzon, M. (2010), 'International Law of Economic Migration—a Ménage à Trois? GATS Mode 4, EPAs and Bilateral Migration Agreements' 44(6) *Journal of World Trade* 1207–52.

Panourgias, L. (2006), *GATS, EU and Prudential Institution Building*, Oxford: Hart Publishing.

Papadopoulos, A. (2008), *The International Dimension of EU Competition Law and Policy*, Cambridge: Cambridge University Press.

Peers, S. (2011), 'The Constitutional Implications of the EU Patent' 7(2) *European Constitutional Law Review* 229–66.

Pelkmans, J. (1984), *Market Integration in the European Community*, Martinus Nijhoff Publishers.

Pelkmans, J. (2007), 'Deepening Services Market Integration—a critical assessment' 7(4) *Romanian Journal of European Affairs* 5–31.

Pelkmans, J. (2012), 'Mutual Recognition: economic and regulatory logic in goods and services' (2012) Bruges European Economic Research Papers, 24/2012. Available at: https://www.coleurope.eu/sites/default/files/research-paper/beer24.pdf.

Perez Pugatch, M. (2007), 'A Transatlantic Divide? The US and EU's Approach to the International Regulation of Intellectual Property Trade-Related Agreements', ECIPE Working Paper, No. 02/2007. Available at: http://www.ecipe.org/media/publication_pdfs/a-transatlantic-divide.pdf.

Peterson, J. and Young, A. (2006), 'The EU and the New Trade Politics' 13(6) *Journal of European Public Policy* 795–814.

Piris, J. (2010), *The Treaty of Lisbon: a legal and political analysis*, Cambridge University Press.

Poiares Maduro, M. (2001), 'The Constitution of the Global Market', in F. Snyder (ed.), *Regional and Global Regulation of International Trade*, Oxford: Hart Publishing, 49–70.

Poletti, A. (2012), *The European Union and Multilateral Trade Governance—the Politics of the Doha Round*, Routledge/Garnett Series.

Pomorska, K. and Vanhoonaker, S. (2015), 'Europe as a Global Actor: the (Un)Holy Trinity of Economy, Diplomacy and Security' *Journal of European Public Policy* 1–14.

Prada, G. and Rossi, A. (2002), 'The Regulatory Framework of Regional Trade Agreements', in W. Lim and R. Torrent, 'Multilateral and Regional Frameworks for Globalization: WTO and Free Trade Agreements', Korea Development Institute and Observatory of Globalisation, University of Barcelona. Available at: http://www-dev.kdi.re.kr/kdi_eng/database/report_read05.jsp?1=1&pub_no=9916.

Radaelli, C. (2004), 'The Puzzle of Regulatory Competition' I *Journal of Public Policy* 1–23.

Ramalho, A. (2011), 'The European Union and ACTA—or making omelettes without eggs (again)' 42(1) *International Review of Intellectual Property and Competition Law* 91–101.

Ranjan, P. (2008), 'International Investment Agreements and Regulatory Discretion: Case Study of India' *The Journal of World Investment & Trade* 9(2) 209–43.

Raustiala, K. and Munzer, S. (2007), 'The Global Struggle over Geographical Indications' 18(2) *European Journal of International Law* 337-65.

Rege, V. (2001), 'Transparency in government procurement: issues of concern and interest to developing countries' 35(4) *Journal of World Trade* 489–515.

Reich, A. (1997), 'The New GATT Agreement on Government Procurement: the Pitfalls of Plurilateralism and Strict Reciprocity' 31 *Journal of World Trade* 125–51.

Reich, A. (2009), 'The New Text of the Agreement on Government Procurement on Government Procurement: An Analysis and Assessment' 12(4) *Journal of International Economic Law* 989–1022.

Reichman, J. (1998), 'Securing Compliance with the TRIPS Agreement after US v India' 1(4) *Journal of International Economic Law* 585–601.

Reinisch, A. (ed.) (2007), *Standards of Investment Protection*, Oxford: Oxford University Press.

Reinisch, A. (2013), 'The Future Share of EU Investment Agreements' 28(1) *ICSID Review* 179–96.

Roberts, C. (2007), 'Liberalising International Trade in Services Through the WTO: how rich and poor countries alike will gain' 13(3) *International Trade Law and Regulation* 51–6.

Robles, A. (2008), 'The EU and ASEAN: Learning from the Failed EU-MERCOSUR FTA Negotiations' 25 *ASEAN Economic Bulletin* 334–44.

Roessler, F. (1996), 'Diverging Domestic Policies and Multilateral Trade Integration', in R. Hudec and J. Bhagwati (eds.), *Fair Trade and Harmonization: Pre-requisites for Free Trade?*, Cambridge, MA: MIT Press, 21–56.

Rolland, E. (2012), *Development at the World Trade Organisation*, Oxford University Press.

Roy, M (2009), 'Endowments, Power and Democracy: Political Economy of Multilateral Commitments on Trade in Services', WTO Economic Research and Statistics Division, Staff Working Paper ERSD-2009-07. Available at: http://www.wto.org/english/res_e/reser_e/ersd201011_e.pdf.

Roy, M. (2011), 'Services Commitments in Preferential Trade Agreements: an Expanded Data Set, WTO Economics Research and Statistics Division', WTO Staff Working Paper ERSD-2011-18. Available at: http://www.wto.org/english/res_e/reser_e/ersd201118_e.pdf.

Rubini, L. and Trybus, M. (eds.), *The Treaty of Lisbon and the Future of European Law and Policy*, Cheltenham: Edward Elgar Publishing.

Ruggie, J. (1982), 'International Regimes, Transactions and Change: embedded liberalism in the postwar economic order' 36(02) *International Organization* 379–415.

Ruggie, J. (1994), 'Trade Protectionism and the Future of Welfare Capitalism' 48(1) *Journal of International Affairs* 1–11.

Sahu, S. and Gupta, N. (2007), 'Competition Clauses in Bilateral Trade Treaties: Analysing the Issues in the Context of India's Future Negotiating Strategy', Report Prepared for Competition Commission of India, November 2007. Available at: http://www.cci.gov.in/images/media/completed/bilateral_trade_treaties_20080508105059.pdf.

Sakoui, A. and Politi, J. (2013), 'China antitrust push draws ire of US companies and regulators', 22 August 2013, *Financial Times*.

Salacuse, J. (2007), 'The Treatification of International Investment Law' 13 *Law and Business Review of the Americas* 155–66.

Sampson, G. (2005), 'The Future of the WTO in World Economic Affairs' 4(3) *World Trade Review* 419–28.

Santa-Cruz, M. (2007), 'Intellectual Property Provisions in European Union Trade Agreements: Implications for Developing Countries', ICTSD IPRs and Sustainable Development Issue Paper No. 20, International Centre for Trade and Sustainable Development. Available at: http://ictsd.org/i/publications/11387/.

Santos, A. (2012), 'Carving Out Policy Autonomy for Developing Countries in the World Trade Organization: The Experience of Brazil and Mexico' 52 *Virginia Journal of International Law* 551–632.

Sauvé, P. (2009), 'A Plurilateral Agenda for Services? Assessing the Case for a Trade in Services Agreement' NCCR Trade Regulation, Working Paper No 2013/29, May 2013. Available at: http://www.nccr-trade.org/publication/a-plurilateral-agenda-for-services-assessing-the-case-for-a-trade-in-services-agreement-tisa/.

Sauvé, P. and. Ward, N. (2009), 'The EC–CARIFORUM Economic Partnership Agreement: Assessing the Outcome on Services and Investment', ECIPE January 2009. Available at: http://www.ecipe.org/media/publication_pdfs/the-ec-cariform-economic-partnership-agreement-assessing-the-outcome-on-services-and-investment.pdf.

Sbragia, A. (2010), 'The EU, the US and Trade Policy: competitive interdependence management globalisation' 17(3) *Journal of European Public Policy* 368–82.

Schaeffer, G. (2005), 'The Under-Examined Trade-Environment Linkage: Domestic Politics and WTO Disputes', Conference Paper for the Festschrift for Jagdish Bhagwati, Columbia University, August 5–6, 2005. Available at: http://www.columbia.edu/~ap2231/jbconference/Papers/Shaffer_Bhagwati%20Conference.pdf.

Schepel, H., et al. (2013), 'Statement of Concern about Planned Provisions on Investment Protection and Investor–State Dispute Settlement (ISDS) in the Transatlantic Trade and Investment Partnership (TTIP)', Available at: https://www.kent.ac.uk/law/isds_treaty_consultation.html.

Scherer, F. and Watal, J. (2001), 'Post-TRIPS Options for Access to Patented Medicines in Developing Nations' 5(4) *Journal of International Economic Law* 913–39.

Schill, S. (2009), *The Multilateralisation of International Investment Law*, Cambridge: Cambridge University Press.

Schloemann, H. and Pitschas, C. (2008), 'Cutting the Regulatory Edge? Services Regulation Disciplines in the CARIFORUM EPA', GTZ, Trade Programme, Division of Economic Development and Employment. Available at: http://www.acp-eu-trade.org/library/library_detail.php?library_detail_id=4822&doc_language=Both.

Schnitzer, J. (2005), 'The External Sphere of Public Procurement Law: bi-regional trade relations from the perspective of the European Community' 14 *Public Procurement Law Review* 63–90.

Schreuer, C. (2007), 'Introduction: Inter-relationship of Standards', in A. Reinisch (ed.), *Standards of Investment Protection*, Oxford: Oxford University Press.

Scott, J. (2000), 'Trade and Environment in the EU and the WTO', in J. Weiler (ed.), *The EU, the WTO and the NAFTA, Towards a Common Law of International Trade*, Oxford: Oxford University Press, 126–68.

Seid, S. (2002), *Global Regulation of Foreign Direct Investment*, Farnham: Ashgate Publishing.

Sell, K. (2003), *Private Power, Public Law: The Globalization of Intellectual Property Rights*, Cambridge: Cambridge University Press.

Seuba, X. (2009), 'Border Measures Concerning Goods Allegedly Infringing Intellectual Property Rights: the Seizure of Generic Medicines in Transit, ICTSD Working Paper. Available at: www.iprsonline.org.

Seville, C. (2009), *Enforcement of Intellectual Property Rights*, Cheltenham: Edward Elgar.

Shabalala, D. (2007), 'The European Approach to Intellectual Property in European Partnership Agreements with the African, Caribbean, and Pacific Group of Countries', Trade and Sustainable Development Program. Available at www.ciel.org.

Shan, W. and Zhang, S. (2010), 'The Treaty of Lisbon: Half way toward a common investment policy' 21(4) *European Journal of International Law* 1049–73.

Simon, F. (2012), 'EU to confront China with "reciprocity" in public contract', Euractiv 9 March 2012. Available at: http://www.euractiv.com/innovation-enterprise/eu-confront-china-reciprocity-pu-news-511404.

Simmons, B. (2006), 'Bilateral Challenges for Multilateral Trade', in E. Newman, R. Thakur, and J. Tirman (eds.), *Multilateralism under Challenge? Power, International Order and Structural Change*, Tokyo: United Nations University Press, 442–3.

Simmons, B. (2014), 'Bargaining over BITs, Arbitrating Awards: The Regime for Protection and Promotion of International Investment' 66(1) *World Politics* 12–46.

Smith, K. (1998), 'The Use of Political Conditionality in the EU's Relations with Third Countries: How Effective?' 3 *European Foreign Affairs Review* 253–74.

Smith, K. (2000), 'The End of Civilian Power EU: A Welcome Demise or Cause for Concern?' 35(2) *The International Spectator* 11–28.

Snidal, K. and Snidal, D. (2011), 'International "Standards" and International Governance' 8(3) *Journal of European Public Policy* 345–70.

Smith, M. (2010), 'Single Market, Global Competition: Regulating the European Market in the Global Economy' 17(7) *Journal of European Public Policy* 936–53.

Snyder, F. (ed.) (2001), *Regional and Global Regulation of International Trade*, Oxford: Hart Publishing.

Sokol, D. (2007), 'Monopolists Without Borders: The Institutional Challenge of International Antitrust in a Global Gilded Age' 41 *Berkeley Business Law Journal* 37–122.

Sokol, D. (2008), 'Order Without (Enforceable) Law: Why Countries Enter into Non-Enforceable Competition Policy Chapters in Free Trade Agreements' 83(1) *Chicago Kent Law Review* 231–92.

Sornarajah, M. (2004), *The International Law on Foreign Investment*, Second Edition, Cambridge: Cambridge University Press.

Sornarajah, M. (2010), *The International Law on Foreign Investment* (Cambridge: Cambridge University Press.

Sornarajah, M. (2011), 'Evolution or Revolution in International Investment Arbitration? The descent into normlessness', in C. Brown and K. Miles (eds.), *Evolution in Investment Treaty Law and Arbitration*, Cambridge: Cambridge University Press, 629–30.

Spears, S. (2011), 'Public Interest in International Investment Agreements', in C. Brown and K. Miles (eds.), *Evolution in Investment Treaty Law and Arbitration*, Cambridge: Cambridge University Press, 271–97.

Spears, S. (2011), 'Making way for the Public Interest in International Investment Agreements,' in C. Brown and K. Miles (eds.), *Evolution in Investment Treaty Law and Arbitration*, Cambridge: Cambridge University Press.

Ssennoga, F. (2006), 'Examining Discriminatory Procurement Practices in Developing Countries' 6(3) *Journal of Public Procurement* 218–49.

Steger, D. (2012), 'Institutions for Regulatory Cooperation in "New Generation" Economic and Trade Agreements' 39(1) *Legal Issues of Economic Integration* 109–26.

Steger, D. (2013), 'Enhancing the legitimacy of international investment law by establishing an appellate mechanism', in A. De Mestral and C. Levesque (eds.), *Improving International Investment Agreements*, Abingdon: Routledge, 247–65.

Steinicke, M. (2012), 'Government Procurement—can the WTO learn from the EU Regime', in S. Gaines, B. Egelund Olsen, and K. Emsig Sorensen (eds.), *Liberalising Trade in the EU and the WTO, A legal comparison*, Cambridge: Cambridge University Press, 360–84.

Stephenson, S. and Robert, M. (2011), 'Innovations and Regionalism in Services in the Americas', NCCR Trade Regulation Working Paper No 2011/34. Available at: http://www.nccr-trade.org/fileadmin/user_upload/nccr-trade.ch/wp2/people/WPInnovations%20of%20Regionalism%20in%20Services%20-%20Americas%20-%20May%202011%20FINAL.pdf.

Stern, S. (2001), 'The Overlaps between Trademarks and Geographical Indications in Australia' (2001) 1 *Melbourne Journal of International Law* 224–40.

Stevens, C. and Kennan, J. (2011), 'Who will benefit from GSP graduation?', International Centre for Trade and Sustainable Development, 10(5) Trade Negotiations Insights. Available at: http://ictsd.org/i/news/tni/110546/.

Stiglitz, J. (2000), 'Two Principles for the Next Round or, How to bring Developing Countries in from the Cold' 34(4) *The World Economy* 437–54.

Stiglitz, J. and Charlton, A. (2005), *Fair Trade for All: How Trade can Promote Development*, Oxford: Oxford University Press.

Stoble, J. (2013), 'Japan and EU to start talks on trade deal', *Financial Times* 25 March 2013.

Stopler, W. and Samuelson, P. (1941), 'Protection and Real Wages', 9 *The Review of Economic Studies* 58–73.

Sugden, R. and Wilson, J. (2012), 'Economic Development in the Shadow of the Consensus: a Strategic Decision-Making Approach' 21 *Contributions to Political Economy* 111–34.

Sykes, A. (1999), 'The (Limited) Role of Regulatory Harmonization in International Goods and Services Market' 2(9) *Journal of International Economic Law* 49–70.

Sykes, A. (2002), 'Domestic Regulation, Sovereignty, and Scientific Evidence Requirements: A Pessimistic View' 3 *Chicago Journal of International Law* 353–6.

Telò, M. (2007) (ed.), *European Union and New Regionalism: Regional Actors and Global Governance in a Post-hegemonic Era*, Aldershot: Ashgate Publishing.

Tiejte, C., Finke, J., and Dietrich, D. (2010), 'Liberalisation and Rules on Regulation in the Field of Financial Services in Bilateral and Regional Integration Agreements', German Federal Ministry for Economic Cooperation and Development and German Technical Cooperation, November 2010. Available at: www2.jura.uni-halle.de/INSTITUT/Abstract_97.pdf.

Tinbergen, J. (1954), *International Economic Integration*, Amsterdam: Elsevier.

Thorne, R. and Doucleff, J. (2010), 'Disregarding the Corporate Veil and Denial of Benefits Clause: Testing Treaty Language and the Concept of "Investor"', in M. Waibel (ed.), *The Backlash Against Investment Arbitration: Perceptions and Reality*, Alphen aan de Rijn: Kluwer Law International.

Tienhaara, K. (2011), 'Regulatory Chill and the threat of arbitration: A view from political science', in C. Brown and K. Miles (eds.), *Evolution in Investment Treaty Law and Arbitration*, Cambridge: Cambridge University Press, 606–27.

Trakman, L. (2014), 'Investor–State Arbitration: Evaluating Australia's Evolving Position' 15 *The Journal of World Investment & Trade* 152–92.

Trepte, P. (2004), *Regulating Public Procurement, Understanding the Means and the Ends of Public Procurement Regulation*, Oxford: Oxford University Press.

Trionfetti, F. (2000), 'Discriminatory Public Procurement and International Trade' 23(1) *The World Economy* 57–76.

Vadi, V. (2013), *Public Health in International Investment Law and Arbitration*, Abingdon: Routledge.

Van den Gronden, J. and De Waele, H. (2010), 'All's well that bends well? The constitutional dimension to the Services directive' 6(3) *European Constitutional Law Review* 397–429.

Van den Hoven, A. (2002), 'Interest Group Influence on Trade Policy in a Multilevel Polity: Analysing the EU Position at the Doha WTO Ministerial Conference', EUI Working Papers RSC No. 2002/67. Available at: http://www.eui.eu/RSCAS/WP-Texts/02_67.pdf.

Van den Hoven, A. (2004), Assuming Leadership in Multilateral Economic Institutions: The EU's "Development Round" Discourse and Strategy 27(2) *West European Politics* 256–83.

Van den Hoven, A. (2007), 'Bureaucratic Competition in EU Trade Policy, The EPA as a Case of Competing Two-Level Games', in G. Faber and J. Orbie (eds.), *European Trade Politics and Development, Everything But Arms Unravelled*, New York: Routledge Studies in Development Economics, 60–73.

Van Eechoud, M., Bernt Hugenholtz, P., Van Gompel, S., Guibault, L., and Helberger, N. (2009), *Harmonizing European Copyright Law, The Challenges of Better Lawmaking*, Alphen aan den Rijn: Kluwer Law International.

Vandevelde, K. (2005), 'A Brief History of International Investment Agreements' 12(1) *University of California Davis Journal of International Law* 157–94.

Vandevelde, K. (2012), 'Model Bilateral Investment Treaties: The Way Forward' 18 *Southwestern Journal of International Law* 307–14.

Vanduzer, J., Simons, P., and Mayeda, G. (2013), *Integrating Sustainable Development Into International Investment Agreements*, London: Commonwealth Secretariat.

Vicenti, D. (2014), 'US Ambassador: Beyond growth, TTIP must happen for geostrategic reasons' *EurActiv*, 17 July 2014. Available at: http://www.euractiv.com/sections/trade-industry/us-ambassador-eu-anthony-l-gardner-beyond-growth-ttip-must-happen.

Vicenti, D. (2015), 'European Parliament committee signals opposition to ISDS' Euractiv 14 January 2015. Available at: http://www.euractiv.com/sections/trade-society/european-parliament-committee-signals-opposition-isds-311189.

Viju, C., Yeung, M., and Kerr, A. (2013), 'Geographical Indications, Conflicted Preferential Agreements, and Market Access' 16(2) *Journal of International Economic Law* 409–37.

Villalta Puig, G. and Al-Haddab, B. (2011), 'The Common Commercial Policy After Lisbon: An analysis of the reforms' 36(2) *European Law Review* 289–366.

Viner, J. (1950), *The Customs Union Issue*, Carnegie Endowment for International Peace.

Viner, J. (1999), 'The Customs Union Issue', in J. Bhagwati, P. Krishna, and A. Panagaryia (eds.), *Trading Blocs: alternative approaches to analysing preferential trade agreement*, MIT Press, 105–18.

Vivas-Egui, D. and Oliva, J. (2010), 'The WTO Dispute on Trademarks and Geographical Indications: some implications for trade policy-making and negotiations', in C. Correa (ed.), *Research Handbook on the Interpretation and Enforcement of Intellectual Property under WTO Rules, Intellectual Property in the WTO Volume II*, Cheltenham: Edward Elgar Publishing, 122–43.

Voigt, C. (2009), *Sustainable Development as a Principle of International Law, Resolving Conflicts between Climate Measures and WTO Law*, Leiden: Brill Publishing.

Von Brau, J. and Munyi, P. (2010), 'New Enforcement Mechanisms Challenge the Legality of Generics in the Name of Public Health: the emergence of anti-counterfeiting legislation in East Africa' 18 *African Journal of International and Comparative Law* 238–53.

Wallace, H., Wallace, W., and Pollack, M. (eds.), *Policy-making in the EU*, Oxford: Oxford University Press.

Wallach, L. and Woodall, P. (eds) (2004), *Whose Trade Organization?*, New York: The New Press.

Wang, P. (2009), 'China's Accession to the WTO Government Procurement Agreement—Challenges and The Way Forward' 12(3) *Journal of International Economic Law* 663–706.

Wang, P. (2011), 'Accession to the GPA: The Case of China', in S. Arrowsmith and R. Anderson (eds.), *The WTO Regime on Government Procurement: Challenge and Reform*, Cambridge: Cambridge University Press, 92–116.

Wang, P., Cavallo Perin, R., and Casalini, D. (2011), 'Addressing Purchasing Arrangements Between Public Sector Entities: what can the WTO learn from the EU's experience?', in S. Arrowsmith and R. Anderson (eds.), *The WTO Regime on Government Procurement: Challenge and Reform*, Cambridge: Cambridge University Press, 252–82.

Warman, M., (2012), 'European Parliament rejects ACTA piracy Treaty', *The Telegraph*, 4 July 2012.

Weiler, J. (2000), 'Cain and Abel—Convergence and Divergence in International Trade Law', in J. Weiler (ed.), *The EU, the WTO and the NAFTA, Towards a Common Law of International Trade*, Oxford: Oxford University Press, 1–4.

Weinrauch, R. (2004), *Competition Law in the WTO, The Rationale for a Framework Agreement*, Antwerp: Intersentia.

Welfens, P. (2000), 'Globalization of the Economy and International Organizations: Developments, Issues and Policy Options for Reform', in R. Tilly and P. Welfens (eds.)

(2000), *Economic Globalization, International Organizations and Crisis Management*, Springer-Verlag.

Whalley, J. (2004), 'Assessing the Benefits to Developing Countries of Liberalisation in Services Trade' 27(8) *The World Economy* 1223–53.

Wigger, A. (2008), 'The External Dimension of EU Competition Policy: Exporting Europe's Core Business', in J. Orbie (ed.), *Europe's Global Role: External Policies of the European Union*, Farnham: Ashgate, 181–202.

Wolf, S. (2008), 'The Regulation of Foreign Direct Investment Under Selected WTO Agreements—Is there a Case for a Multilateral Agreement on Investments?', in C. Tietje (ed.), *International Investment Protection and Arbitration*, Berlin: Springer, 71–104.

Woolcock, S. (1993), 'The European Acquis and Multilateral Trade Rules: Are They Compatible?' 31(4) *Journal of Common Market Studies* 539–58.

Woolcock, S. (2000), 'Civil Society and the World Trading System', in D. Kelly and W. Grant (eds.), *The Politics of International Trade in the 21st Century*, London: Palgrave Macmillan, 30–46.

Woolcock, S. (2003), 'The Singapore Issues in Cancun: a failed negotiation ploy or a litmus test for global governance?' *Intereconomics* 38(5) 249–55.

Woolcock, S. (2005), 'Trade Policy from Uruguay to Doha and Beyond', in H. Wallace, W. Wallace, and M. Pollack (eds.), *Policy-making in the EU*, Oxford: Oxford University Press, 377–98.

Woolcock, S. (2007a), 'European Union Policy towards Free Trade Agreements', ECIPE Working Paper, No. 03/2007. Available at: http://www.ecipe.org/publications/european-union-policy-towards-free-trade-agreements/.

Woolcock, S. (2007b), 'Competing Regionalism—Patterns, Economic Impact and Implications for the Multilateral Trading System' *Intereconomics* September/October 2007, 236–59.

Woolcock, S. (2008a), 'The potential impact of the Lisbon Treaty on European Union External Trade Policy', (2008) Swedish Institute for European Studies, European Policy Analysis, Issue 8. Available at: http://www.sieps.se/sites/default/files/427-20088epa.pdf.

Woolcock, S. (2008b), 'Public Procurement and the Economic Partnership Agreements: assessing the potential impact on ACP procurement policies', May 2008, Commonwealth Secretariat, 4-6. Available at: http://www.thecommonwealth.org/shared_asp_files/GFSR.asp?NodeID=179104.

Woolcock, S. (2009), 'The EU and the Rise of Regionalism', European Foreign Policy Unit, Working Paper No. 2009/2, 14-16. Available at: http://www.lse.ac.uk/internationalRelations/centresandunits/EFPU/EFPUpdfs/EFPUworking paper2009-2.pdf.

Woolcock, S. (2012a), *European Economic Policy Diplomacy, The Role of EU External Economic Relations*, Farnham: Ashgate Publishing.

Woolcock, S. (2012b), Public Procurement in International Trade, Directorate-General for External Policies of the Union, 25 October 2012, 14. Available at: http://www.europarl.europa.eu/activities/committees/studies.do?lamguage=EN.

Woolcock, S. (2014), 'Differentiation Within Reciprocity: the European Union Approach to Preferential Trade Agreements' 20(1) *Contemporary Politics* 36–48.

Wouters, J. and Coppens, D. (2006), 'Domestic Regulation Within the Framework of GATS', Institute for International Law 2006 Working Paper No 93. Available at: http://www.law.kuleuven.be/iir/nl/onderzoek/wp/WP93e.pdf.

Wouters, J., Goddeeris, I., Natens, B., and Ciortuz, F. (2013), 'Some Critical Issues in EU–India Free Trade Agreement Negotiations', Leuven Centre for Global Governance Studies, Working Paper No. 102 February 2013. Available at: http://ghum.kuleuven.be/ggs/

publications/working_papers/new_series/wp101-110/wp102-wouters-goddeeris-natens.pdf.

Wu, C. (2011), 'Foreign Direct Investment as Common Commercial Policy: EU External Economic Competence After Lisbon', in P. Cardwell (ed.), *EU External Relations Law and Policy in the Post-Lisbon Era*, The Hague: TMC Asser Press; Springer, 375–400.

Yackee, J.W. (2008), 'Bilateral Investment Treaties, Credible Commitment and the Rule of (International) Law: Do BITs Promote Foreign Direct Investment?' 42 *Law and Society Review* 805–32.

Young, A. (2007), 'Trade Politics Ain't What it Used to be: The European Union in the Doha Round' 45(4) *Journal of Common Market Studies* 789–811.

Young, A. and Peterson, J. (2006), 'The EU and the New Trade Politics' 13(6) *Journal of European Public Policy* 795–814.

Yu, P. (2006), 'TRIPS and its Discontents' 10 *Marquette Intellectual Property Law Review* 369–410.

Yu, P. (2009), 'The Objectives and Principles of the TRIPS Agreement' 46 *Houston Law Review* 797–1046.

Yu, P. (2012), 'Intellectual Property and Human Rights in the Nonmultilateral Era' 64(4) *Florida Law Journal* 1045–100.

Zanthaki, H. (2001), 'Centros: is this really the end for the theory of the siege reel?' 22(1) *Company Lawyer* 2–8.

Ziegler, A. (2013), 'Is it necessary to avoid substantive and procedural overlaps with other agreements in IIAs?' in A. De Mestral and C. Levesque (eds.), *Improving International Investment Agreements*, Abingdon: Routledge, 158–76.

Zielonka, J. (2008), 'Europe as a Global Actor: Empire by Example?' 84(3) *International Affairs* 471–84.

Zoellick, R. (2001), 'The United States, Europe and the World Trading System' Speech given to the Kangaroo Group, Strasbourg, France. 15 May 2001. Available at: http://www.ustr.gov/archive/assets/Document_Library/USTR_Speeches/2001/asset_upload_file206_4282.pdf.

# Index

The manufacturer's authorised representative in the EU for product safety is Oxford University Press España S.A. of el Parque Empresarial San Fernando de Henares, Avenida de Castilla, 2 – 28830 Madrid (www.oup.es/en or product.safety@oup.com). OUP España S.A. also acts as importer into Spain of products made by the manufacturer.

www.ingramcontent.com/pod-product-compliance
Lightning Source LLC
LaVergne TN
LVHW011820200926
848484LV00005B/1255
* 9 7 8 0 1 9 8 7 5 3 3 8 4 *